THE CROSS AND THE BO-TREE

Catholics and Buddhists in Vietnam

The CROSS
and the BO-TREE

CATHOLICS AND
BUDDHISTS IN VIETNAM

by PIERO GHEDDO
translated by Charles Underhill Quinn

SHEED AND WARD: NEW YORK

Introduction

There already exists an important bibliography on the war in Vietnam.[1] A new book on Vietnam therefore might seem at first sight to be superfluous or quite useless.

But when we examine more closely the real flood of publications on Vietnam, we remain struck by the fact that the religious aspect of this country is almost completely neglected: not religious life in se, but the religions which are embodied in the local scene and which thereby have assumed noteworthy importance also in the area of politics. For those who know the East in general and Vietnam in particular this fact causes no surprise, since these peoples—much more than ours in the West—are still profoundly immersed in the "age of the sacred," so that the religious component marks not only the individual and family life of the country but also its political and social life. And this, I repeat, is valid not only for Vietnam but for almost all Asian countries: in fact it would be absurd to think that one could write the present-day history of countries like India, Pakistan, Ceylon, Indonesia or Burma without taking into account the influences exerted by the local religions upon their peoples and governments.

This, then, is why this book has been written: to report the Vietnamese situation from a point of view essential for our understanding of it—namely, the religious dimension, since we already

v

have many publications on the other aspects of the Vietnamese conflict, such as the military, political, sociological, ideological, diplomatic and economic.

A second justification for the book which I feel would be useful to communicate to the reader is this: on visiting Vietnam[2] and having close contacts with the local Church, I was astonished how we, Christians of the West, ignore the Christian realities of Vietnam and how much bishops, priests and lay Christians there suffer from the neglect of their brothers in the faith who at times accuse them unjustly of faults of which they are objectively not guilty. The voice of bishops and Vietnamese Christians on problems that concern them so immediately is almost totally ignored in the West, even by Christian writers and newspapermen: only a very small number of them take into account, in their judgments about the Vietnamese situation, what the local Christian community is thinking, nor do they bother to find it out.

I have written this book, then, to bear witness to the Vietnamese Church, to make known its tortured history and the present situation in which it finds itself, the positions it has assumed toward the ravaging war and, finally, the contribution it has given—and even more, could still give—to a peaceful resolution of the conflict.

There are certainly some points in the book with which Vietnamese Catholics will not agree (the basic judgment I have given about Diem, my presentation of the Buddhist movement, certain criticisms of the local Church I thought it necessary to make, the need—of the Catholics—for dialogue with the Buddhists and the Communists, etc.), but I am also confident of having rendered a service to the Church of Vietnam, at least insofar as this is possible for a foreign visitor who knows Vietnam only from what he has read and heard, and not from what he has lived! And we know that there is a certain distance between writing and living.

The book also says much about Buddhism and the other religions, both from an historical and a present-day point of view, in a spirit of complete sympathy and brotherly appreciation and with respect for historical truth. In no country more than Vietnam does it seem clear today that the different religions must unite to contribute— together—to the winning of the peace[3] and to giving men that "re-enforcement of soul" which they increasingly feel they lack. The time of intransigence and refusal to dialogue is definitively over in the Catholic Church with Vatican II and the last two popes: but we Christians—in the East as in the West—are still quite far from understanding the "others" since the study of non-Christian religions and personal contacts for dialogue are still only beginning.[4] I hope that what I have written on Buddhism and the other Vietnamese religions will cause us to appreciate—in the West and in the East—how much there is that unites Christians to non-Christians; it is much more than what divides us.

One other point, so that the reader may understand the spirit of this book. I should be most unhappy were it to be superficially interpreted as an old-style, anti-Communist "pamphlet." There is nothing further from my intention than to contribute to a new "anti-Communist crusade," which would not only be stupid and harmful but also contrary to the directives of the council and to the spirit of tolerance and dialogue for which our whole age cries out to us. If the anti-Communist crusade spirit is still quite alive in the Vietnamese Church, I unequivocally condemn it: I have written positively (see the final chapter) that the local Christian community must become open to dialogue not only with the other religions but also with the Communists and be ready to face, in the hopefully close *post-bellum* period, a calm and loyal collaboration with all the forces that are active in Vietnam, and therefore also with the Communists. Whoever studies the Vietnamese problem is in fact easily convinced that the Communists are a particularly alive nationalist force that can give a noteworthy contribution to the building of a better Vietnam that is independent and more just. It is therefore indispensable, as I have clearly stated, to accept the Vietcong as participants in a national coalition government if people want peace: arms will never shut off ideas!

Surely, this Communist participation in the government of South Vietnam must come about with respect for the freedom of all: what happened in North Vietnam ought not to be repeated. There, when the Communists came to power with ample promises of democratic freedom for all, they soon eliminated whoever was opposed to their dictates. What is wanted are serious guarantees that this will not happen again. But in any case, within these limits, I have clearly stated that the Vietcong, as a live and popular force in South Vietnam, have a full right to participate in a national coalition government and to collaborate with the other national forces in the rebuilding of the country.

However, all this has not prevented me from bringing together in this book a plentiful documentation on the behavior of the Vietnamese Communists in regard to the local nationalist movement and to religion. And it is a documentation, as might easily be imagined, that clearly condemns the Communists' modes of action and their goal, which is to impose on everyone their own dictatorship.

In Italy (and generally in the West) among certain progressivist Catholic groups, there is an attitude toward Communism and Communist regimes that seems neither just nor honest to me. In favor of dialogue—doubtless best if we are dealing with real dialogue—they are inclined to betray the reality of irrefutable, historical facts; in other words they think that to have a dialogue, in order that there be understanding, they have to be silent about or by-pass the truth, close their eyes to reality and understand and defend to the bitter end the others' positions, even those which are in greatest conflict with the data of good sense and objectivity (even though the Communists themselves—or at least a part of them— are inclined to admit the errors and excesses of their regimes).

I found myself faced with a mentality of this kind in the course of not a few conferences and debates on Vietnam these last months with Catholic groups. If it is mentioned that the Americans are seriously guilty morally in their waging of the Vietnam war (the bombings, etc.), there is immediate applause; if it is stated that Diem was a dictator and that the succeeding governments have not been very popular, there is ample agreement in the audience; if the Church is reproached for lacking dialogue with the Buddhists and the other nationalist forces, the hearers will surely and easily agree with you.

But when the statement is made that even the Communists have their faults; when it is documented that one of the most profound causes of the Vietnamese war is the express will of the local Communists to impose their regime upon the Vietnamese people; when you reveal factual data about the massacres wrought by the Communists against the nationalist patriots during the war against France, and by the Vietcong against the peoples of the South, then the least that can happen to you in certain Catholic circles is to be accused of "fascism" (as if speaking the truth about the Communists was a "fascist" ploy and not simply an act of honesty and clarity).

With the mentality of this kind of "dialoguing," it is clear that real dialogue will never make any progress: to be authentic, dialogue must always start with factual reality,[5] however agreeable or disagreeable the facts may be, and not be based on preconceived myths[6] that do not correspond with objective historical truth. Otherwise it is not called a dialogue but a fraud.

Any dialogue with the Vietnamese Catholics is excluded a priori unless we fundamentally understand their tragic experiences with local Communism; the general massacre of the Catholic and nationalist patriots during the anti-colonial war against France; the exodus of a million Vietnamese from the North and the antireligious persecution; the "scientific and systematic" terrorism of the Vietcong in the South, etc. Should we minimize, or worse, capsize the significance of these dramatic experiences, we would not only be sinning gravely against objective historical reality, but we would also be precluding any possibility of dialogue and beneficial influence with the Vietnamese Catholics.

To take an example, the progressivist French Catholic press—it is useless to cite the names of the papers and reviews to which I am alluding—is closely followed by Vietnamese Christians, but only to indicate as much as possible how bad it is insofar as it has assumed positions on the Vietnamese problem that are in no way objective and above all unreal; they take no account of the concrete reality of the Vietnamese situation. This blanket dismissal of the most animated press the post-conciliar Western Church has sent to Vietnam is most negative, since with it, it naturally brings the dismissal of all the most open conciliar statements and closes the Vietnamese Church in an intellectual, psychological and theological isolation that is very harmful in many senses.

On the contrary, I am convinced as I clearly state in the last two chapters of this book, that the Western churches (and in particular those of France and Italy, since all the bishops and many priests know Italian as well) can render great service to the Vietnamese Church (and to the Asian Churches in general, who often find themselves in very similar situations) by stirring our brothers to a thorough examination of conscience on the untenability of certain positions: for example, a fanatical and negative anti-Communism, their scanty interest in social reforms, closing off dialogue with Buddhism and the other local religions, their failure to collaborate with the other nationalist forces, etc.

But to have this contact and fraternal dialogue, it is absolutely indispensable that we have a basic understanding of the dramatic experiences of Vietnamese Christians and their authentic terror—experienced also by the great majority of the faithful of other religions—of falling under a Communist dictatorship.[7] This is what I have sought to do with this book, which is written also for the Christians of Vietnam who, I hope, will be able to read it in French or English.

In correcting the proofs of the book, I was somewhat horrified at its length. We live in a time when, although everyone tells us we have more "leisure time," there are always fewer people disposed to read a 400 page book, crammed with quotations and documents. I apologize to the reader, but to a short work with unproved statements I preferred a book of documentation because a great part of these documents, noted in a fragmentary way, have never been collected organically.

For the hurried reader I would advise beginning with the last two chapters of the book (IX and X) in which there is a partial summation of the content of the whole book and above all a mention of the conclusions to be retained (or discussed). Afterwards, if there is question about the "whys" of certain statements, the preceding chapters of a more documentary nature will have to be read.

Finally, I am obliged to express my thanks to many friends without whose aid I should have been unable to write this book, especially the Apostolic Delegate in Saigon, Mgr. Angelo Palmas, and the Vietnamese bishops, particularly the Archbishops of Saigon (Mgr. Nguyen-Van-Binh) and of Hué (Mgr. Nguyen-Kim-Dien), the Bishops of Dalat (Mgr. Nguyen-Van-Hien), Kontum (Mgr. Seitz) and of Nha Trang (Mgr. Van-Thuan-Nguyen), and to Mgr. Ngo-Dinh-Thuc and Mgr. Urrutia, both of whom were former bishops of Hué. I am thankful to Mgr. Pignedoli for his encouragement in my undertaking this task and to many Vietnamese priests, among whom I particularly remember Frs. Phan, Vui and Vi, all of whom are from the Saigon diocese; the missionaries of the Missions Etrangères of Paris in Vietnam, especially Frs. Dozance, Parrel, Arnould, Dujon and Hirgoyen, and to two dear friends, Cressonnier and Poncet, who were killed in February 1968 at the Tet offensive in Hué; the rector of the pontifical seminary of Dalat, Fr. Raviolo, S.J., and Fr. Angelo Pittau, a professor in the same seminary; and finally, many Catholic and Buddhist Vietnamese laymen, including the editors of *Song Dao*, various Buddhist figures (the Venerable Tri-Quang in particular) and members of the Vietnamese Confederation of Labor and the Y.C.W.

In Italy, I must thank Professor Mario Gozzini for his advice during the drafting of the book, and Frs. Renzo Bonaudo and Angelo Lazzarotto, my colleagues from the Pontifical Institute for Foreign Missions and now missionaries in Hongkong, for having looked over the text and brought to it substantial corrections.

I dedicate this English-language edition of my work to my American colleagues of PIME, in the hope that it may serve to make their work better known. One of the oldest exclusively mission-sending societies in existence, PIME (the initials stand for Pontifical Institute for Foreign Missions as written in Latin) was formed under the direction of Pope Pius IX in 1850. PIME Missionaries act as trailblazers or "shock troops" for the missionary Church. They enter a new mission territory, work among the potential Christians as doctors, educators, builders—(and priests)—providers to the homeless and hungry—and then, when sufficient native clergy have been trained to conduct the diocese, the PIME Fathers move on to a new territory to begin their work afresh.

Founded in Italy, the PIME Missionaries were invited to set up United States headquarters in Detroit, Michigan, by the late Edward Cardinal Mooney, who had known the work of the Society firsthand through his visits to the missions. In the intervening twenty years since coming to the States, PIME has established two minor seminaries (one in Newark, Ohio and one in Oakland, New Jersey) and a college seminary (Maryglade College, Memphis, Michigan), as well as a central headquarters and promotional center in Detroit.

PIERO GHEDDO
*The Pontifical Institute
for Foreign Missions of Milan*

Notes

1. A recent bibliography listing hundreds of books is the following: Nguyen The Anh, *Bibliographie critique sur les relations entre le Vietnam et*

l'Occident (Paris: G. P. Maisonneuve et Larose, 1967), pp. 310. Another full and critical bibliography is given by J. Buttinger, *Vietnam; a Dragon Embattled* (London: Pall Mall Press, 1967), vol. II, pp. 1258-1282. And finally I wish to mention R. Jumper's mimeographed volume, *Bibliography on the Political and Administrative History of Vietnam* (Michigan State University: Vietnam Advisory Group, 1962).

2. I was in Vietnam as a correspondent for the Milan daily *L'Italia,* and expressly invited by Mgr. Nguyen-Van-Binh, the archbishop of Saigon, in November–December 1967. With the truly providential aid of the apostolic delegate, Mgr. Palmas, the Vietnamese bishops and priests and the French missionaries (from the Paris Missions Etrangères), I was able to visit the whole of South Vietnam, including country, city, mountain and forest regions, and to have very numerous contacts with Catholics and Buddhists, students and syndicalists, newsmen and politicians, representatives of the people and the government. Before going to Vietnam I already had contacts in Rome with Vietnamese bishops; and after the trip, in preparing this book, I was able to have a detailed and frequent correspondence with friends in Vietnam. The written sources I used for the book are almost all quoted in footnotes: at times, however, I was unable to quote the confidential documents given to me by bishops and priests for my private information, since I was not authorized to reveal the name of the informant (thus, I must say that although to my pleasant surprise I found many people who were disposed to tell me their ideas, let me see documents in their possession and discuss with me the problems of Vietnam, I found myself confronted frequently with refusals when I suggested the names of my interlocutors. In Vietnam many people speak and share intimate confidences, but nobody wants his name to appear in papers or books; the very lengthy war years taught them above all to be incredibly prudent).

3. It is a pity that in Italy, even on the level of informed public opinion, while we note a praiseworthy interest in the Vietnamese problem and a most praiseworthy protest in favor of peace, there is not an adequate impartiality of information in newspapers, periodicals and books. Unfortunately, a great part of what is published on Vietnam, such as translations and original works, is marked by partiality in favor of one or other side in the conflict: either they exalt the Americans and the Saigon military government, upholding the solution of the "just war" and the "war to victory," or else, in the opposite camp, they exalt the Communist regime in North Vietnam and the Viet Cong, asserting that the sole solution is the victory of Communist nationalism. Very few seem to perceive that in Vietnam there exists a "third force" held in two by the arms of the two opposing forces but supported by

the great majority of the people who want neither a militaristic regime subjugated to America nor a Communist regime. In reference to what I have said about current opinion in Italy with regard to Vietnam, read the statement made at Rome by Vo-Van-Ai, the secretary-general of the Vietnamese Buddhist Associations Abroad. (Chapter X, note 9.)

4. In an interview granted to me during the Council, Cardinal König, a student of non-Christian religions, told me: "If we want to go out to meet other peoples, we must first have a good knowledge of their thought and their religious traditions. Unfortunately in the Catholic camp up to today, very little has been done to get to know the religious spirit of non-Christian peoples. I am always asked why our great theologians and thinkers together with our theological and philosophical faculties do not devote more time to these studies; in our own seminaries we ought to have a training in universality precisely through a knowledge of the religious thought of men not only of the past, of the Greco-Roman world but also of men of our own day. I become richer when I know what others think . . ." P. Gheddo, *Concilio e Terzo Mondon* (Milan: Editrice Missionaria Italiana, 1965), pp. 22–23.

5. In the document *Dialogue with non-Believers,* published on October 1, 1968 (but dated August 28, 1968) by the Secretariat for non-Believers (directed by Cardinal König) we read among other things this essential condition for the dialogue's success: "The dialogue, in order to attain its proper objectives must respect the exigencies of truth and freedom. It must therefore sincerely seek the truth."

6. With regard to the "myths" about Vietnamese Communism, read (Chapter IX, note 12) what Robert Kennedy thought of the myth that certain current American progressives had made out of the Ho Chi Minh regime.

7. The oldest and most cultivated persons I met in Vietnam—whether Catholics, Buddhists or belonging to other religions—often stated that the Vietnamese have the same terror of Communism that Europeans had of Nazism in the years 1940–1945. Certainly the Vietnamese Communists possess values, at least ideally (since in practice it is often quite another story!), that neither the Nazis nor the Fascists had. Therefore it would be erroneous to identify in an absolute way Vietnamese Communism with Nazism. But this does not do away with the fact that the Vietnamese, caught in the vice of Communist violence that has characterized all of their recent history and of the perspective of a ruthless "dictatorship of the people," have the same negative reactions towards Communism as we did towards Nazism. And we must be aware of this psychological position, if we want to understand anything about Vietnam.

Contents

Contents

THE CROSS AND THE BO-TREE

Catholics and Buddhists in Vietnam

I

A Colonial
and Persecuted Church

In the countries of the Far East, the Church was born and developed amid persecutions: in China, Korea and Japan, in the lands of South East Asia, and, naturally, also in Vietnam. What is not generally known is that the persecutions in Vietnam were the longest and the most cruel of all those that afflicted the Christians of the East in the last centuries.

The decisive importance of the laity in the first Indochinese mission. The preaching of the gospel in Vietnam from the beginning encountered an exceptional receptivity on the part of the poorest elements of the local population, while it gave rise in the upper classes at first to a diffident curiosity and then to violent reactions that turned into bloody persecutions which were first motivated by religious and social reasons and then, after the French intervention, by political considerations.

However, the Vietnamese encounter with Christ is considerably prior to the colonial intervention of the French. The first missionaries to embark for Vietnam were the Spanish and Portuguese in the sixteenth century, and they founded Christian communities there; this first evangelization (made by Franciscans, Dominicans and Carmelites) was renewed by the Jesuits in the seventeenth century,[1] and especially by the French Father de Rhodes who is

looked upon as the real founder of the Indochina mission. He
landed on the coast of Tonkin in 1627 and his apostolate, along
with that of his confreres who followed him, had rousing success:
in 1639 there were already 100,000 Christians in Tonkin and a
hundred odd churches (in that year 12,300 adults were baptized!);
in 1663 Christians numbered 200,000 among some two million
Tonkinese (according to the most common estimate of historians).
Fr. de Rhodes founded the Domus Dei, an organization of lay
catechists trained in a special seminary that was quite strict: these
catechists were to keep the faith among the Christians even when,
after Fr. de Rhodes, there was a dearth of priests. For example,
in 1658 the whole of Vietnam had 300,000 Catholics and only two
priests, but with a great number of lay coworkers. The Domus Dei
is a characteristic institution of the Church of Indochina and for
many centuries made up the basic structure of the mission.

In 1640 Fr. de Rhodes founded Christianity in Cochin China, in
the far South of present-day Vietnam, where he activated the same
methods he used in Tonkin but with less success, although even
here Christians numbered 50,000 in a short time.

But the missions in Indochina soon met with their first persecutions: the kings of Tonkin and Cochin China had hoped that in
welcoming the foreign missionaries they would bring with them
the Portuguese merchants whose reputation, especially in trade, had
spread as far as Indochina from China via Macao. But when they
saw that the missionaries were not concerned with attracting the
merchants, but rather that with their religion they were destroying
the bases of local society by achieving great success among the
people, they hastened to expel them from the country, initiating
severe persecutions.

The Paris missionaries and the native clergy. Fr. de Rhodes was
also expelled from Cochin China and went to Rome in 1649 to
plead for the cause of the Indochinese missions and the establishment of the local clergy. He then went to Paris, where his fiery

words caused the foundation of the Missions Etrangères, an institute of secular priests totally dedicated to the work of the missions with the specific goal of training native priests. Some ten years later, in 1660, the first group of French priests set sail from Marseille for Indochina, reaching Ayuthia, the capital of Siam, after twenty-six months: of the 14 who left, only 6 remained. Eight, including one bishop, perished on the voyage!

With the reenforcements arriving in the following years, these new missionaries immediately undertook the principal work for which they had been sent, the training of the native clergy. At Ayuthia they founded the first Collège général, the first seminary in South-East Asia. The Vicars Apostolic guiding them, taken from the Portuguese patronage of the East and solely dependent on *Propaganda Fidei,* had specific instructions: "The chief reason the Sacred Congregation is sending you as bishops to these regions is the instruction of the youth, that they may be promoted to the priesthood and also to the episcopacy." The pope granted ample faculties to the Vicars Apostolic; they could ordain priests, at their discretion, even those who "did not understand Latin, as long as they knew how to read and knew the meaning of the canon of the mass and the forms of the sacraments."

In 1668 at Ayuthia there were the first four ordinations of Indochinese priests, two from Tonkin and two from Cochin China, and the following year Mgr. de La Motte, one of the Vicars Apostolic, ordained at Tonkin itself, still in a state of persecution, seven catechists: the youngest was thirty, the oldest sixty-six. Undoubtedly these were priests who had no knowledge either of scholastic philosophy, Latin, or the theological disputes that at the time so captivated European scholars; but as a compensation they were fortified with a great faith and a practical sense and were an integral part of the community of their own Christians.

In this way, despite periodical persecutions, the Indochinese Church continued to survive with the help of the missionaries who secretly entered the country. There were the French from the

Missions Etrangères of Paris, the Portuguese Jesuits from Macao and the Spanish Dominicans from the Philippines. But above all, the Church survived because of the lay catechists who with great courage and a sense of responsibility took the Christian communities in hand and guided them, especially throughout the eighteenth century, when the arrivals of foreign missionaries gradually diminished.

It would be superfluous to reiterate the history of these years which involved a continual succession of persecutions and periods of tolerance in conditions of general if precarious safety for faithful and priests. In Tonkin, for example, violent persecutions were begun in 1696, 1713, 1721, 1736, 1773, 1778, etc., depending upon the emperors who were more or less tolerant about the religious question and more or less influenced by the mandarins who saw Christianity as a revolutionary religion, with its principles of respect for the human person, monogamy, social justice, etc.

Although the foreign missionaries were appreciated for the scientific innovations they brought into the country (astronomical, mathematical and mechanical knowledge, clocks, etc.) and for their first attempts at romanizing the Vietnamese language,[2] they were subsequently opposed in their efforts at propagating religion, which were looked upon as destructive to local society and custom.

The "rites question" closed Vietnam off to Christianity. Towards the end of the eighteenth century a new fact brought the Church of Indochina a long period of peace and prosperity: after thirty years of wars and rebellion, the whole of Vietnam was unified under one Emperor, Gia-Long, who granted freedom to the missionaries and to Christians since he had conquered the country with the aid of the French. Here we have the first entrance of France onto the scene. At this time, Gia-Long himself called France "the protectress of Christians."

At this time in Vietnam there were three major kingdoms and various secondary principalities divided among themselves and at continual civil war for supremacy. The nephew of the king of Cochin China (who was killed in one of these wars) took refuge in Cambodia, where he was helped by the vicar apostolic, Mgr. Pigneau de Béhaine, who was afraid he would turn to Holland or England; he offered him the aid of France for the reconquest of his kingdom. Nguyen-Anh was the name of the youth, who was only seventeen. He entrusted the bishop with making an alliance in his name with the King of France, which was the Versailles treaty of 1787. Two years later, with the help of the French from Pondicherry (India), Mgr. Pigneau de Béhaine arrived with two ships at Saigon, which had already been reconquered by Nguyen-Anh's own forces; the French volunteers organized the army of the King of Cochin China, which permitted him, after a ten year struggle, to unite Vietnam under his rule. In 1802 Nguyen-Anh took the name of Gia-Long and, in 1806, proclaimed himself emperor of the country.

In exchange for their help, the French held the port of Tourane (today Danang) and had freedom of trade throughout the country, while the Christians gained tolerance from Gia-Long and thereby had a long period of peace, during which the Church was able to regain its strength and prepare itself for future persecutions that were bloodier than the previous ones. It is interesting to note that during the reign of Gia-Long, Christianity would have been able to reach the cultivated classes and the mandarins and, perhaps, would have become the religion officially recognized in the country even under the subsequent emperors had it not been for the prohibition of the famous "rites question" that really ruined the missions not only in Vietnam but in all the countries of the East.

The "rites question" is acknowledged today as papal Rome's most serious error in the direction of the missions *ad paganos*, particularly in the East. The "quarrel" tied up the Roman Congregations for more than a century, as well as a great part of thinking Europe. It naturally involved the missionaries[3] who were more directly concerned, since it included not only pastoral and methodological problems but also theology and basically the approach to be taken by evangelical activity. The two opposing tendencies, that fought one another for many decades, were the conservative idea of the *tabula rasa* (the method followed, for example, in Latin America, which met with little difficulty but which caused enormous cultural harm) and the progressive notion of "adaptation." The problem involved not only the use of the "Chinese rites" (the civil and also religious ceremonies in use in China) but also the various "rites" of the Eastern countries, particularly India, Japan and Indochina. One side held that these ceremonies were "pagan" and therefore should be condemned, their use forbidden to Christians. The other side insisted on looking upon them only as an expression of the local religious sentiment or of merely civil ceremonies (like the signs of veneration given to Confucius).[4]

The difficulties in solving this problem came chiefly from the little knowledge Europeans had of these "rites," which each missionary described differently, and from the fact that even the "natives" of the various countries of the Orient, questioned by papal emissaries, did not agree in giving the rites religious or merely civil significance. For nearly two centuries the universities and theologians of Europe were deeply engaged in a discussion of the problem, which even became politically involved. At the same time, in the countries of the Orient, despite some papal instructions, the missionaries adjusted their conduct somewhat at will according to their personal judgments or their particular religious order or the region to which they belonged. The question was resolved, conservatively, by Pope Benedict XIV with the bull *Ex quo* (1742) on the Chinese rites and *Omnium sollicitudinum* (1744) on those of the Malabar coast, which meant the condemnation not only of the "rites" themselves but also of those principles of adaptation of the mission that were stated and defended by *Propaganda Fidei;* (see the preceding note 3), which in turn delayed or impeded missionary studies and methods, and condemned the evangelization of the great eastern countries to almost complete ineffectiveness.[5]

The prohibition for Christians to take part in the ritual ceremonies of ancestor worship—the real national religion of Vietnam, originating in China—contributed to keeping alive the suspicions with regard to Christianity as a "foreign religion" and constituted the major obstacle to the conversion of the upper classes of the kingdom who were still hostile to the Church. Although the same Gia-Long tolerated the presence of Christians as a debt of gratitude toward Mgr. Pigneau de Béhaine, he was not converted, particularly because of the Church's intransigent position toward ancestor worship, rather than the other norms of Christian morality (like the prohibition against having several wives). For more than half a century his successors were pitiless towards the Christian religion and abandoned themselves to excesses of violence rarely encountered elsewhere in the numerous persecutions suffered by Christians at different times and places; a violence that then provided France with the opportunity to intervene in defense of the missionaries and the Christians by occupying the whole of Vietnam and depriving it of its independence.

Persecutions for political and social reasons. The French colonial sway over Vietnam, which became stabilized towards the end of the last century, resulted in the Vietnamese having to bear a bitter yoke. When they arrived in Indochina, the French did not understand that they were dealing with a nation that had an ancient and already well organized civilization but treated the Vietnamese as if they were primitive tribal peoples that were to be subjected to the colonial yoke and assimilated into "Western civilization." Hence the whole drama of Vietnamese nationalism with its veiled hostility toward France and unfortunately toward the Church and the Christians, who somehow were considered to be responsible for the French intervention in the country.

After the death of Gia-Long in 1820, his son, the Emperor Minh-Mang, came to power and, contrary to his father, fostered a profound mistrust towards foreigners, particularly missionaries. In 1825 he published the first edict hostile to Christianity[6] and, in 1833, a second edict that announced a general persecution: it was this year that began the systematic "hunt of the Christians" which lasted for half a century until France intervened to put a stop to it.

The persecution raged throughout the country with savage cruelty, causing agitation and indignation in Europe where the Emperor of Hué's behavior was judged to be an affront to Christians and to France (almost all the foreign missionaries were French).

In reality Minh-Mang was driven to persecute the Christians not out of religious reasons but for reasons that were chiefly political and social. As an intelligent and strong-willed man, he proposed to unify the whole of Vietnam under his scepter by reenforcing his power over all the regions and races of the country. To this end the Christian religion was viewed as a revolutionary obstacle toward bringing order into the country on the principles of Confucian law. Minh-Mang was thwarted in his plan by many internal revolts (many, even among the mandarins, would not put up with his despotic absolutism) and foreign wars, and he therefore raged against the Christians to remove an element of divisiveness, to affirm his own authority and to satisfy the mandarins and the men of letters who asked for the greatest severity against the Christians.

Faith in the "civilizing mission" of Europe. At Minh-Mang's death in 1841, he was succeeded by his son Thieu-Tri, a weaker character, who mitigated the fury of the hunt for Christians. But unfortunately Thieu-Tri's reign was also marked by the intervention of French ships in order to obtain the freedom of various missionaries still in prison under the death sentence: in 1843, 1845 and 1847, French ships stood off-shore at Hué, demanding the liberation of the missionaries and freedom for the Christians without obtaining anything more than a few promises but also arousing the wrath of the Emperor and the reaction of the court and the mandarins against the "foreign priests" and the Christians "who had sold out to a foreign power." Thus, missionaries and Christians became the first victims of an intervention they had not sought and whose sole aim was to secure their freedom (later, other interventions by France had quite different aims, as we shall see).

Before going on to what happened subsequently, we must make some preliminary remarks about these ever more frequent interventions of France on behalf of the missionaries. Today, naturally, we would condemn a similar policy and feel that we could not agree with the requests made later by the missionaries for protection by the French military power. Nevertheless, to be just, we must seek to understand the mentality of the time which fully explains, though by no means justifies, this collusion between religion and politics.

The mentality of the time was one of "Europe's civilizing mission," and the West, which was then invincible, undefeated and much more advanced than the rest of the world, had no reason to doubt the superiority of its own civilization over all the others; it was therefore unthinkable that citizens of European countries, priests or laymen, could suffer insults or persecutions in any country from what we call today the "third world." And this was equally true for both Protestant and Catholic countries. Armed intervention or the threat of intervention to protect the missionaries and their Christians from persecution was considered not only the right but the duty of the State, even when the government professed a religious neutralism at home.

Again, we must add that for the bishops and the missionaries the intervention of France was desired for the real good of the country, at least as they saw it and conceived of it. At a time when Asian and African (and therefore "pagan") countries were falling one after the other under European domination, which brought them modern progress and "civilization," and at a time when Vietnam was dominated by a caste of mandarins and intellectuals that kept the people in a state of semi-serfdom and troubled by wars and bush-fighting, the missionaries thought spontaneously of the liberation of the country by the French and believed that under the spur of an advanced nation like France, Vietnam would also make rapid progress.

The Emperor Tu-Duc and the French intervention. Returning to
our historical account, Thieu-Tri was succeeded in 1847 by his son
Tu-Duc, who almost immediately resumed the persecution under
a form that was still more cruel than Minh-Mang's after the edicts
of 1851 and 1855: "The European priests"—we read in the first—
"are to be thrown into the depths of the sea or the rivers. The
Annamese priests, whether they trample on the cross or not, will
be cut in two that all may know the severity of the law."

After these edicts, the hunt for Christians and priests once more
broke out, with the destruction of churches and the burning of
Christian villages; the faithful were forced to trample on the cross
and to build pagodas and offer sacrifices to the idols; under torture,
some revealed the hiding places of the priests and missionaries, who
suffered horrible deaths. These excesses of cruelty, known in
Europe through the letters of missionaries, drove Napoleon III to
intervene.

But the French expedition, led by Montigny, had its ships damaged in bad weather and arrived on the Annamese coast in reduced
formation, without causing any impression. Since Montigny's mission did not show the proper strength it was also unsuccessful in
making contact with Tu-Duc, and Montigny himself advised the
French bishop, Mgr. Pellerin, to go to France and inform Napoleon
III personally. Pellerin left immediately and Napoleon promised
him effective action.

Meanwhile, another wave of persecution broke out in Vietnam,
and one of the victims was a Spanish bishop, Mgr. Diaz, O.P. The
relief expedition therefore took on the character of a Franco-
Spanish demonstrations, with ships and soldiers from both nations.
On August 31, 1858, the port of Tourane surrendered after a short
bombardment from the sea, and in the February of 1859 the French
and Spanish conquered Saigon, but the violence of the persecutions
increased in the rest of the country and new imperial edicts ordered
every kind of cruelty against the Christians (for example, while the
Christians who refused to abjure were killed by torture, those who

trampled on the cross were branded: on the left cheek with the words *Ta dao*—perverse religion—and on the right with the name of their prefecture, making flight impossible).

On June 5, 1862, at Saigon, Tu-Duc signed the first treaty with France which granted freedom of worship to Christians and settled the French occupation of the provinces in Cochin China. It is not possible for us here to follow step by step the French occupation of Vietnam, which by this time had nothing to do with the anti-Christian persecutions. Our concern here is only to point out that the article of the 1862 treaty dealing with the granting of freedom to the Christians was in no way respected: thus from 1862 to 1885, when the French sway over the whole of Vietnam was complete, in those regions still under the control of Emperor Tu-Duc (who died in 1883) the persecutions knew practically no respite, since to the hatred of Christianity—a religion that revolutionized a whole ancient concept of life and ancient traditions—was added the hatred of the French.

This is the origin of the whole drama of Vietnamese Christianity which is still going on today: the Christians were not only hated as Christians but also as supposed allies of the French, and therefore traitors to their country.

Full religious liberty under France. At the end of the last century, Vietnamese Christianity enjoyed complete religious liberty, and its organization and "nationalization" were far advanced. Despite the persecutions of the previous century, which had given to the Church some 130,000 martyrs—of whom 125 were beatified by various successive popes[7]—Catholics never ceased increasing in number: 310,000 in 1800, with 20 European priests and 119 native; 420,000 in 1840, with 24 European priests and 144 native; 708,000 in 1890, with 270 European priests and 398 native; (in 1890 there were 10 vicars apostolic and one vicar coadjutor, 2,886 churches or chapels).

Has the freedom of worship and religious propaganda obtained with the intervention of France really been a gain for Vietnamese

Christianity, or has it rather been a loss? This is a question asked even at the end of the last century by a priest of the Paris Foreign Missions in an extremely lucid passage on those times, which sums up many other citations that could be given in this regard. The historian Louvet made a special point that the French had not gone to Vietnam from the beginning of the century at the request of the missionaries, and their interventions solved nothing but rather contributed to unleashing still further persecutions of the Christians:

To announce the Gospel to the non-believers we did not expect the support of the civil power; I shall even go further, we did not want it. We had already been working for two hundred years in China, Siam and Annam: we were persecuted many times and we always triumphed over the persecutors by patience and death. But since they gratuitously came to compromise us without our having asked them, was it not then right for them to come to our aid? Should our 500,000 Christians have been the victims of the generous intentions of our fellow-countrymen and pay with their blood for the sterile interest that they awakened?[8]

After detailing the massacres of the Christians after the intervention of the French until their total occupation of the country, Father Louvet continues:

At such a sacrificial price, did our Christians at least obtain religious freedom? Alas! In Saigon and in the colony the presence of our fellow-countrymen made us secure from persecution and permitted us to work out our tasks in peace. This is an important result, and we must realize it. Unfortunately, the religious indifference and the bad example given by the great majority of the European population created new difficulties for the propagation of the Gospel, difficulties that may be worse than those of the past . . . . And there is a further problem, for many of us, of knowing whether, when all is said and done, religion gained anything from the presence of our countrymen. On my account, I am one of those who think that religion lost out, and that it continues to do so day after day.

And then he adds another reason, besides bad example and immorality, which until then were unknown and were brought by the French; a reason that ought in the future to prove to be most valid:

Previously, Catholicism, even though proscribed, enjoyed the sympathy of the people, and more than once the missionaries found shelter among the good pagans. Today the situation is much changed. The presence of the French in Saigon and the growth of their power in Annam injured the heart of national pride, especially with the intellectual and cultivated class. Hence the implacable hatred which could not vent itself against our fellow-countrymen fell back most heavily on our wretched Christians. . . . And as the climax of this adventure, our poor Christians who had been pillaged, oppressed and massacred solely because of hatred for France, found unjustifiable mistrust from the French. Not only did they let them be massacred without anyone's seeking to help them, but they even accepted the accusations of the pagans against their own people, saying that they were the cause of wars, and often prevented them from defending themselves. The missionaries who courageously risked their lives to protect their Christians saw themselves written up in the French papers as ringleaders and brigands.

Was French colonization a boon for the Church? That the period of French colonization did not represent for the Vietnamese Church an excessively prosperous period is demonstrated simply by statistics: the Christians had almost the same rate of increase as they did in the previous half-century amid a full and bloody persecution: 1840: 420,000 baptized; 1890: 708,000 baptized; 1933: 1,365,000 baptized; 1941: 1,638,000 baptized.

If the conversions of this long period did not correspond in peacetime to those in the preceding period of persecution, it is due chiefly to the fact that the Church appeared to the Vietnamese people to be bound up with colonial domination, and therefore a "foreign religion." On the other hand, in the preceding period of persecution the Christian community was evidently revolutionary in regard to the established power, the bearer of revolutionary novelties (the rights of the human person, the equality of all men, the emancipation of women, the freedom of marriage, etc.), and therefore favorably viewed by the people; the heroism of the priests and the Christians under torture could only increase the admiration of the pagans and their fascination for a religion capable of producing such heroism.

The vicar apostolic of Vinh, Mgr. Eloy, said in 1925:

What are the impressions caused among the pagans by these conversions to Christianity? The new convert is looked upon as a traitor to the country; by accepting a foreign religion, he denies his country and, at times for months, he is made to feel the weight of this supposed betrayal. Time finally extinguishes this animosity; but before conversion, there are numberless obstacles in the way and the pagans only leave them in peace when the will of the neophyte is seen to be irrevocable; but this sometimes takes years. The pagans' horror for the foreign religion still remains instinctive.[9]

This animosity toward the "foreign religion" came also from the fact that the French colonization, as we have already said, was a heavy burden to bear for the Vietnamese, especially for the intellectual and affluent classes, among whom in fact conversions were always extremely rare. The colonial organization in Vietnam was characterized by an administration entirely in the hands of the French, without the local population having any means to express itself.

Unfortunately, on the part of the Church during the colonial period there was an absolute enfeoffment to the French authority, for it was commonly thought at the time that colonial expansion was a providential aid to the work of the missions, despite the papal *monita* on the question, which clearly distinguished colonialization from evangelization and recommended that the missionaries keep far away from any political action.[10]

Mgr. de Guébriant, superior of the Paris Foreign Missions and a man of great worth (whom Pius XI called "the greatest missionary of our time"), wrote around 1930: "The presence of the French (in Vietnam) gave to the missionaries and their work the security they lacked and with security a large measure of freedom. And this is already appreciable. Moreover, the French regime by and large is sufficiently beneficent to do honor to the religion of France."[11] At the Missiological Week of Louvain in 1925, Mgr. Eloy, whom we have already quoted, declared: "If France were to get out of Indochina tomorrow all the Christians would be exterminated."[12]

However it would be false to think that the Church got other advantages from the colonial power besides freedom. France, as we also pointed out in the case of the African colonies where it protected and favored Islam, always followed the policy of assisting the local religions as a means of subduing the natives: in Vietnam the chief support of the government and the colonial functionaries—for the most part Freemasons and anticlericals—went always to Buddhism, which was considered to be the only organized religion of the country. In 1932, at a meeting of the International Colonial Institute, Gourdon, the French delegate, in speaking of the colonial policy in Indochina, stated: "It is impossible to count on Christianity, whatever its intrinsic value, to give these populations a morality or an effective rule of life. Christianity says nothing to them. Therefore the government policy consists in ignoring the Catholic mission and in intensely favoring Buddhism which has great intrinsic value, and is furthermore perfectly adapted to the native mentality and tradition."[13]

An historian of the French missions writes that after the French occupation of Vietnam, there was a complete reversal of sides between Christians and non-Christians: the persecutors of yesterday, enemies of France, passed themselves off as friends of the French and as victims of the Christians by bringing against them numerous accusations of disturbing public order and oppressing the majority of the population, forcing conversion, etc. These accusations, which came especially from the mandarins, are absolutely improbable since the Christians are dispersed among the pagans in the proportion of one to thirty. . . . These completely calumnious and still unproved accusations were too often received favorably. Circulars, with a really disastrous moral effect, were sent out several times at the request of the mandarins but with the signature of the French authorities, either to besmirch the honor of the missionaries, by lightly accepting the accusations brought against them, or to forbid pagans to embrace Christianity and to order the newly baptized to return to their old religion.[14]

The path of the Church under the colonial regime. The progress of the Vietnamese Church during the colonial period was noteworthy for the organization and the "nativization" of the Church more than on the level of conversions.

Following the "apostolic visitation" to the missions in Indochina, which was made by Mgr. Lécroart, a bishop from China, in 1922–23 at the behest of Pius XI, Mgr. Aiuti was chosen apostolic delegate at Saigon in 1925 (the see was later transferred to Hanoi in 1951), and in 1934 the first national council was held, presided over by the new apostolic delegate Mgr. Dreyer. The 8 vicariates apostolic became 14 in 1939, while throughout the country parishes, schools (65,000 pupils in 1939) and other charitable and missionary works were being organized. At this period in Vietnam we have the appearance of numerous congregations, both of men and women, especially for the schools, the works of charity, or for specialized apostolates: Redemptorists, Brothers of the Christian Schools, Trappists, the Sisters of St. Paul from Chartres, the Franciscan Missionaries of Mary, etc.

The progress of the local clergy was one of the first concerns of the Church, and perhaps in no other mission country did the Christian people give such an inspired answer to the call of ecclesiastical and religious vocations. Since the "jungle seminaries" of persecution times, in 1941 there were eight major and some twenty minor seminaries, with 482 clerics and 1,298 seminarists. In 1941 there were the following religious forces in Vietnam: 1,406 native priests and 340 foreign; 74 native religious priests; 635 native nonpriest religious and 45 foreign; 4,684 native sisters and 371 foreign; 2,956 native catechists.

On the eve of the Second World War, Vietnam had also three native bishops (vicars apostolic), and the first, Mgr. Nguyen-Ba-Tong of Phat Diem, was consecrated in 1933.

The evangelization of the country was extended to the whole territory with the inauguration of new missions, especially on the central plateaux inhabited not by Vietnamese but by the Montagnards, who were primitive mountain tribes.[15] Vietnamese Christianity, although well organized and very fervent, remained composed almost solely of poor countryfolk and tribal peoples: the upper classes had rejected Christianity.

We wish to point out one last negative aspect that the persecutions of the past and the colonial era produced in the shaping of the Christian community: the ghetto mentality and the closedness to the outside that made, and partially still makes today, the Catholics strangers to the national community. Partly responsible for this is also the missionary methodology of the past not only in Vietnam but also in other parts of the world (in Africa for example), which tended to form "Catholic villages," i.e., to convert entire villages, or else to regroup the converts in special villages separate from the others, in order to make a better spiritual atmosphere for them and to prevent their contamination by pagan practices of life and religion. An historian of the Vietnamese Church points out that:

the unanimously inevitable consequence was that these united Christian communities did not at the time succeed in avoiding certain characteristics of closed communities. In fact, they worked out a Catholic language, not only in writing but also in daily conversation. Many Vietnamese were Christianized, but the faith caused them to adopt their own calendar, the use of saints' names, and a whole "culture" that remained alien to the non-Catholics. And these differences could more

easily become separations insofar as the Christians had undergone the
bloody persecutions of the imperial power for two centuries. The
colonial era was only partly favorable to the social integration of
Catholics, who were always suspected of favoring the foreign power.[16]

Notes

1. On the history of the first missions to Indochina see the basic work, H.
Chappoulie, *Aux origines d'une Église—Rome et les missions d'Indochine
au XVII siècle,* vol. I (Paris: Bloud et Gay, 1943), vol. II, 1948.

2. Fr. de Rhodes is generally considered the chief author of the romanization of the Vietnamese language, which previously had been written in
ideographs derived from the Chinese. In practice, this was the work of different missionaries of his time, but the first book in the romanized Vietnamese language is by Fr. de Rhodes, printed at Rome in 1651 by the
Typographia of *Propaganda Fidei;* and reedited in the original Vietnamese
and Latin text in 1961 at Saigon (Alexandre de Rhodes, S.J., *Catechismus pro
iis qui volunt suscipere Baptismum in octo dies divisus,* reedition of the
work published at Rome in 1651 (Saigon: Thinh-Viêt, 1961). We must point
out that the romanization of the language, which came into general use
throughout Vietnam (today the ancient ideographic characters are only
studied in the Faculties of Letters in the university), gave the country a
wonderful instrument for expression and diffusion of the national culture.

3. It is enough to think of Streit-Dindinger, in vol. V of the *Bibliotheca
Missionum,* Aachen, 1929, who catalogues and sums up the content of more
than a thousand titles (books, pamphlets and articles) on the rites problem.

4. The question was naturally not so simple: there was, for example, the
translation of the terms of Christian theology into the Eastern languages and
the name of God itself (whether to use the terminology and the name of
God of the "pagans" or to invent new terms); the problem of certain Christian ceremonies, even sacramental ceremonies, that were ill-adapted to the
sensibilities and the traditions of the East (saliva, which in the East is
looked upon in the same way as excrement, while we use it for baptism;
the anointing of the sick, which obliged the priest to touch certain parts of
the bodies of the dying, with grave scandal to the orientals, etc.); whether at
least to take account of certain prohibitions of the caste system in India that
are deeply rooted in popular custom, etc.

5. In our century the evolution of missionary thought first produced a

mitigation of the severe norms set down by Benedict XIV, and caused them to be abolished with the instruction of *Propaganda Fidei* in 1939. See D'Elia, "La recente Istruzione della S.C. di Propaganda Fide sui riti cinesi," in *La Civiltà Cattolica*, 1940, pp. 123–127, 191–202.

6. In the decree we read: "The perverse religion of the Europeans corrupts the heart of men. For a long time various European ships have come here to make trade and left behind teachers of the religion of their kingdom. The teachers have seduced and perverted the heart of the people and have adulterated and corrupted good customs. Is this not a real calamity for our kingdom? Therefore it is fitting that we oppose similar abuses in order to lead our people back on the right path."

7. Among the martyrs of Indochina in the 19th century the most famous was Blessed Théophane Venard, whose letters from prison are among the most beautiful pages of Christian hagiography of all times.

8. L. E. Louvet, *Les Missions Catholiques au XIXe siècle* (Lyon: Oeuvre de la Propagation de la Foi, 1894), pp. 211–213.

9. *Les aspirations indigènes et les Missions, compterendu de la troisième Semaine de Missiologie de Louvain*, Louvain, 1925, p. 30.

10. Read, for example, the encyclical *Maximum Illud* (1919) of Benedict XV, and various documents of Pius XI (especially the letter *Ab ipsis* of 1926).

11. *Missi*, no. 2, Lyon, 1956, p. 42.

12. P. Charles "La crise du Vietnam" in *Revue de l'Aucam*, Louvain, September, 1948, p. 220.

13. Charles, *art. cit.*, p. 216.

14. J. B. Piolet, *La France au dehors; les missions catholiques françaises au XIXe siècle*, vol. II (Paris: Colin, 1902), p. 475.

15. On the missionary epic of the Vietnamese plateaus, read P. Dourisboure, C. Simonnet, *La Mission des Grands Plateaux* (Paris: Editions France-Empire, 1961).

16. A. Marillier, in *La Missione*, no. 29, Milan, 1961, pp. 92–93.

II

Catholics in the anti-French Resistance

The fact that the Church obtained freedom of worship as a result of the intervention by the French armed forces was long a source of concern for Vietnamese Catholics, accused by their fellow-countrymen of being "serfs of the French" and members of a "foreign religion." Vietnam's declaration of independence in August 1945 offered Catholics the opportunity to free themselves from this inferiority complex which they felt was profoundly unjust, contrasting as it did with their feelings as good nationalists.

A new situation after the war. First of all, we must specify that Catholics knew they were good patriots, on an equal footing with other Vietnamese: not a few intellectuals had belonged to the various associations and movements that created a national awareness and that fought for independence. For example, the famous nationalist movement Viet Nam Quoc Da Dang, which in 1929–31 succeeded in raising armed revolts against the French, had among its most prestigious leaders two Catholics, Nguyen Gia Luan (brother of two priests from Phat-Diem) and Le Huu Canh, both of whom paid with their lives for their attachment to the national cause.[1]

It was therefore no wonder that during the last war (when Vietnam was occupied by the Japanese forces but was still in great part run by Vichy French functionaries), in the general agitation of the nationalists for independence the Catholics aligned themselves with the other exponents of patriotic movements.

At this time many nationalist movements rose up in Vietnam, and to two of these the Catholics gave their support: the Dai-Viet Dan-chinh (People's Party of Greater Viet), founded and led by the two Nguyen-Tuong-Tam brothers, who were Catholics and members of the group Tu Luc Van Doan, a literary school very much in fashion at the time, and the Dai-Viet Quoc Xa (National Socialist Party of Greater Viet), which attracted the Catholic Ngo Dinh Diem, an already outspoken nationalist personality, who led the nationalist agitations in Annam (central Vietnam).[2]

The most organized nationalist movement (and the only one with very clear ideas and programs) had its leaders not in Vietnam but in China: Vietnamese Communism, which had enjoyed the support of the Chinese nationalist regime of Chiang Kai Shek, as his ally in the war against Japan. Under the leadership of its founder, Ho Chi Minh, the Vietnamese Communist party founded in May 1941 at Tsingsi in southern China the Law for the Independence of Vietnam (in an abbreviated form, *Viet Minh*) with the collaboration of many Vietnamese nationalist parties, including Catholics as well. In the following years, despite the fact that Ho Chi Minh was put into prison for thirteen months by the Chinese nationalists, the Viet Minh initiated in Vietnam guerrilla action against the Japanese and the French under the leadership of a young history professor who was also a Communist, Vo Nguyen Giap, and with the help of Chiang Kai Shek's Chinese and the Americans.

With the defeat of the Japanese on August 15, 1945, the Viet Minh controlled almost all of Vietnam without a shadow of opposition and with the support of a great part of the people, especially after the foundation of the first national government on August 29, 1945, with Ho Chi Minh at its head. He declared the country's independence on September 2 of that year.[3]

Enthusiastic Catholic support for the Ho Chi Minh government.
The Catholics—who numbered some 1,600,000, or some 18 percent
of the whole Vietnamese population, representing the most organized and active group—supported the Viet Minh en masse and the
Ho Chi Minh government, formed with a majority of Communists
but also with representatives from the other political and religious
forces: one of the ministers was a Catholic (Nguyen Manh Ha,
economy minister), together with two Buddhists and others from
non-Communist political parties. In 1950 one missionary magazine,
very well informed on Vietnam, wrote:

After the Japanese overturned the French authority in Indochina in
1945, the Vietnamese clergy and Catholics took an active part in the
national emancipation movement of which the Viet Minh had taken
command. If we must judge harshly certain excesses and the xenophobia
that certain fanatics confused with patriotism, this action was legitimate
in itself and can in no way be condemned. At that time the Viet Minh
did not claim to be a party but rather the Front for National Independence, and many people then did not see that because of its leaders, its
doctrine and its methods, it was nothing else but the Vietnamese
Communist party, whose chief aim, even though it was disguised, was
the setting up of a Marxist regime in Vietnam, profiting to this end
from the aspirations for national independence.[4]

And in 1946 another missionary publication explained the tenacity
with which the Catholics supported the Viet Minh government,
even after it was abandoned by other nationalist forces:

If the Catholics succeeded in proving their patriotism to all nations, they
are sure of filling in the trench separating them from their non-Christian
fellow-countrymen. . . . The duty of the Christians, therefore, is no
longer in doubt and the greater part of them have already made their
choice. Enlightened and sustained by bishops of their own kind, they
were no longer willing to commit the error of their forebears of the
last century and they refused to compromise their faith by making

common cause with the metropolitan power. They wanted to preserve the independence of Christianity by working with their fellow-countrymen for the legitimate cause of the independence of their homeland.[5]

In the beginning relations between the Viet Minh government and Catholics were of the best. The Vietnamese bishops—four at that time—besides sponsoring the Catholic demonstrations in favor of the government, wrote two collective letters to Pope Pius XII (September 23, 1945) and to Christians of the whole world (November 4, 1945) to seek their aid in the struggle for independence:

Our people [wrote the Vietnamese bishops to Pius XII] has asked its four bishops to offer to your Holiness the homeage of its profound respect and to ask your blessing . . . upon our independence which the people has acquired and intends to keep at any price. . . . We, Vietnamese bishops, beg your Holiness . . . and all the Catholics of the world, especially in France, to uphold the decision of our dear homeland.

In the second message the bishops asked the English and American Christians to

Intervene effectively in order to keep us from the horrors of war. . . . Our country at present is invaded and is defending its independence, the cause of justice and freedom . . .[6]

The support of the Catholics for the independent government of Ho Chi Minh was enthusiastic and total. On September 23, 1945, a great demonstration was called at Hanoi by Catholics in favor of the Ho Chi Minh government. About 40,000 faithful and priests participated and filed through the center of the city singing hymns to the independence of the country. The following October 8, another manifestation of Catholics brought together 30,000 faithful in the city of Vinh, the episcopal see of a strongly evangelized region, in support of the national government. The unitary adhesion of the

Catholics during this period to national independence and the government presided over by Ho Chi Minh caused Bernard Fall, the most authoritative historian of modern Vietnam, to write: "It is without doubt that the Catholic Church of Indochina was at a certain time in the vanguard of Vietnamese nationalism . . . and it is no less certain that it simply was expressing the profound feelings of its faithful."[7]

Also, the Vietnamese priests residing as students and as chaplains of the Vietnamese communities in France took a position that was in favor of the independence of their country:

All the Annamese priests living in France, 20 in number [said their statement] met on the fourth and fifth of January 1946 in Paris. . . . At this occasion, they offered Holy Mass for their so sorely tried country. . . . In the difficult situation through which the whole of Indochina is passing today, they thought it their duty to echo the Annamite bishops who shared and upheld the legitimate aspirations of their people for national independence, according to natural and divine right . . .[8]

The nationalist sentiment of Catholics took on a clearly anti-French coloration, like that of all the Vietnamese, and was skillfully used by the Viet Minh's propaganda against the French missionaries in Vietnam:

The Vietnamese Catholics [writes the *Bulletin des Missions*] from the very beginning enthusiastically united for the cause of independence. . . . Unfortunately their hearts did not always remain pure. Feelings were so high that the local priests avoided contact with the missionaries. . . . Moreover, from the beginning, the propaganda campaign against the French was orchestrated in a special way against the missionaries. The Viet-Minh radio and press not only accused them of being agents of a foreign colonial power, but spread the most absurd accusations about them, such as polluting the wells, hiding arms, destroying the dikes of the Red River to cause floods and famines, etc. Truth obliges us to say

that a certain number of Catholics associated themselves with these
loathsome manoeuvers in the wish, legitimate in itself, to show their
fellow citizens that they were no less patriotic. . . . They were secretly
stirred up by agents of the Viet Minh, who saw the influence of the
missionaries as an obstacle to the expulsion of the French and sought to
launch a movement among the Catholics in favor of the autonomy of
the Vietnamese Church.[9]

At the top level, between Catholics and Communists, a fruitful
collaboration seemed to have been initiated, with Catholics in the
Communist dominated government and in responsible posts, and
with the Vietnamese bishops who with their pastoral authority
among the Catholics, supported the first steps of the independent
government. But basically the Viet Minh militants, indoctrinated in
materialism and in the struggle against religion, performed acts of
vandalism against churches and religious houses, ill-treated foreign
missionaries and disturbed religious functions.[10] The bishops intervened with the head of the government, and Ho Chi Minh himself
promised that the antireligious vandalism would stop immediately:
the decree of September 20, 1945, which threatened severe penalties
for those who damaged churches or pagodas and disturbed functions or exponents of religion, bore his signature.

Ho Chi Minh showed his appreciation of the Catholics' support
of his government. As soon as he was in power, he adopted as the
national holiday for the whole of Vietnam—the independence day
—the first Sunday of September every year, a date which coincided
with the Catholics' national day, celebrated for many decades in
remembrance of the martyrs for the faith of previous centuries. At
Christmas of the year 1945, Ho Chi Minh sent a warm message to
the Catholic community, praising Catholic participation in the
independence movement and in national reconstruction.

An already mature but ungranted independence. More than
twenty years ago, Vietnam could have joined the independent na-

tions, with a government supported by the majority of the people. On the contrary, two facts prevented the attainment of this goal, which in August 1945 seemed so imminent.

In the first place, there was the attitude of France, which did not want to recognize independence (although it was already more than ripe) in Vietnam and in the other countries of French Indochina (Laos and Cambodia). In October 1945, de Gaulle charged Admiral d'Argenlieu with the "reestablishment of French sovereignty in the territories of the Indochinese Union," offering the Vietnamese people broad internal autonomy in the framework of a close dependence on France. All the French governments up to 1954 composed or sustained by the Socialists and at times also the Communists (the first government of de Gaulle which refused independence was also supported by the Communists) continued to fight a colonial war that was ill-timed and out of place.

The second fact that prevented the attainment of a stable systematization in Vietnam (not only in 1945, but also today) was the Communist aim to make the whole country a "people's democracy" of the Chinese variety, suppressing non-Communist nationalist movements and thereby driving them into the opposition's camp since they decided to sell their skins dearly, first with the support of the French and then the Americans.

This is the basic point of the Vietnamese question and explains the desperate resistance of the non-Communist nationalists, especially the Catholics, to the Communists' will to dominate. Joseph Buttinger, who assembled an impressive documentation on recent Vietnamese history, makes this basic judgment about the origin of the conflicts between the various nationalist political parties in Vietnam in regard to the year 1945 and afterward:

This government [i.e., of 1945, P.G.] was firmly in the hands of the Communists. The danger that they would participate in a war directed by other nationalist forces was, from the beginning, improbable. But the Communists were not satisfied with being only the lead group within the national movement. They in no way wanted to share its control. Since they were sure enough of achieving their goal, they insisted upon a monopoly of leadership. The Communists were not interested in a free Vietnam dominated by their political enemies in the nationalist camp. The policy they followed either toward their nationalist adversaries or in regard to France, proved that they were in favor of the war only if and when they could be sure that it could aid their plans to become the leading party in a liberated Vietnam. In reality, the struggle for independence was for the Communists only a vehicle for the conquest of power. If they fought hard, as they did, it was because their political control of the country during the war would have made the achievement of independence the equivalent of the establishment of a Communist regime.[11]

The political panorama of Vietnam, which declared its independence in the last months of 1945, was most varied: in addition to the Communists, there were numerous parties or small, national political groups. The following are the three major ones that enjoyed the support of the nationalist Chinese:[12] the VNQDD (The Democratic Nationalist Party of Vietnam), an old anti-Communist movement, the DMH (Dong Minh Hoi, Revolutionary League of Vietnam), founded in 1942, grouping together other minor parties and movements, and the Dai Viet (Party of Greater Vietnam), founded in 1941. These three parties, together with other minor ones, took part in the national coalition government, which respected a certain democratic freedom: freedom of the press and assembly, of worship and thought, etc.

On the other hand, on the military level, things went differently: the government troops were solidly in the hands of Communist elements (Giap was the minister of the interior and of defence) and occupied the whole country, everywhere establishing the party organization and seeking to absorb the non-Communist patriotic groups. This ploy began to cause the leaders of the non-Communist movements to worry, and they defended their autonomy at least within the framework of the united struggle against the French colonial troops. The Catholics, who previously had joined *en masse* with the Viet Minh organizations, also began to seek political and military autonomy. In October 1945, at Phat-Diem, a strongly Christianized zone south of Hanoi, two Catholic political and social organizations were founded. The first, Cong-Giao Cuu-Quoc (Catholic Association for National Salvation) had all the character-istics of a political party; it participted in the Viet Minh National Front and began to organize the Catholics militarily into autono-mous groups for the purpose of fighting the French; these were dependent on the government military command (i.e., General Giap) but were also ready to defend the national freedoms even against eventual Communist attacks, whenever this might be thought necessary. Moreover, this was the plan of the other non-Communist political movements and of the various Buddhist sects (especially the Cao-Dia and Hoa-Hao) who had organized or strengthened their own military groups.

The second of the Catholics' movements, Lien-Doan Cong-Giao Viet-Nam (Federation of Catholics of Vietnam) had a more social and cultural character: its plan was to act in the social and cultural field by means of trade-union action or the cooperative farms and by using the press to diffuse Christian ideas.

The only general elections in Vietnamese history. The coalition of the nationalist government, dominated by the Communists, went from before August 1945 to the Spring of 1946, when the coalition broke up and the Communists, little by little, took power and eliminated the opposition. The most important events of this period are the general elections of January 6, 1946, and the formation of the second Ho Chi Minh government, which was still more rep-resentative than the first.

The elections gave rise to strong conflicts among the parties, since they took place under the control of the army and the Viet Minh government, which meant the Communists, in the greater part of the country. The non-Communist movements claimed democratic

control for the election machines and sought as much as possible
to insure themselves against the eventuality of corruption and
trickery: an agreement of December 22 between the Viet Minh and
the other parties assigned to the latter a certain number of seats in
the future national assembly, whatever the result of the elections.
They developed peacefully, however, and produced unexpected
results: although Ho Chi Minh experienced great personal success
in many districts (even 100 percent of the votes), the national
estimate was not favorable to the Communists.

The national assembly resulting from the elections, which met
for the first time on March 2, 1946, was made up as follows:[13]

	seats
The independent nationalist parties (union of small groups and movements, including Catholics)	90
Viet Minh (Ho Chi Minh's Communists)	82
VNQDD	26
DMH	22
Democrats	15
Socialists	27
Marxists (Trotskyites)	10

Even if the Viet Minh had not had the overwhelming majority
that the non-Communist nationalists feared, its control over a great
part of the country would not be in doubt.

At the meeting of the National Assembly on March 2, 1946, the
president of the Assembly, the Catholic, Ngo Tu Ha, proposed to
entrust Ho Chi Minh with "the mission of forming a government
of national union." This was how the second Ho Chi Minh government was formed, which was even more representative than the
first, with only four Communists (including Ho Chi Minh) among
the twelve ministers, two of whom were Catholics, and with a High
Cabinet, a consultative body presided over by the ex-Emperor Bao
Dai, which also included the nationalist bishop, Mgr. Le Huu Tu

(vicar apostolic of Phat-Diem). However, the command of the army remained in the hands of General Giap.

At this point—March 1946—there is no doubt that the Vietnamese were all united around the coalition government and quite decided to fight the French if they were to oppose independence with arms. But with the spring of 1946 everything began to change, and Vietnamese Communism made clear the goals it would pursue: undisputed domination of the country through the elimination of the non-Communist resistance forces.

This fact is often ignored by the historians of the Vietnamese question, who preferred to give exclusive importance to the relations between the Viet Minh and the French: conferences to discuss independence (Dalat, Fontainebleau, etc.), discussions in the French parliament, armed encounters, etc. These undoubtedly were important events bearing on the war between the Vietnamese and the French, but it seems to us that observing the internal relations among the various nationalist movements within Vietnam was at least as important, since this brings us to the roots of the Vietnamese war still in progress. In other words, few authors explain why in the resistance struggle against the French the Vietnamese began in total unity and then their national front became divided, with the result that the only ones who remained in the fight were the Communists; or why the Catholics, enthusiastic supporters of Ho Chi Minh and the Viet Minh in 1945–46, soon became only a few years later fanatical anti-Communists. There must be some reason for this! And it is this reason that at least partially explains, from the aspect of the internal quarrels among the Vietnamese, why the war in Vietnam is still going on.

The Viet Minh eliminate the non-Communist patriots.

The Communists efforts [writes Buttinger] to obtain the monopoly of leadership by means of persuasion and with the force of their action had notable success during 1945. But in the spring of 1946 the honeymoon of the national revolution was over. The peaceful methods to promote national unity around the Viet Minh, which Ho Chi Minh undoubtedly preferred to the assassination of his political opponents, no longer produced the spectacular results that they did at first. . . . When the Communists became aware that they could no longer broaden the basis of the government . . . they concentrated their efforts more than ever on perfecting their direct organizational control of the masses. Among the means to this end there was the creation of the so-called Lien Viet (National Popular Front) on May 27, 1946. Into this pseudo-coalition the Communists drove every legal political party, dozens of ethnic groups inspired by the Viet Minh and all the cultural, religious and professional organizations of the country. . . . The political "program" of the Lien Viet was "independence and democracy," but its real aim was to take away whatever independence the existent mass organizations still possessed, and to put an end to any democratic competition within the national movement. In fact the Lien Viet was nothing but a kind of super-Viet Minh and whoever refused to join the Lien Viet was denounced as an opponent of independence and democracy, which was equivalent to being doomed to assassination.[14]

The Communists' ploy from March to December 1946, when the war with France was in full swing, was this: while there still was a coalition government and a national assembly composed of various political forces, and while in the cities there was a certain freedom of the press and assembly, in the fighting zones the Viet Minh military forces (i.e., forces that were both official and Communist) were aiming to occupy the whole country, even the regions already held by other patriotic forces deriving from government parties, by eliminating or absorbing those forces opposed to an uncontested domination by the Communists. We must add that the nationalist parties had already previously protested against the use of armed forces in favor of Communism: wherever they arrived, the Viet Minh forces set up "people's commissars" who abolished the old power of the mandarins and the village chiefs, carried on the "indoctrination of the people," set up "people's committees" and "popular assemblies," etc. In brief, by means of the Viet Minh government forces, commanded by Communists and swiftly Communized, they spread the organization, methods, and ideas of the Communist party throughout the country.[15] This caused the other political movements, and the Catholics with them, to form their own armed forces to prevent Communism, through the governmental army and under the mantle of legality, from succeeding in dominating the whole country.

In the spring of 1946, the Viet Minh forces began to attack the non-Communist patriotic bands and to occupy the territories they garrisoned systematically.[16] The first to experience the Viet Minh attack were the two strongest and oldest parties, the VNQDD and the DMH, who, as we said, had their representatives in the government and in the national assembly. In fact, in March 1946, the French arrived also in North Vietnam, after having taken the place of the English in the South, and demanded the withdrawal of the nationalist Chinese troops that garrisoned those areas and above all supported not only the two nationalist parties mentioned but also the Viet Minh government.

The void thus created by the withdrawal of the Chinese [writes B. Fall] gave the Viet Minh an unique opportunity to liquidate what remained of the nationalist opposition parties, since they had now lost their protectors. Since, on account of their anti-French hatred, they broke with their new occupiers [i.e., the French], they found themselves quite suddenly terribly alone, in the face of an implacable enemy that had been waiting for this moment for almost a year.[17]

In the military campaign to eliminate the two nationalist parties, the Viet Minh did not act alone but in full accord and collaboration with the French colonial troops.

Convinced by the militant xenophobia of the Nationalist Party (VNQDD) and the Revolutionary League (DMH) that these two groups constituted a serious threat to internal order to the agreement of the 6th of March 1946 (*signed with the Viet Minh government at*

Hanoi), the French joined with the Viet Minh in the military and police action against them.[18]

Not only were the Communists happy that the French had refused to collaborate with the genuine nationalists, besides the Viet Minh, but they wanted these forces to disappear completely, as they did the French who, for their own reasons, helped the Communists to eliminate the common enemy. . . . All who refused to collaborate, no matter whether their position was anti-Communist or not, were persecuted by the French. . . . As for the Communists, the secret of this unholy alliance was, naturally, in the totalitarian nature of the goals they pursued. No one who had really fought for independence should remain at the end of the war, with the exception of the Viet Minh.[19]

In June 1946 the Viet Minh, with the kind assistance of the French command, occupied the whole zone of influence of the DMH in North Vietnam and in the following July liquidated the centers of the VNQDD force in the Red River valley, incorporating their soldiery or eliminating by force those who showed resistance.

We must remember [writes Ernst Kux] that in Indochina the Communists have pursued and implacably exterminated all the other nationalist elements. We know today that Ho Chi Minh handed his nationalist rivals over to the French secret police, that by 1946 the secret Communist organization had exterminated all the partisans of the national Vietnamese movement of the Kuomintang, and that by means of purges he had got rid partially of the nationalist rivals with whom he presented a common front in the Viet Minh.[20]

Retracing the history of this time, so crucial for the future of Vietnam, *Eglise vivante* writes:

Every day the gulf between Communists and nationalists grew wider. Although they fanatically fought France, the Communists sought to reenforce their domination over the population by implacably eliminating the most indomitable among the nationalists, absorbing the neutralists and organizing the masses. It was in this way that the eminent chiefs of the Hoa-Hao and the Cao-Dai (two Buddhist religious sects) were drawn into an ambush and cravenly assassinated. The very tactic of the scorched earth policy, besides its military effectiveness, seemed designed precisely for a purely political goal: accelerate the proletarization of the masses in order to throw them more securely into the arms of Communism. The scorched earth policy was practiced with the most implacable severity, despite vehement protests from the population, which had been sorely afflicted by the loss of its possessions. It was clear that the Viet Minh wanted to profit from the exceptional circumstances deriving from the war in order to effect a rapid bolshevization of the country.[21]

I have been able to gather first hand testimony about this period from the Buddhist, Tran Quoc Buu, the president of the Vietnamese Confederation of Labor[22] in Saigon, who told me of his personal experiences:

As a young man I was an elementary school teacher and a rabid nationalist. Before the last world war, without joining the Communist party, I worked for a few years with the Communists in the service of their clandestine organization, in order to fight the French colonialists. In 1939 I was arrested by the French police and condemned to ten years at hard labor; In 1940 I was deported, along with a few Communists from Vietnam, to the prison islands of Poulo-Condor in the Pacific Ocean. I stayed there five years: it was a most cruel imprisonment I spent in full brotherhood with the Vietnamese Communist leaders . . . and I too was convinced that only Communism could bring freedom and justice to Vietnam and to all the oppressed peoples.

In 1945, when the war ended, we were liberated and returned to Vietnam, but in that year the resistance to the French began, led by Ho Chi Minh who had with him the majority of the people. I too became a combatant with the Viet Minh and for four years fought side by side with the Communists against the French. It was at this time that I finally realized the truth: the Viet Minh were not interested in the liberation of our country but in the triumph of their own idea, the domination of their party. In fact they were eliminating all their adversaries,

all the patriots that did not think like them. I myself saw scores of
fighters for Vietnam's freedom killed not by the French but by the Communists themselves: entire bands of patriots were drawn into traps and
eliminated or else they were tricked and handed over to the French.
Among the Viet Minh themselves, those who were repelled by these
methods were eliminated. Thus, what in the beginning had been the
fight of a whole people against the colonialists, became the private war
of the Communists to impose their own regime on the people. It took
me a little time to realize that the killing of the non-Communist patriots
was systematic. At the beginning I thought it was only the traitors who
were being killed, but then it was clear as the sun to me that all the
non-Communists were being eliminated. At that moment all I could
think of was flight. . . . (Tran Quoc Buu told me afterwards how he
succeeded in fleeing to France in 1949 where he was trained in trade
union techniques, and when he returned to his homeland the following
year he became one of the founders of the unions he now leads).[23]

*Ho Chi Minh's third government represented only the Commu-
nists.* In eliminating the patriotic bands of their adversaries, the
Viet Minh leaders did not neglect the evolution of internal politics.
In a few months the opposition newspapers were suppressed, and
then the various nationalist parties were purged of their most
prominent personalities who were arrested on the most diverse accusations and suffered the fate of political parties in all the "people's
democracies." They were dissolved or "renovated" and integrated
into the Lien Viet (United National Front) set up in May 1946 by
the government.

When the national assembly that originated with the elections of
January 6, 1946, met on October 30 of the same year, the parties
opposing the Viet Minh had no more than 37 free representatives;
and at the session of the following November 8, the members of
the opposition parties were only 2: "Mass arrests became so frequent [writes Bernard Fall] and were openly admitted even by
the official newspaper of the government of the republic. In fact,
one can read in the *Cuu Quoc* (National Salvation) of November

1, 1946: 'On October 20, our police arrested more than 300 persons during the course of an operation. After close questioning, the majority remained in prison, waiting to be transferred to the concentration camps.' "[24]

On November 2, 1946, the first Constitution of the Democratic Republic of Vietnam (promulgated on November 9, was adopted, with 240 votes for and only 2 against: on November 3, Ho Chi Minh's third government was formed. Now the Communists had all the key ministries, and only three (Public Works, Social Security and Health) were left to representatives of the minority parties that still existed. The "Supreme Counsellors" of Ho Chi Minh—who had assumed the offices of President of the Republic, Prime Minister and Foreign Minister—were still the ex-Emperor, Bao Dai (who soon after fled to Hong Kong) and Mgr. Le Huu Tu, who in his episcopal see of Phat-Diem continued for a few more years his collaboration with the Viet Minh. To reenforce the representativeness of his government after the elimination of many opponents, Ho Chi Minh requested the chief representative of the Catholics, Ngo Dinh Diem, to join with him. But Diem answered by positing specific conditions: give back the freedom of political parties and of the press, rebuild the unity of all the nationalist forces, form a government that would be basically representative of the voting that took place in January 1946, and finally, Diem requested that the government armed forces be headed not only by Communists but also by men from other political views.

The conditions were naturally not accepted, and Diem remained in the opposition camp, choosing soon afterward the road of exile in America, so as not to compromise himself with the French on the one hand and a now clearly Communist government on the other.

The "Republic" of Mgr. Le Huu Tu. For a few years more, the vicar apostolic of Phat-Diem (today in North Vietnam), Mgr. Le Huu Tu, collaborated with the Viet Minh government. At the moment of his joining the government, he said to Ho Chi Minh: "As long as you fight for the independence of Vietnam, I shall always be at your side; but if you wish our country to become Communist, I shall always fight against you."[25]

After the Viet Minh government became clearly Communist in the autumn of 1946 by eliminating many opponents[26] and the war between the Viet Minh and the French broke out violently, the situation of the Catholics became extremely delicate. They wanted independence at any cost, but they also were very much afraid of a Communist victory under the guise of independence. The goal was clear: to become independent but not under a Communist government.

In order as much as possible to prevent the Communists from identifying in the eyes of the people the two terms of Communism and independence, the Catholics rallied around the Bishops of Phat Diem (Mgr. Le Huu Tu) and Bui Chu (Mgr. Pham Ngoc Chi) in a strongly Christianized area (about a third of the inhabitants were Catholics). Under the energetic leadership of Mgr. Le Huu Tu, the local troops and a proper administration were organized. Through an agreement with the Ho Chi Minh government, the region had its own administrative regime and its own police, depending directly on the Bishop of Phat Diem.

The "Republic of Mgr. Tu" counted about 1,600,000 inhabitants, of whom more than half a million were Catholics (who had come from other areas, especially Hanoi), and it was garrisoned by the patriotic forces of the Cong-Giao Cuu-Quoc (Catholic Association for National Salvation), whose members were in great part Catholic. Here there was freedom of the press and of assembly, and into the Phat-Diem region there came as refugees those patriots who had fled from the zones controlled by the Viet Minh in order to escape the political police of the Communists; after the abolition of freedom of the press by the Ho Chi Minh government, the only non-Communist nationalist newspapers that could still be published were those printed at Phat-Diem. They were the *Nhiem-Vu* (Duty) and the *Thieng-Keu* (The Voice that Calls).

In the same issue of *Eglise vivante,* which we have already mentioned, we have the following:

The nationalists, the intellectuals and all those who for whatever reason feared the implacable repression of the Viet Minh came to settle in this region. . . . Phat-Diem became the gathering place for all non-Communist patriots, the point of attraction where all the unsatisfied wishes of the powerless nationalists joined forces. . . . With the growing importance of Phat-Diem, an idea spread abroad in public opinion: the leadership of the future anti-Bolshevik struggle ought to be given to the Catholics who constituted the most cohesive and united part of the nation and whose religious faith was irreducibly opposed to Communism. Among all the nationalists, the Catholics were the most intransigent, and they always refused to take part officially in nationalist governments formed with the support of the French to oppose the government of Ho Chi Minh.

The existence of a nationalist but non-Communist enclave like the ones at Phat-Diem and Bui-Chu could not have pleased the Viet Minh. If they tolerated such a situation in the beginning, it was because they did not have the strength needed to eliminate it and they had other adversaries among the nationalists with whom they had to settle accounts, as we have already seen. But from 1947 on, although they continued to extend a strained hand of friendship to the Catholics officially, the Viet Minh, since they no longer had any groups opposing them except the Catholics, began to turn against them.

The *Fides* agency of those years reports many facts that show the two tactics used by the Viet Minh against the Catholics: the "extended hand" with signs of friendship (messages of condolence at the time of the death of a bishop, assistance given to the Spanish missionaries for their school, honors for bishops within their own areas, etc.) and the "clenched fist," with many serious aspects: missions burned and sacked, real episodes of religious persecution, the killing of catechists and also of priests, and above all the elimination of the bands of Catholic patriots fighting at the side of the Viet

Minh. Here we cannot reflect the whole compass of the news reports appearing between 1947 and 1949, but Bernard Fall, the best student of the Viet Minh movement, wrote: "As for the Catholics in the regions under Viet Minh control during the war, the Viet Minh gave a military resolution to the problem they posed. . . . The province of Thai-Binh was twice marked out for massacre of the Catholic villages. At Cao-Mai it is reported that 180 Catholics, men, women and children, were burned alive in the village church."[27]

In its chronicle of these years, *Eglise vivante* wrote:

No Vietnamese wants the colonial occupation any longer, and all are directly or indirectly involved in the struggle. Unfortunately the Communist "Independence Front" (Viet Minh) stifles resistance and dominates. The people do not want Communism any more than they want colonialism, but in practice there is no third way. Wherever it can, the people struggles against the foreign invader and also resists the Communist leaders, since it is aware that the official troops of the Viet Minh rarely expose themselves to battles with the French; they leave this to be done by the local armies and reserve for themselves the task of internal political domination. The Communists have seen to the killing and disappearance of priests and Christian leaders and the red terror oppresses everyone. But they present themselves as the artisans of independence and national unity. And after failing in a vain attempt to seduce the Christians and to win them over to their ideology, they are content, as they wait for the next phase, with frightening them, rather than making a frontal attack. When they attack their adversaries, Christians or others, they never do so by advancing ideological reasons, but with motives of national interest, and when they burn too undocile a village, they invoke the "scorched earth" principle.[28]

The Viet Minh attack in the Phat-Diem region. In the meanwhile, the region of Phat-Diem and Bui-Chi continued to be administered by Mgr. Le Huu Tu and his bands of patriots, who kept their distance both from the French army, allied with the army of Bao Dai,[29] and from the Viet Minh. They, however, were tightening the ring around the region.

Even in 1947 there was an accurately prepared attempt on the life of the Bishop of Phat-Diem which failed at the last moment. Immediately afterwards the Viet Minh radio began to attack the Phat-Diem Catholics, accusing them of being social reactionaries and not revolutionaries, and of breaking the unity of the national front.[30] Mgr. Tu responded by organizing "people's missions" to combat the Communist propaganda in the region. He wrote pastoral letters that were read throughout Vietnam (he wrote forty-seven up to 1949) and answered the Communist accusations in the region's two free newspapers, which were sent secretly even into the Viet Minh zones. Above all, at Phat-Diem, refuge was given to all who fled from the Viet Minh areas, especially to political representatives and intellectuals who, from Phat-Diem, accused the Ho Chi Minh government of the oppression and bolshevization of the entire country.

In 1949 relations between Catholics and Communists became more tense, since the Chinese problem was added to the others to divide men's opinions even further. The victory of Mao's troops in China exalted the Viet Minh (the Viet Minh radio reported: "*Our* troops have occupied Shanghai . . . *our* army is marching on Nanking . . ."), while it seriously worried the Catholics who were informed about the actual persecution going on against the Chinese Church.

This was joined to the settling of accounts. In September 1949, the Viet Minh occupied the episcopal seat of Bui-Chu, after shooting encounters with the Catholic patriots, and on October 15 they made a direct attack on the episcopal see of Phat-Diem; but on the following day, October 16, parachute troops from Bao Dai's army came to the aid of the Catholics and freed the region from the Viet Minh.

There was much discussion over the intervention of Bao Dai's parachutists to help the troops of the Bishop of Phat-Diem, and the Viet Minh openly accused Mgr. Tu of having requested aid from the "stooge emperor of the French." In an open letter of response, Mgr. Tu indignantly rejected the accusation. Here are a few extracts from the statement: "I never had the idea of calling the French army to help us in ridding ourselves of any danger whatsoever. Even in 1947, in an extremely critical situation, we always refused any help from the foreigners. . . . As we have always repeatedly said, we never had relations with the Bao Dai government."[31]

Mgr. Tu then went on to state that the recent decree of the Holy Office on Communism merely confirmed the line that had been followed for some time:

Both before and after the Decree we condemned Communism as a doctrine opposed to the Catholic religion, and at the same time, together with our fellow countrymen, we fought for our homeland's independence . . .

Consequently, we had hardly seen the parachutists [of Bao Dai], when we sent a message to the leader of the resistance to tell him to unite the national troops and the Catholic defenders to resist together. But the leader of the resistance [i.e., the Viet Minh] informed us that they had already all retreated. It was for this reason that we thought that we too should retreat from Phat-Diem in order to leave no room for false interpretations; and our priests advised us to do so. However, after two days, we changed our mind. Unfortunately, a certain number of Viet Minh in different places engaged in acts of violence, confiscation of property, personal arrests, surrounding of Catholic villages and laying waste to them. They went so far as to destroy the dike built by the missions to protect the rice-paddies of the people. Similar behavior showed us that there was no longer any safe place and that we were obliged to remain. On the other hand, we want also to remain with you [i.e., the faithful], to share with you both joys and sorrows. Thus, priests and faithful can be calm: God is witness that we never made a move nor said a word that could be interpreted as an invitation or an appeal to any army to come to our aid . . .[32]

The drama of conscience for the Catholics. After the violent rupture of 1949 (Mgr. Le Huu Tu was still part of the Ho Chi Minh government, as a "Supreme Counsellor") there began a new act in the troubled history of the Vietnamese Church. The disorientation of the Catholics and the intimate drama of those who had believed in and fought enthusiastically for the freedom of their homeland were well described by a French missionary in Vietnam at that time. After describing the Viet Minh's methods of acting, Fr. Cussac wrote:

At that time, there began for many Vietnamese Catholics a painful drama of conscience: were they to continue to uphold the action of a party whose chief aim was to effect the triumph of Marxist ideology, which was opposed to their religious convictions? Or should they give up their participation in the work of national emancipation, the very object of their patriotic aspirations, which, by so doing, would risk their being thought to be traitors to the cause and to be treated as such? Vietnamese Catholics are ardent nationalists and are no less profoundly attached to their faith and to their religious freedom for which they do not hesitate to sacrifice their lives if need be: we could cite many ancient and recent examples to this effect.[33]

From the political point of view, the bishops resolved the problem by keeping apart from the political problems of the country, while the war between the French and the Bao Dai government on the one hand and the Viet Minh on the other became ever more and more widespread and bloody, especially after the Communists were able to have the assistance of Mao's China. Only the two bishops of Phat-Diem, Mgr. Le Huu Tu, and Bui-Chu, Mgr. Chi, took a clear position in favor of the Bao Dai government. Their aversion toward the Viet Minh, with whom they had been allied for five years, caused them to fight in the opposite camp, with the nationalist government supported by France.

Naturally the bishops' position towards Communism as a materialist doctrine could only be one of condemnation, especially after the Holy Office's decree which we have mentioned, and after triumphant Communism in nearby China had begun a severe persecution of the Church and of all other religions. Meeting in Hanoi from November 5–10 in 1951, the bishops of Vietnam published a collective pastoral letter in which we read the following:

We believe it is our duty to put you on your guard [i.e., the faithful] against the grave danger of atheistic Communism. . . . There exists the most complete opposition between the Catholic Church and Communism, to such an extent that the Holy Father has declared that it is absolutely impossible to be at the same time a Catholic and a Communist, and that every Catholic who belongs to the Communist party is de facto separated from the Church. But not only is it forbidden to join the Communist party: you may not cooperate with it or do anything that in some way might bring the Communist party to power. The danger is so grave and the possible consequences so terrible that we feel obliged to put you on your guard also against the subterfuges and ruses that serve uniquely and solely the Communists' aims. . . . No longer is it the interests of the fatherland that count, but only the interests of Communism . . .[34]

Other important facts forced the Catholics more and more to take sides against the Viet Minh and to come gradually closer to the Bao Dai government. In 1949–1950 it seemed clear to all in Vietnam that the Viet Minh government was closely bound up with the Communist countries (aid from China and Russia, praise of the Chinese regime in the Viet Minh propaganda, etc.) and that it wanted to impose a Communist regime on the Vietnamese people. After having eliminated the non-Communist parties and organizations, as we said, the Viet Minh had reconstituted, with accommodating parties and persons, a "National Front" that presented a non-Communist façade. But, as *Témoignage chrétien* recently pointed out:

. . . under the influence of China, which is giving increasing assistance to the Viet Minh, an important political evolution is coming about in Vietnam. Although up to about the end of 1949, Ho Chi Minh's government included both Communists and nationalists, grouped together in the "National Front," the Chinese claimed that the Communist party had a predominant role. Everything that up to then had been able to keep up the appearance of a nationalism that was of course "on the Left," although independent, had now to be put aside. Hence, the creation of the Lao Dong (the Workers' Party, which was in effect Communist), the great purge of 1950–51, and the progressive transformation of the Democratic Republic of Vietnam into a people's democracy . . .[35]

The Viet Minh's action against the Christian communities. In the regions under the control of the Viet Minh armed forces, the Marxist indoctrination of the people had become customary and the methods of fighting and agrarian reform were clearly inspired by those used by the Chinese Communists. Moreover, the oppression brought against the Catholics and the religious institutions augmented in proportion as the war turned in favor of the Ho Chi Minh government. A missionary wrote from Vietnam:

No longer hoping to attract Catholics into their camp, at the beginning of 1953 the Viet Minh modified their tactics and no longer hid their real face. From then on they officially aligned themselves with the Russian bloc and professed to "study Russia and China" in order to imitate them as much as possible. Actually, in the areas subject to their control, we note, with some nuances due to the state of war, the same policy that in China attempted to snuff out the Church and to divide her in order to destroy her: an economic attack on the missions which were ruined by exorbitant taxes and tariffs, resulting in the closing of schools and other Catholic welfare projects; the teaching of Marxism in the government schools and in the army; the suppression of Catholic Action; the systematic denigration of the Vietnamese clergy (there is no other clergy in the Viet Minh zones); the forbidding of priests to go into neighboring Christian areas without prior authorization, which had the effect of depriving these areas of religious instruction and the sacraments; arrests of priests accused of collusion with the enemy, of hostility to the democratic government. . . . People's trials accompanied by torture; condemnations to prison and forced labor, etc. Whoever has read

the accounts written by missionaries expelled from China is struck by
the similarity of what went on there to what we are told by those who
were able to flee from the Viet Minh zones . . .[36]

Another missionary gives an account of certain types of harassment used in this period by the Viet Minh against the Catholics
and the Church:

In certain Churches a large picture of Ho Chi Minh was exhibited; in
other places the catechism children were obliged to add the name of the
President to the beginning of the sign of the cross. . . . In one place
mass stipends were suppressed, in another they were increased and distributed: one third to the priest and two thirds to the "community"
which in this instance was represented by the political commissar. Taxes
on hearing mass, taxes on crucifixes that were hung in houses or worn
at the neck. . . . Some no longer dare to come to church . . .[37]

Other more serious incidents were reported by the *Fides* agency
during these years, although it was not yet possible to speak of a
real action of persecution in regard to the Church. For example,
priests were removed from their faithful and at times imprisoned or
held in semi-internment in far off provinces;[38] in 1954, at the
moment of the Geneva accords, some 116 priests, almost all Vietnamese, were in the prisons of the Viet Minh.[39] We shall record
a few extracts of a long study made by the *Fides* agency, which
describes very well the situation of Catholics in the Viet Minh
zones during these years:

The Communist regime (in Vietnam) is characterized as a regime of
controlled freedom: the freedom is all the greater and the control all the
weaker when they are dealing with a new group of people which they
do not yet have completely in hand; on the other hand the control is all
the more rigid and freedom all the more restricted when the regime
feels surer of itself. The consequence is that the control increases to the
point of a dictatorial regime, while freedom decreases to the point of

disappearance. . . . In the beginning the Catholics were left religious freedom with the intention of winning them to the cause of the regime, which presented itself simply as an incarnation of the national soul; at the same time, however, their religious ceremonies were spied upon and inspected, and traps were laid for them. If by chance complaints happened to be leveled against the regime, if they assumed ambiguous attitudes, they were accused: propaganda seized upon the situation . . . and then it was ready, against the guilty priest or Christian layman, with the indictment of a people's trial entirely favorable to the regime. . . . In certain regions, in Langson, for example, courses in Marxism were regular and obligatory. . . . In order to reach adolescents and the youth, the regime imposed its own schools and programs on everyone. . . . The fundamentals of the faith and the reasons for obedience to the hierarchy were attacked . . . the representatives of Rome were denigrated, from the simple priest to the apostolic delegate . . .

The study then speaks of the tactic of dispersing the Catholic groups and of separating the priests from the faithful so that the isolated individuals would be easier to "reeducate":

Defections, however, are an exception. Among a dozen priests with somewhat ambiguous attitudes, three or four are perhaps suspect of apostasy or punished with suspension. On the 2nd of December 1952, Fr. My was shot at Hué; another ten or so priests were condemned and possibly also killed and a few are under house arrest, waiting for trial; some who were too stubborn to be . . . re-educated are in forced labor. The faithful too have given proof of their fidelity: four leaders of the "Catholic Federation" were killed and 25 are in prison; some individual apostasy is noted as well as the unfaithfulness of a few catechumens, although there is no mention of any defection of Catholic groups.[40]

The most important historical period in modern times. What was the attitude of the Catholics towards the government of Bao Dai? We have already pointed out that the bishops—with the exception of the two from Phat-Diem and Bui-Chu—abstained from taking any political position.[41] As for the Catholic people, up to about

1950–1951 they remained outside the government because it was clearly supported by the French colonialists; but soon afterward, since the Communist threat was growing, they in great majority supported it. Again in 1950, Bao Dai had requested various Catholic public figures (among whom were the brother of Bishop Le Huu Tu and Bishop Ngo Dinh Diem) to join his government, but all he got were refusals. In the new government launched in June 1952, however, five of the ministers were Catholics (once again, Diem did not accept the invitation).

The historical period we have studied (1945–1954) is undoubtedly decisive in our understanding the position of the Church and Catholics in the following years, i.e., the mistakes made and the good opportunities that they will see slip away, especially the spirit of the ghetto and a closedness to the world, the defensive attitude, the fanatical anti-Communism that will prevent the Christian community availing itself of other aspects of the Vietnamese reality.

All of this derives either from the past history of the Church, from the persecutions in past centuries and from the inferiority complex that matured during the French colonization, or from the frustration of the nationalistic sentiments that the Catholics felt after 1945. After the last war they dedicated themselves to the death to upholding the nationalistic idea and the national government of Ho Chi Minh in order to prove to their brother Vietnamese that they were not second class patriots, but their hopes were brutally betrayed by the partisan politics of the Viet Minh, who used the national idea to impose their dictatorial regime upon the people by exterminating all the non-Communist patriots who wanted a country free not only from the foreign yoke but also free from any other oppression. Unfortunately, the non-Communist nationalists were no longer successful in rebuilding their ranks after the massacres suffered in the years after 1945. Buttinger puts this sad consequence in bold relief: "The Communists' policy of killing all true nationalists who opposed the Viet Minh also had profound and lasting consequences on the future of Vietnam. In fact this is one of the reasons for the weakness of the non-Communist movements which, with their best and most important young candidates assassinated, were deprived of the formation of qualified leaders, who would have been enough to govern them for many years."[42]

And this, in reality, is the drama not only of the Catholics but of all the non-Communist Vietnamese, especially with those who are bound to a religious notion of life (Buddhist Confucianists, etc.); it is the drama of modern Vietnam to have found on its way, at the most delicate moment of its history (the transition from colonialism to independence), a Communist party that was already well organized under a personality of the highest prestige, who knew how to take hold of the banner of nascent nationalism and to use it solely in his own favor.

Notes

1. The Viet Nam Quoc Da Dang (VNQDD, Nationalist Democratic Party of Vietnam) was the first modern party to fight for the independence of the country. Founded in 1927 (the Communist Party was founded in 1930), it was inspired by Chiang Kai Shek's *Kuomintang*. This party organized the major anti-French revolt before the last world war, that of Yen Bay, when a few divisions of Indochinese troops rebelled together with part of the population. The revolt, however, was put down with bloodshed, and even though it was followed by other minor skirmishes, it signaled the end of the VNQDD, at least temporarily: its leaders fled to China, others were killed by the French and the party was reconstituted in China under the aegis of Chiang Kai Shek. Tonkin was thereby left free to organize another large party, the Communist, which never made the mistake of rising against the French before the proper time and thereby risking massacre of its leaders and the destruction of the organization. When the Second World War broke out, there were many parties and nationalist movements in Vietnam, but the best organized and most widespread was the Communist. For the history of Vietnamese nationalism, see the most complete treatment in a Western language on Vietnam: J. Buttinger, *Vietnam: a Dragon Embattled* (London: Pall Mall Press, 1967), in two volumes and 1346 pages.

2. The participation by some Catholic representatives and groups in the anti-French resistance before the last world war was, however, purely inci-

dental and did not induce the Catholic masses, much less the official Church, to take sides for Vietnamese independence. Elsewhere, the rest of the people, the non-Christian masses, also did not actively take part in the resistance, which was always the work of an intellectual elite. On the other hand, during and after the world war it was really the whole people that became aware of the national idea and vigorously supported it.

3. The independence of Vietnam had already been declared for the first time by Bao Dai in the preceding March, when the Japanese had overwhelmed the French forces and incited Bao Dai, Emperor of Annam, to set up the first independent government of the country under their protection. With the defeat of the Japanese, Bao Dai abdicated in favor of Ho Chi Minh who named him his counsellor.

4. *Missionaires d'Asie,* a review of the Paris Foreign Missions, March-April, 1950, p. 38.

5. *Le Bulletin des missions,* no. 1, Bruges, 1946, p. 17.

6. See the integral text of both messages in *Le Bulletin des missions, op. cit.,* pp. 39–40.

7. B. Fall, *Le Viet Minh 1945–1960* (Paris: Colin, 1960), p. 165.

8. Integral text in *Missi,* nos. 9–10, 1947, p. 230. The letter was signed by the group leader of the Vietnamese priests in France, Rev. Cao Van Luan, who was later rector of the University of Hué and an opponent of the Ngo Dinh Diem regime.

9. No. 1, 1948, p. 64.

10. P. Devillers, *Histoire du Vietnam de 1940 à 1952* (Paris: Ed. du Seuil, 1952), p. 187.

11. Buttinger, *op. cit.,* vol. 1, p. 399.

12. At the Potsdam Conference (July, 1945) it was decided that, at the defeat of the Japanese, Vietnam would be occupied by the Chinese North of the 16th parallel and by the English in the South; a provisional occupation which, for want of French troops, was to cease when the French arrived. In the South the English handed over the country to the French, while Chiang Kai Shek's Chinese nationalists in the North made an agreement with the Viet Minh and handed over to them the arms taken from the Japanese as well as all administrational control. Therefore, before the French were able to set foot in North Vietnam, the Communists had already spread out their organization network, which was later to serve in the anti-French guerrilla war; this mini-war, in fact, was waged more in the North than in the South of the country.

13. We are reported this data from Fall, *op. cit.,* p. 47. Fall is quoting the official sources of the Viet Minh government.

14. Buttinger, *op. cit.,* vol. I, pp. 399–400.

15. In the laudable effort to stamp out illiteracy, the government charged the army with setting up schools for children and adults everywhere, with obligatory attendance: the school text books, however, were all of Marxist inspiration.

16. On the Viet Minh fight against the nationalist non-Communist movements up to their total elimination, see *France et Viet-Nam. Le conflit franco-vietnamien d'après des documents officiels* (Geneva: Ed. du Milieu, 1948), pp. 22–24 and 35–38.

17. Fall, *op. cit.,* p. 50.

18. E. J. Hammer, in *Vietnam, History, Documents and Opinions on a Major World Crisis,* ed. by M. E. Gettleman (London: Penguin Books, 1966), p. 74.

19. Buttinger, *op. cit.,* pp. 418–419.

20. E. Kux, in *La Chine et le Vietnam, Un problème pour la conscience chrétienne,* collaboration (Mulhouse: Salvator, 1968), p. 58.

21. *Eglise vivante,* no. 3, Louvain, 1950, p. 300. On the extermination of the leaders and the troops of the Cao-Dai and Hoa-Hao religious sects, see the full description given by Buttinger with the relative documentation, *op. cit.,* pp. 410–415. While the extermination of the patriots of the VNQDD and the DMH nationalist parties came about in North Vietnam on the borders of China, the elimination of the politico-religious sects deriving from Buddhism took place in the South, in the Mekong delta south of Saigon. Still today the Hoa-Hao and Cao-Dai sects, numbering about three million faithful, are the fiercest adversaries of the Communists, who in 1946–7 killed their leaders and prophets.

22. In South Vietnam there exist four national trade unions, but the one that includes the vast majority of the labor force is the Vienamese Confederation of Labor which has some 600,000 members and is organized on the international plan similar to the Italian CISL. The Confederation was founded in 1950 as a "Christian trade union" by Catholics, with a few Buddhists (among whom was Tran Quoc Buu), but it subsequently became a union open to men of all religious faiths (today 70 percent of its membership is non-Catholic).

23. That the Communists eliminated the non-Communist patriots in Vietnam ought not to cause wonder when we think that the same method was used in various countries of Eastern Europe (e.g., Czechoslovakia), where at the end of the Second World War the non-Communist parties represented the majority of the population but were also reduced to silence, while their more prominent leaders were killed or condemned in various ways.

24. Fall, *op. cit.,* p. 51.

25. Mgr. Le Huu Tu was born in 1897 in the Hué region. He came from an old Catholic family (two of his brothers are priests and two sisters nuns), became a Trappist at Phuoc-Son, where he was distinguished for his piety and studiousness, and became the superior of that monastery. After fifteen years he was nominated vicar apostolic of Phat Diem and consecrated bishop in October 1945, after he had already became known as an exponent of nationalism; a few months later, Ho Chi Minh named him his "Supreme Counsellor." Mgr. Le Huu Tu took refuge in South Vienam after the Geneva agreements in 1954 and died near Saigon in May 1967.

26. An observer living in Vietnam wrote in 1948, giving the story of this period: "At the end of 1946, there remained only one party, the Viet Minh, which was of a very Communizing tendency, and which, under the label of national union against the foreigner, governed with extremely detestable totalitarian methods" (in *Rythmes du monde*, 1948, p. 70).

27. Fall, *op. cit.*, p. 167.

28. See, *Eglise vivante*, no. 1, Louvain, 1949, pp. 101–102. We do not have available the numbers of *Témoignage chrétien* (hereafter *T.C.*). for those years, but we read in other periodicals of the time that at this period *T.C.* was conducting a press campaign against Vietnamese Communism, denouncing the terrorist methods and the stifling of all the non-Communist resistance forces. Today, with the Americans involved in Vietnam and the French out, it seems, according to *T.C.*, that the Vietnamese Communists have totally changed their fighting methods and their aims and that they are now bent on upholding them unconditionally.

29. In July 1949 the French succeeded in forming the "Bao Dai government," recalling the ex-Emperor from Hong Kong and placing him at the head of a nationalist government which for all practical purposes was under their control.

30. After eliminating the most influential personalities in the nationalist political parties, the Viet Minh created the Lien Viet (United National Front), which included stooge parties under the close control of the Viet Minh, who dominated the government and the armed forces.

31. The text of the letter is found in *L'Actualité religieuse dans le monde* (the periodical that changed its name later to *Informations catholiques internationales*), fasc. of September 15, 1954, pp. 16–17.

32. The decree of July 1, 1949, condemning Communism, AAS, 1949, p. 334).

33. G. Cussac, "La situation du catholicisme au Vietnam," in *Missionnaires d'Asie*, Paris, March–April, 1950, p. 40.

34. *L'Actualité religieuse dans le monde*, Paris, September 15, 1954, p. 17.

35. *T.C.*, August 10, 1967, p. 13 (quoting in part Lacouture amd Devillers).

36. Cussac, in *Les Missions catholiques*, Paris, May–June, 1954, p. 130.

37. C. Simonnet in *Missionnaires d'Asie*, Paris, 1954, p. 153.

38. *Agenzia Fides* (Italian edition), February 9, 1952, p. 44.

39. Abbé Bourguignon, *op. cit.*, p. 78.

40. *Agenzia Fides*, "Le cristianità della zona vietminh nel Vietnam," December 19, 1953, pp. 394–396.

41. At the end of 1953 the bishop-vicars apostolic addressed a common pastoral letter in which they asked Catholics to assume their responsibilities on the political plane without involving the Church and to act always as Catholics in temporal activities for the welfare of the whole country. The bishops did put the faithful on guard against claiming to possess, as Catholics, formulas that were valid absolutely. The letter was published because a few groups of Catholics were founding political movements and claiming to represent the Church.

42. Buttinger, *op. cit.*, p. 412.

III

Anti-Christian Persecution in North Vietnam

The long war between the Viet Minh and France ended with the Geneva agreements of May–July 1954, after the French troops had suffered the grave defeat of Dien Bien Phu. The least that can be said about these agreements is that they were the best of the still possible solutions, even if they resulted in the absurdity of a country divided in two (at the 17th parallel). But the greater absurdity was undoubtedly the manner of partitioning the country: the North to the Communists and the South to the nationalists. The North (Tonkin and North Annam) was the region that had the most anti-Communists because for many years the population had known the cruel methods of guerrilla warfare used by the Viet Minh and was witness to the elimination of the non-Communist bands effected during the mini-war against the French (see the foregoing chapter); the masses of Vietnamese Catholics, who were clearly anti-Communist, flocked to the North. In the South, on the other hand (South Annam and Cochin China), which passed into the hands of the non-Communist nationalists, the population had little knowledge of the action of the Viet Minh since they had operated mostly in Tonkin (remember that Ho Chi Minh's first and second governments were in Hanoi), and also because, since 1949, assistance to the Viet Minh had come from China, i.e., the North. The regime and the person of Ho Chi Minh therefore enjoyed a great reputation in the South as the nationalists who had won the war against French colonialism.

The Geneva accords and the right of option. Each of the two governments, in the North and the South, received that part of the country that was most hostile or at least indifferent to them, while their respective populations would have preferred to live in the other half of the country (i.e., the Northerners in a non-Communist regime and the Southerners under the national hero Ho Chi Minh, free from any foreign patronage that had a colonialistic flavor). One fact of grave importance should immediately show the absurdity of a partition of the country that was so opposed to popular feeling: the flight to the South of about one million North-Vietnamese, two thirds of whom were Catholics.

One clear statement of the Geneva agreement of 1954 foresaw the exchange, between the North and the South, of persons who had the intention of opting for one or other regime. This clause (14 d) stated: "From the date of enforcement of the present agreement until the troop movements are completed, any civilian, living in a region controlled by one side and desiring to go to live in the zone assigned to the other side, will have the right to do so, and must be aided in his aim by the authorities of the particular region."

The right of option, then, was limited to some 300 days, from July 21, 1954 to May 21 1955, the date on which the troop realignments were supposed to be at an end (i.e., the French troops from the North to the South and the Viet Minh from South to North). When the accord came into force (July 21, 1956) a mass exodus had already begun from the Northern provinces near Hanoi, still held by the French, where tens of thousands of refugees were thronging in search of a way to get to South Vietnam. The French navy and air force put itself at the disposal of the refugees by transporting them to Saigon: but in the following month, as the population of the interior began to know the possibility open to them of getting to the South, new waves of fugitives reached Hanoi and the port of Haiphong, overloading all the services made available by the French and creating great confusion in both cities (there were also revolts, and desperate fighting for food and for places on the ships and in the aircraft that were leaving for the South). The French then requested the aid of a few American ships stationed in the Philippines, the first of which the *Montague,* arrived at the Bay of Along on August 14, 1954; a few days later, five American ships were ready to transport the refugees.[1]

Aboard the *Montague* was Tom Dooley,[2] the Navy doctor who subsequently became a lay missionary in Laos and died of cancer in 1961 after having founded MEDICO (Medical International Cooperation Organization), the medical missionary organization that still continues his work. Tom Dooley immediately disembarked from the *Montague* and along with other American physicians and Navy men organized two medical missions for the aid of the refugees, which were in operation until May 1955 at Haiphong. He has left us the most vivid and moving account of the flight of hundreds of thousands of North Vietnamese from the regions occupied by the Viet Minh in his diary, *The Night They Burned the Mountain.*[3]

The refugees were mostly (although not exclusively) Catholics, and they fled to villages in the interior. Their massive exodus toward the South took on the aspect of a popular plebiscite against the Viet Minh, who were well known during the long years of the anti-French war. Even the Viet Minh had foreseen that a certain number of Vietnamese would flee to the South, just as others would come from the South into the North.[4] But no one would have imagined at the time of the signing of the Geneva agreements that the refugees from the North to the South would have numbered one million in that first year after the accord especially since a good part of those who had compromised themselves too much with the French (political figures, leaders of the Vietnamese army that fought with the French), or the great landholders who did not lack the means, had already fled to the South before the enforcement of the agreements in May and June 1954. Those who fled afterward were poor peasants and fishermen, the very people whom the Viet Minh were claiming to have "liberated"!

There was no true freedom of displacement. Although the Geneva agreements gave the right to the people to shift from one part of the country to the other, they unfortunately did not provide for any concrete guarantee that the right of option could be concretely realized (since no one, as we said, foresaw such a massive exodus). The peoples living in the zones controlled by the Viet Minh army (which with the exception of the Red River delta held almost the whole of North Vietnam) had therefore to depend, for the exercise of their right to flee, upon the Viet Minh army itself, which naturally had no intention of allowing masses of people to flee, after the first moment of confusion at what was happening.

Evidence in this regard is very considerable. We shall report only what was most characteristic. The Reverend Tran-Nam-Bac, the procurator of the Bui-Chu diocese, wrote from exile in Paris at the beginning of 1955:

These flights are taking place under truly moving and heartrending conditions, since in clear violation of the Geneva agreements the Viet Minh have tried and continue to try to oppose them. They first used persuasion and then force, and many refugees were wounded by Communist bullets. Inhabitants of entire villages were seen marching toward the sea, crossing the rice fields in order to avoid the roads controlled by the Viet Minh, and then building emergency rafts which they put out into the open sea at great risk, without any certainty that anyone would come to their aid. Hundreds of refugees were drowned. One could not imagine the moving spectacle of last November 6, when a group of 2,000 refugees were waiting on a sand bank at Cua Tra Ly for ships of friendly nations to come and save them.[5]

Frank N. Trager, a teacher at New York University who visited Vietnam, stated recently[6] that North Vietnam had imposed restrictions and brutal punishments on people seeking to go to the South.

There were summary arrests, refusals of permission, intimidations by means of "public trials" of those who were the leaders of the exodus, and executions, which all served to prevent the exercise of the option. The last petitions of those who wanted to go to the South concerned some 95,000 persons from the North. They were presented to the International Control Commission but achieved no result. Therefore, according to Trager, an unknown number of persons never succeeded in leaving the Democratic Republic of Vietnam.

In the years 1954-55, the *Fides* agency reported very copious evidence, and we shall quote some of it:

In the first days of October the refugees continued to arrive in Hanoi, but in reduced numbers . . . because of the serious obstacles put in the way of their leaving; they were forbidden boats, carts, tricycles, and the barges for the river crossings; on the highways the Communist authorities made all those who had chosen to remain stop the columns of refugees: the only ones to arrive were a few dozen who had been able to flee in secret, taking advantage of the night. How many families were broken up for this reason! One refugee from Nam Dinh, 90 kilometers from Hanoi, told us that he was the only member of his family of eight to succeed in getting to the city. . . . All the hopes of these thousands of people who had abandoned everything and were stranded on the highways were expressed to the International Control Commission. They did not request people to come for them with ships or motor-cars: all they wanted was their right of transit to be made secure; they would willingly make the journey even on foot . . .[7]

In the beginning of 1955, *Fides* cited a few methods used by the Viet Minh to impede the flights from the North:

Among the procedures used by the Viet Minh we may note the following, whose oppressive and inhuman character is inescapable:
   formal prohibition to the barges to transport the refugees from one bank to the other and the forbidding of the coast-dwellers to harbor

them or to sell them anything when, while waiting for a boat they were
obliged to camp on the riverbanks for weeks at a time;

   inciting the crowd to bar the refugees' way by blocking access to the
bridges and trestles over the rivers;

   the illegal arrest of elements considered by the Viet Minh to be group
leaders and seducers of youth, in order to disorganize the movement;

   the use of troops to terrorize and scatter the refugees;

   a close surveillance by the regular troops along the coasts . . . in order
to prevent the refugees from getting to Haiphong by sea, etc.[8]

Bloody fights to flee to the South. We shall give some more
quotations from *Fides* which brought together some evidence
widely reported even by the newspapers of the time. This is the
famous Ba-Lang episode:

During the first days of January, 10,000 Catholic refugees who were
concentrated at Ba-Lang in order to get to South Vietnam were stopped
by force and ultimately led into the interior before the International
Commission was able to intervene. In this operation, 5,000 Viet Minh
soldiers were involved in taking over by assault the church where the
refugees were intrenched. In the battle there were losses on both sides
but the refugees, who had only improvised armaments, were quickly
overwhelmed. All were taken to an unknown destination and a part,
among whom was one priest at least, was arrested. . . . The mobile section of the International Control Commission, which was detained at
Thanh Hoa under the pretext of guaranteeing their safety, until Ba-
Lang was no longer being "combed," finally arrived on the spot with
the decision to search out with every means the refugees that had dis-
appeared.[9]

Here is more evidence from the village of Luu My in the vicariate apostolic of Vinh. I apologize to the reader for the length
of these examples, but it is precisely in the reading of these texts
that we can understand the anguish of these times, since all these
passages are from eyewitnesses of the events described. *Fides* says
once more:

The bloody incidents of Ba-Lang were verified also at Luu My, a parish of 3,000 Catholic inhabitants and of more than 30 pagan families in the province of Nghe An, vic. ap. of Vinh. There were twelve dead, fifty wounded and 200 arrested.

The inhabitants of this region had been under Viet Minh domination since 1945, and therefore they knew them well. Only on December 18 (1954) were they aware of the Geneva agreements and it was at this time that all the inhabitants of Luu My presented their request to the Viet Minh authorities to leave for the South. The Viet Minh responded by ordering the troops to surround the village whereupon the police arrested six of the most important persons. Seeing this, the inhabitants threw themselves at the soldiers to disarm them and a battle ensued. This was January 8. The soldiers withdrew to obtain reenforcements . . .[10]

Naturally reenforcements came and they severely punished the rebel village. In another parish of the same vicariate of Vinh, Phu Yen, the Viet Minh arrested all the young men and deported them to unknown places.[11] The arrests of the village chiefs and the most important persons in the Catholic villages was the order of the day, with the aim of preventing an organized flight:

The arrested persons were mistreated systematically; they were chained up, beaten, starved, and after a certain time, freed. . . . In the coastal parishes, made up of fishing villages, the Viet Minh sought to prevent the Christians from attempting to flee by sea by having a scout ship nearby their boats. With this goal in mind they constituted a kind of marina for the sampans, acting as a barbed wire defence, and allowing of only one way out. The sampan owners were obliged to put their boats in these marinas, which were under the surveillance of the troops. Not content with this, in order to prevent the fishing boats from seeking escape, the Viet Minh took away all the masts and sails from the sampans.[12]

The impotence of the International Control Commission. Theoretically, the freedom of the right of option and of leaving for the

South ought to have been guaranteed by the International Control Commission, formed by representatives from Poland, India and Canada, but the commission had neither a way of policing nor means of transport which were its own, and in the process of displacement it relied on the local authorities, which meant the Viet Minh. Furthermore, how could a Commission control the whole of a large country that had only few roads and see to it that all those who wanted to reach the South would actually have the possibility to do so? It is due to the honesty of the Indian and Canadian members of the Commission that everyone knows, despite the Geneva pacts, that the Viet Minh did not allow freedom of evacuation to those who so wished.[13] But the Commission was able to do little more. In his book, Tom Dooley tells how the Commission had to act according to his experience. Apparently, when the CIC representatives visited a village, they set up a table in the public square and advertised that anyone who wished to speak with them could do so. Right outside the village, however, the Viet Minh had set up roadblocks which were supposedly for the protection of the Commission members. The result was that it was only a limited number of persons who were able to voice their complaints and what information they had. And even those who got through were later subject to reprisals. Consequently, the only way to get out of a village was to leave immediately after the Commission's decision, since it was unable to furnish means of transport. But there was a further problem, since within the Commission itself often insoluble problems arose which seemed to arise in all organizations that had Communist representatives. It seems that the Poles were particularly disposed to put obstacles in the way of any official activity. Dooley, as he tells us in his book, seems to have observed this personally on many occasions.

When the CIC succeeded in coming across a case of persons who wanted to leave, it gave the order to the local authorities to permit them to leave and to furnish their means of transport. Tom Dooley also tells us of a case of this kind that took place at Phat Diem.

So they would not bring world public opinion against them, the Viet Minh ordered the local authorities to let the peasants go free. But here too there was a catch. The Viet Minh set up a processing center that could take care of one hundred persons a day. An office gave out passports, but only after dozens of documents had been filled out by the parties concerned. Another office sold tickets for the buses supplied by the Viet Minh, and these tickets cost 8,000 Ho Chi Minh piastres, the equivalent of $8.00. For a family the problem became insoluble. However, in the world it was said that the Viet Minh was supplying everything, even the means of transport. The first group of refugees left for the South on November 15, and the buses took side roads, stopping for mysterious repairs. . . . There were other delays and frustrations. . . . Thousands of other refugees were led a merry chase throughout Vietnam until their fifteen day permit was declared expired and they were sent back to their original villages.

Marvin E. Gettleman writes: "For its part, the Viet Minh regime in the North greeted the Commission enthusiastically and the documents prove that it generally cooperated with it. One exception to the compliance of the Viet Minh was the occasional oppression of the refugees who wanted to go to the South."[14] Then the author quotes partially from a CIC document (February, 1955) in which we read: ". . . Similarly, although the High Command of the People's Army of Vietnam cooperated with the Commission and took measures to insure the freedom of movement in the case of some 8,000 refugees from Phat Diem,[15] up to today it has done little to develop adequate administrative measures with the result that complaints are continually coming in (to the Commission) . . ."[16]

In a report in *Civiltà Cattolica* we have the following:

. . . Among those who preferred to abandon their land there were a great number of Catholics who were fleeing religious persecution. They represented about ten percent of the population in the northern regions . . . Of these it is calculated that about three quarters remained, almost all of them because they were obliged to do so by the Communist authorities. To convince ourselves of this we have only to look at what happened in the Dong Hoi region, immediately north of the 17th parallel, where the inhabitants could easily have left: out of some 30,000 Catholics only 200 requested to remain. For those residing in the interior, the Communist authorities did not lack the means to detain them; they forbade them to move about without a permit, which was given only to some members of a family, and they blocked the river banks. Even those who did leave were molested along the way, and others who requested to go to the South were arrested. Against these abuses the International Armistice Commission can do practically nothing because they were never "official" abuses.[17]

In an article in the *Tablet,* an English observer, Robert Cardigan, describes the importance of the Commission, citing the various cases in which the Commission was unable to intervene and guarantee to groups of North Vietnamese the right of option, or else it intervened too late when the unsuccessful refugees had already been transferred to regions deeper in the interior. He states that the wretched condition of these innocent people so moved French public opinion that the Paris government gave instructions to the chief of the French delegation to the Armistice Commission, General Brebisson, to protest.[18]

Various commentators are of the opinion that if there had been absolute freedom in choosing for the South—and the concrete possibilities of really getting there—the refugees from the North would have been several millions and not only the million that succeeded in reaching their destination before June 21, 1955. After this date, however, others did flee the North, especially the fishermen from the southern coasts of North Vietnam and the Montagnard tribes from the central plateaus.[19] It is difficult to say how many refugees there have been since 1955. The most common estimates, in South Vietnam, are in the hundreds of thousands, which refer to the period between 1956 and 1964. In the most recent years, however, with the war fought on the 17th parallel, flights have become practically impossible.

Fanciful interpretations of the escape of the Catholics. That the Viet Minh tried with every means to prevent the exodus of masses of people to the South is a fact that is easily explained and humanly understandable: all those people who were fleeing constituted the most brutal slap in the face for the Communist propaganda about the favor with which the people greeted the "liberation" brought to them by Ho Chi Minh's army.

Consequently, to justify these flights before the world the international Communist press dedicated itself to spreading abroad fanciful and fantastic interpretations of the flights from the North. Subsequently, when the war in the South broke out, these interpretations were taken up even by non-Communist publications and writers, although at the time the flights were being verified very few (with the natural exception of the Communists) thought to interpret them differently from what was logical and precise,[20] namely, the terror of the Communist dictatorship, the fear of losing one's life, freedom, or faith, etc.

A correspondent from the Italian Communist daily *L'Unità* (December 27, 1954) summed up almost all of the versions bruited about by the Viet Minh government to explain the flight. According to the Communist paper, the Catholics were not fleeing to the South out of fear of Communism but because they were driven to do so by terrorist pressures from the "ecclesiastical hierarchy" which, naturally, was in the employ of the Americans. Not the least purpose of this pressure was to get a cheap labor supply for the American plantations in the South . . . The Church forced the faithful to leave by declaring invalid those sacraments that were administered in the Viet Minh regions, by handing out holy cards "made in the U.S.A.," which focused the eyes on the South, by promising every family a "fabulous land of milk and honey on the outskirts of Rome," and by circulating rumors that the war would soon be resumed with the dropping of American atomic bombs north of the 17th parallel . . .

Today, in the interpretation of the exodus to the South, it must be said that in addition to the Communists or self-confessed "Marxists" (e.g., Burchett and Chesneaux), many non-Communist writers have come to accept, at least in part, this version they give. It is curious, however, that they never delve more deeply into the problem but rather dismiss it with a few lines or a footnote, either because they lack proof for their statement, or perhaps because they are ashamed to admit that they are convinced that the flight of one million Vietnamese can not be explained merely as a result of propaganda and promises of receiving monetary rewards. We shall quote one author, although we do not agree with his interpretation since it does not seem to us to be well-founded:

After the armistice signed in Geneva [writes Segio Ciuffi] Ngo Dinh Diem organized with the help of the Americans a campaign to promote the transferral of the Catholics to the South. In particular, a Father Khue, one of the commandants of the Catholic troops, had set up at Haiphong a Central Evacuation Committee financed by the United States; one of his messages, diffused in duplicated copies through the villages, expressed an attempt at psychological violence: "Dear Catholic brothers and sisters, hundreds of gigantic airplanes are waiting to transport you gratis to Saigon. In the South the cost of living is three times less, you will receive twelve piastres a day and in addition you will be given fertile rice fields and other means of livelihood. By remaining in the North you will experience famine and will damn your souls. Set out now, brothers and sisters. Hurry so as not to miss the opportunity. To miss it would be like burying yourselves alive with your own hands."[21]

Ciuffii then quotes in a note some other leaflets of this kind and states that the purpose of such a transferral to the South was to give supporters to Diem and to create a mass of malcontents who were disposed to taking part in a crusade for the conquest of the North.

Ciuffi then concludes that "the expectations [of Diem] were disappointed," since the refugees were less than a million. . . . To explain in a few short paragraphs, by a few leaflets of questionable authenticity, the mass displacement of one million persons seems hardly worth taking seriously to me. That Diem organized the flights seems still less proved: certainly the South Vietnamese dictator was happy with the exodus and may even have done something to promote it, but to attribute to him the major responsibility for it is against historical truth. In the first place, when the flights began at the beginning of June, Diem was still in France and not yet in power; then, once in Saigon (June 25, 1954), Ciuffi himself tells us that he was an isolated man, imposed by the United States, and that he had to fight for more than a year in order to assert his power (*op. cit.,* pp. 125, 126, 146). That such a man, without power and without a popular basis in his struggle to assert himself, could have forcefully and deceitfully extracted one million persons from a strong and organized regime like the Viet Minh seems to me a bit too unbelievable, especially when this assumption is not proved, except with apodictic statements.

As for the hypothetical participation of the Americans in the organizing of the flight, we have already seen that the first two American ships arrived in the port of Haiphong on August 14, 1954, when the exodus had already become massive (and the ships themselves were requested by the French, who were not succeeding in transporting all the refugees). It is true that the Americans had a consulate at Hanoi, but even if we admit (through an unproven hypothesis) that members of this consulate involved themselves in organizing the exodus, we still have to explain why this came about, and on such a massive scale.[22]

But we still have to explain all the more why the majority of the refugees came not from the regions held by the French troops (part of the Red River delta) but precisely from those areas controlled for many years by the Viet Minh, where it was obviously impossible to any overt propaganda for flight and even more impossible to spirit the refugees away in trucks: "A humiliating observation [for the Viet Minh, writes *Missi*] was that the most impulsive and persistent push toward the South came from those provinces that until 1946 were entirely under the Viet Minh regime."[23]

Therefore we must consider as unproven fantasy the statement made by some people that American agents were offering the North Vietnamese the sum of $89 a person if they would flee. In such a case we would still have to explain why it was chiefly the Catholics who were fleeing and not the others (dollars ought to have been of interest to everyone). The fable may have arisen from the fact that when the refugees arrived in South Vietnam, after many ups and downs and in total deprivation, they were assisted with moneys from both Catholic and non-Catholic charitable missions: i.e., they were given a small subsidy in order to start their lives anew. But to assert that the people from the North fled, giving up everything in order to receive this subsidy—they probably had no idea even that it existed—is exceedingly absurd.

They fled in order to preserve their faith. What really did happen? Let us say first of all that the official position of the Church in North Vietnam was declaredly against flight, at least in the case of the clergy. On July 23, 1954, the apostolic delegate, Mgr. Dooley, an Irishman, addressed a letter to Mgr. Khue, the vicar apostolic of Hanoi, to remind the bishops and priests of North Vietnam of "the special obligations of those who are charged with the care of souls." Among other things, the letter said: "All those who have the charge of caring for souls—after the example of the perfect Priest who did not abandon his flock—must remain with their own faithful, with the exception, naturally, of cases in which for special reasons they have received written authorization to leave, given by the competent authorities."[24]

The hierarchy's attitude was that of requesting the priests to remain at their posts, even after the departure of the French troops from the North. Symbolic of this was the declaration of Mgr. Mazé, of the Paris Foreign Missions, vicar apostolic of Huong-Hao, who said: "At the moment that the flock finds itself in danger the shepherds must not abandon it." The Paris missionaries were given the order to remain at their posts, whatever happened.[25]

Many Vietnamese priests did flee to the South: according to a

French periodical that was very well-informed about Vietnam, the Vietnamese priests who escaped to the South were practically in the same proportion as the Catholics, two thirds (619 escaped as against 375 remaining in the North).[26] Two bishops, who were seriously compromised by the government of Bao Dai, immediately set out for the South at the beginning of July 1954: they were Mgr. Le Huu Tu of Phat Diem and Mgr. Pham Ngoc Chi of Bui Chu, about whom we have already spoken. Mgr. Cooman of Than Hoa, after four years spent under the Viet Minh regime, returned to Europe for a period of rest (after a half century of uninterrupted work in the apostolate in Viet Nam); Mgr. Ubierna of Thai Binh died at that time. The other bishops, four Vietnamese and two foreigners, remained in the North, as did the apostolic delegate, Mgr. Dooley, at the seat of his delegation in Hanoi.[27]

As for the behavior of the faithful, the ecclesiastical authorities gave no general instruction: the movement toward the South arose quite spontaneously out of the awareness of the parish clergy and the faithful. Pastors and people left together or stayed behind together, depending upon the concrete possibilities of flight and the judgment that they had formed with regard to the Viet Minh regime during the years of the anti-French guerrilla war. There were also priests who thought it was possible to collaborate with the Communist government, and they restrained the people's desire to flee.[28]

We now come to the reasons that determined the Catholics' flight from the North.[29] The opinion of the Vietnamese priests and the foreign missionaries, as well as the concerned Catholics themselves, was united: the Catholics left because they had known the Viet Minh for many years and judged that it was impossible to collaborate with a Communist government and maintain religious freedom. The essential reason for the flight was therefore the fear of losing the faith: the religious future of North Vietnam in the following years will tell, as we shall see, whether or not this fear was justified.

The purely religious interpretation of the exodus (that they fled
in order to preserve their faith) could seem "triumphalistic" and
perhaps even ingenuous, but it seems to me most exact psychologically as well, when we are familiar with the congenital "triumphalism" of the Vietnamese Christian community (we shall
be speaking of this at length in the following chapters). We now
live in a secularized world, while they are still in a sacral period,
like our Middle Ages. Furthermore, the most copious evidence,
both written and spoken, that we have gathered agrees on this
point: the strongest stimulus to flight for the masses of Catholics
was precisely this fear of religious persecution and, therefore, the
impossibility of preserving the faith and Christian practice for
themselves and their children. That, subsequently, there may have
been other secondary motives influencing one million refugees
seems logical: the fear of losing civil liberties, the mirage of more
sumptuous earnings (for the intellectual elite), the desire of saving
one's skin (for those who were compromised politically and for
the rich), the example of those who had escaped becoming a cause
of excitement, the excitation of general panic through pertinent
propaganda, etc. However the fact remains that one million North
Vietnamese had such terror of the Communist domination, for one
reason or another, that they fled their country; for the Catholics
this fear was chiefly religious. Here is what one Vietnamese priest
wrote:

What then is the reason for their leaving? [i.e., the faithful]. First of
all, for the Catholic faith. Vietnamese Catholics have suffered and are
ready to accept still other sufferings to defend the most noble of all freedoms, that of their faith. . . . To remain behind is to risk being en-
snared in dangerous compromises, in a difficult situation from which
they cannot extricate themselves. For Communist tactics are the same
everywhere, in Russia, China, or Vietnam. Their methods can be dia-
grammed in this way [a] separate and turn away the faithful from the
hierarchy [b] make no martyrs [c] introduce class struggle into Christian milieus [d] use and promote, at least for a time, that religion that

is least consistent and least hierarchical against the most solid religion, and to take hold of the ecclesiastical organization itself. The ultimate aim of these tactics is to seduce, compromise and corrupt the Christians in order to subsequently destroy the Church. The serious element in all of this is the systematic and generalized degradation of souls before the structures themselves are degraded. The Church does not disappear all at once, *en bloc,* but progressively. It is the Church in one region, in one vicariate, seeing its visible structures breaking down: the elimination of influential Christians, of the catechists, the disappearance of the priests, etc. With these maneuvers of persecution it is very difficult for an ordinary Christian not to succumb. It is for this reason that many Vietnamese Catholics see themselves forced to abandon their own hearth. . . .[30]

And a Paris missionary wrote:

But—someone will ask—if these refugees did not leave for their own particular interests, did they leave out of fear? Of course, out of fear, but a fear that is quite special; not for fear of losing their possessions, since they gave up everything in order to leave; not out of fear of suffering, since they rushed headlong into misery and faced the worst physical and moral sufferings in order to escape; nor was it even out of fear of death, since rather than remain they accepted death, preferred it, and thousands of them actually suffered it.

Then why this flight? The answer is simple. . . . The refugees had had the direct experience of the way in which the Communists practice religious freedom: their priests silenced, imprisoned or killed; whole Christian communities deported and scattered; the word of God fettered, false doctrines imposed, religion persecuted. . . . In a few places it had become impossible to hear mass or celebrate it, to teach or learn catechism. In the schools the study of Marxism was obligatory. The whole vast Communist apparatus of constraint was put in motion in order to exert over individuals and institutions its inexorable hold, and to bend them to the regime's way of thinking or destroy them in case of resistance.

This is what the Vietnamese Catholics fear, and for this reason they left. . . . If there really did exist real freedom of choice in accordance with the Geneva agreements, North Vietnam would be emptied of every one of its million Catholics.

Someone might say that they ought to have stayed to bear witness to the Church. But it is precisely in leaving that they gave a full-voiced witness to Christ and his Church. And it is just because this witness is so efficacious that it seems intolerable to some few who are striving to suffocate, scorn and destroy it. If only the movement had taken place in the opposite direction! If only the Catholics of the South had taken refuge in the North, what a fanfare would have acclaimed their choice! . . .[31]

Fr. Gian, rector of the Vietnamese mission in Paris, writes:

If so many Catholics fled the new regime, it is especially because they, more than the other people, were conscious of the difficulties that the Marxist government would have created for their conscience and for that of their own children in regard to the Christian faith. Many who had lived for years under Communist law had learned this by experience. The Christians of Thanh Hoa or Vinh, for example, who witnessed with bloody struggles against the Viet Minh and lived under their law until the beginning of the war, reported on the religious policy of the Communists in terms that are the precise echo of what was told by the missionaries who were expelled from China. They fled because, above all, they wanted to remain Catholics and practice their religion as they wished.[32]

Mgr. Jean Rodhain, of the Secours Catholique, in an article in *Osservatore Romano,* wrote after a sojourn in Vietnam:

Whatever the reasons [for the exodus], I ask only one thing: to which side did these people go? If, after the Geneva accord giving them the faculty to choose the region, 600,000 Vietnamese were seen rushing, at the risk of their lives, by land and sea, toward the Communists in the North, this popular referendum could have been explained as manifest evidence against our civilization, against the missions, against a century of work by the French. But this exodus took place in the opposite direction, and therefore, agrees with me in saying that this signifies something quite different. Just as the rats leave a sinking ship, this mad flight demonstrates a popular instinct: these people smelled danger . . .[33]

A concrete experience of the Communist regime. The determining reason for the flight of the Catholics, therefore, was the experience they had of the Communist regime and the fear that the situation would undoubtedly worsen once the regime was in full control of the country. Let us see what this experience was that forced them to flee. This is referred to, among others, by a Vietnamese priest of Vinh, who tells that his town fell to the Communists early in September, while he remained at his post with his Christians. In regard to religious freedom, he writes that despite the promises and every kind of assurance about respect for religion, it was fettered and oppressed. He gives concrete examples:

As for preaching, the police copied out the sermons given in Church, at times distorting their sense. . . . If the priest spoke on the fourth commandment, the children should obey their parents, he was accused of praising slavery and of going counter to the spirit of independence. If he spoke of pardoning offenses, he was accused of protecting the rich and of sabotaging the spirit of struggle. If he preached the seventh commandment, he was reproached for sabotaging the government program. . . . Whatever he said, he was accused of political error. Under these circumstances it is better not to preach at all in the parishes for fear of losing the pastor who risked being arrested. As for the catechism, it was impossible to study it for want of time or because we could no longer meet together without authorization.

Outside the Church it was not possible to organize any religious manifestation; for an extraordinary feast we needed an authorization given beforehand and difficult to obtain. . . . Masses and prayers had to be ended quickly, at times after political meetings, or be interrupted or suppressed on account of a political meeting. . . . Fake penitents were sent to confession, to lay traps for the priest. . . . The most painful fact is the question of separation from the Holy See. It is claimed and calumniously taught that the Holy See is in the employ of the Americans, of imperialism, and priests and faithful were obliged to protest against this attitude and to request the Holy See to take the side of the Communists. . . . It is impossible to tell you everything we suffered under the Communist regime. Only those who live under such a yoke can form an idea about its cruelty.[34]

The priest goes on to say how, little by little, his Christians became convinced about the impossibility of continuing to live in similar conditions, and they organized their flight which, despite the "severe surveillance" to which they were subjected, was successful. It is evidence like this that gives a concrete idea as to why the Catholics fled en masse from the regions occupied by the Viet Minh. We are not dealing with "anti-Communist propaganda": for people living under the Communists for many years there is really no need! Here is some more evidence: "If we had to abandon our country [reports a man of 56, the father of six children] it is because we were no longer able to bear the Communist regime: religious freedom was not recognized, our children were commandeered for unpaid "people's" services (they always told us that it was for three months but a year went by and they are still not free), they levied such heavy taxes on us that it left us almost nothing of the products of our labor on which to live."[35]

The situation at our mission [writes a Vietnamese priest] is painful at present. The priests have to suffer all sorts of insults; three are dead, a few are in prison. As for the others, their situation is most wretched, it is as if they were in prison: they are under surveillance by people in their own house. . . . Christians are detained in prison in great numbers. . . . Once the exodus to the South had begun, the Viet Minh watched the Christians more rigorously and imprisoned them in great number. Everywhere people had decided to leave: they could no longer bear the Viet Minh yoke; then they sold their lands, their houses, their furniture and all their possessions at ridiculous prices, happy if they found someone to buy them. In other words, they abandoned everything without any regrets. All they wanted was to leave, to go and live some-where else and to be free to practise their religion; nothing else was im-portant. Since Christmas no one had been able to reach the high sea to leave since the surveillance was everywhere strictly organized: it was no longer possible to leave one's own village and one's own parish; the police and the army were watching every house, exerted a dragon-like control and allowed no one any longer to go fishing. Since the sea route was now blocked, the Christians left on foot in small groups . . . and in this way made three or four hundred kilometers in order to reach Haiphong. . . .[36] Those unable to leave appealed, in vain, to the inter-national Commission. Then they tried by force to break their chains. Recently there have been bloody battles. The Christians say: "If we have to die, let us die for God and for religion."[37]

Ho Chi Minh's hand extended to the Catholics. The first acts of the Ho Chi Minh government towards the Christian community were a period of rest and ample promises about religious freedom. In reality, even before the end of the war with France there had been declarations in favor of religious freedom. Unfortunately, however, in the zones controlled by the Viet Minh this was con-tradicted by the facts. In any case, in the first week of August 1953 —to recall but one important happening—the Viet Minh govern-ment organized a National Congress of Religions in which some "progressivist" clergy and laymen took part. They themselves had established the Association of Catholic Resistants (Hoi Song Giao Khang Chien). At the end of the congress, which had met to study the "religious policy of the government and the Lien Viet front," the representatives declared among others things that the government and the front never ceased showing their solicitude in regard to religion (i.e., of the participants). Religious freedom, they continued, was inscribed in the constitution and expressly acknowledged by the statutes of the National Front.

After the Geneva agreements, at the time when the unexpected and unforeseen flow of refugees to the South had begun (most of these were Catholics, at least at the beginning), the Communist

leaders were surprised and embittered. Ho Chi Minh was especially
affected and went to see Mgr. Khue, the vicar apostolic of Hanoi,
with whom he had good personal relations. He asked him, quite
grieved, why the Catholics did not trust in his government.
Probably the man was sincere in promising religious freedom insofar as it depended personally upon him; in his speeches and declarations in the months following the Geneva agreements the religious
freedom theme frequently recurred.

Ho's first appeal to the Catholics was in July 1954, in which,
according to the *Agence France-Presse* version, he requested the
Catholics to believe in the policy of freedom of faith as stated by
the government, and he gave the order to the combattants and the
military cadres to act correctly with the people.

On July 24, a second document defined the attitude of the government with regard to religion: "Every citizen enjoys freedom of
faith. No one has the right to violate this freedom. Every citizen
has the right to propagate any religion, on condition that it is not
harmful to independence and national freedom, in the social order
and in the laws of the government of the Democratic Republic of
Vietnam. . . . The government protects churches and pagodas and
watches out for the safety of religion. No one has the right to
disturb worship or to intrude into the places reserved for the worship of the various religions. . . ."[38]

On October 10, Ho Chi Minh made another solemn declaration,
proclaiming religious freedom and respect for holy places. For
Christmas in 1954, he addressed a letter to Catholics, promising
them full religious freedom but asking in exchange for fidelity to
the fatherland and the government, participation in the struggle for
peace and a condemnation of the American imperialists, colonialists
and capitalists—all those people whom Jesus had already condemned in his time.[39] For Christmas, the government lifted the
curfew and there were exceptional crowds at midnight mass.

The law granting full religious freedom. Two official texts came
to sanction the "extended hand" of the Communist regime toward

the Catholics and the adherents of all religions. The first was a resolution of the National Assembly of North Vietnam on March 26, 1955, in six articles[40] dealing with religious freedom, very broadly conceived (art. 5 asserted that "in the agrarian reform, one part of the rice fields will be reserved for the parishes, pagodas and Cao-Dai temples" . . . at a time when everything had been confiscated in those areas long occupied by the Viet Minh).

The second document is the basic law on religious freedom in North Vietnam, still in force today, and we must give it an especially close examination.

It is a decree signed by the president of the republic, Ho Chi Minh, on June 14, 1955, and is called "Decree on the religious question."[41] It offers full guarantees of religious freedom, and there is no doubt that if the Hanoi government had respected it, the differences between the Catholics and the Communists would have been all ironed out.

The first chapter of the law is on the "guarantee of freedom of faith" and states: "The government guarantees freedom of faith and worship to the people. No one has the right to trample on this freedom. All Vietnamese have the right to follow a religion or to follow none. The ministers of worship have the freedom to preach religion in religious places [churches, pagodas and other places of worship . . ."], art. 1.

Article 3 admits the principle of the presence of foreign missionaries, "who are authorized by the government" (from 1960 on it no longer gave authorization to anyone!) and article 4 allows religious denominations freedom "to publish and diffuse prayer books and catechisms, book and newspapers of a religious nature" (this one, like the following one, as we shall see, is an article that for a long time has been of no use). Article 5 grants religious denominations "the opening of schools of religious training for those who devote themselves to religious activities," while the last two articles of the first chapter state that the churches are under the protection of the law, which will punish all who: ". . . under the pretext of religion disturb the peace, unity, independence and democracy, in order to make warlike propaganda, break the union of the people, prevent the faithful from doing their duty as citizens ... or commit any other infraction of the law."

The second chapter speaks of the economic, cultural and social activities of the religious denominations and grants them the right to run their economic, cultural and social organizations which are looked upon as private property (art. 8); article 9 on the other hand allows all churches "to open private schools which must conform their teaching to the educational program of the government."

The third chapter treats of the agrarian properties of the religious denominations and says expressly: "In the agrarian reform . . . there will be left to the churches, pagodas and other places of worship a part [of the rice fields] sufficient for worship and so that the ministers of worship will be in circumstances that will enable them to fulfill their religious activity. The extent of this part of the rice fields shall be determined by the local people and approved by the administrative authority of the province [art. 10]."

The other two articles say that the ministers of worship who have private rice fields are not considered "landholders" if they observe the laws of the government in agrarian matters (art. 11); and that the government will "show its good will" to the churches and pagodas and "will grant a mitigation of taxes on the crops for the portion of the rice fields left to the disposal of the churches, pagodas . . ." (art. 12).

In the fourth chapter it is stated that "the civil authority will not interfere in the internal affairs of the religious denominations. In regard to Catholicism in particular, the religious relations between the Church of Vietnam and the Holy See of Rome are the internal affair of the Catholics [art. 13]." The final two articles say that the religious organizations must respect all the laws of the State (art. 14) and that "freedom of faith and worship is a right of the people. The authority of the Democratic Republic of Vietnam always respects this right and helps the people to exercise it [art. 15]."

The law on religious freedom—signed by Ho Chi Minh and

Pham Van Dong, the two supreme heads if the DRVN, then as now—was satisfactory to the Catholics who had not expected this goodwill gesture on the part of the government, all the more since the bishops were not questioned before passing the law. A short time after its promulgation an unsigned editorial in the official party newspaper *Nhan Dan* confirmed the fact that not only the government but also the party had decided to respect the law on religious freedom. Although it asserted that the party followed dialectical materialism and "did not recognize the existence of a divinity," the article specifies that "the Party has always recognized that religion for the people is an affair of free belief and free thought and that there can be no recourse to prescriptions or constraint that would violate this right or abolish it. . . . The policy of respect for freedom of belief and assembly that guides the Workers Party of Vietnam is sincere and firm. . . . From its foundation the Party has always firmly upheld this policy as it does today.[42]

The difficult period of "agrarian reform." The law of June 14, 1955, on religious freedom was well received throughout the Catholic world and even *Osservatore Romano,* in an anonymous article (*Vietnamese Panorama*, August 13, 1955), noted the importance of the thaw in the religious question that had taken place in North Vietnam. Actually, during the course of the year in 1955 there were churches and seminaries opened in Vietnam and even religious processions through the city streets, especially in the capital, Hanoi; but, as *Osservatore Romano* pointed out in the same article, "freedom of worship and the official authorization to celebrate religious feasts and solemn processions are merely external manifestations of a reality that is quite different."

In other words, despite the law of June 14 and all the declarations of respect for religious freedom (I could cite some others besides those already mentioned), the action of the government and the party against the Church practically never ceased since it was begun years before during the guerrilla war against the French.[43]

The first difficult period for the Church in North Vietnam was in the years 1955–1956 until the autumn of 1956, when the persecution was attenuated (and resumed again in 1958). 1955–1956 were the years of the agrarian reform, which had been launched more for political than socio-economic reasons and with the same methods that had already been experimented with some years before in Communist China: people's trials, public executions, violence of every kind not only against the landholders but also against every opponent of the regime, mobilization and indoctrination of the masses, etc. In the year and a half of agrarian reform more people died in North Vietnam (by executions, and suicides in the forced labor camps and the prisons) than during the long years of the war against France: according to some estimates some 200,000 people died.[44] The bloody excesses of the reform, carried out with violence, were subsequently repudiated by these same Communist authorities. For example, General Giap, in a speech reported in the official paper of the Communist party in Hanoi (the *Nhan Dan*) on October 31, 1956, had this to say about the period of agrarian reform: "We suppressed too many upright persons. . . . Terror was too widespread. . . . Even worse, tortures were considered normal practice in the party organization . . ."

We should not be surprised by this. Is there any Communist regime in the world that has not had excesses of this kind? They were verified even in the countries of Eastern Europe, which were already much more highly developed economically than Vietnam when the Communists rose to power. Evidence of the terror during the agrarian reform was considerable, and we even find some mention of it in the North Vietnamese papers themselves, especially in the two most official ones, the *Nhan Dan* and the *Hoc Tap*, which reported numerous incidents of peasant rebellions during the people's trials of the agrarian reform.[45] Here is how J. Buttinger sums up the characteristics of this period, which above all was one of economic failure in the agricultural field:

The chief reason for this resounding economic failure was the policy adopted by the regime towards the peasants who represented more than four fifths of the population living in the 15,000 villages of the country. This is the story of the agrarian reform in Communist North Vietnam, a story not only of economic failure but of unbelievable terror, disastrous mismanagement on all levels of the Party, and a crisis brought about by widespread popular discontent, which the regime was capable of surrounding only with brutality and a rapid political retreat.[46]

In the following pages, Buttinger describes how and with what terrorist means the agrarian reform was promoted and how poor peasants with two or three acres of land were condemned as capitalists and publicly punished ("the difficulty was this," writes Buttinger (p. 912), "that North Vietnam had always had few real landowners and most of these had already long since been expropriated as traitors"); and Buttinger concludes with the statement that:

Nothing in the history of the Communist persecutions can equal the projected plan to get rid of as many peasants as possible who possessed more than two or three acres of land. . . . In order to have a sufficient number of condemnations to prison, the forced labor camps, or death, crimes had to be invented and charges made in sequence, even against those who had always supported the Viet Minh. Undoubtedly there were some landowners who had cruelly exploited and badly treated the poor, but the Party was not interested in dispensing justice. Its goal was to eradicate a social class, and to this aim it mobilized hatred and greed and the desire for personal revenge (pp. 912–913).

Here is how a French missionary who had remained in North Vietnam until 1959, and whom I interviewed in Saigon in December 1967, describes the excesses of the agrarian reform which he was able to witness personally in a town near Son-Tay:

Once the Communists were absolute masters of the country in 1955, they launched their "Campaign for Agrarian Reform," which in reality was a campaign to impose itself through terror. Under the pretext of the agrarian reform all the opponents or supposed opponents were eliminated, or more simply, there were killings in every village in order to terrorize the people.

First of all there was the prohibition for anyone to move from his own village so that news could not be circulated or an opposition be organized. . . . Then, to every village or to every quarter of the cities, there came a people's commissar with many soldiers and Communist militants. Over a period of several days, in the public square, they organized the people's tribunal in which everyone had to take part. They set up a platform with a loudspeaker and then began the accusations: everyone was called upon to make a self-criticism and to accuse others of "sins against the people." . . . Once the accusations were over, some were condemned to death. . . . The condemned persons, who had already been beaten several times in the course of the trial when the opportunity presented itself, were killed immediately in the sight of everyone by a rifle shot. . . . These actions were systematic, and were part of the system of imposition by terror. . . . What was important to the regime was to nip in the bud any thought of opposition and to force the people to accept order at any cost. And in reality these people's verdicts destroyed an individual's spirit, and even destroyed mutual trust within families since no one any longer dared trust anyone else. You would have had to see the terror in the eyes of the people in order to understand these situations! Then came the order to give the State all the agricultural crops, and the State gave each family the bare necessities of food. This created so much discontent and even at times open rebellions, which however were unable to spread and were immediately stamped out in each of the villages. As long as I was in North Vietnam until 1959, I had news of these popular rebellions, but the opposition was never able to organize itself beyond the base of a single village.[47]

The attempt to create a patriotic and national Church. The anti-Catholic movement [reports *Fides*] is particularly violent in the vicariate of Vinh. Catholics are accused of being "hindrances to the historical progress of Marxism," people who are rotten in spirit and heart, people who have to be re-educated. Following this campaign many Catholics were sent to re-education camps. It is known that recently several priests from the city of Vinh . . . along with 70 young seminarians and 700 secular students . . . were deported to these camps.[48]

If in the beginning there was no general open persecution of the Church throughout North Vietnam, there was the attempt to bring to life a "patriotic Church," cut off from Rome, in order to wage from inside an attack against the faith of Catholics. In March 1955, on government initiative, a congress of progressivist Catholics met at Hanoi, with 14 priests (9 from the North and 5 who had arrived from the South with the Viet Minh troops) who had already joined the Viet Minh in 1945. Thus the "National Union of Catholic Peace-Loving Patriots" was formed, with a directive committee composed of 8 priests and 21 laymen. It was installed in a luxurious villa in Hanoi and began the publication of the weekly *Chinh-Nghia* ("The Just Cause") and the development of a great propaganda effort among Catholics to found parochial committees, form discussion groups, etc. A few months later, when the Viet Minh were the absolute masters of the country, the bishops and priests had no longer any means of communicating with Rome by mail.

The Union of Catholic Patriots did not have the success hoped for by the government. Its aim was to create confusion among Catholics, especially in their relations with Rome and their bishops, and to spread about the government propaganda themes and to create troubles of various kinds in the Church. For example, during the outdoor processions to the churches, Catholic patriots carried red banners behind the Blessed Sacrament; when the priests and especially the bishops were preaching, the Catholic patriots took down what they said in order to have "proof" of the clergy's infidelity to the fatherland. In the beginning of 1956 they bitterly criticized the vicar apostolic of Hanoi, Mgr. Khue, for his Christmas pastoral letter, in which the bishop recalled the precept of charity and the duty to forgive offenses; in the beginning of 1958, the Catholic patriots began to arrange campaigns against the

foreign missionaries, who were then expelled; in their paper the
Vatican is always presented as imperialistic, a servant of the
Americans, etc.

The response of Vietnamese Catholics to this creation of a Church
separated from Rome and the bishops was and still is minimal. For
all practical purposes the only people (whether priests or laymen)
who joined it were already connected with the Viet Minh before
the Geneva peace. Those few who joined afterwards did so more
to avoid troubles and persecutions than out of deep conviction.[49]

It is possible, however, and we can at the very least admit it as
an hypothesis, that in the Union of Catholic Patriots there were
(or are) still priests and laymen of good faith who wish to integrate
the Church within Socialist society by bringing it into collaboration
with the government in the "building of Socialism." In one of the
first communiqués from the leaders of the Union of Catholic
Patriots, we read that "the bishops of our country ought to commit themselves with every means to upholding the people's government and to giving their full approval to the agrarian reform; we
wish to offer to the goverment of the people the mass of Catholics
who are ready to serve the common goals."

The intention, perhaps, was good, but everything was asked from
one side and nothing from the other. Relations between the
Church and the Viet Minh were already compromised by at least
five or six years of reciprocal hostility—which were surely not
initiated by the Catholics or the Church—and the bishops' goodwill
would certainly not be enough to renew their cordiality (provided
the bishops felt like approving a so-called "agrarian reform" which
was exterminating all opponents of the regime with inhuman
methods later disavowed by the Communist authorities themselves).
The government, it is true, had made a gesture of goodwill with
the law on religious freedom of June 14, 1955, but unfortunately
what happened did not correspond to the legislative guarantees.

The "Hundred Flowers" period. In the autumn of 1956 a strong reaction burst out among the people against the government and particularly against the atrocities of the agrarian reform which had sowed terror in the country regions: the peasants rebelled, and there were armed encounters with the "people's" army, which for the first time hesitated to fire on the peasants armed with clubs. Even some Catholic villages rebelled, in particular Nghe-An and Thanh-Hoa, whose male population had been taken to "reeducation camps." Here is what a French author writes (he could hardly be accused of preconceived hostility in regard to the Ho Chi Minh regime):

1956 is the year of crisis for the agrarian reform, which is shaking violently the still unsolid structures of the regime. . . . Everywhere [i.e., the reform] is carried out with brutality and incompetence, letting loose a discontent in the country areas which in some regions is taking on the dimensions of a real revolt. There are excesses committed against poor peasants . . . out of political revenge or personal hatred . . . inopportune zeal on the part of suspect functionaries who are seeking to rehabilitate themselves in the eyes of the government by cruelty; so many reasons that discredit the agrarian reform in the eyes of those very people who ought to benefit from it. The discontent reached its paroxysm at the moment that the events in Budapest and the "Polish October" shook the Communist world. The Hanoi government was wobbling on its very foundations.[50]

At the end of 1956 there happened in North Vietnam the same phenomenon that was verified at the same time in China: the Period of the Hundred Flowers, i.e., a certain liberalization not only in literature and the arts but also on the level of political discussion, with self-criticism by the chief persons responsible for the cruelties of the agrarian reform. The organizer of this reform, Truong Chinh, became for a few months the scapegoat for all the errors of the regime. After having made his self-criticism, he was deposed, accused of all the misdeeds, insulted and finally expelled from the party. In the meanwhile, on November 1, 1956, the

Council of Ministers decided to free 12,000 political prisoners (this figure alone shows the extent of the repressions accomplished in the name of the agrarian reform) and on November 8 Radio Hanoi announced a Decree of liberalization: "By decision of the government, all persons who have been unjustly condemned will be freed, whatever their social class, and the sentences pronounced against them cancelled . . . Freedom of worship must be scrupulously respected."

The decree goes on to say that the errors in the matter of religious policy "will be rectified," and actually from Autumn 1956 there began the period of greatest freedom for the Church of North Vietnam, which enjoyed a certain calm until 1958. One observer wrote: "Many of the priests in prison were released;[51] permissions for them to leave were granted more liberally: the priests were thus able to visit the sick and the people were no longer obliged to bring the dying over long distances on foot to the nearest priest, as they had done previously so as not to die without the sacraments."[52]

At this period the Catholic press of St. Theresa, the only one remaining in the hands of the Church, was able to print catechisms and prayerbooks freely. The seminaries, especially the minor ones, could reopen their doors and free themselves from the guardianship of the priests of the Union of Catholic Patriots.[53] The liberalization period, which lasted a little more than a year (i.e., all of 1957), gave the optimum opportunity to the Church to close ranks and prepare for new storms.

The missionaries were expelled. At the beginning of 1958, the Period of the Hundred Flowers and of liberalization was over and even for the Church hard times began again, only this time the persecution was much more open than in the past. In the first place there was the expulsion of the twenty-one foreign missionaries who remained in the country and who had not been expelled previously, evidently for reasons of political expediency. Almost all of them were French, with the exception of two Canadians. In fact at

Hanoi the French ambassador closely followed the plight of the missionaries and intervened several times to get their release from prison or to obtain permission for them to come into the capital or to visit their own bishop. From 1956 on these missionaries lived confined to their parishes, with permission only to celebrate mass and administer the sacraments.

Even the members of the Apostolic Delegation at Hanoi left the country. The government first sought to obtain a certain number of Catholic signatures requesting the expulsion of the apostolic delegate and his secretary, but obtained too few—even among the "Catholic patriots"—to be able to say that they represented the "Catholic people." In July 1959, the apostolic delegate Mgr. Dooley fell gravely ill, after years of confinement to his residence, and was transferred to a French hospital in Cambodia (since in North Vietnam there were no adequate facilities).[54] He left the delegation, however, in the hands of Fr. O'Driscoll, also an Irishman, and his secretary. Three weeks later Fr. O'Driscoll was invited to the police station and brought under armed guard to the Chinese border, with the accusation of "subversive activities."[55]

The plight of the seminaries and the Catholic schools. Another important aspect of the action against the Church and the Catholics was to deprive them of every means of mass communication. The St. Theresa press in Hanoi was requisitioned, and the circulation of books and religious pamphlets was forbidden. Fr. Marillier, who in 1958 was still in Vietnam, writes: "One risked one's freedom by transporting a package of religious publications as if it contained explosives. Religious conferences were forbidden as well as the study centers, and their leaders were condemned to forced labor. The young people or the mothers of families who brought the children together secretly for catechism were persecuted by the police and were obliged, whether they liked it or not, to suspend their activities."[56]

The Catholic schools that were still free, although strictly controlled, followed the same lot. After 1957 the government monopolized education on all levels: the teachers were functionaries of the State, obliged to take long courses of political indoctrination and to teach Marxism; in the schools it was forbidden to give any other ideological teaching, including Christianity; the Catholic schools were occupied one by one, and then "ideological integration" took over the seminaries.

The problem of ecclesiastical vocations was, and still is, the weakest point of the North Vietnamese Church, not that there was any lack of young men ready to dedicate themselves to the priesthood (although almost all the clerics and seminarians of 1954 had fled to the south), but the possibility of adequate training was lacking. From 1955 to 1960 there were reports of twenty ordinations to the priesthood in the whole of North Vietnam, and certainly after 1960 they diminished still more. The last figures that we have, from July 1959, speak of about 500 minor seminarians and 70 clerics in philosophy and theology. Up to that year at least, half the diocesan seminaries had been able to function, although with many privations and annoyances (especially from the "priest patriots").

Consequently, with the national educational reform and the absolute monopoly of the State, even the seminaries were obliged to take the courses imposed by the State, and the professors and students were forced to study Marxism, taught by political commissars with the help of Catholic patriots. In August 1959 the religious authorities of Phat Diem refused the courses of political indoctrination and the Phat-Diem seminary had to close its doors (it had 170 students), followed in September by the seminary of Hanoi (172 students), while the government school authorities with the help of the police occupied the seminary of Thai-Binh by force. Later, with the beginning of the American bombing of North Vietnam it seems that the government granted a little more liberty to the Church, and that today the seminary of Vinh is still open (Stalin did the same thing during the war against Nazi Germany by granting more freedom to the Russian Orthodox Church).

The priests, however, continued to be closely watched, even though after 1960 the number of priests condemned to prison or forced labor seemed to diminish (also on account of the fact that the clergy were getting old). Fr. Marillier writes:

While the priests imprisoned by the Viet Minh numbered in the tens at the end of the war, in 1960 only half a dozen remained. But this ought not to create any illusions. In a regime in which there was always less difference between freedom and imprisonment with forced labor, the all-powerful police, obligatory political studies, the Catholic clergy was anything but free. . . . The priest was shut up in his church and became increasingly more isolated, both physically and morally. He could rarely visit the sick, assist the dying, go to celebrate mass in other villages. He was denied the possibility of visiting his confreres or of knowing the directives of the bishop. He had no other information than that given him by the government propaganda. It was up to him to find out a way to reach his deluded and deceived parishioners. Old and tired, he had to suffer repeated visits from the "Catholic patriots," with their alluring or threatening speeches in which quotations from the Gospel went hand in hand with the dogmas of Karl Marx. The police dragged him along, either by force or deceit, to follow the sessions of political studies where he was enjoined to take a position on the farm cooperative, the new marriage law, the enemies of the people, or even on events taking place in the Congo or Cuba. . . . After years of effort to put the moral authority of the clergy, which was acknowlededgd to be very great, in the service of the regime, it is a miracle that the North Vietnamese Communists gained to their cause hardly more than about fifteen priests. . . . But the clergy as a whole gave proof of its fidelity. There remains the fact that the Catholic Community is increasingly losing more priests each year and it is methodically torn away from those that remain.[57]

The spiritual renewal of the Christian Community. Very rarely do we get any news about the Church in North Vietnam in these latter years, i.e., from 1960 to today (as is true in the case of the Church in China). Yet we know that the Catholics and the Church have resisted well the undue pressures of the State and the party, and this is all the more remarkable if we realize that all the other religions have long ceased to exist as organisms independent of the State.[58]

The Church experienced a good spiritual renewal even under the Communist regime, especially an inward deepening of the faith and a more lively sense of belonging to the Church.[59] The sparse bits of information coming to us from the North permit us to affirm that the endurance of the Catholics in the faith still remains very much alive despite many difficulties. Let us quote in particular a few witnesses from these last years. The first is the account given by a few foreigners who remained behind for a while in Hanoi and who were afterwards interviewed by Fr. O'Connor of the NCWC News Service:

In Hanoi one sees in church "young people and couples with children as well as old people." . . . "I knew that the Communists were not interested in the religious feelings of the old people but sought to prevent the young from going to church." From what the visitor saw, however, he noted that a good number of the Catholic younger generation had not given in to the anti-religious pressures. "The hardships for fervent Catholics are many, but they endure very well," stated another foreigner. Yet many of those who were not fervent no longer go to Church. "Very few faithful had prayerbooks [observed a visitor assisting at mass in Hanoi] but they recited the prayers from memory."[60] Travellers who had assisted at the Christmas midnight mass of 1962 in Hanoi cathedral, reported that the doors of the cathedral were closed at 11:30 P.M. At that time the church was full, and outside there was a crowd of some 5,000 people who were gathered in the square in front and in the convergent streets.[61]

One other episode was told by the Archbishop of Saigon, Mgr. Nguyen-Van-Binh, in an interview given to me during the first session of the Council in Rome; after speaking of the courage of the Catholics of North Vietnam, the archbishop said:

Some time ago a village priest was arrested by the police for imaginary offences against the security of the State. The inhabitants of that village, a few hundred people, are almost all Catholics; they all followed their priest to the city prison, men, women, children and old people. . . . They sent a delegation to the chief of police saying that if the priest had done something worthy of condemnation, then they were all guilty because they had followed him in everything: then they too should be arrested! In the face of such a solid manifestation, the priest was released.[62]

Uncertain statistics on the Church in the North. On December 8, 1960, John XXIII established the ordinary episcopal hierarchy in all of Vietnam. In the North he set up an archdiocese (Hanoi) and nine dioceses, nominating new bishops, three of whom have not yet been able to be consecrated because they were prevented by the civil authorities from abandoning the residence in which they were confined.

Here are the latest statistics on Christianity in North Vietnam, published in the *Annuaire catholique du Vietnam,* 1964 (printed at Saigon):[63]

Dioceses	Bishops	Priests	Parishes	Population	Catholics	%	Rel. men	Rel. women
Langson	1	4	11	350,000	2,500	0.7	—	—
Bac Ninh	1	6	48	2,000,000	35,423	1.7	1	24
Hung Hoa	1	34	23	1,920,000	70,181	4.1	—	34
Haiphong	1	8	61	1,500,000	54,617	3.6	—	—
Hanoi	2	53	112	2,500,000	155,000	6	1	13
Thai Binh	1	13	14	1,660,891	88,652	5.3	—	26
Bui Chu	1	30	117	895,000	165,000	18	1	90
Phat Diem	1	24	61	450,000	58,900	13	7	34
Than Hoa	1	27	44	1,500,000	47,000	3	—	50
Vinh	2	124	135	1,890,000	156,195	8.2	—	64
Total (North Vietnam)	12	323	626	14,665,891	833,468	5.6	10	35

A Church scattered but still alive. In recent years external contacts with the Church in North Vietnam have diminished to almost nothing.[64] No bishop from the North was able to come to Rome for the sessions of Vatican II, and there is reason to believe that not only were the council's deliberations not put into effect in the North, but were probably not even known. There is no communication possible any longer between Rome and the Vietnamese bishops.

A recent and symptomatic fact of the situation in which the Church lives in Hanoi, the capital—in the other cities and in the country it is even worse—is this: in January 1967, Mgr. Huessler, the director of the German *Caritas* organization, went for fifteen days to Hanoi, in the company of Pastor Niemöller of the World Council of Churches, to bring to North Vietnam aid from the German Christian communities. Both were received by Ho Chi Minh and treated with every courtesy as guests of honor, but Mgr. Huessler was unable to visit the Archbishop of Hanoi or any other bishop or Catholic church. Officially, returning from his trip, Mgr. Huessler declared at Rome that he would have wanted "to make contact with the Catholics of the country and especially with the episcopate. But his program was so crowded and had been worked out from a purely humanitarian point of view that there was no opportunity to have contacts of this kind."

At Saigon I found out from someone who knows the city of Hanoi that the residence of the archbishop and the cathedral were not more than five minutes away on foot from the hotel in which Mgr. Huessler was staying. This "lack of time," therefore, that prevented the German prelate from paying an official call on the Archbishop of Hanoi is quite curious, especially since there had been little precise news about him for many years. What really happened was somewhat different, and I was able to find out what the same Mgr. Huessler had said in private. He insistently asked to see the archbishop, but with one excuse or another the visit was not allowed him. One morning, very early, Mgr. Huessler left the hotel and went to the cathedral; he went in, asked where the archbishop was, and was directed to a confessional in the back of the church. Pushing aside the curtains of the confessional, Mgr. Huessler introduced himself and asked Mgr. Khue for news. The bishop did not want to speak with a foreigner, perhaps fearing some trap by the police, and his diffidence barely lessened when Mgr. Huessler showed his passport and said to the bishop that he had come on the part of the pope. Mgr. Khue said simply: "Greet the pope for me and tell him to pray for us," then he closed the curtains. The pressure and the surveillance must have been very strong and severe if such things could take place in Hanoi itself.

However, to compare the Church of North Vietnam with that of China, where all the churches are now closed and the bishops and priests scattered or imprisoned, would be unjust. The Hanoi government, despite many antireligious measures, continues to allow a certain religious freedom. This can be attributed above all to three factors that are not present in China:

(1) First of all the Catholics are rather numerous (5.6 percent of the population of North Vietnam), concentrated in a few dioceses and well organized. This makes it difficult to eliminate religious freedom completely for the Catholics.

(2) As long as Vietnam is divided into two parts and as long as the government of the North cultivates the hope and the aim to "liberate" the South, it is inevitable that there will be a certain moderation toward the Church, in order to demonstrate to the Catholics of the South that even under a Communist regime they would have the possibility of living the faith.

(3) Finally, the Communist leaders of North Vietnam, especially Ho Chi Minh, were much more influenced by Christianity than the Chinese, given the importance the Church has always had in Vietnam. It is enough to say that a good number of the older leaders had studied in Catholic schools during the French occupation of Vietnam, when the Catholic secondary schools were the most important and the most numerous.

The Church in North Vietnam enjoys greater freedoms than it did in China, but there is still no sign of a relaxation in the relations with the government, as may be seen in a few Communist countries of Eastern Europe (Yugoslavia, Czechoslovakia, Hungary, etc.). There is no news of any contact between government and religious authorities.

The magazine *Frères du monde* gives this description of the Church of North Vietnam:

The situation in North Vietnam is not comparable with that of the Church in Poland, East Germany, etc. The relations between Church and State are far from any climate of relaxed tension. Practically no effort has been made by either side.

For the clergy's part, their training, the age of the priests, the forced isolation of each priest from the others (the Archbishop of Hanoi himself cannot make his pastoral visits), the impossibility of keeping pace with the *aggiornamento* of the Church in the rest of the world, especially in the conciliar period (the bishops were unable to take part in Vatican II)—all of these factors did not favor a search for any attitude other than a self-imposed withdrawal into one's self in order to preserve the faith. Cut off in time and space from the general movement within the Church, the Christians of the North must cling to the "letter"—even when this is dead in the rest of the world and even when it creates useless problems of conscience for them—as the supreme proof of their fidelity.[65]

Even the regime itself is not free from a certain archaism. In many aspects the Communists of North Vietnam could make one think that the world has not evolved since Marx and Lenin. It is enough to read certain articles from the newspapers and magazines of Hanoi to be convinced of this. And whatever they may say to justify their refusal to let the bishops go to the Council, this fact remains the disquieting sign of a certain meanness and narrow-mindedness. The leaders of the North will have to understand that meanness and narrow-mindedness solve nothing and that the Christians of South Vietnam—and the Buddhists as well—cannot be deceived for the simple reason that they have seen many things from 1945 to today. If they want us to believe that religious freedom is respected in North Vietnam better than Diem respected it in the South, then as a beginning, let them open the doors to the young North Vietnamese priests who have finished their studies in Rome or Paris and ask for nothing better than to be able to "re-enter"; and also let them open the doors to the bishops who have the right to sit beside the bishops of Poland. Before accusing the Christians of being more Catholic than the pope, let them begin by showing themselves to be no more Marxist-Leninist than Khrushchev.[66]

In substance, in a Church like that in North Vietnam, about which we know so little but which remains alive;[67] in a Church that is dispersed, especially in the country areas, but still not snuffed out as an institution, as happened in China; in a Church that no longer has any contact with the outside world but which continues to live in silence and suffering; in such a Church the witness of its faithful will one day bear its fruit.

Notes

1. This fact alone, that even though the flights had been in progress for about two months, the first Americans arrived in North Vietnam on August 14 would be enough to demonstrate the falseness of the assertion of some writers that the flights were provoked by an "intense anti-Communist propaganda by the Americans" and by the offer of money that the Americans would have made to the refugees.

2. On the life and work of this young American physician (he died at the age of 37), see Christiane-Fournier, Tom Dooley (Turin: Borla, 1964).

3. (New York: Farrar, Straus and Giroux, 1960).

4. About 10,000 persons migrated from the South to the North; they belonged to the Viet Minh forces stationed in the South but were originally from the North. On the other hand, the Viet Minh, who originated in the South, remained there and years afterward joined the army of the NLF (Viet Cong).

5. See Tran-Nam-Bac, "Le drame des réfugiés catholiques vietnamiens" in *Les Missions Catholiques,* Paris, March, 1955, pp. 1–2.

6. F. N. Trager, *Why Vietnam?* (London: Pall Mall Press, 1966), p. 97.

7. *Fides* Agency (communiqué in Italian), November 20, 1954, pp. 379–380.

8. Communiqué of January 15, 1955, p. 10.

9. Communiqué of January 29, 1955, p. 28.

10. *Fides,* February 5, 1955, p. 38.

11. *Ibid.*

12. *Fides,* February 19, 1955, p. 51.

13. The documents of the CIC relative to the problems we are examining are contained in the *Quarterly Review* published at Ottawa after 1954 by the CIC itself.

14. M. E. Gettleman, *Vietnam: History, Documents and Opinions on a Major World Crisis* (London: Penguin Books, 1966), p. 173.

15. The "case" of Phat Diem is reported by Tom Dooley. We have given what he said above. This case in which the CIC asserts that the Viet Minh collaborated in the evacuation of the refugees developed actually in quite a different way, despite the formal collaboration as Dooley precisely relates. It is easy to imagine what happened in the other cases in which the Viet Minh did not collaborate . . .

16. *Op. cit.,* p. 175.

17. *La Civiltà Cattolica,* December 18, 1965, p. 728.

18. *The Tablet,* London, February 12, 1955, pp. 152–153.

19. The Montagnard tribes from the central plateaus fled the North especially because the promised concession of administrative autonomy was not forthcoming, even though these people had always enjoyed it, even under the French domination. Hence the revolts against the Communist regime and the consequent repressions and deportations of the mountain peoples and their flights to South Vietnam and Laos.

20. *T.C.* published in April 1955 a bulletin on Vietnam in which we read: "Between the 1st and the 20th of September in one refugee center there came 23,000 refugees, but the Viet Minh took swift measures to stop the movement. . . . In my opinion, if the Geneva agreements were applied and the inhabitants of the North had had the effective possibility of choosing freely, more than three million Vietnamese would have left the People's Republic. . . . The Viet Minh did everything to stop this mass emigration. Its papers stated that the refugees had to serve as slaves on the rubber plantations or would be sent to Madagascar or Morocco . . ." (*L'Actualité religieuse dans le Monde,* April, 1955, p. 13).

21. S. Ciuffi, *Storia politica e sociale della civiltà vietnamita* (Florence: Cultura, 1967), pp. 141–142.

22. In his book, Tom Dooley relates that the refugees from the Communist zones arriving at Haiphong were so influenced by anti-American propaganda (which accused the Americans of poisoning the wells, giving lethal injections, etc.), that they did not want to let themselves be seen and

cared for by the doctors from the American mission. The people were so afraid of them that it was enormously difficult even to get them to go into the tents for medication. Dooley felt it was unnecessary to insist on the fact that they never compelled even one person to emigrate against his will. Quite the contrary was true. After spending fourteen to fifteen hours in the first-aid station he would have been happy to have seen the evacuation stopped since he was incapable of doing more.

23. *Missi*, no. 2, 1956, p. 41.

24. Text in *L'Actualité religieuse dans le monde*, Paris, September 15, 1954, p. 19.

25. *Ibid.*

26. See *Missi*, no. 2, 1956, p. 40; *Eglise vivante*, nos. 3–4, 1955, p. 197.

27. Of the four Vietnamese bishops, Mgr. Hoan-Van-Doan, O.P., of Bac-Ninh, succeeded in reaching Hong Kong after five months under the Ho Chi Minh regime; the two foreign bishops were later expelled in the following years.

28. See, for example, *L'Actualité religieuse dans le monde*, September 15, 1954, p. 22.

29. According to the director of the refugee commission at Saigon, there were 928,152 refugees, of whom 794,867 were Catholics. According to Catholic sources, however, there were 676,384 Catholics that had fled to the South out of a total of 860,206 refugees (*Informations catholiques internationales*, April 15, 1956, p. 17). In his ponderous work *Vietnam: A Dragon Embattled*, J. Buttinger discusses in volume II (pp. 1116–1117) the figures given by various sides on the numbers of the refugees and concludes that it is still impossible to reach a definitive answer since the archives of the refugee Commissariat at Saigon were destroyed by fire in 1955 during the struggle of the government against the Binh-Xuyen. However, it is interesting to note that the military refugees (i.e., Vietnamese from the colonial army) were not computed with the civilian refugees, but separately: "About 124,000 persons," Buttinger writes, "in the flight to the South were military or quasi-military personnel, in addition to the 900,000 that includes all the civil refugees." There is no agreement on the military refugees in the various sources: some say there were 120,000, some 212,000, some only 70,000. The total number of Vietnamese refugees was certainly over one million, counting both civilians and military. The civilians were: peasants, 706,000; fishermen, 88,000; craftsmen, small businessmen, students, government employees and professionals, 133,000, after the general total of 927,000 (see Buttinger, *op. cit.*, p. 900).

30. In *Les Missions catholiques*, Paris, March 1955, p. 2.

31. In *Missionnaires d'Asie,* Paris, March–April, 1955, pp. 33–36.

32. F. Gian, "The Church in Vietnam," in *The Clergy Monthly Missionary Supplement,* Kurseong, India, December 1955, p. 312.

33. J. Rodhain, "La lezione dei profughi del Vietnam," in *L'Osservatore Romano,* March 3, 1955.

34. In *Missionnaires d'Asie,* May–June, 1955, pp. 67–70.

35. In *Les Missions catholiques,* March, 1955, p. 6.

36. A Canadian missionary of the "Fatebene" brothers, Norbert Lacerte, who today is a physician in South Vietnam but who was in the North until 1955, was interviewed by me on the topic of the flights and answered: "When the Viet Minh perceived that the people were fleeing en masse, they had hardly become familiar with the guarantees offered by the Geneva agreements and they began to stop the fugitives by force. Particularly in the villages of the interior garrisoned solely by the Viet Minh, only a very small number of those who wished to flee actually fled. At that time we had a hospital at Bui-Chu, and we sheltered dozens of persons wounded by the Viet Minh as they were fleeing. Along the coast, on the other hand, it was easier to organize escape, which often took on a tragic aspect: junks loaded with starving and indigent people setting out on a voyage to freedom that meant hundreds of kilometers to the South! Not a few of these junks capsized under their excessive load and those who were not picked up by passing French ships returned desperately to the shore or ended up being torn to bits by the sharks." When I asked the medical missionary whether the escapes were caused by anti-Communist propaganda, he answered: "The people who fled were in great part peasants, extremely attached to their land and their village. In Vietnam the national feeling of the poor and the peasants had begun to count in these latter years; at that time the peasant was much more attached to his village, his house, his field, his family tomb, than to the country in general. If people like this left everything to undertake a mass exodus toward unknown lands and an uncertain future, it is a sign that a stronger and more concrete reason motivated them: they would never have been moved by a hypothetical anti-Communist propaganda, if they did not have a real terror of living under a regime dominated by the Viet Minh, whose methods of oppression during the guerrilla war against the French they well knew." (*L'Italia,* Milan, December 23, 1667).

37. In *Missionnairs d'Asie,* March–April, 1955, pp. 37–38.

38. See both documents in *L'Actualité religieuse dans le monde,* September 15, 1954, p. 18.

39. See the text of Ho Chi Minh's message in *Mission Bulletin,* Hong Kong, March, 1955, p. 241.

40. See the text of the resolution in *Missi*, no. 2, 1956, p. 42.

41. The integral text of the Decree was published in *Fides-Documentazioni*, vol. III, no. 19, on August 27, 1955, pp. 173–175. In *Bulletin de la Société des Missions Etrangères de Paris* Hong Kong, January, 1956, pp. 15–23, there is the text of the Decree with full commentary.

42. See the integral text of this important article in *Fides-Documentazioni*, *op. cit.*

43. In the preceding chapter we have already alluded to the Viet Minh's harassment of the Church and Catholics even before the end of the war with the French. Reports of this would be very numerous if we had the space to quote them. One will suffice. Fr. de Soras, S.J., in an article in *La Croix* of July 23, 1954, after having spoken of the guarantees of religious freedom made by the Viet Minh, wrote: "But what were these guarantees worth? Certainly a clause in the armistice provided that there would be no violence or reprisals by either side against its adversary. This was maintained, perhaps until 1956. But afterward? And on the other hand, what effective guarantees existed for such impartiality and moderation? Was anybody naive enough to believe that the control commissions would see everything that was plotted and carried out in the depths of the tropical forest or along 1,300 kilometers of the Annamese mountain chain? . . . The future is particularly black for the wonderful Christians of Vietnam. Let us admit that the Viet Minh professed to observe 'religious neutrality.' We have innumerable facts that permit us to diagnose what hidden forms that future would take. At Tan-Hoa and Vinh, which at the beginning of the hostilities were situated in the Viet Minh zone, 'respect for religious opinions' was officially assured. The Viet Minh made no frontal attack on the Catholic religion which had remained 'free.' But, with every kind of measure [obligatory taxes that were impossible to pay, refusal of displacement visas, systematic and trumped up trials, organized calumnious accusations, etc.] priests found themselves de facto incapable of exercising their ministry. All the procedures of Mao-Tze-Tung's China had crossed the border into the peninsula."

44. The estimation that 200,000 died is given, among others, by Fr. Paquette who was expelled from Vietnam in 1958, as we shall see. He wrote: "A year and a half of agrarian reform caused more deaths than seven and a half years of war. More than 200,000 executions and suicides were attributed to the agrarian reform, and it would be impossible to calculate how many hundreds of thousands of persons were thrown into prison and condemned to forced labor." (Cf. D. Paquette, "Religious Persecution in North Vietnam," *Asia,* Hong Kong, January, 1960, p. 14.) The figure of 200,000 dead caused by the Communist regime in order to impose itself on

the population ought not to cause wonder and seem excessive. In May 1968, the official Czechoslovak sources stated that in the Stalinist period between 1948 and 1952 in Czechoslovakia the tribunals of Prague and Bratislava issued 130,000 condemnations. At that time Czechoslovakia had some 10 million inhabitants, which is less than North Vietnam at the time of the agrarian reform; and furthermore, we should point out that the European Communist regimes, perhaps with the exception of some time under Stalin, never achieved the ruthlessness of the Asian ones.

45. The best documentation on the agrarian reform and its excesses, taken partly from the official press and documents of North Vietnam, is to be found in Hoang Van Chi, *From Colonialism to Communism. A Case History of North Vietnam* (New York: Frederick A. Praeger, 1964), chapters XIII-XXVII.

46. From the economic point of view, the regime of North Vietnam, like the other Communist regimes, had good success in the industrial field but failed in the area of agriculture. Buttinger (p. 910) gives these figures: in 1955 the rice production of North Vietnam was 3.6 million tons, and the regime's program was to double this figure by 1960. But that year the rice production, instead of being more than 7 million tons, as the plan provided, was only 4.1 million. P. J. Honey explains the basic reason for this economic failure in *North Vietnam Today: Profile of a Communist Satellite* (New York: Frederick A. Praeger, 1962), p. 11: "Oppressed in this way, the peasants reacted in the only way possible to them. . . . They stopped caring for the rice fields in the way they had done previously, and this brought about a dramatic fall in food production. . . . Consequently, they tried to get money by selling part of their produce clandestinely, and from this developed the black market in food, which reached its zenith in the terrible famine of 1961." On the agricultural difficulties in North Vietnam, see R. Dumont, "Au Nord-Vietnam: production 3 percent, population 3.6 percent," *Chine surpeuplée, tiersmonde affamé* (Paris: Du Seuil, 1965), pp. 17–24; R. Dumont, *Problèmes agricoles au Nord-Vietnam,* no. 183 (Paris: France-Asie, 1964), pp. 138–40.

47. For reasons of prudence I cannot give the name of the missionary interviewed, who today lives in a guerrilla area of South Vietnam. The interview was published in *L'Italia,* Milan, January 28, 1968.

48. Communiqué of August 13, 1955, p. 254.

49. On the Catholic patriots and other aspects of the Church in North Vietnam, see "Les catholiques au Nord-Vietnam," *Informations catholiques internationales,* December 15, 1961, pp. 17–28.

50. G. Chaffard, *Indochine, dix ans d'indépendance* (Paris: Calmann-Lévy, 1964), pp. 138-40.

51. As is natural, the priests were the prime targets in the preceding period of anti-Catholic pressure either by limiting their freedom of movement (even to the imprisonment because of the least compliant) or by accusing them in front of the people: "The crimes for which the priests are reproached are almost always the same: direct or indirect murdering, poisoning the wells, extortion of money, raping of women, actions against the government. By condemning such criminals the authorities showed themselves to be defenders and vindicators of the honor of religion." (*Informations catholiques internationales,* September 1, 1955, which quotes a *Fides* comm., French ed.)

52. T. O'Driscoll, "Eight Years in Vietnam," *The Far East,* St. Columbans, February, 1960, p. 9.

53. Some seminaries fell under the direction of these priests who reopened them on their own initiative after the government had closed them for hiding priests faithful to the bishops (for example, the minor seminary of Phat-Diem); in other seminaries which remained open, there was some "progressivist" priest who kept his confreres under surveillance and controlled the programs of study and the lessons.

54. In *Missionnaires d'Asie,* January–February, 1960, pp. 16–19, can be read the account of the expulsion of this French missionary bishop.

55. T. O'Driscoll, *op. cit.,* pp. 7–9.

56. A. Marillier, "Evangelizzazione coraggiosa nel Vietnam del Nord dopo il 1955," *La Missione,* para. 29, Milan, 1961, p. 88.

57. A. Marillier, "Les chrétiens du Nord-Vietnam en 1960," *Missionnaires d'Asie,* May–June, 1961, pp. 23–30.

58. It does not enter into our discussion to speak of the persecution of the Buddhists, which was more drastic and total than that of the Catholics, in as much as the anti-Buddhist measures in the North never aroused the least international reaction, and therefore the government felt more free to go all the way in their anti-Buddhist action even from the start; furthermore, since the Buddhists did not have a centralized organization, they showed less resistance than the Catholics. In Saigon, December 1967, a high Buddhist leader told me that about 90 percent of the Buddhist pagodas and monasteries in the North had been closed by government order and the bonzes scattered. A few pagodas in the major cities remained open, with the bonzes completely subjected to the regime.

59. In regard to the spiritual renewal, see the study "Les Catholiques au Nord-Vietnam," *Informations catholiques internationales,* December 15, 1961, especially the part "Renouveau catholique" on pp. 21–24, where it speaks of

new relations between Christians and pagans; the pagans admired the endurance of the Christian faith, despite all the hardships.

60. In *Le Monde,* December 27, 1966, a correspondent from Hanoi described the midnight mass at Christmas of that year at Hanoi and spoke of the full cathedral and of five or six hundred faithful following the mass outside.

61. See the summary given in *Le Missioni cattoliche,* Milan, May, 1963, p. 271.

62. *L'Osservatore Romano,* December 10–11, 1962, p. 8.

63. Three of the twelve bishops have still not been able to be consecrated: those of Thai-Binh, Than-Hoa and Langson.

64. On November 25, 1967, p. 611, *Fides* published the information that the Diocese of Vinh had been severely damaged by American bombs in recent years; four priests were killed and the coadjutor bishop wounded. Moreover, the cathedral, the archibishop's residence and the two seminaries suffered damage from aerial bombardment. At Saigon, refugee priests from the North showed me letters from their confreres who had remained in the North, and they were strongly accusatory in regard to the American bombings which were aimed, especially in the Diocese of Vinh, slightly north of the 17th parallel, at churches and Catholic buildings. For this fact, which otherwise would seem inexplicable, I heard the following explanation: the North Vietnamese military set up the antiaircraft equipment in the towers of the churches and in the cover of the large buildings belonging to the Church (seminaries, bishop's residence, etc.).

A communiqué from Kipa (June 4, 1968) reported a declaration of the Liaison committee of Catholic Vietnamese patriots and friends of peace, located in Hanoi, according to which over the last years the American planes destroyed or damaged with their bombs 437 churches in North Vietnam, killing four priests, among whom was a vicar general, and wounding two others; many nuns and male religious also perished.

65. Knowing the Church in South Vietnam—of which we shall speak at length in the following chapters—it is not hard for me to imagine that the Church of the North also remained closed in a solely defensive position with regard to religious freedom and religious traditions, without attempting any opening out to or inclusion in the Socialist system. This is certainly a limitation, a defect of the Church, especially if it is pushed to the extreme, since the Church would run the risk of remaining totally cut off from a society that for good or ill is evolving. We must also take into account the opposite risk, of becoming an *instrumentum regni* of a regime that is everywhere striving to acclimatize religions and men for its own exclusive use.

The example of the Church in the Communist countries of Eastern Europe can teach us something. In Czechoslovakia, for example, for almost twenty years, the Movement of Priests for Peace has fully collaborated with the government, supporting everything it did; its president, Mgr. Plojhar, was minister of health and a deputy in parliament, although he never succeeded in getting the least concession of religious freedom either for the Church, or for any other religion; these priests, who for so many years have boasted about dialoguing with the government and being within the Socialist regime, have obtained practically nothing more than getting themselves implicated in all of the offenses of the Gottwalds and the Novotnys, which they always applauded, even though what these leaders did was hated by the people as much as by the leaders themselves. The new Czechoslovak government that came out of the 1968 revolution immediately bypassed the "priests for peace" and dealt with those who had resisted the regime and had refused to be forced into being part of a system now repudiated. The same is happening in Poland with the Pax Movement, which has practically become the long arm of the government in religious matters. The history of the Church reveals once again that service is rendered to Christianity by a man who commits himself to living it consistently and not by one who sells himself for a "mess of pottage." But this does not mean that in Communist countries—and therefore also in Vietnam—the Church must always and in everything oppose the government and its social and cultural initiatives: it is necessary to collaborate in everything that is good and for the welfare of the people, but one must also know how to resist when it is contrary to the Christian principles of love and justice.

66. *Frères du Monde,* no. 28, Bordeaux, 1964, p. 46.

67. That the Church is still alive is demonstrated among other things by the fact that when the Hanoi government denounces the "enemies of the revolution," there is always special mention of those who use religion to combat the revolution. For example, the official paper of the Communist party, the *Nhan Dan,* in an editorial on March 21, 1968, commenting on the "Decree for the punishment of counterrevolutionary crimes" signed by Ho Chi Minh a month or so before, states that among the various types of counterrevolutionaries there are also "reactionary elements that profit from the mask of religion . . . to undermine the building of Socialism . . . The counterrevolutionaries in the North of our country are only a small force, but the aim they are pursuing is wicked and their activity very dangerous."

IV

The Church
under the Diem Regime

The history of the Diem[1] regime, which lasted almost ten years (from June 25, 1954 to November 1, 1963), does not enter into the scope of our work, since our purpose is to study the position of the Church and its members and the progress of Christianity at this period. But we must synthesize the negative and positive aspects of the regime in order to better understand the central theme of this chapter.

The assertion of a non-Communist nationalism. Diem (pronounced Z-yemm) was called by Bao Dai to form the Saigon government on June 16, 1954. The Annamese emperor would have preferred to entrust the task to Tran Van Huu, a more conciliatory man who promised to seek an accord with the Hanoi government, rather than to Diem, who was an indomitable anti-Communist. But Diem got the post as a result of the decisive support given to him by the United States, which saw no possibility of colloquy with the Communist government of the North, and which discerned in Diem the "new man" who would be able to keep the South free from the influence and the occupation of the Communists.

And undoubtedly, whatever judgment we might wish to make of it, this was the greatest success of the Diem regime, when everyone thought in 1954 that the attempt to save half the country from

Communist domination would be a wretched failure. We must remember that after the victory of Dien Bien Phu and the Geneva agreements, the Viet Minh were the sole organized force in the whole of Vietnam (besides the French troops which were on the verge of leaving), and the Ho Chi Minh regime made no mystery about its wish to unify all of Vietnam under his rule. July 28, 1954, two days after the closing of the Geneva conference, Ho Chi Minh addressed a message to the Vietnamese people, clearly revealing his plan:

During the cease-fire, we must systematize the military zones, and look upon them as the first step toward final victory. . . . The line of demarcation ought not be understood as a political and territorial boundary line. The northern, central and southern sectors of Vietnam are inseparable parts of our territory—i.e., the Democratic People's Republic of Vietnam—and we assure the people of the three regions that they will be liberated. The people of southern Vietnam is one that dared to undertake the patriotic war: I guarantee to this people that we shall fight shoulder to shoulder with them to gain peace, unification, independence and democracy for the whole of Vietnam. . . . The fight is long and difficult: all the populations of the North and South must unite to win the victory.

Between 1954 and 1955, declarations of this kind by the leaders and the newspapers of North Vietnam abound. They reflect the real situation in the country, with the North strongly controlled by the victorious Viet Minh and the South on the brink of chaos on account of the withdrawal of the French troops and the lack of leaders and organizations that were on a popular basis and with a national spirit. The South was compared by a French newspaperman to a "ripe pear" that at any moment was ready to fall under the domination of the North (the intellectual and political elite of the country had fled to France).

The blackest pessimism reigned at that time [a missionary reports] with all the Vietnamese intelligentsia. Many of its members, and even personalities who had remained resolutely neutralist during the whole war in Indochina, decided to go and settle in France. One eminent French journalist, whose predictions carried weight in Indochinese matters, wrote at the time: "Ho Chi Minh will be in Saigon at the end of 1956, or perhaps even well before." The emperor Bao Dai himself had set up his capital at Cannes in preference to Saigon.[2]

Thus, Diem saved a desperate situation[3] by reenforcing the State and nationalism in the South and by acquiring in a short time a great popularity that he was later to lose. He is given his accolade for this even by writers and observers who could certainly never be suspected of being pro Diem. One Italian historian of Vietnam, Sergio Ciuffi, in referring to Diem's sustained struggle to assert the authority of the State throughout the South during his first year in power, states: "From the viewpoint of organizing and stabilizing a State organism in South Vietnam, we must acknowledge the positive value of the results obtained by Ngo Dinh Diem in the liquidation of the politico-military apparatus of the sects."[4] The Buddhist bonze Nhat Hanh wrote: "Under the Diem government there came to light an awareness of a distinction existing between the Communists and the national resistance, and this was Diem's most valid contribution to the country. In the cities, especially, the intellectuals and the middle classes began to understand and support the anti-Communist policy of the Diem government."[5]

The rising of the Diem regime. From the very beginning Diem found himself confronted with grave difficulties. In the climate of dejection and capitulation that was created after the Geneva accords, no one had confidence any longer in a resistance to Communism. Diem's great merit was that of having instilled, first in his closest collaborators and then in broad masses of the population, a decided will to survive and not to succumb to the stronger adversaries. Without this force of his spirit, the whole of Vietnam would have in time been under Communist domination.[6]

In the beginning, Diem's most dangerous adversaries were the national army, the French and the feudal sects. The army still depended upon the head of State, Bao Dai, who was living in exile in Cannes but following closely the political situation of his country. Bao Dai leaned toward a moderate solution and an accord with the Viet Minh; the leaders of the army, tied as they were to France, were also of this frame of mind and wrote to Bao Dai, requesting Diem's resignation; General Hinh declared himself openly against the prime minister, after having surrounded his palace with troops several times.

The French colonists, who were still powerful in the South, and the troops of the French expeditionary corps frowned upon a "protégé of America" who was outspokenly anti-French and who boycotted the solution proposed by the Paris government, which was a rapprochement and an accord with the Viet Minh. Finally, the third adversary, the feudal-religious sects (Binh-Xuyen, Hoa-Hao, Cao-Dai) each had its own military organization and controlled part of the national territory.

Diem was able to win out over these adversaries thanks to three supports of remarkable force: American aid, which in the beginning was primarily financial (there were no American troops in Vietnam until 1961); the refugees from the North who, having had concrete personal experience of the Communist regime, were disposed completely not to have the experience repeated; and finally, the support of the majority of the people, which grew in the first two years of the regime but diminished later, as we shall see.

In October 1955, Diem decided to launch a popular referendum to resolve his differences with Bao Dai, which were becoming ever more acute. The dilemma proposed to the voters was a clever one: the choice between Diem and Bao Dai, without any middle course. The result of the referendum—even if the plebiscite itself were not completely free and democratic—was expected beforehand. Very few chose the emperor, who was too compromised with French colonialism and living abroad while the country was in grave crisis. Strengthened with this popular support, Diem proclaimed the fall of Bao Dai (October 26), instituted the Republic and became its first president. During the following months, one step at a time, he succeeded in settling accounts with the leaders of the army, who were Francophiles and too bound to the ex-emperor, defeated in real pitched battles the armies of the sects and sent home the French expeditionary corps (France, involved in the Algerian war, made no opposition).

Was it good or bad not to have a poll in 1956? Having stabilized the internal conflicts, Diem reestablished his authority over the whole country—although allowing the discontented and the opposition to be still free to express themselves. In 1956 he faced the problem of electoral consultations in all of Vietnam, as provided for by Geneva as a means of unifying the two halves of the country under one government.

From the very beginning, Diem always refused any contact with North Vietnam and drastically excluded the possibility of holding the projected elections, either because the nationalist government of South Vietnam had not signed the Geneva agreements,[7] or because in the North, free elections were clearly unthinkable after the Viet Minh had done away with even the slightest opposition to their regime. Article 7 of the final declaration of the Geneva Conference declares that

it will be permitted to the Vietnamese people to enjoy basic freedoms, guaranteed by democratic institutions resulting from free general elections with a secret ballot. In order to assure sufficient progress for the re-establishment of peace and because all the conditions necessary for the free expression of the will of the nation have been achieved, there will be general elections in July 1956, under the control of an international commission composed of representatives of the States who are members of the International Control Commission.

It is beyond any reasonable doubt that in July 1955, when the two parts of the country had to make contact in view of the elections the following year, there did not exist in North Vietnam any possibility of "free elections" that would be the "free expression of the will of the nation." As we saw in the previous chapter, as soon as the Communists took power the only liberty left to the people of North Vietnam was to declare themselves Communists.

In the South, on the other hand, Diem still had much internal opposition to his regime, which, at least until July 1956, was certainly much freer and much more democratic than that which had been set up by the Viet Minh in the North. The press was gagged completely in 1957, and the "Communist hunt" began only at the end of 1956 (the foreign observers agree on the estimate that, still at the beginning of 1955, practically the majority of the country villages were controlled by elements faithful to the Hanoi government that had not been repatriated to the North but remained in the South, waiting for the elections in order to prepare the way for the inevitable Communist victory). To agree to electoral consultation under these circumstances would mean resigning oneself to giving the country into the hands of a Communist government if only because the North was more densely populated than the South and no one doubted that it would have voted en masse for a Viet Minh representation. (Has it ever happened in any Communist country that the electors voted differently from the will of the party?)

After declaring in May 1955 that his consent to have elections would "depend on the conditions in which the elections themselves would be held," Diem declared on August 9:

The Vietnamese government considers the principle of free elections as a peaceful and democratic institution. But it is necessary that the circumstances of life and the vote be satisfactory before we can speak of the voting itself. From this point of view, nothing constructive will be done until the Communist regime of the North permits each Vietnamese citizen the enjoyment of democratic freedoms and the basic rights of man.

And in reality no one up to today has succeeded in demonstrating how it would be possible for the people of North Vietnam to express themselves freely in accordance with the prescriptions of the Geneva Convention. It would be completely naive to think that the International Control Commission (we have already seen how it functioned to guarantee freedom to the North Vietnamese to go to the South) would have been able to check the freedom of the polls in the thousands of polling places in the cities and the 15,000 rural and mountain villages. In addition, the conditions of terror brought about by the agrarian reform still existed, as the Communist leaders themselves acknowledged (see the preceding chapter), conditions which in July 1956 certainly did not exist in South Vietnam, although they were to come some time later. As we said, after the Communists took power the only freedom in North Vietnam was to declare oneself a Communist.

It seems to me, then, that the many criticisms generally leveled at Diem for not having wanted the elections of 1956 as provided at Geneva are valid only in this sense: if one wanted all of Vietnam to fall under Communist domination through bogus elections, then Diem is to be condemned for his stubbornness in going against the constitution; but if one wanted to safeguard the Vietnamese people's freedom of decision (at least in the South), there is no doubt that Diem is to be praised. Diem, as we shall see, was certainly no champion of the idea of democracy, but we have to acknowledge that he left the opposition free enough to organize themselves and ultimately overthrow his regime; in the North this is unthinkable, since the opposition was completely eliminated and had no possibility of rebirth or reorganization.

On the other hand, the following year the Moscow government proposed the admission of both Vietnams to the UN, with the intention of canonizing the definitive division of the country.[8] And in the South, as an anti-Diem observer writes, Diem's decision won him many followers from the people:

The *sine die* postponement of the elections had remarkable psychological consequences in South Vietnam. A noticeable part of the non-
committed (who hesitated to commit themselves since they expected
an eventual victory of the Viet Minh) now sided with those in power.
In the country regions, the frustrated and sentimental masses who never
stopped believing in the accession of the Viet Minh and in the infalli-
bility of uncle Ho, suddenly discovered in amazement that there was
another president in Saigon, who dared oppose the Communists and
that the Communists were not so all-powerful as they thought, since
their political cadres, disseminated throughout the South, were incapable
of forcing the elections on Diem. . . . In all strata of the population
there then arose a movement of support for the regime, which the
mandarin Diem and his proud retinue did not know how to receive,
or what was soon going to happen.[9]

A fanatical and intransigent anti-Communism. Towards the end
of 1956, Diem really had the country in hand, in a state of almost
complete calm,[10] and was able to govern it and build it up with the
diplomatic support and financial aid of the United States. But it
was precisely during these years that the Diem regime revealed
its major flaws, which caused him to lose the people's favor and
ultimately dug his grave.

The mistakes of the South Vietnamese dictator were grave and
many. We shall record them summarily. The first, relating to
Diem's personality, is of a psycho-religious nature. As a good
practicing Catholic of great faith, a man of the greatest integrity
and a convinced nationalist, Diem felt himself invested with a divine mission to save the country from the threat of Communism
and based every action of his government on this one anti-
Communist platform, refusing any advice and any meeting of ideas,
even with those who were closest to him and wanted to advise him
for the good. In South Vietnam, one bishop, whom I am not at liberty to name but who was close to the dictator, made the following
declaration to me verbatim:

Diem was undoubtedly an upright and honest man, but one of the worst kind of fanatics there could be: he considered himself to be directly and personally aided by God, with a mission to fulfill that was inspired by God himself, and he never wanted to discuss or accept advice. Once, I told him in confidence—this was in 1959—that in the country areas of my diocese the Communists were making enormous progress, indoctrinating the people, distributing antigovernment pamphlets, and profiting from the people's unhappiness with the dictatorship, Diem did not even let me finish and went off in a rage, calling me a pessimist and a defeatist; in the following years, every time he met me he immediately brought up my pessimism and defeatism. . . . It was impossible to speak with him, to have any dialogue: he liked only monologues. Towards the last years of his power he became hard and intractable with a few bishops and leaders of the Catholic laity who recommended moderation to him and requested greater democratic freedom.

A newspaperman gave this judgment, which agrees with the foregoing:

An energetic and informed leader, with an intuitive intelligence, animated by unquestionable patriotism, pugnacious, upright but unpliable, very stubborn, President Ngo Dinh Diem did not know his people well enough. This statement, borne out by the facts, is all the more surprising if we think that he was continually travelling about the country. As a Catholic, mystical enough to think that he was aided by heaven . . . the attempts on his life that he escaped convinced him that he was under heaven's protection. The price of such doggedness was that his character seldom allowed for opposition. Very few people would dare contradict him; and some even felt that cricitism would not even be understood.[11]

Closed within his unshakeable convictions, Diem made his first mistake by neatly cutting off any possible dialogue with North Vietnam not only for the electoral consultation of July 1956 but also for other aims such as the reestablishment of postal and commercial relations. There are those who say that this totally closed mind was advised and practically imposed on Diem by the American advisers at his side, but given the obstinate and intransigent nationalism of the dictator, who could always withstand any American pressure, we should think that this political tack was chosen quite autonomously and out of personal conviction.

The fact was that North Vietnam, especially in the years immediately after 1956, had an absolute need to trade with the South in order to obtain the foodstuffs of which the disastrous agrarian reform and the meager agricultural productivity of the land had deprived it. On the other hand, the South could at least have used the mineral and industrial products of the North, which the Americans were now supplying them. Thus, while the South was exporting rice and other farm produce, the North was reduced to starvation, and this enraged the leaders of Hanoi, who were already disappointed in their hopes by the failure to have the electoral consultations of 1956. Diem's intransigence contributed to sharpening and not to alleviating (as would have been good on all sides) the conflicts between the North and the South, which were further widened by the aid the North gave to the guerrillas in the South who were rebelling against the dictatorship.[12]

A family regime and a stifling dictatorship. Diem's second error was to want to fight Communism by Communist methods, which were dictatorial and oppressive, and J. Buttinger points out the mistake of those Americans who supported Diem to the end, asserting that many Americans reached the conclusion that Diem would have been successful if he had been more efficient instead of an incompetent dictator and if his dictatorship had achieved the level of perfection boasted by Ho Chi Minh.[13]

But this, Buttinger goes on to say, was pure illusion, since in the struggle and the confrontation between democracy and Communism, democracy can be victorious only if it is the champion of freedom of opinion and if it gives the people the progress and the social justice it expects.

All observers, even those who were best disposed toward the Diem regime, reproached him for not having broadened the representative basis of his government after having assured the country internal peace and unity. That he used undemocratic methods during the 1954–1956 period is understandable, and the "hard" line was his success in the reestablishment of the State's authority over a country in rack and ruin and in restoring the courage of the non-Communist nationalists. But from 1957 to 1960, Diem had four years to democratize the regime and permit a gradual return to the freedom of expression and democratic education of the people. On the contrary, it was precisely in these years that the regime became more intransigent, physically eliminating every opponent and indulging in that "Communist hunt" which was the determining factor that caused the outbreak of the guerrilla war in 1960.

Robert Scigliano, of Michigan State University, who was in South Vietnam from 1957 until 1959 and then again for many months in 1961 on official duty, gives a full description of the "democracy" (one wag called it "diemocracy") that was functioning in the country. He gives a fund of particulars which we cannot quote here, but according to him, the Republic of Diem was practically a one party government with its camps for political re-education, its denunciatory manifestations against Communism, its omnipresent propaganda that exalted the "leader" and condemned the enemy, its mass organizations, etc.[14] Naturally, there was no lack of "guided" elections, secret police, intolerance even toward the non-Communist opposition. Whoever opposed the regime was arrested, detained without trial and at times tortured. The press, even though up to 1962 it enjoyed a certain freedom, became adulatory of the regime, etc. As the supreme irony, the Republic of the South—like the North—also had a "superbly written!" constitution, with the fullest and most solemn guarantees of civil and political freedoms." Scigliano's conclusion is that Diem's regime had become but the pale reflection of its rival,[15] "pale" in the sense that Diem lacked the strength and the dexterity to deprive the people of all their freedoms and to compel them in all things and

by every means to do the will of the leader, thus losing the few
advantages that a "perfect dictatorship" can possess.

All in all, Diem went in the opposite direction from the one he
ought to have chosen. Not only did he not give Vietnam a true
democracy,[16] which perhaps in so short a time and with the many
difficulties encountered may have been impossible, but he did not
even give his people a strong government that would have been
bearable and popular and more representative than the one that
remained in power for nine years. Diem governed by essentially
trusting only those people who were part of his "family" (because,
as we said, in the beginning no one had confidence in him).
"Diemism" is the reign of a family, the Ngo: Diem was the president, Nhu was the political head of the regime as an ingenious
thinker, gifted, like Diem, with an iron will for power; behind
these two, there was brother Can, the governor of Hué province,
brother Luyen who was ambassador in London, and finally, brother
Thuc, the Archbishop of Hué and the family's spiritual counsellor;
then there was the sister, Ca-Le, who headed the rice companies.
But in addition to the Ngo family, with a generous supply of
nephews and various relatives, there was the Tran family, closely
allied and related to them. The wife of Ngo Dinh Nhu, the famous
"Madame Nhu," was a Tran by birth: intelligent, courageous,
ambitious and very beautiful, she directly intervened in politics by
assuming the role of moral arbiter of public life and by fighting
for women's emancipation. (Behind her relatives and friends, she
also sought to divide the political pie, since her father was ambassador in Washington.)

The Diem family, therefore, had become a center of power and
corruption. Although everyone respected the president and his
closest relatives, knowing them to be upright people (like all the
fanatics who "have an idea"—in this case, anti-Communism), into
the ruling hierarchy there was an intrusion of every kind of ad-
venturer, all intransigent supporters of Diem and sworn enemies
of Communism but quite capable of taking care of themselves as

well. The people saw corruption in all the workings of the state but could not speak of it since even the minor leaders were protected by the regime as an exchange for their services. J. Buttinger, who seems to me to be somewhat exaggerating, wrote that actually to ask the Diem regime to punish lazy, corrupt or brutal functionaries was tantamount to asking it to change what it already was, namely, a self-liquidation.[17]

The political philosophy of the regime: "personalism." All of this alienated the people, especially the city elite who were witnesses of the bureaucratic corruption and suffered from the lack of political freedom, despite the grandiose propaganda and ideological explanation organized by Nhu for the "indoctrination of the masses," after the example of what the Communists were doing in the North (Nhu prided himself on his desire to imitate the "efficient" methods of Communism). As a matter of fact, as its own political philosophy, the regime had a "communitarian personalism" derived from the Left-wing French philosopher, Emmanuel Mounier, an obscure and much discussed derivation. Jean-Marie Domenach, the editor of the review *Esprit* and spiritual heir of Mounier, protested many times against the usurpation of the Mounier name and the distortion the South Vietnamese regime had made of the philosophy of personalism.[18]

The many authors I have consulted on this argument agree in saying that the "personalism" of the Diem regime was more or less a vague blend of ideas, as one of Diem's supporters, Anthony T. Bouscaren, calls it.[19] Robert Shaplen, a very serious-minded American journalist, asserts that a few Americans, including some students visiting Vietnam, spent considerable time trying to understand and explain personalism, but they had to give up because it had all the aspects of a mixture of heterogeneous elements that did not blend together, and also because, whatever it was, it was merely a theory; in practice it was what Nhu wanted it to be.[20]

While he claimed that personalism was a "respectable philosophy," John Mecklin recalls a conversation between the American ambassador Nolting and Diem in which the diplomat said that the Vietnamese leader might possibly be surprised to learn that most Americans, who had never heard of personalism, thought that it meant the glorification of Diem's person as head of state. Mecklin adds that those Vietnamese who never knew anything about personalism had the same attitude. Personalism died an unforeseen death, without regrets, the moment the Diem regime fell.[21]

The most exhaustive writer on the Diem period, Robert Scigliano, gives a description of personalism.[22] Noting that the personalist Labor Party has a philosophic basis known as "personalism," he goes on to point out that this is the official doctrine of all pro-government parties, and that it is studied (in diluted form) in the civil service and proclaimed as the stronghold of the Constitution. Personalism chiefly emphasizes the harmonization of the individual and spiritual aspirations with the social needs of the community and the political needs of the state in order to find a middle way between individualistic capitalism and Marxist collectivism. Although, as Scigliano says, this personalism claims to have gotten its inspiration largely from the Asian tradition, it also strongly relies on the Western tradition of the social encyclicals of popes Leo XIII and Pius XI.

Also on this question I have an exchange of correspondence with a person very close to Diem, about whom I have mentioned a few things previously, who sent me two long memoranda on personalism, both in theory and in practice (49 closely packed pages); I shall try to sum them up since I think they are interesting insofar as there is very little on this question in studies in Western languages.

During the Diem period, the political doctrine in South Vietnam was called Chanh-sach Nhan-Vi (i.e., the ideology of the dignity of man), translated into French by the word *personnalisme,* and wrongly likened to Mounier's doctrine precisely because of this French word chosen to signify a different meaning in Vietnamese. Mounier, however, was partially the inspiration for the political doctrine, as were other Christian thinkers and Roman pontiffs, interpreted in accordance with the mentality and the traditions of Asia and particularly of Vietnam. In practice, the Nhan-Vi was an attempt to translate the most modern Christian social teaching into Vietnamese terms, so that it might be understood and lived even by the poorest peasants of Vietnam.

The Nhan-Vi is opposed both to Communism and capitalism (we are still summing up the memorandum) since capitalism is as materialistic as Communism; it cannot satisfy man fully since man is not only matter but also spirit. The Nhan-Vi does not admit that man's happiness can be realized only materially; man must also be able to realize himself spiritually. Therefore, the dignity of the single human person must be respected and is at the center and basis of Nhan-Vi political philosophy, which both in its goals and its means wishes to be differentiated from both Communism and capitalism. In fact, Communism sacrifices human freedom, private property, the family and religion, while capitalism sacrifices justice, permits exploitation, etc.

In order to realize the human person and to respect his dignity, the Nhan-Vi starts with the lowest to reach the highest: it guarantees the rights of a single man (freedom in all its aspects, including freedom from want and from exploitation, freedom of ownership, etc.); it recognizes the family and its rights (autonomy, education of children, etc.); it establishes democracy, beginning with the village (village assemblies, election of the village chiefs), and then passing to provincial, regional and national democracy.

On the level of labor, it wishes to increase national production through "community labor"; not, however, like Communism, which makes the people work for the gain of the whole State, but by giving immediate and personal profit to the worker in proportion to his capacity and by taking into account the needs of the community. In this way personal interests are joined to those of the community.

On the social plane the principle of "collective ascent" prevails, limiting the property of individuals on a basis of the richness of the particular area but assuring every family of two to three hectares of land, a house, farm tools supplied by the State or the cooperatives, etc. Social justice is brought about by revolutionary means that are also moral and humane, preserving man's dignity and eschewing the brutalities of Communism.

On the national level, the Nhan-Vi wishes to defend the country from Communist aggression and from submission to capitalism and capitalist countries by instilling anticolonialism in the minds of the people, along with anti-Communism and the virtue of nationalism.

On the cultural and spiritual levels, the Nhan-Vi is based on ancestor worship, the national religion of Vietnam, understood as the veneration of the fatherland and the national culture, and as a rebirth of traditional Vietnamese virtues.

The "Communist witch-hunt." After the popularity it enjoyed until 1956, as we said, the regime gradually lost this precious capital, partly because of its failure to broaden its democratic basis, partly because the social reforms came too slowly (especially the agrarian reform), and partially also because of the reorganization of the opposition parties, particularly the Communists (which drove Diem and his followers to increasingly harsh forms of dictatorship and oppression). There is almost something pitiful about the effort the regime made to give a faith to the people by teaching it "personalism." In this way it thought it could regain the confidence it was losing on account of the corruption, the inefficiency and the lack of democracy that it was experiencing. Courses of indoctrination for public officials were organized; personalism was taught in the schools; books were printed and university faculties established with the intention of giving South Vietnam an ideological impetus superior to what Communism gave to the North.

But all was in vain: "personalism" did not catch on with either the poor villagers or with the city elite. The people wanted more freedom, more democracy, more social justice. In the cities, especially, discontent with the dictatorship was growing, anti-Diem manifestations were organized, pamphlets and newspapers were printed in secret against the regime, and the opposition began to close ranks. Buttinger writes: "Fought by the intellectuals, scorned by the cultivated middle classes, rejected by businessmen, hated by the youth and by all nationalists with political ambitions, and completely lacking the support of the masses, the Diem government had to rely for its survival on an apparatus of coercion."[23]

And, Buttinger continues, in order to dominate by force, qualified men are needed. While in its first years the regime had attracted many capable men dedicated to serving the country and the people, as it gradually became more and more dictatorial and unpopular it had to rely chiefly on less honest men who were ready for anything. This is the logic of all dictatorships!

The antidemocratic oppression was ideologically styled as a "Communist witch-hunt," which gave the coup de grace to the regime not only internally but also externally in the countries of Western Europe and America where the Diem regime, which in its early years was looked upon favorably, was increasingly losing its universal esteem. From this point on, even the most unthinkable calumnies against Diem found world public opinion ready to accept them unconditionally.[24]

In 1961, Robert Guillain, a noted journalist and expert on Asian problems, wrote: "It is decidedly a fascist regime. . . . Three years ago, writing about this country, I accentuated the hopes that it still aroused and avoided bringing up the political problem. In brief, I had practised in my report at that time that self-censorship that a responsible journalist has at times to impose on himself. But today the hope of a reformation of the regime is completely gone: this kind of self-censorship is no longer admissible."[25]

Up to 1956, the Communist cadres that had been left in the South remained spread out among the people in expectation of the elections and the unification of the country: although they made intensive political propaganda and at times took over full power in remote regions, they did not cause much trouble for the Saigon government. After 1956, if political life had been liberalized, Diem would have broadened the basis of his power and pulled the rug out from under the malcontents. However, immediately after 1956 the purge of the Communists began: "Communist" meant not only real Communists but also all opponents of the government and all who in the old fight against the French had had anything to do with the Viet Minh. Quite a sizeable number of people! "In 1955 [writes Lacouture] every opponent of the government was denounced as a hold-over from the sects of 'feudal rebels,' supported by colonialism. Beginning with 1956, every opponent was called a Communist."[26]

We can easily imagine the methods used in this violent and indiscriminate repression of political adversaries: arresting of suspects, torture, killings, abuses of power, etc.[27] This is the face of all dictatorships, and in the case of Diem, it was especially antipathetic and damnable insofar as he wanted by these means to save the country from the "Communist peril" by leading a crusade that also had a religious flavor in defense of a "civilization" that declared itself to be at least nominally Christian.

In 1960 the ministry of information at Saigon published a revealing document entitled *Balance sheet of six years of government activity*. In the chapter concerned with civic activity, we find the following figures referring to the years 1954–1960:

893,291 sessions of "personalist education," with 18,759,111 participants [which meant for all the Vietnamese, over the six year period, an individual average of one and a half sessions of indoctrination: this is very slight for a regime that wished to keep up with the "brainwashing" of the Communist regime in the North but too much for one that claimed to be the defender of freedom].

The national police arrested 25,700 Communists, while the local police arrested another 22,500 [Here, too, the above observation obtains: the Communists of North Vietnam arrested and eliminated many more persons, but some 48,000 political arrests in six years are too many for a government that pretended to be defending the country against dictatorship!].

In a word, the Diem regime ended up by representing in the eyes of the peoples of the South a kind of rival that was both equal and opposite to the Hanoi regime. This brought about a radicalization of the political struggle in Vietnam insofar as the possible choices were reduced to two: a Communist dictatorship or the dictatorship of Diem (and following Diem's fall, military dictatorships). Diem's died-in-the-wool defenders asserted that he was forced to use dictatorial and oppressive methods because of the constant ideological and terrorist pressure of the Communists, but it still has to be demonstrated whether the escalation of terror was the best means for fighting the guerrilla war, instead of the democratization of the regime, the opening up of trade and negotiations with North Vietnam, more courageous social reform, etc. The latter way was the opposite of the one followed by Diem!

Positive aspects of the Diem regime. Not all of the balance sheet of Diem's work is negative, however, as people generally tend to think and write. Thus, we can say, in the circumstances in which he had to operate, leaving aside the serious mistakes about which we have spoken, Diem was able to register some noteworthy points to his credit, which should be recalled.

Among the positive aspects of the regime, we must first point out the placement of one million refugees from the North, an enterprise of great importance in a disorganized country that had little resources, which was praised even by the regime's severest critics (except, naturally, for the Communists or the pro-Communists). Diem committed himself thoroughly to this work of refugee placement in the years 1954–1955, since he understood that if such a mass of people had not found suitable living conditions in the South, they would have rebelled. New villages were founded by deforesting entire regions and cultivating them; agricultural cooperatives were developed along with centers for handicrafts and small industry; industrial factories were set up on the periphery of the large cities in order to provide work for the refugees who came from cities in the North and did not want to settle in the country areas.

If we look at the period from 1954 to 1961, on the socio-economic level the Diem regime registered notable success in contrast to the degradation of the farm economy in North Vietnam (after 1961, the guerrilla war and the insecurity of the country areas worsened the economic situation in the South, the same thing happened in the North after 1965, following the American bombings). At the Paris talks with the North Vietnamese, the American ambassador, Harriman, in answer to the first declaration of the Northerners, May 15, 1968, defined as "false and ominous" the picture of South Vietnam painted by the Hanoi delegation in 1955–1960.

According to Harriman, during these years the per capita food production in South Vietnam increased by more than 20 percent, while in the North it decreased by 11 percent. Textile production registered many enormous increases: more than 20 percent in 1960 alone. Sugar production rose by 100 percent. The refugees who had fled Communist domination in the North found a new peaceful placement in the South. The number of pupils in the elementary schools quadrupled during these years. In 1960 the per capita income had risen in the South to about $110, which is a level more than 50 percent higher than in the North. In short, there has been a continual betterment in the living standard of the people of South Vietnam. It won out by far over the North in this peaceful rivalry.

That this was not just diplomatic propaganda is shown by the unanimous opinion of impartial observers. The South registered more rapid progress than the North in the economic and social fields despite the very serious handicap of the guerrilla war, which broke out in force in 1960, although it had already been spreading previously in the rural regions. One author, who is not suspect of being sympathetic toward Diem, Georges Chaffard, writes the following in a magazine that is even less suspect:

The respective evolution of the economies of South and North Vietnam after 1954, the year of the Geneva agreements, contradicts the hypotheses that we should be tempted to formulate *a priori* on the rhythms of development on one or other side of the 17th parallel. However astonishing it may seem, nine years of almost constant disorders have caused relatively little disturbance to the situation in South Vietnam. On the other hand, nine years of peace and socialist construction have only modestly bettered the lot of the people of Tonkin and the industrial and agricultural potential of the Democratic Republic of North Vietnam.[28]

Chaffard continues and examines the factors favoring the South over the North: a more benign climate, American aid, and especially the absence of those mistakes which slowed evolution down in the North. For Chaffard, the ideological factor is a serious pall on North Vietnamese economy, while a free economy favors the development in the South.

Looking at the 1955–1962 period as a whole [Chaffard concludes] the South Vietnamese economy has suffered less from the civil war than it might have been feared, and in the last analysis the Vietnamese living south of the 17th parallel, favored by nature and foreign aid, lives better than his compatriot to the North, bound to a killing work routine, subject to the rationing of food, and authorized to hope only in a distant future in order to get the fruits of his labor. The resumption of peace and an honest government administration, devoted entirely to accomplishing its development, will undoubtedly give South Vietnam the winning cards in the competition with the Hanoi regime.

Robert Scigliano fully describes the economic and social progress of the country, although he does not refrain from severely criticizing the government in this field and states that after 1960 the guerrilla war stopped progress and in some sectors caused the results already achieved to disappear (the closing of schools in the country areas, the insecurity of business, abandoned fields, etc.).

The economic balance sheet of Diem's government, however, is positive, thanks especially to American aid.[29] This is the practically unanimous judgment of those studying the field, who acknowledge that, despite the almost constant state of insecurity in the country, the economic and social progress has been higher than it would have been possible to foresee (there are, however, differences of opinion with regard to the agrarian reform, as we shall see). Various observers, then, put forward the hypothesis that one of the basic reasons why North Vietnam elicited and fully supported the guerrilla war by means of the Communist cadres left behind in the South after 1954 is this: that the encounter with the fully developing economy in the South was becoming burdensome for the North,[30] deprived as it was of substantial economic aid from the Communist countries and beset by serious economic difficulties, especially following the failure of the agrarian reform and the policy of indiscriminate nationalization, which completely killed individual initiative and deprived the country of foreign (especially French) capital and technology that would have been so very necessary!

Conflicting judgments about the agrarian reform. On the level of social works, we must first of all mention the scholastic program and the fight against illiteracy, an area where the Diem regime equalled Ho Chi Minh's, for whom education represents his major success.[31] Diem, however, trained a lesser number of technicians and engineers than the North, where industry had always been more developed. Here are the figures of the progress made from 1955 to 1962:[32]

secondary schools		number of pupils
1955	162	61,500
1962	437	229,800
primary schools		
1955	2,886	581,000
1962	7,302	1,505,605

Illiteracy affected 2,284,144 persons in 1954 but only 592,316 in 1962, while the national education budget went from .79 percent in 1954, in a percentage relative to the whole State budget, to 6.22 percent in 1961. I myself was able to confirm, even in the smallest country villages and in the mountain regions, the schools built during the Diem period, although today, unfortunately, in part at least, they are no longer functioning because of the dearth of teachers willing to expose themselves to Vietcong terrorism and to live in places not protected by the national army. University students increased from 2,451 in 1954–1955 to 7,496 in 1960, and in that year there were some 2,000 other young people studying in universities abroad.[33]

Again on the social field we must not forget the work of Mme Nhu for the emancipation of the Vietnamese woman who, like all Asian women, still lived in a state of extreme subjection; the most deserving from the social and moral point of view were the campaigns against opium, gambling, prostitution, polygamy, etc.[34] Buttinger enumerates rapidly, quoting other authors as well, the progress attained in other areas: the antimalaria and antitrachoma health campaigns, the great growth of hospitals, dispensaries, maternity stations and other health facilities, the setting up of rudimentary medical stations in some 3,300 villages, etc.[35]

On the agricultural plane, students and observers are not in agreement. Undoubtedly, up to 1960 production experienced rapid increases (while in the North, as we say, it was decreasing or increasing slowly). Rice production, for example, went from 3.4 million in 1956 to 5 million in 1959, while the increase in the production of coffee, rubber, tea and other industrial products was most noticeable.[36] The agricultural development policy can only be praised: setting up numerous farm cooperatives and fisheries which, aided by the State and under the direction of American technicians, modernized agriculture and the fishing industry (in this project of the cooperatives the Vietnamese Confederation of Labor was also involved). Through the work of the refugees from the North, the government set up throughout the country, especially on the central plateaus, several hundred "agricultural development centers" which gave South Vietnam new crops and more modern growing methods.

The criticism is centered on the agrarian reform carried out in various stages by Diem, beginning in 1955. There were two basic stages. The first (with the ordinances of January 8, 1955 and February 5, 1955) was directed toward improving the life of the tenant farmers by means of a more just arrangement of their relations with the owners, retilling the lands that had been abandoned during the war of the preceding years and deforesting new areas. The second stage (ordinance of October 22, 1956) limited property to 100 hectares per person, expropriating the other lands to distribute them to the peasants, with accommodations for the expropriated owners to invest the proceeds in industry. In all, the reform made available about one million hectares for cultivation and distributed another 428,000 to 115,000 families without property, while on the plateaus about ninety new land reclamation centers were set up for the settling of some 200,000 persons.[37]

The verdict about this reform—very summarily described—varies from author to author. Some maintain that it was too timid a reform either because of the modesty of the predetermined goals or because of the slow pace with which it was put into effect; for others, however, this slow and prudent pace was correct, considering the catastrophic example of the reform in the North, which wanted to overturn centuries-old situations in two years. Diem lacked the time to bring his work to conclusion, since in 1960, when the guerrilla war broke out, the State machinery began to come to a standstill, even in the area of the agrarian reform. However, from the beginning we may conclude that if there had been the needed time, the reform would probably have been more widespread and would have had greater success. According to Scigliano, who does not share this judgment at all, the agrarian reform is generally looked upon as one of the great successes of the Ngo Dinh Diem government.[38]

It is hard to make a competent and impartial judgment about a technical problem like this, which ought to be studied in depth and seen under all its aspects. Undoubtedly Diem's agrarian reform was insufficient, especially for the zones held by the Viet Minh during the war against France, where the peasants had already received all the available lands and, at times, were later obliged to return them to the owners. Some think that this insufficiency was due to a lack of time (practically only four years, from 1956 to 1960) and to many technical or political difficulties. For example, the expropriation of the rubber plantations did not come about so that production would not be harmed (which, in fact, was a boon); the founding of new villages and land reclamation centers on the plateaus was stopped by the Americans who held that they were too close to the borders of Laos and Cambodia and therefore easy prey to the guerrillas who came out of these two countries. It was not sufficient to give land to the peasants, they had to learn to be self-sufficient and at the same time to set up cooperatives, be given work implements, etc.

On the other hand, other people attribute the insufficiency of the agrarian reform to the fact that Diem and his men were too conservative. J. Buttinger claims that Diem was radical only in two senses: nationalism and anti-Communism; everything else was of secondary importance. While recalling that in the years preceding his rise to power Diem had manifested reformist tendencies in the social field, and acknowledging that the agrarian reform as effected had many merits, Buttinger says that Diem was not radical in this reform because he did not understand that this was the only way to win the favor of the peasant masses. If Diem had understood that the reform was indispensable for the fight against Communism, he would have swept away the landowners and made all the farmers landowners, no matter what the price. But it was precisely his conservative nature that prevented him from thoroughly understanding this simple truth:[39] that he was actuating only half a reform that was not sufficient for the revolutionary atmosphere of the country (even if in other countries of the third world—Latin America, for example—this would have been greeted as a revolutionary reform).

The American mistake of eliminating Diem. As we said, there is no doubt that Diem was a dictator. His dictatorship was essentially directed towards warding off the "Communist peril," but he ended up designating every political opposition to his regime by this term. However, we must also say that the peoples of the South under Diem always had greater democratic freedoms than those granted in the North under the regime of Ho Chi Minh. One example was the freedom of the labor unions and their right to strike: the Vietnamese Confederation of Workers, founded in 1950, was one of the major unions of Asia with more than half a million members, and under Diem it succeeded in obtaining a social legislation that was one of the best on the continent. From 1956 to 1963, the confederation caused large social strikes throughout the country in areas of industry and trade most neglected by the Diem regime. In 1961 alone, the confederation was successful in settling 870 claims, in 97 of which it was necessary to use strikes.

At Saigon, in December 1967, the Buddhist, Tran Quoc Buu, secretary of the Vietnamese Confederation of Workers, gave me some precise information about the union's relations with the Diem regime and the ones that followed. To my question as to whether the confederation always had freedom of action during Diem's time, Tran Quoc Buu answered:

Then, there was certainly not the freedom in the political field to criticize the government, found political parties, have elections, etc., which we have now. But from the point of view of the union we always had full freedom to organize and to strike. In the first years of his power, Diem founded a government union for the farmers, which represented 70 percent of the laborers, with the intention of subsequently abolishing our union; but his maneuver did not succeed and he gave up, possibly because he feared international reactions, since we had openly denounced the maneuver. During the last year of Diem's dictatorship, we also had some unionists in prison.[40]

And then he told me:

We are completely independent of the government, both the present government and the previous ones. . . . The frame of mind of the ruling classes, in Vietnam as in the countries of the third world, is one of fear toward mass organizations like ours and of striving with every means to get control of them. You know that in most of the countries of the third world there is only one union, dependent on the government. Here in Vietnam this is not so, since we have a long tradition and an optimum organization on the mass level; up to now we have maintained our independence, but we do not concern ourselves with political problems: we only make union claims and are interested solely in social problems.[41]

Among the other freedoms granted by the Diem regime there was that of religion (we shall see in the next chapter the conflict that took place with the Buddhists), of nonpolitical assembly, freedom to demonstrate,[42] a certain freedom of the press and finally the open admission into the country of many foreign journalists of every political stripe who were able to report abroad the opinions of the opponents of the regime, and the regime's mistakes. In North Vietnam the foreign newspapermen remain in Hanoi and are under strict surveillance wherever they go: their visits are planned by the authorities themselves. It is hard even to imagine a case where a foreign journalist in Hanoi could interview persons opposed to the government, and in fact such a case has never been verified, while in the South during the Diem regime foreign newspapers reported interviews with Buddhist bonzes, opposition leaders, and persons hostile to the regime. Even during the conflict of the summer of 1963 with the Buddhists, which resulted in Diem's downfall, the Buddhist leaders were still able to grant interviews and write articles. Is it possible that there is not even one opponent of Ho Chi Minh's regime in North Vietnam? Or is it that no one can speak out any longer?

Thus, under Diem the South Vietnamese were able to go abroad, and in fact many exponents of the opposition established themselves in France, from where they conducted a vast campaign against the Diem regime. Out of North Vietnam—it is almost superfluous to repeat[43]—no opponent has ever come to tell us about life under the Ho Chi Minh regime.

To conclude this examination of the Diem regime, it seems to me that it would be wrong and unfair to make Diem into a blood-thirsty dictator, hated by the people, as is done at times by writers who have not impartially delved into the story of this period. As we said, Diem was certainly a dictator, and his mistakes were serious and many (at times attributable to those around him rather than to him personally). But we must take into account, with a balanced judgment, not only his successes and the difficulties he met with in reestablishing the authority of the State and in defending the country against subversion but also the normal level of efficiency and honesty in the countries of the "third world," which are evolving after a long period of colonial oppression. In other words, we cannot start with a model of efficiency that is proper to more evolved Western nations. We have to refer to those circumstances common to countries which are trying to find their way after colonialization.

The fall of the regime was attributed above all to its mistakes, as we have already said, and chiefly to the error of not having broadened the democratic basis of the government and parliament. But in any other country of the third world, a regime like Diem's would have had better fortune and would have been judged much more benignly. In Vietnam, however, the opposition of the city elite (more than the people in the rural zones),[44] frustrated in their legitimate desire for democratic freedoms, and the presence of a strong Communist organization aided from abroad, were fatal for Diem.

The fall of the dictator, greeted at the beginning with joy by the

Vietnamese as the grounds for a quick peace and a better government, is regretted by many today as an unpardonable mistake which has deprived the country of its most prestigious non-Communist nationalist leader. The same Buddhist bonze, Tri Quang, who was the principal architect of his downfall, no longer takes responsibility today for having overthrown him. In a long interview granted to me, he asserted that it was not his intention to have Diem fall; all he wanted was for him to concede greater democratic freedoms and not to patronize the Catholics openly. But, Tri Quang went on, Diem was overthrown by a coup d'etat of the military, supported by the Americans and not by the Buddhists (which in fact is true).

The fact that they contributed to Diem's downfall is regretted by the Americans as an unpardonable error. Actually, the dictator was a convinced nationalist and did not want the Americans to gain a footing in the country. This is our war—he said frequently to the American ambassador—not yours; give us arms and military advisers, but not soldiers. In fact in November 1963, when Diem was killed, there were only 16,000 Americans in South Vietnam, principally diplomats and advisers of various kinds (military men, advisers for the aid programs and agricultural development, etc.), while today there are more than half a million!

When Diem realized that the guerrilla war was becoming fiercer every day and that it was impossible to put a stop to it, he made contact with Hanoi and the NLF to begin secret negotiations.[45] It was at this point that his assassination, attributed generally in the South to the Americans, threw the country into chaos, demoralized the army, led the Americans to involve themselves deeply in the Vietnamese snare and removed the tenuous prospects for peace. The mistake of overthrowing the one nationalist who had authority and who was capable of resisting the Communists and dealing with them—despite all his limitations and faults—was dearly paid for both by South Vietnam, which no longer found a leader to rise to the situation[46] and saw the Americans invade the country, and by the Americans themselves, who were forced to throw themselves into the Vietnamese furnace in order to fill the void left by the death of the dictator.

For all these reasons a man who was open and sensitive to the contemporary situation, Cardinal Frings, the Archbishop of Cologne, in a pastoral letter to his people issued in June 1965 and focused on peace in Vietnam, praised Diem's work and asserted that "only today, in the midst of these grave incidents (in Vietnam), do we realize that the greater part of the world has not given just recognition to the life and death of this noble man."[47] And he concludes by saying that those who at one time thought that Diem's death would have brought salvation and peace to South Vietnam have had the experience, unfortunately in a tragic way, of finding out now that they were wrong. The situation, as the cardinal said, was constantly worsening. Nor could we say anything different today, three years after the German cardinal's letter.

The Catholics' enthusiastic support of Diem. What was the attitude of the Church and Catholics toward Diem and his regime? The South Vietnamese Church was profoundly influenced by some 700,000 Catholic refugees who had fled to the South in 1954–1956 and who doubled the number of local Catholics. As we can easily imagine, such an imposing mass of people, organized with their priests and catechists (and sometimes also with their bishops), immediately because the most animated and dynamic expression of the Catholic community, bringing along with them the Catholics from the South, who were more spread out throughout the national territory.

It is natural that these disinherited masses be exploited by the political power, as a Vietnamese Catholic writes:

In regard to the exodus of the Vietnamese, we witnessed an authentic political exploitation of the drama of the refugees. In South Vietnam, the evacuation of the Vietnamese from the North constituted the political strength that was essential to Diem's government. The refugee clergy openly gave it their support. Once again, the destiny of the Church was bound to a specific political system which depended, like all political systems, on many imponderable factors, and therefore on a system of uncertain success.[48]

For the Catholics, Diem's rise to power was a moment of triumph after years and centuries of persecutions and humiliations. The man was a convinced nationalist and anti-French to the heart (then people feared French colonialization: the American version had not yet arrived); he was honest and had never been compromised in the past with double-dealing ventures of any kind; furthermore, he was anti-Communist and was fighting for a country free from any oppression and colonialism. What more could one want? The Catholics acclaimed him en masse as the savior of the country and put themselves entirely at his service.

At the beginning, it was the enthusiasm of all the Catholics, not merely a minority. One journalist wrote:

When we go back to the Vietnam of 1956 we find with dismay certain young Catholic intellectuals whom we knew well some years before when they were JEC (Young Catholic Students) militants, who, as enthusiastic supporters of the new regime, gloried in being organizers of "spontaneous" demonstrations that tended to exert psychological pressure on the people: the ransacking of neutralist newspapers, meetings for the rejection of the general elections provided for at Geneva, etc.[49]

Diem was not insensible to the support of his coreligionists, the only ones who acclaimed him and who were ready to support him personally, in the midst of the general rejection or at least disinterest and lack of confidence that South Vietnamese society manifested in his regard at the beginning of his power. Referring to the demonstrations of September 21, 1954, Fr. Naidenhoff wrote:

In the poisoned atmosphere of Saigon these wretched refugees, with hurriedly scribbled posters, come to proclaim their trust and are a great comfort for him (Diem). He is therefore not alone in his Norodom palace, as certain people insinuate. The refugees cluster about by means of simple passwords. They know that their father, their support, their guardian, is president Diem; they know that the president is on the verge of being put into a fix by his adversaries: then they come, peaceful, without arms, to shout out their attachment to him. Is this provocation? But then the head of the government is no longer the head of the government. Men armed with machine guns and in trucks, the Binh-Xuyen, are revolutionaries of a quite different type. In this way the refugees, most of them Catholics, signified by means of a demonstration that was dispersed by machine gun bullets their connection with the government.[50]

Thus, spontaneously, there was created that convergence of interests, sentiments, and reciprocal support and favor that from the beginning characterized the relations between the dictator and the community of Catholics taken as a whole. It had two negative results: Diem was accused of partiality toward the Catholics (which was not at all true), and he aroused the anger of the Buddhists, while the Catholics, who were ever more taken by the exclusive anti-Communist mystique of the regime which they themselves contributed to reenforce, ended up by becoming a "sect" within the body of the nation, closing themselves off from any dialogue with the "other" South Vietnamese.

We shall say more in the next chapter, when speaking of Buddhism, of how the close relations between Diem and the Catholics stirred up Buddhist reactions. Here it is sufficient to point out that from the beginning of Diem's power, despite the Catholics' enthusiasm for the rise to power of the nationalist who was most representative of their religious community, there were already some people who warned of the danger that he would be facing. Following a trip to Vietnam, Fr. Naidenhoff wrote, after stating that no one in Vietnam, from the religious majority, reproached Diem for being a Catholic: ". . . on the condition, however, that the confessional minority, strongly crystalized around such a leader, not be tempted to look upon itself as a majority, and that it repudiate any sectarian spirit. Many Vietnamese Catholics are very aware of this danger. If certain members of the clergy are not very careful to avoid any confusion between Church and State, there are others who are very watchful . . ."[51]

The same observation was made by another missionary, Fr. Simonnet, who wrote in 1956:

That the Catholics of South Vietnam see their sole hope of salvation in the success of president Diem is undeniable and furthermore, up to today, Diem, who started out as a loser with everyone against him, showed himself to be the only Vietnamese personality who succeeded in keeping the Communists in check. . . . The great temptation and the grave danger today for many Catholics and for certain members of the clergy in South Vietnam consists in conceiving of the Church *qua* Church as a political power. In this way they would become a Catholic politicio-religious "sect," in the manner of the Binh-Xuyen sect which has now been defeated. This illusion is all the more serious since Catholics here represent only 10 percent of the population.[52]

Prudence of the Church hierarchy towards the Diem regime. Unfortunately, in international and internal public opinion, the Church ended up by finding itself compromised with the regime, although, with its most representative exponents, it never gave open approval of the regime, with the exception of the acts of homage that each bishop made to the civil authorities, and which, further-more, were made by the leaders of the other local religions. If it would be false to say that the bishops opposed the Diem regime openly when it became more and more dictatorial, we must not underestimate the fact that in private various bishops as well as priests pointed out to Diem the mistakes he was making, as we have already mentioned, but with no result.

The official Church, the hierarchy, was much more prudent in its relations with the dictator than was the Catholic community and also some priests, especially those who were refugees from the

North. Typical was the example of Diem's opposition to the nomination of Mgr. Nguyen-Van-Hien as vicar apostolic in Saigon in
the autumn of 1955. It was reported by various sources.[53] Considered to be too much of a francophile and too little involved
politically in the anti-Communist crusade, Mgr. Hien was initially
refused by Diem as the bishop of the capital, Saigon, and the successor to the Frenchman, Mgr. Cassaigne, who had resigned from
the see in order to make room for a Vietnamese.[54] There were
interventions with the Vatican, calumnious campaigns in the press,
hostile demonstrations, and the refusal of the president to receive
the new bishop: but Rome did not give in. "This Diem affair [the
ICI wrote, *art. cit.*] in any case had the unexpected result of a
'customs clearance' of the Church by the government."

But the case of Mgr. Hien was not the only one. According to
Fr. Simonnet—who was writing in 1956 (i.e., in an unsuspect year,
art. cit., pp. 83-84)—and according to the American Catholic
NCWC news service (quoted by Fr. Simonnet), the nomination of
Mgr. Nguyen-Van-Binh to Cantho in October 1955 was also dis-
pleasing to Diem, since the new bishop, like Mgr. Hien of Saigon,
"also resolutely held himself aloof from any political activity, while
he [i.e., Diem] would have been happy with two agents for his
political policy."

It was precisely Mgr. Binh, who had later become Archbishop of
Saigon after Mgr. Hien had been nominated Bishop of Dalat, who
separated the responsibilities of the Church from those of the State
with a courageous pastoral letter in the "hot summer" of 1963, at
the time of the Buddhist revolt:

During the popular revolt against president Diem's regime [writes the
bonze Nhat Hanh] the resisters numbered in their ranks some illustri-
ous Catholic progressives. While Archbishop Ngo Dinh Thuc, the
primate of Vietnam [he was 'dean' of the episcopate, i.e., its eldest
member, while the primate was actually the Archbishop of Saigon,
Mgr. Binh] sided decidedly with the Diem government. Archbishop

Nguyen-Van-Binh of Saigon had the strength to declare that, just as the Church at times had its limitations, so also should the State. Archbishop Binh's position, although it was not so decisive as to constitute a real and proper form of opposition or resistance to the Diem government, did reveal an awareness of the difficulties that the Catholic Church was facing by showing support for such a regime.[55]

There are numerous examples of the episcopate's prudence in its relations with the triumphant regime and in the tendency of the Catholics to become a "sect" and to use religion in the political arena. In the first months of 1954, the bishops signed a common pastoral letter in which we read:

The episcopate is solely authorized to speak in the name of the Church of Vietnam and to take responsibility for it. . . . The ecclesiastical hierarchy of Vietnam, as elsewhere, is not subjected to any political party and is not opposed to any regime that recognizes the inalienable rights of the Church. . . . As citizens, Catholics are free to join any political group or movement of their choice, provided that these groups in their principles and programs in no way contradict the imperatives of the duly enlightened Catholic conscience. . . . But in this, Catholics are always acting in their own personal name and on their private responsibility.[56]

It is a clear letter that neatly separates the responsibility of the Church from that of Catholics involved in politics and, at that time, committed to the support of Ngo Dinh Diem. On the occasion of the election of members to the Constitutive Assembly that took place in South Vietnam on March 4, 1956, Mgr. Pham Ngoc Chi, the bishop of the Northern refugees (those who were most prone to form a separate caste), published a pastoral letter in which he reminded Catholics of their duty to elect ". . . competent and virtuous persons, capable of working usefully for the Fatherland, prescinding from whether they belong to our religion or not." And the bishop continued by disproving that a list had been prepared of Catholic candidates chosen from the refugees, as had been reported.[57]

There remains the fact, however, among the 10 Vietnamese bishops of Diem's time (now there are 14), of the Archbishop of Hué, Mgr. Ngo Dinh Thuc, the brother of the president, a very good pastor of great intelligence and organizational abilities but undoubtedly closely connected with the president and the government, perhaps more than would be expedient for a bishop. A French weekly wrote that Mgr. Thuc "had the family spirit,"[58] and the observation is most exact: whoever knows what "the family spirit" means throughout the Orient can find it understandable that the Archbishop of Hué became an open supporter and an active propagandist of his brother's regime. This is certainly a questionable position, even presuming the prelate's right intention; for him, Diem represented to the last the only salvation of the country.[59]

A priest wrote me from Vietnam, in response to a request of mine for a judgment about the Archbishop of Hué that would reflect the general opinion of the local Church:

Diem had a brother who was a priest and then a bishop. He had a superior intelligence that joined to the mandarin spirit of his family the spirit of the bishops of the Middle Ages, a fighter, a crusader and a feudal lord. Monseigneur Thuc often identified the Church with his brother's regime, and in this he was quite different from the other Vietnamese bishops[60] who refused to follow him along this path, even though he was the eldest and the one with most authority. If we prescind from the political problem, Monseigneur Thuc was without any doubt an excellent bishop: on the level of personal religious practice, on the pastoral level, in taking new initiatives, in organizing the diocese, he was an excellent pastor. But his meddling in political affairs, and his propagandizing for the Diem regime harmed the Church more than any Communist persecution from which he wanted to save the country and the Christians.

Diem's was not a "Catholic regime." We must honestly recognize that President Diem, if he was especially supported by the Catholics, strongly resisted any untoward attempt at the "clericalization" of the regime. The dictator was a man sure of himself and of the mission entrusted to him of rebuilding the State of South Vietnam in order to make it able to resist Communist pressures. Just as he always resisted the untoward interference by America, he did not allow his regime to become defined as "Catholic." In many speeches, he himself explicitly stated that he was the president of Vietnam, of all Vietnam, and not only of the Catholics.[61] A few facts demonstrate that these were not only words.

On the religious plane, we see the aid given to the Buddhists and the other Vietnamese religions (to which we shall return in the next chapter), as well as to the Catholic Church, for the rebuilding of churches and religious works destroyed by the war; his presence at Catholic and non-Catholic ceremonies on the occasion of great festivities; his not having wanted the name of God in the 1956 Constitution, as the Catholics requested, but only the name "Most High," as the representatives of Buddhism and the Buddhist sects asked. This problem was very important at the beginning of the Diem regime in order to see whether the president would give in to the pressures of the Christians or not. In promulgating the Constitution in October 1956, Diem said: ". . . I took an oath before the Most High and before the people. The Most High is also invoked in the preamble of the text of the Constitution. It is true that the Christian Democratic Party[62] had proposed the word God, but since the majority of Vietnamese are not Catholics, the parties agreed on a more general term."[63]

Diem was very discriminating with the Vietnamese and entrusted the most important positions only to most trusted persons, but this was not on the basis of the individuals' religious persuasion but on the basis of their anti-Communism. The Diem regime could in no way be called "Catholic," as *Eglise vivante* states:

In Belgium, would Spaak be happy if the government of which he was a part was presented as "Catholic"? Yet some of his colleagues and the prime minister himself are Catholics. . . . Then, why speak of the "Catholic" government of South Vietnam when the non-Catholic ministers are more numerous?[64] When an archbishop is the brother of a head of government, it is very delicate for him to support the government politics. His pastoral charge seems to require great discretion from him. But if he still believes that he must take a public position, it is obvious that his political opinions only involve himself, since then he is no longer acting as the archbishop but as a citizen, and his words in no way commit the Church or the mass of South Vietnamese Catholics who are not necessarily warm supporters of the regime.[65]

Lacouture, who can certainly not be suspected of being pro-Diem, agrees with this judgment when he writes:

Clericalism is much talked about in regard to Diem. On this point we must be prudent. Certainly, Ngo Dinh Diem is a very fervent Catholic. . . . But one who stays any time with well-informed religious will find out that relations between Church and State and between the State and the Vatican are not the most serene. Relying on Diem's reputation, members of the clergy tried in 1954–1955 to "colonize" the regime, but they met with a man who was well aware of the reality of power, irritated by the fact that Vietnam was still kept by Rome under a mission territory regime (a reminder of the colonial period),[66] and disappointed that his brother the bishop had still not received the cardinal's hat. Therefore we cannot speak so much of clericalism, i.e., of a domestication of the regime by the clergy, as of a kind of "Josephism," since the political leader was trying to use the religious power. . . . If in South Vietnam there is a State religion, it can only be anti-Communism.[67]

A Vietnamese priest, a native of the South, who occupies an important position in the Church of Vietnam and had lived through the Diem period as a priest, wrote me:

After Diem had vanquished his enemies and gotten firm control of the
country [i.e., around 1956], there were priest refugees from the North,
leaders of important refugee communities, who presented themselves
to him to ask him the price of the support they had given him up
to then. Diem refused any aid and sent some of them away with bitter
words; one of them was so disappointed and humiliated that he began
to propagandize against Diem within Christian public opinion. . . .
When Diem was at the beginning of his power, or even afterwards,
other priests offered to organize Christian committees to support his
politics, but the president repeated to all the clergymen that they ought
to be thinking about religious matters solely and not meddle in politics.

I travelled throughout Vietnam and spoke with many Christian
and non-Christian representatives, with bishops and priests, and I
must say that I frequently heard it repeated that Diem was
opposed to any clericalization of the regime. And although he
had profited politically from the Catholics' support in order to
strengthen his power, he did not want the clergy to mix actively
in politics, even were it in his favor.

The most irritating aspect: Catholic "triumphalism." If during
the Diem regime the Church did not make the mistake of binding
itself unconditionally to a political regime, we must say that on
the other hand many Catholics and priests, especially the refugees
from the North, profited fully and shamelessly from the fact that
the head of State was a Catholic. Catholics had privileged positions
that were not easily definable, although they were quite real: State
aides for good works and schools, the military employed to build
or repair Catholic institutions, the first places in public functions
reserved for the bishops, Catholic propaganda transmitted over the
national radio, and finally, the supremacy of Catholics in the army
and the State bureaucracy, who formed a caste apart and helped
one another up the ladder to more important and more remunera-
tive posts. Certainly a good part of the Vietnamese Catholics did
not heed the warning of Mgr. Nguyen-Van-Binh, Archbishop of

Saigon, who wrote in a pastoral letter in 1963: "We freely practise our religion in South Vietnam, just as the followers of other confessions can do; let us rejoice in this freedom. But let us not try to add to it exaggerated rights and privileges. Let us not confuse the spread of the faith with the development of political influence or social prestige . . ."[68]

For the Catholics, then, and especially for the refugees from the North, both priests and laymen, the Diem period represented compensation for all the persecutions and humiliations of the past. A community of believers that for the last centuries had lived on the fringes of national life, closed into itself, suspected of serving the interests of the foreigner; a community which, after expressing enthusiastically its own dedication to the national cause in 1945 and the following years, was then brutally tricked and oppressed by triumphant Communism, found itself unexpectedly the most prominent exponent of nationalism, with a Catholic head of State and with full religious freedom. The temptation to "triumphalism" was strong, and the Church as a whole, with few and irrelevant exceptions, gave in.

It is certain [a missionary wrote me] that in the Vietnamese Church there exists a tendency to triumphalism which, even though it suffered so much in the past, is not excusable. But this tendency comes rather from the Asian psychology, for which the spectacular and the institutionalized are extremely important. Even in colonial times there was too much insistence on the need for power, for force that comes from the Truth of our religion, and the Diem regime merely reenforced this fundamental idea. Furthermore, the number of Christians was growing from year to year in such a way that if there had been more priests, it was thought that the majority of the people of the South could have been converted in a few years . . .

In the Diem period, Catholic triumphalism assumed forms that certainly proved irritating to the more aware believers of other religions, even though they had their own religious demonstrations in full freedom. But for the Catholics there was in addition the prestige that came to them from the devout head of State, the larger organization, and the greater capacity for putting its policy into effect; interminable processions even in the cities, with the traffic blocked for long hours on the main arteries; pilgrimages of "oceanic" crowds of believers to the major shrines, especially to the Marian shrine of Lavang near Hué; congresses of associations that had the first place in the national press, with participation by State personalities; blatant advertising of the conversions made throughout the country, etc.

The two national Marian Congresses of 1959 (Saigon) and 1961 (Lavang)—to cite only two cases among many—brought together huge crowds of believers, and these were treated as two events that interested the whole country. The Christians left their villages with banners and flags, openly celebrating their faith; they crossed the country in trains or in Pullmans, carrying everywhere the Christian standards; they returned to their tiny rural communities with the pride of belonging to a world religion, the chosen people of the nation. When the whole of Vietnam was consecrated to Mary, no one thought that Vietnam was neither Italy nor Poland but a land in which the Christians represented only about 10 percent of the national community.

Another aspect of Catholic "triumphalism" that we must recall was the exploitation, in the worst sense of the term, of the Diem regime by the Catholics and the priests. That these "exploiters" were a tiny minority in the complex of the Christian community does not lessen the scandal roused by their undertakings; once they were known (even during the Diem regime), they gave rise to the suspicion of corruption that was even more widespread than it actually was. The reference is to the economic exploitation of the regime. The term "Catholic," or the supposed friendship with the president or some particular leader, was used to make money at the expense of the State or of private persons who were in need of support or recommendation. The stories of this kind, which are

still heard today in Vietnam, are many and varied; they go from
the priest who asked money in order to get a job within the State
bureaucracy to the story of another priest who "guaranteed" absolu-
tion to people who were implicated in some wrongdoing, naturally
after due compensation. There were those who obtained from the
local leaders the exploitation of forest areas without paying anything to the State; others set up committees for religious celebrations or for festivities for Diem, taxing the people of a given place
and then going off with the money; still others, as the local military
leaders, made the soldiers build the church or the parish house, etc.
Some of these stories are gossip, and it seems impossible for us
today to investigate their veracity. It is certain, however, that during the Diem regime, if only through the fault of a tiny minority
of Catholics and priests, the Church as a whole made an unsavory
reputation for itself.

Spontaneous or forced conversions? Beyond the external and
"triumphalistic" aspect, we must also point out that during the
Diem regime the Vietnamese Church was able to work zealously
for the missionary spread of the faith and the growth of Catholic
institutions of training and charity.

There was first of all the phenomena of conversions which
assumed truly extraordinary proportions. Undoubtedly, part of the
appeal exerted by the Church at this time with the non-Christians
was attributed to the prestige of the Catholic community as a result
of the Catholic president and a successful regime chiefly supported
by Catholics, and also, perhaps, precisely on account of the "triumphalism" about which we have spoken, which for simple folk
constituted a forceful element of appeal. We must immediately
add, however, that if the initial reasons for this burst of faith were
not always completely spiritual (and this is difficult in any case
in mission countries), the new Christians immediately proved the
strength of their faith in the following years, when the Catholics
passed through some very difficult times after the fall of Diem.

Still, none of the baptized lagged behind, although the catechumens soon swiftly diminished in number. Again, it must be pointed out as a cause of conversions that these came about especially among the Buddhist refugees from the North and in the regions that were under the Viet Minh in the South during the period of the guerrilla war against the French (e.g., Qui-Nhon, Binh-Dinh, Danang, and the central plateaus), while there were almost none in the zones dominated by the Buddhist sects (Mekong delta, Hué). In other words, even in Vietnam we have a verification of that movement toward the Church that has in the last fifteen years characterized other regions of the Far East which have had real experience with Communist regimes and where the Catholic resistance to Communism has been particularly esteemed (e.g., Hong Kong, South Korea and Taiwan among the refugees from China).

The reasons for conversion in South Vietnam are varied [*Fides* points out]. Undoubtedly, there is the eloquent example of convinced Catholics like President Ngo Dinh Diem, but the chief reason is sought in the fact that the trials themselves have brought the people closer to Christianity. Experience has taught non-Christians that for those who are unhappy, 'the faith is a solid support along life's road.' It is the Communists themselves, contrary to the aim they pursue, who have helped the people to wake up from their sluggishness. Those unfortunates who had been subject to the persecutions of such a cruel regime experienced its horror and set out to search for the truth. The non-Christians understood that among religions only Christianity does not change, despite persecutions; they compare its stability to the opportunism of other religions, like the Cao-Dai and the Hoa-Hao, who change their doctrine according to what happens.[69]

The same news service reports the response of a young convert:

People wonder why we embraced the faith. We were drawn to the Catholic faith by what we saw with our own eyes. For ten years the

Communists in Vietnam have tried by every means to persecute Christ and his Church and to ridicule his religion. But the more they increased their efforts to destroy Catholicism the more it progressed, and the barbarous systems of Communism were miraculously transformed into means of growth and expansion for Catholicism. The Communists themselves have actually smoothed the way for the Church. The Vietnamese people had the opportunity to see and admire the Christian virtues heroically practised by Catholics: patience, sacrifice, stoutheartedness and charity. We were convinced and won over especially by the Catholic exodus of 1954 and by the example given by the Catholics in the red prisons.[70]

The "mass conversion" movement that manifested itself after 1954 produced a good number of adult baptisms (30,000–35,000 a year), although we have no certain statistics,[71] with the exception of some information on the "catechumens" (i.e., adults preparing for baptism), who on June 30, 1961 numbered 111,324. The majority of the conversions, as we said, took place among the Buddhist refugees from the North and in a few dioceses that had suffered Communist domination in the past, Qui-Nhon, Danang and Kontum especially. At Qui-Nhon, in the four years 1957–1960, there were 70,000 baptisms, and in 1961 another 16,000; Danang, a new diocese created in January 1963, was ahead of Qui-Nhon with 86,000 Catholics, almost all of whom were recent converts; Kontum went from 45,000 Catholics in 1957 to 101,000 in 1963. Especially noteworthy during this period was the evangelization of the central plateau regions, which was accomplished by the Paris missionaries among the primitive Montagnard tribes through a profound study of their cultures, which were so different from the Vietnamese.[72]

The regions of South Vietnam that were the stronghold of the Buddhist sects and never had direct experience of Communist domination were excluded from the conversion movement. It is amazing, for example, that the Archdiocese of Hué went from 78,417 Catholics in 1957 to 100,225 in 1963, an increase of only 22,000

Catholics in six years, which seems to be almost the natural demographic increase of Christians. If we remember that Hué was the diocese of Mgr. Thuc, the brother of president Diem, we must point out that precisely here, where we should be able to verify the greatest politico-social pressure for ulteriorly motivated conversions (in accordance with the accusations of some writers), the increase of the Christian population was minimal. This clearly proves that if it is true that a certain impetus to conversion came from the prestige of the Catholic head of State and, perhaps, from the not completely disinterested aims of some converts, it is true on the other hand that the bulk of the new Christians who came into the Church during the Diem period were much more highly and nobly motivated.

In all, according to official statistics (which in my opinion are very questionable and conservative), the Church in Vietnam experienced this increase: 1957: 1,230,755 Catholics, 1963: 1,454,842 Catholics.[73]

The conversions barely diminished when the guerrilla war began, since it had an anti-Catholic tone at first which was subsequently attenuated. From 1959 on, there began to appear in the *Fides* news service increasingly numerous reports of Viet Cong attacks on Christian churches and villages, killings of priests, sisters and catechists. In 1961 alone, the country regions saw the killing of Fr. Bonnet of the Paris missions (Diocese of Kontum), a Vietnamese priest from the Diocese of Vinh-Long, two sisters, and seven Catholic Action militants who were returning from a meeting in Dalat. Another Vietnamese priest and two Paris missionaries were gravely wounded, in addition to various catechists and Christians killed or wounded in ambushes (one ambush attack against the Bishop of Vinh-Long failed).

Gradually, in the years after 1960 it became clear even to the simple peasants and Montagnards that the guerrilla war led by the Communists and directed against Diem and his regime also had a strong anti-Catholic component either because the Catholics had supported Diem from the beginning or because by their massive

flight from the North they unmasked the unpopularity of the Communist regime. Therefore conversions diminished: those who were
already Christian remained strong in their faith, but there were no
more mass movements of conversions to the Church and, especially
after Diem's fall in 1963, even many catechumens abandoned their
study of the Christian religion.

A more adult and self-sufficient Church. The most important
and basic thing that happened in the Vietnamese Church from
1954 to 1963 was the setting up of the ordinary ecclesiastical hierarchy by John XXIII on December 24, 1960, which, as *L'Osservatore
Romano* wrote in its court style, "crowned three centuries of
apostolic labors." Actually, this transition from a "missionary regime" of vicariates apostolic to the ordinary Church regime constituted a prize that was well-deserved by the Church of Vietnam,
although, in comparison to many other "mission countries" of Asia
and Africa, it was very late in coming due to reasons of political
expediency. In South Vietnam 2 archdioceses, Saigon and Hué,
were set up, as well as 8 dioceses, all with native bishops (except for
Kontum, among the non-Vietnamese Montagnards, which still has
as its bishop the Frenchman, Mgr. Seitz, from the Paris missions).
Of these dioceses, 3 were newly created by the act of instituting the
hierarchy itself, Dalat, Mythe and Long-Xuyen, and four new
Vietnamese bishops were consecrated in January, 1961.[74]

The progress of the Church during this period we are studying[75]
went hand in hand with the increase of conversions and the solemn
recognition by the pope, especially in regard to the encouragement
given to the local Church institutions and the socio-educational es-
tablishments. On the other hand, the cultural-theological renewal
in the Vietnamese Church was sparse. This came about after
1963, following Diem's fall, when the Church was obliged to make
a greater effort at reflection, and also as a result of the Ecumenical
Council (but we shall say more about the scanty apostolic *aggiornamento* of the Vietnamese Church in Chapter VI).

Among the most important institutions of the Diem period was the national pontifical seminary of Dalat, with its theological faculty begun in 1964 and entrusted to the Jesuits, the two regional major seminaries of Saigon and Hué, and the reconstruction in the South of several minor seminaries filled with refugees from the North. Ecclesiastical vocations abounded, so much so, in fact, that the idea was launched to found a national missionary institute for the Vietnamese clergy, with the purpose of sending priests to other Asian countries (where European missionaries were no longer in good odor) and to Africa. Nothing was subsequently done, but the fact that the project was discussed and given serious consideration indicates the maturity that the Vietnamese Church had achieved. We must recall that the Vietnamese Church in the South had practically to start from zero in its recruiting of seminarians in 1954 since the war had scattered what work had been done previously.

Most remarkable was the increase in the number of Catholic schools, and these too started out almost from zero in the South. For example, there were only 3 middle and upper Catholic schools in 1953 in South Vietnam, while there were many more in the North, and by 1963 there were 145 with 62,324 pupils. At the same date there were 1,060 Catholic elementary schools with 209,283 pupils. At Saigon alone, there were built some 30 Catholic secondary schools. To the old *Institut Taberd* (run by the Brothers of the Christian Schools, and still today the most famous school in the Vietnamese Church) were added many others of a much more popular kind but no less efficient. For example, the upper school that was named after the first Vietnamese bishop, Nguyen-Ba-Tong; it has some 4,000 students and is run by the diocesan clergy and Vietnamese sisters.

In connection with the touchy nationalism of the Diem regime and its marked anti-French feeling, the "nativization" of the Church was pursued resolutely. While previously the foreign missionaries were almost exclusively French, Vietnam was now receiving missionaries from every nationality, generally for specialized works (the Jesuits for the pontifical university and the theological faculty, the Italian Salesians for technological schools, etc.).

The Church's social commitment was carried out by the establishment of many health and charitable institutions (orphanages, etc.), which by 1964 had reached the total of 435. On the more specifically social level, there was the Social Secretariat founded in 1956 at Dalat by Fr. Fernand Parrel, of the Paris missions, and then transferred to Saigon in 1962. Its aims were the documentation and study of the social problems of Vietnam in the light of Catholic teaching. Unfortunately, it has not had any great effect in shaping a socially open and modern mentality among Vietnamese Catholics, who are still more sensitive to the appeals of charity than to those of justice.

This is all the more curious, since in South Vietnam the most important trade union on the national level is the one founded by the Catholics in 1950, the Vietnamese Confederation of Christian Workers, connected internationally with the CISC (Confédération Internationale des Syndicats Chrétiens), which was able to function very well and obtain one of the best social legislations in all Asia. In April 1960, the Confederation celebrated the tenth anniversary of its foundation with an extraordinary congress in which 500 delegates represented about 450,000 members of the union.[76]

We must also recall the Catholic University of Dalat, begun in 1957 and run completely by Vietnamese personnel. The University, which in 1963 had 500 students and faculties of language, philosophy and natural sciences, had its first 25 graduates in 1961 and became the stimulus for other cultural initiatives (yearly study weeks for Catholic intellectuals, etc.). There were also many Catholic professors in the two state universities of Saigon and Hué: in fact, the rector of the University of Hué (who was also its founder) was Fr. Cao-Van-Luan, a progressive priest who defended the Buddhists in their 1963 conflict with Diem.

Notes

1. Ngo Dinh Diem, who later became head of state in South Vietnam, was born in 1901 at Hué in a mandarin family (his father had founded the free university of Quoc Hoc) that had long been Catholic. After studying abroad, he was called by Bao Dai in 1933 to fill the post of minister of the interior in the French protectorate of Annam, but he resigned a few months afterward when he saw the government's intention to stamp out bloodily a revolt of the peasants, who were asking for greater justice in the administration of the country areas. Diem withdrew from active politics, remained a bachelor and made contact with the anti-French cultural and nationalistic movements. In 1934 he refused to join a government that was under Japanese protection; in 1945, and again in the following years, he refused Ho Chi Minh's invitation to join the Viet Minh government as the representative of the Catholics since the Communist leader had posited unacceptable conditions. A few years later, in 1948 and 1949, he again refused to support the government of Bao Dai, which was supported by the French ("I do not wish to join a government of Bao Dai unless Vietnam is completely free"). In 1950 he visited the United States, preceded by his reputation as an intransigent nationalist and a man of integrity; there he met Cardinal Spellman, who became his supporter, and various American political figures.

2. C. Simonnet, "Vues sur le drame du Vietnam," *Missions étrangères de Paris,* Paris, March–April, 1967. p. 18.

3. In the West, very few people thought that it was possible to save the South from Communist occupation. Here is what *Relazioni Internazionali* writes, Milan, December 18, 1954, pp. 1441–1442: "Washington still hopes that it will be possible to make South Vietnam the equivalent of South Korea and Ngo Dinh Diem a second Syngman Rhee. The probabilities of success in such a policy seem very meager to the majority of observers. While the 38th parallel and the armistice line in Korea are a solid and stable frontier, the 17th parallel in Indochina is merely a line on a map . . . from the political point of view it is nonexistent in the sense that the Viet Minh has spread to the South. Foreign observers are in agreement in estimating that almost all the villages in the South are controlled and administered by commissars or committees linked to the Hanoi government. This is not due to the superior organizing ability of the Communists—who withdrew from the South only the young trainees of their troops, leaving behind in their homes, like civilians, the old, experienced and militant soldiers—but especially

to the total dearth of administrative ability of the Saigon government, which left whole areas unguarded at the very moment of the transferral of power [from the French to the nationalist government]." This was the situation in South Vietnam when Diem rose to power.

4. S. Ciuffi, *Vietnam, storia politica e sociale della civiltà vietnamita* (Florence: Cultura, 1967), p. 149.

5. Nhat Hanh, *Vietnam, la pace proibita* (Florence: Vallecchi 1967), pp. 86–87.

6. The American senator, Mansfield, a bitter opponent of the American presence in Vietnam and of Diem, in a report to the Senate dated February 1963, strongly criticized the "authoritarian methods" of the dictator, but in regard to the first period of his regime he expressed his great admiration for President Ngo Dinh Diem for the exceptional accomplishments he was able to achieve during the transitional period to independence. During this period, Mansfield stated, his personal courage, his integrity, his determination and his genuine nationalism were factors essential for preventing a complete collapse and establishing a certain order and they permitted us to hope for an end to the chaos, intrigues and general corruption.

7. This was just one of the many inconsistencies in the Geneva accords of 1954. The government of South Vietnam never felt obliged to apply the accords which it had not signed. Of course, the fact that it refused to have the elections provided for July 1956 offered Hanoi the best reason (or pretext) to send men and supplies to the South in order to undermine with every means in its power a government that "did not respect the agreements."

8. A fact quoted by Devillers in M. E. Gettleman, *Vietnam: History, Documents and Opinions on a Major World Crisis* (London: Penguin Books, 1966), p. 213. In the preceding and following pages Devillers asserts that Russia and China did little toward the application of the Geneva convention on the question of the general elections, and even in Asia, the "Bandung countries" (i.e., the neutralists: India, Burma, Sukarno's Indonesia, etc.) made no gesture of support for Hanoi's thesis, since they had no interest in seeing the Communist troops reach Saigon.

9. G. Chaffard, *Indochine, dix ans d'indépendence* (Paris: Calmann-Lévy, 1964), pp. 98–99.

10. In the first months of 1956 it was possible to take the bicycle road of Camau-Benhai—a distance of some 1,500 kilometers—which led a very large party from the farthest point of Cochin China to the border of the 17th parallel, through forests and country areas, without the slightest incident.

11. M. Percheron, in *La Croix*, November 15, 1960.

12. The extreme defenders of the Diem regime affirmed that Diem re-

fused to establish contact with North Vietnam because by means of trade, postal exchange and other approaches, the Communists would have spread their propaganda to the South. The justification is ridiculous, when we remember that in the South there remained tens of thousands of Communist cadres, especially in the country villages: there was certainly no need for propaganda sent through the mails in order to maintain the Communist presence in the country! Another reason often given is that by closing the doors to trade with the North, Diem wanted to weaken that dictatorship and favor the revolt of the people. But this means only that Diem did not calculate the means of persuasion a Communist dictatorship could use, since it would be absurd to think that one could rouse revolts in the North by reducing the country to famine (when, in addition, there was China and the other Communist countries available). However one looks at it, the refusal to trade and establish good relations with North Vietnam—scornfully rejecting the many offers of the rulers in Hanoi—was one of the so many tragic mistakes of Diem which led to the guerrilla war and the test of strength with the North.

13. Buttinger, vol. II, *op. cit.,* p. 940.

14. R. Scigliano, *South Vietnam, Nation under Stress* (Houghton Mifflin Co.: Boston, 1964), pp. 88, 91.

15. R. Scigliano, *op. cit.,* p. 91. "In the end South Vietnam became . . . a country of a Communist type without Communism," writes D. Halberstam, the *New York Times* correspondent in South Vietnam, in *The Making of a Quagmire* (New York: Random House, 1965), p. 52.

16. Following my articles on Vietnam, I had an exchange of letters with a high personage who was very close to Diem and who still today defends his memory. This person wrote in regard to the lack of democracy in the regime: "You call Diem a dictator more than once. We must reach an understanding on vocabulary. We had emerged from a long colonial oppression and then from the war, and we were unable immediately to have a democratic regime as exists in the West, which comes about through a slow process of maturation. . . . Diem wanted to accustom the people to govern itself in accordance with democratic principles. He therefore began with the communal assembly, then the provincial assembly and, finally, the national assembly. He was familiar with the individualism and the argumentativeness of the Vietnamese elite, especially in the South, and sought to put a brake on the division of the country by not only imposing unitary organizations and a few lesser parties but also by always calling to the government people who seemed best prepared and devoted to the national cause (some did not accept the invitation since they did not want to compromise themselves with the

regime). . . . You do not remember that Diem sent thousands of students abroad for their preparation, that he opened the country's doors to news-papermen from every country and tendency, that he respected some basic liberties, like that of the trade unions or the freedom to strike, as well as religious liberty: do you call this dictatorship or democracy? And you forget also that our first aim was to save the country from Communism, which had deep roots going back to colonial times. If we wanted to get rid of this weed, it was necessary because of the situation to suspend certain freedoms and constitutional guarantees. When Diem took power, the great majority of the country villages were strictly controlled by the Viet Minh. In order to conquer these wily and ruthless forces it was also necessary to act outside of the constitutional freedoms. . . . Diem's intention, I assure you, was to elevate the people gradually and to accustom it to govern itself demo-cratically; if he used strong methods, it was because he thought that in this way he would have more easily conquered the number one enemy of our country, not because he chose a dictatorship out of principle and as a method of governing." This impassioned defense of Diem coming from a person very close to him can perhaps preserve the president's ultimate in-tention but certainly not, it seems to me, his concrete mode of acting.

17. Buttinger, *op. cit.,* p. 953; he adds that Diem and his followers were honest and scorned even financial corruption, but they made use of it for political aims. Some authors report that Diem's family had deposited great sums in foreign banks. For those who know the survivors of the regime— Mme Nhu, with her daughters, living modestly in Rome, helped by Mgr. Thuc, a guest of the shrine of Pompei—this accusation is obviously false.

18. G. Chaffard, *Indochine, dix ans d'indépendence* (Paris: Calmann-Lévy, 1964), p. 160.

19. A. T. Bouscaren, *The Last of the Mandarins: Diem of Vietnam,* (Pittsburgh: Duquesne University Press, 1965), p. 57.

20. R. Shaplen, *The Lost Revolution* (New York: Harper & Row, 1965), p. 131.

21. J. Mecklin, *Mission in Torment: an Intimate Account of the U.S. Role in Vietnam* (Garden City, N.Y.: Doubleday, 1965), p. 37.

22. Scigliano, *op. cit.,* pp. 75–76.

23. Buttinger, *op. cit.,* vol. II, p. 952.

24. For example, the "persecution" of the Buddhists, as we shall see in the next chapter. Or the other absurd accusation, that Diem was preparing to attack and invade North Vietnam since his was a "militarist" regime. In this regard it is enough to say that not only did Diem encounter the strongest resistance to his regime right in the army (which made several attempts at a

coup d'etat and which finally succeeded in eliminating him), but also that the army of South Vietnam numbered 150,000 men at the time of "triumphant Diemism," and raised to 270,000 only at the end of 1961 when the guerrilla war was spread throughout the country (see *T.C.,* September 14, 1967, p. 13). On the other hand, the regime of North Vietnam was much more militaristic. On April 9, 1956, with a diplomatic note from Great Britain to the Soviet Union, the English government accused the authorities in Hanoi of having raised the forces of the regular army, from the armistice of that date, from 7 to 20 divisions. In March 1958, the French Minister of Foreign Affairs denounced the Hanoi government for having increased the forces of the regular army to 350,000 men and those of the "people's police" to 200,000 men. At the same period, the government of South Vietnam brought its active servicemen from 242,000 to 150,000 men, without substituting for the 180,000 men from the French expeditionary corps (see *Fides,* May 31, 1958, p. 179). Finally, as denounced by the International Control Commission of Geneva in 1961, North Vietnam was sending armed men and munitions to the South, and not vice versa (see the quotations in Ciuffi, *op. cit.,* p. 219).

25. R. Guillain in *Le Monde,* Paris, April 6, 1961.

26. J. Lacouture, *Le Vietnam entre deux paix* (Paris: Ed. du Seuil, 1965), p. 46.

27. The systems of repression used by the Diem regime are widely known and condemned by all, and we shall not dwell on a description of them.

28. G. Chaffard, "Un Viet-Nam Sud plus riche que le Viet-Nam Nord," *Croissance des jeunes nations,* no. 28, Paris, December 1963, pp. 4–6.

29. Scigliano, "Economic and Social Development," *op. cit.,* pp. 101–129.

30. Some authors assert that one important cause of the slow economic progress in North Vietnam would not be the mistakes of the Communist regime in the economic field or the noncooperation of the people but rather the noticeable harm the partition of the country brought to the North. This is true up to a certain point. The North lost the agricultural resources of the South, but the South found itself without mineral resources and almost without any industry, since the mines and the industrial potential were in the North. Furthermore, there is the considered fact that by nature the peoples of the North are much harder workers than those of the South, more tenacious and more industrious. Human capital favored the Communist regime more than Diem's (see: Buu Hoan, "Vietnam: Economic Consequences of the Geneva Peace," *Far Eastern Economic Review,* Hong Kong, December 11, 1958, pp. 753–757).

31. Buttinger, vol. II, *op. cit.,* p. 928.

32. Statistics taken from *Lumen Vitae,* no. 3, Brussels, 1965, p. 523.

33. Buttinger, vol. II, *op. cit.,* p. 928.

34. It is curious that some journalists and authors of studies on Vietnam, when they refer to the moralization accomplished by the Diem regime, accuse him of bigotry and of wanting to impose Christian morality on a non-Christian people (calling him "paternalistic," a "hack moralizer," etc.). But when the same journalists and authors describe the institutions of the Ho Chi Minh regime, they boast of its ascetical morality, approving enthusiastically the severe measures of the government against opium smokers, prostitutes, gambling, etc. In brief, if Diem did certain things, they were bad, but if Ho Chi Minh did the same things, they were very fine. . . . The authoritative *Far Eastern Economic Review* wrote in January 1962, (Hong Kong, January 11, 1962, p. 47): "Few regimes of modern times have had a worse press than that of President Diem. Accusations of corruption, nepotism, incompetence, authoritarianism, are hurled at him with untiring vigor. Some of these accusations are true, or true in part, but others are clearly false, and in general the obvious discrepancy between the defects of the regime and the volume of the accusations made against it is patent. A small investigation is enough to make it obvious that many of the accusations are merely malicious and irresponsible gossip, and undoubtedly a great quantity of this arose simply from the propaganda of the Communist enemy. At times it seems almost as if the regime is accused more in connection with its merits than in respect to its insufficiencies." If all of this were true in January 1962, it is all the more true today.

35. Buttinger, vol. II, *op. cit.,* pp. 927–928.

36. *Ibid.,* vol. II, pp. 928–929.

37. Hoang Ngoc Than, "La réforme agraire au Viet-Nam," *Rythmes du monde,* no. 3, 1964, pp. 150–162; F. N. Trager, *Why Vietnam?* (London: Pall Mall Press, 1966), pp. 150–154; W. Ladejinsky, "Agrarian Reform in the Republic of Vietnam," *Problems of Freedom: South Vietnam since Independence,* ed. W. R. Fishel (Free Press of Glencoe: 1961), pp. 153–175.

38. Scigliano, *op. cit.,* p. 121.

39. Buttinger, vol. II, *op. cit.,* pp. 934–935, 937.

40. The interview was published in *L'Italia,* Milan, January 18, 1968.

41. Tran Quoc Buu spoke to me about the trade union in North Vietnam in these terms: "After the Geneva Conference of 1954, our Confederation had a good organization in North Vietnam, since it was in the North especially that there were the large industries and the mines. Even then we already had more than 130,000 members in the unions in the North which were dependent on us, a school of leader training, a newspaper, various centers and

professional organizations. Yet in less than two years everything was lost and many union leaders were condemned to death, among whom was Phan-Nam, the head of the miners' union (one of our best member unions), a man who had spent his whole life in the service of the workers. In North Vietnam there does not now exist any autonomous union organization and no right to strike: the Communist Party thinks of everything!"

42. For example, on May 1, 1958, at the height of "triumphal Diemism," about 500,000 persons met at Saigon, creating a large demonstration against the Diem government and requesting the end of political repression in the country regions, the granting of democratic freedoms and the resumption of relations between North and South with a view toward general elections. On May 1 of the following year (1959), another 200,000 workers paraded through the streets of Saigon demonstrating against the Diem regime (see Ciuffi, *op. cit.*, p. 179; and *T.C.*, September 7, 1967, p. 13). The "savage" dictatorship of Diem, ready for all kinds of repressions, is therefore understood in this sense: that it gave a wide margin to popular demonstrations of dissent, a margin that would be unthinkable in truly and ruthlessly dictatorial regimes in the style of those of the Communists or Nazi-Fascists.

43. To some, this continual reference, as a term of comparison, to the Communist regime of North Vietnam may seem tiresome. We are doing it deliberately, since in the West, and even in Italy, there is the established habit of unconditionally condemning the Diem regime—as if it were a new form of Nazism or something similar—while, also unconditionally, the Ho Chi Minh regime is praised. Without wanting to defend Diem completely, and recognizing his mistakes, it seems to me that this way of looking at things is completely erroneous.

44. "Practically all the peasants" (wrote the *Far Eastern Economic Review* on January 11, 1962, p. 48, in a study on Vietnam) "live in places which, during the war of Indochina [against France] were occupied [at least by night] by the Viet Minh, and they certainly did not remember this experience with pleasure. These peasants were drawn to supporting the government by the agrarian reform enacted in 1957. Except where it was sabotaged by the Viet Cong, it proved on the whole to be a success, at least socially if not economically. Although the behavior of the civil and military functionaries was not such as to confirm the peasants in their loyalty to the government, it seems that it generally enjoyed greater popularity in the rural zones than in Saigon. . . . Saigon did not experience such marked changes for the better as the rural regions in recent years, since the city population was exposed to every kind of propaganda and more aware of the censurable aspects of the regime." In Vietnam I often heard repeated by competent persons that the

real enemies of the Diem regime—besides the Communists, naturally—were the intellectual elite of the cities. With the country people and the city dwellers, to whom political freedom was of little importance and who had the country pacified and in constant economic progress, Diem was at times even popular and almost never strongly opposed. As proof of this they told me that in the first years of the guerrilla war those who took up arms against the regime were almost all educated persons aided by the Communist cadres. In the early days the peasants denounced the rebels and courageously defended themselves against their night attacks. It was only afterwards when the army showed itself incapable of defending the country villages from the nocturnal terrorism of the Viet Cong that the people from the rural areas were forced to follow the rebels (we shall speak more about this in chapter IX).

45. According to what I heard from various authoritative sources in Saigon, there can be no doubt that there were contacts between Diem, Hanoi and the NLF. According to some, the determining factor was that Diem, weakened by the Buddhist revolt and fearing the loss of American support and being thus dismissed from power, was disposed to come to some agreement, although this was completely contrary to his previous political line (in the Orient, as someone pointed out to me, such compromises and bargaining are quite natural). According to others, however, it would have been the Viet Cong who made contact with President Diem through the Polish member of the Geneva Control Commission, since the "fortified village" strategy had taken away their many hopes for victory and the war was on the verge of being stopped in 1963. In fact we might add that in that year Kennedy assured the Americans that by the end of 1963 the American military advisers would be withdrawn since the war was at the point of stopping and therefore their function became useless.

46. With all his limitations and faults, Diem, even by the fact that he had remained in power for almost ten years, succeeded in becoming a popular figure with a broad strata of the population, especially with the simple country people who did not suffer much from the lack of political freedom. Several times in South Vietnam, I heard it asserted in different parts of the country that among the little people there are a few who still believe that Diem is not dead, but that he fled to the mountains with a few followers and that he will return sooner or later to save the country. This indicates that the dictator had become part of popular legend (like Lumumba in the Congo, for example), which happens with leaders who capture the imagination of the masses.

47. The document is reported in the *Sunday Examiner,* Hong Kong, July 30, 1965, p. 12.

48. *Église vivante,* 1955, pp. 136–137.

49. G. Chaffard, "Les adversaires de Diem," in *Le Monde,* August 23, 1963.

50. G. Naidenhoff, "Les impasses tragiques du catholicisme vietnamien," in *Missi,* no. 9, 1954, p. 299.

51. *Missi,* no. 2, 1956, p. 46.

52. C. Simonnet, "L'Église du demi-silence: au Vietnam," *Cahiers Charles de Foucauld,* no. 3, Paris, 1956, pp. 82–83.

53. *Informations catholiques internationales,* April 15, 1956, p. 25; *The Economist,* December 17, 1955; *America,* December 10, 1955.

54. Mgr. Cassaigne, of the Paris missions, resigned from the see of Saigon and went to live in the leprosarium of Ben-Sa near Dalat, where he still lives. Another French bishop, Mgr. Urrutia, also of the Paris missions, resigned the see of Hué in order to make way for a Vietnamese and went to live in the parish of Dong-Ha, near the demilitarized zone, as a simple parish priest, and he is still there. Two remarkable examples of poverty and service in the spirit of the Council, *ante litteram.*

55. Nhat Hanh, *Vietnam, la pace proibita* (Florence: Vallecchi, 1967), p. 56.

56. Text of the pastoral letter in *Missi,* no. 6, 1954, p. 184.

57. *Fides,* March 3, 1956, p. 65. Other indications of the bishops' refusal to accept government protection are cited in *Informations catholiques internationales,* March 15, 1963, p. 21.

58. *T.C.,* September 16, 1963, p. 14.

59. Mgr. Thuc, who was in Rome for the second session of the Vatican Council, never returned to Vietnam when his brother Diem was killed (November, 1963): he was forbidden to go back by the new Vietnamese government and, we think, also by the Roman ecclesiastical authorities. Recently replaced in the see of Hué by Mgr. Nguyen-Kim-Dien, Mgr. Thuc lives today as a guest at the shrine of Pompei.

60. In this regard Lacouture speaks of "permanent conflicts between the 'state' hierarchy, personified by Mgr. Thuc, brother of the president, and the Vatican, represented particularly by the Archbishop of Saigon, Mgr. Binh," *Le Vietnam entre deux paix* (Paris: Ed. du Seuil, 1965), p. 105.

61. In 1957 there was a strong conflict between President Diem and the Catholic refugees from the North who were organizing clamorous demonstrations against the dictator. He told Fr. Naidenhoff at the time: "I am not the president of the Catholics; I am the president of the whole Vietnamese people. Don't they (i.e., the Catholics) know that they are a minority? Why

these pretensions? Why these demands for favors? Why do they put themselves above the law?" *Missi,* no. 4, 1968, p. 136.

62. I have been unable to find any sign of the existence of a "Christian Democratic Party" in Vietnam. We are probably dealing here with a wrong translation by the news service.

63. See *Fides,* 1956, November 10, p. 335. See also *Eglise vivante* 1956, pp. 453-454.

64. In the beginning of 1956, i.e., in the period when Diem had most need of the help of the Catholics to support his still unsteady regime, of the 14 cabinet ministers only 2 were Catholics. In 1963, at the moment of Diem's fall, there were 5 Catholics among the 17 ministers; 3 generals out of 19 were Catholics and only 2 provincial governors among some 15. However absurd it may seem, the presence of Catholics in directive positions in the country did not stop increasing, as compared with the Diem period, as we shall see.

65. May-August, nos. 3-4, 1963, p. 309.

66. Lacouture refers to the fact that in Vietnam the ordinary ecclesiastical hierarchy had still not been set up (Pope John instituted it in December 1960).

67. *Le Monde,* December 29, 1959, p. 1.

68. *Fides,* no. 522, September 4, 1963.

69. *Fides,* February 1, 1958, p. 39.

70. *Fides,* May 10, 1958, p. 155.

71. In Vietnam, as in almost all the other countries of the world, the Church statistics are quite approximate and uncertain. To give but one example, for ten years it was printed even in official texts that the Catholics in South Vietnam were about one and a half million, i.e., 10 percent of the local population. In December of 1967, the apostolic delegate in Saigon, Mgr. Palmas, showed me the official Church statistics sent in a report to the Vatican in which the Catholics were listed as some 2,100,000, i.e., 13-14 percent of the South Vietnamese. We must add, however, that in not a few "mission countries" the exact statistics of the Catholics and the progress of the Church are never given in order not to arouse jealousy and resentment (the present cases of Indonesia and India where today data on the numerous conversions are kept carefully secret) are typical.

72. In regard to this beautiful epic of the Paris missionaries, see the volumes of Fr. Jacques Dournes, a missionary of Kontum (*Dio ama i pagani,* and *La missione contro le missioni,* ed. (Milan: Jaca Book, 1966 and 1967); and *L'Offrande des peuples* (Paris: Cerf, 1967). In addition, the articles: C.

Simonnet, "Westerns vietnamiens," *Bulletin M.E.P.*, Hong Kong, 1958, pp. 295–301, 383–390, 521–526.

73. The statistics are taken from *Fides* for 1957 (September 21, 1957, p. 297), and for 1963 from the *Annuaire catholique du Vietnam,* Saigon, 1964. It seems to me that the statistics for 1963 sin by defect, perhaps because those responsible for the *Annuaire* did not wish, in that very delicate year for the Church, to reveal to everyone the progress made by the Christian community during the Diem period. If in 1967 the Catholics were more than two million in South Vietnam—as I was personally assured by the apostolic delegate, Mgr. Palmas, who had detailed figures at hand—it is impossible that from 1963 to 1967 (when there were few conversions of non-Christians) the Catholic community could have grown from 1,454,842 to more than 2 million! It is probably the 1963 statistic that sins considerably by defect.

74. On the consecration of four new bishops and the erection of the ordinary episcopal hierarchy, see *Missions Etrangères de Paris,* Paris, May–June, 1961, where we also have Pope John's letter addressed to the Vietnamese bishops and faithful on the occasion.

75. An exhaustive general view of the Church during the Diem period was published in the dossier of March 15, 1963, by the *Informations catholiques internationales,* to which we are indebted for some information.

76. Afterwards, the Confederation became "of Believing Workers" (no longer "Christian") in that the majority of its members were not Christian; later it took the definitive name "Vietnamese Confederation of Labor" (CVT).

V

A War of Religion
in Vietnam?

Among the many students and journalists who have written on Vietnam, the greater part almost completely neglect the religious problem or treat it only from the viewpoint of the immediate political situation. To me this seems a mistake since in Vietnam—as in all the other countries of the "third world" that have still not been desacralized by modern progress—religion has deep roots in the spirit of the people and conditions many aspects of civil and political life. One of the basic characteristics of Vietnamese culture is the profound religiousness of the people. One scholar of this civilization writes: "With the Annamese, and in all classes of society, the religious sentiment is manifested in a powerful way and dominates their whole life; with its tightly knit practices, this feeling permeates every daily action, from the most lowly to the most important."[1]

The religious spirit of the Vietnamese people manifests itself in various forms which are not too easy to define. This is a consequence of the long history of this civilization which has undergone many cultural and religious influences without one religion ever succeeding in rooting itself deeply to the detriment of the others.

The worship of spirits and ancestors. Ancestor worship is at the basis of Vietnamese religiousness and constitutes its most ancient and most commonly practised religion today. It is celebrated on the family altar, on which are placed the wooden tablets that bear the names of the family's deceased members, by burning incense, offering gifts from nature, and praying. The family altar—for the very rich an imposing and finely worked piece of furniture—is the symbol of family unity and continuity. Around it the family members come together for prayer, to settle quarrels, and to discuss the most important problems. This exerts a great influence on the daily existence of the Vietnamese people: the remembering of ancestors, the fear of offending their honored name, the desire to make them happy, to follow their examples, to have them as protectors, are all sentiments that regulate the behavior of individuals. Even for the most callous malefactor, to lack respect for one's own dead is considered the gravest sin he could commit. ⌝

Upon this family religion, which represents the Vietnamese tradition and the religious belief in the immortal soul, are grafted the historical religions, Confucianism, Taoism and Buddhism, all imported from China but by now deeply rooted in the local culture and mingled with many superstitions and with belief in spirits.

These three historical religions, mingled with the ancient beliefs and local superstitions, gave rise to a kind of popular religion that is not clearly characterizable but which includes elements and aspects of various religions. According to the president of the Society of Buddhist Studies in South Vietnam:

. . . theoretically there are three principal religions in Vietnam: Taoism, Confucianism, and Buddhism. In practice there is only one religion, which is a kind of outcome of the interpretation of the three doctrines cited, each of which can be considered as a particular aspect of the whole. The persistence of this state of affairs creates the difficulty, not to say the impossibility, of distinguishing among the Vietnamese three distinct communities. Undoubtedly, a few convinced adepts, religious or lay, practise Taoism or Buddhism exclusively, but these are only a small number. The masses, as a whole, are without prejudices and refuse bewildering distinctions. One family might belong to Buddhism but frequent the Taoist temples no less often, while at the same time performing the rites imposed by ancestor worship. It cannot be denied that this confusion is at the origin, too often, of superstitious practices and favors and maintains ignorance.[2]

It is not within the scope of this book, dedicated to the Vietnamese Catholic Church, to study the origin, historical spread and the various ups and downs of the non-Christian religions of Vietnam.[3] Here it is enough to say that the very fact that there is no dominant religion, along with the other reality of a deeply religious people, has done more to promote the spread of Christianity than in any other country of the Asian continent. Not only this, but the Christian missionaries never found any opposition to their preaching on the part of the non-Christian religions and their most qualified exponents but always found broad religious tolerance. Perhaps, again, in no other country of the Asian continent has religious tolerance for Christian preaching been so general and absolute (let us remember that the anti-Christian persecutions of the last centuries were caused more out of political and social reasons—Christianity was destroying the foundations of traditional order by preaching human dignity, the equality of all men, etc.—more than out of religious motives in the strict sense).

The religious syncretism proper to the Vietnamese people,[4] however, created for Christianity the difficulty of forming in the faithful a knowledge of the uniqueness and the exclusiveness of the Christian faith. It is here that we should look for the origin of the "closedness" of the Christians, the Christian "ghetto," a result of the necessity for camouflage in order to escape persecution.

The modern rebirth of Buddhism. In the last fifty years Vietnam witnessed a Buddhist rebirth, parallel with the same phenomenon verified in almost all the Buddhist countries, while Confucianism and Taoism did not show equal strength of renewal and even today do not count for much in the country. Buddhism experienced a long period of decadence, especially beginning with the Nguyen dynasty (16th century), when religion became a political instrument and the bonzes were reduced to the role of guardians of the pagodas and supporters of the imperial power. The relaxation of discipline in the monasteries, the enthralment before the political power, the abandonment of studies, the lack of contact with other Buddhist countries and the general decadence of Buddhism in the world of that time are elements that explain why, when the French conquered Indochina in the last century, they found a dying Buddhism, at least as an organized religion (not in popular traditions).

The modern Buddhist rebirth goes back generally to 1891, when in Colombo, Ceylon, the Maha Bodhi Society was founded. Among Asian Buddhists it aroused a renewal of study and organization that in 1950 became the World Federation of Buddhists. In Vietnam, the influence of the Buddhist world renewal made itself felt around 1920, when the first initiatives at study and the first timid attempts at organization on the regional and national levels began, but it was only in 1931 that there was established in Saigon the first Society of Buddhist Studies, which spread the following year to Hué and Hanoi. These associations had the purpose of giving the country educated monks and bonzes who were faithful to religious practice, ready to rebuild the "Buddhist community" (*saṁgha*). This project produced numerous translations of sacred texts from Sanskrit and Pali, the two "sacred languages" of Buddhism (the first was for the Mahayana group or the "great vehicle" and the second for the Hinayana or "lesser vehicle"). The Buddhist renaissance was favored in Vietnam by the French colonial authorities, certainly not for religious but for political reasons:

The French [writes the bonze, Nhat Hanh] consented to the formation of very many Buddhist associations in the three parts of the country; thereafter, these associations were even sponsored by the French themselves. Their reasoning was very simple: instead of allowing the local population the initiative to establish its own associations and to use them against the government, the regime supported these associations in order to get its own men into their ranks and thereby control them. Moreover, such a generous religious policy would have procured for the government the favor and the gratitude of the Vietnamese themselves . . . and the attention of the people, so involved with religious practices, would have been diverted from patriotic agitation.[5]

Fr. Cadière, writing in 1913, lamented the support given by the colonial government to Buddhism:

The Buddhist religion remains alien to the Annamese, their intimate religious lives, their soul. Buddhism is an official religion, recognized, approved and sponsored by the state: the Annamese therefore make use of it, but in general only very little. I daresay that in the provinces of the kingdom almost all the Annamese live and die without ever having made one act of Buddhist religion their whole lives. . . . No, the Annamese cannot be catalogued among the Buddhist peoples since Buddhist religious life remains alien to the great majority of the people and even those who more or less take part in it do not grasp either the dogma or the morality of Buddhism.[6]

From 1930 to 1940, Buddhism experienced a widespread renewal and above all became aware of its being a real, organized religion and not merely a moral philosophy, like Confucianism or a super-stitious and magic practice like Taoism. At this period there were founded many higher institutes of Buddhist studies, associations of faithful were formed, books and magazines printed and, finally, the younger bonzes were sent abroad to study, and thus began the formation of young Buddhist militants who subsequently made re-ligion a part of the politics of the country.

The war interrupted the ardor of the renewal of Buddhism and its cultural and religious activities, which were resumed about 1948. At Hanoi in that year and the following one, an association of Buddhist laymen was founded, an orphanage, a private secondary school, a press, and charitable institutions for the war victims. In 1951 there was inaugurated at Saigon a new society of Buddhist studies, in substitution for the preceding one, which for some time had stopped all activity; in general, throughout the country the Buddhist communities were reorganized.

On May 6, 1951, at Hué, a national congress brought together about fifty delegates from all over Vietnam, religious and laity, who decided to unify the associations of the North, Center and South of Vietnam in a new unitary organization, Tong Hoi Phat Giao, which began the publication of the magazine *Vietnamese Buddhism* (*Phat-Giao Vietnam*). The Hué congress made other important decisions as well concerning the codification of rites, the religious education of the bonzes and adults, the formation of societies for the youth, etc.

But the most important element of this congress was the ratification of the membership of the Vietnamese Buddhist movement in the World Federation of Buddhists, founded not long before in Ceylon. For the first time in its history, the Buddhism of Vietnam made official contacts with the nascent world Buddhist organization.

A reaction to colonialism: the prophetic sects. From right and proper Buddhism, we must distinguish the sects that arose out of it and which have a different history and different characteristics. Above all, there is the characteristic of reaction against colonial domination, which gave these sects a strong nationalistic tone and an aspect of prophetic liberation from colonial slavery; other characteristics were primarily religious, while still others were chiefly political on the order of the Chinese "secret societies."

One example among the many originating in the colonial period, which did not acquire national influence and renown,[7] was the Binh-Xuyen sect, taking its name from the region South of Saigon, where it originated around 1930. A band of nationalist extremists, they were bound into feudal and brigandish groups which suc-

ceeded in occupying an important position in the piracy of South
Vietnam, especially during the Japanese occupation and up to 1955,
when Diem dissolved it and did away with its armed bands. The
Binh-Xuyen owned or controlled all the gambling houses and
houses of prostitution in the cities, controlled the markets by imposing heavy taxes on the businessmen, and devoted itself to other
activities of this kind. According to one writer, the Binh-Xuyen
was a racket, a gang in the pure Mafia style, a large company of
genuine pirates.[8]

During the anti-French guerrilla war, the Binh-Xuyen allied
themselves with the Viet Minh until 1945, but in May 1948 the
Communists organized the assassination of their leader and the extermination of their troops.[9] After having escaped this abortive
attempt, the Binh-Xuyen became fiercely anti-Communist, allying
themselves with the Bao Dai government. Ngo Dinh Diem did not
accept their alliance and deplored their highwayman tactics: not
successful in integrating their troops legally, he exterminated them
in real pitched battles, especially in the Cholon quarter of Saigon,
which was dominated by this sect.

The Hoa-Hao are a typical prophetic-religious sect, halfway between a regional protective association for its members and a me-
diumistic Church practicing magic and sorcery. The sect originated
in 1937 in the village of Hoa-Hao in the Mekong delta, where its
founder, Huynh-Pho-Sô, had received from a hermit-monk teachings about "the practice of sorcery, the principles of magnetism and
hypnotism, the making of talismans that brought good fortune."
Cured from an incurable illness, Huynh-Pho-Sô gained the reputation of being a wonder-worker and prophet, and began to preach a
new religion, the *Phat-Giao Hoa-Hao,* calling himself Phat Thay
(i.e., "Master Buddha"), a successor of the Buddha.

During the Japanese occupation the Hoa-Hao, supported by the
Japanese, took action against the French troops and residents with
genuine massacres. With the end of the war, they allied themselves
with the Viet Minh against the French occupation troops until their

founder was led into a trap and killed by the Viet Minh at the end of April 1947.[10] The Hoa-Hao abandoned the Viet Minh to support, albeit with many reservations, the "national" government of Bao Dai. After the Geneva agreements of 1954, the Hoa-Hao refused to integrate their troops in the national army and were defeated by Diem, and subsequently the sect abandoned active politics and developed as a religion. In the period of peace after 1956, it succeeded in spreading throughout the Mekong delta and to Saigon, until it had some million members and an excellent centralized organization.

The last sect of national importance, the Cao-Dai is certainly the one that comes closest to the Western concept of a Church, with a rather well defined doctrine, a rubricized worship form, an ecclesiastical hierarchy almost entirely borrowed from the Catholic Church, and a national diffusion, although it was chiefly centered in the Mekong delta, where the directive center of the sect was set up and where it was founded in 1926. According to some authors, the sect would have originated at the beginning of the century, and in 1926 a bold opportunist who was "miraculously" cured from opium addiction, Le-Van-Trung, took control and had himself named pope, with the support of the colonial government who wanted in this way to be sure of its control over the sect.

The political history of the Cao-Dai is completely similar to that of the Hoa-Hao. From 1930 the sect took sides against colonialism and incited resistance action against the French. During the world war, with Japanese help, the Cao-Dai armed some 3,000 men who took part in the anti-French coup d'etat of March 9, 1945. Then it allied itself with the Viet Minh, took part in the first Ho Chi Minh government and participated in the anticolonial struggle until January 1947, when the Viet Minh attacked the "Holy See" of the Cao-Dai.[11] From that moment, the 15,000 armed men who were members of the sect gave themselves to hunting the Communists in the regions controlled by them, aligning themselves with the Bao Dai government. Under the Diem government, the Cao-Dai also lost interest in politics and prospered as a religion, having some two million members today throughout South Vietnam.

The religious doctrine and organization of Caodaism are most interesting, but here we can only give a brief outline.[12] The Cao-Dai (which means "Supreme Being" or "Supreme Palace") preaches faith in one God, the existence of the immortal soul and its successive reincarnations, along with the posthumous consequences of human acts, in accordance with the law of *karma,* so well-known in the Hindu and Buddhist worlds. It taught respect for the dead, family worship, the love of good and righteousness, the practice of virtue. It preached the coming of a Messiah, Minh-Vuong, the just and wise King, who would establish an age of peace and goodness.

The Cao-Dai was defined as a "typically Vietnamese syncretism," insofar as it claims to sum up and to surpass all the local religions, Buddhism, Taoism, Confucianism and Christianity; it considers the principal founders of religions as incarnations of the one God in different periods of history. It is therefore absurd to set one religion against another since all are valid, even in their diverse rites and truths. Today Caodaism constitutes the strongest and most organized sect in Vietnam: more than 3,000 "priests," 72 "bishops," 36 "archbishops," and 6 "cardinals," with an equivalent number of feminine dignitaries. All are grouped around the "pope," who resides at the shrine of Tay-Ninh, the central seat of the sect, in whose pantheon are venerated Sun-Yat-Sen and Churchill, the Vietnamese prophet Trang-Trinh and St. Joan of Arc, Victor Hugo, Buddha, Christ and Confucius. With two million faithful, the Cao-Dai is the third religious force of Vietnam, after Buddhism and the Catholic Church.

Buddhist expansion under Diem. But let us return to Buddhism proper and its movement of rebirth, which resumed its development in South Vietnam after 1954 and especially when peace was assured to the country after 1956.

Under Diem there is no doubt that Buddhism enjoyed the fullest religious freedom. This is so true that never in its long history had it recorded such a grandiose rebirth in so short a time. We shall soon see the conflicts that gave rise to the Buddhist revolt in the summer of 1963 against the Diem regime, but in the meanwhile we must say that from 1954 to 1963, Buddhism amply developed in South Vietnam and became clearly aware not only of its religious identity but also of its political strength.

As for the rebirth and spread of the Buddhist religion, a few data given in 1962 by the General Association of Buddhists of Vietnam will suffice. In the period of 1956–1962, the upper schools for bonzes in South Vietnam increased from 4 to 10; of the 4,766 pagodas in the country, 1,275 were built after 1954 and 1,295 were renovated or rebuilt after that year. The Diem government at that same time gave nine million piastres for the building of Buddhist pagodas (about $1,600,000), and President Diem himself gave a major contribution for the reconstruction of the famous Xa Loi pagoda, the national center of South Vietnamese Buddhism. Still according to the data given by the Buddhist association, from 1956 to 1962 the associations of Buddhist faithful grew by 32 percent.

The essential data indicating the Buddhist renaissance under the Ngo Dinh Diem regime are taken from an authoritative publication of the president of the Society of Buddhist Studies at Saigon.[13] Under the direction of the General Association of Buddhists of Vietnam, three communities were organized, including 3,000 bonzes and 300 nuns, and another three communities of lay followers, even in the most deserted villages; these three communities grouped together about one million Buddhist laymen, to whom were joined the nonaffiliated laymen, "whose numerical importance was three times greater" (i.e., about another 3 million).

For the "propagation of the faith"[14] and the spiritual formation of the Buddhists, weekly conferences at Saigon are mentioned, periodical preaching in the provinces, with motor cars furnished with loudspeakers and movie projectors, and the wide sale of magazines and pamphlets (about 30,000 copies were published monthly by the General Association of Buddhists alone). Then there were specialized lectures organized, "for those who desire to deepen their knowledge of doctrine," and numerous libraries were set up.

Another aspect recorded by Mai Tho Truyen was the formation of cadres, with the multiplication of schools for the bonzes, 4 in 1956, 10 in 1962, the creation of a corps of specialized preachers, and the sending of young bonzes to the Buddhist universities in India and Japan. In the bonze schools the teaching followed the official programs for the schools of the same level, to which was added religious material, especially the study of the scriptures.

The young Buddhists, from eight to twenty years of age, are incorporated into a youth movement, Gia Dinh Phat Tu, founded in 1940 with the aim of instructing and vitalizing Buddhist young people. In 1962, the movement was directed by 3,000 instructors and counted 70,000 young people in 1,000 city and country areas; about one quarter of these young Buddhists went to the private Buddhist schools, elementary and secondary, founded in recent years. In addition to the schools, the Buddhist community founded various medical and charitable institutions. Mai Tho Truyen's pamphlet cites the medical dispensary built near the Xa Loi pagoda, which takes care of some 200 sick poor every day; at Saigon and Dalat there are two children's homes directed by Buddhist nuns, at Saigon a maternity clinic and a hospital, etc.

The WFB magazine, *World Buddhism,* printed in Ceylon, published up to the May 1963 number (when the violent conflict with the Diem regime broke out) news and articles on the Buddhist renaissance in South Vietnam. Let us mention a few important happenings in the last months before the conflict. In December 1962 the fourth national congress of the Vietnam Buddhist Association was held at Saigon at the Xa Loi pagoda. New directors of the association were elected with the new president, the Venerable Thich Tinh Kiet, and two vice-presidents, Mai Tho Truyen and the Venerable Thich Tam Chau.[15] In September 1962, a report

from Vietnam on the occasion of the inauguration of a new Buddhist building claimed that at that time there was a great deal of
Buddhist activity and signs of a Buddhist renaissance.[16]

On March 9–10, 1963, at Cap Saint-Jacques, to the south of
Saigon, a "colossal image of Buddha" was inaugurated, with the
participation of some 25,000 faithful and 300 bonzes from every
part of Vietnam; 800 automobiles and buses brought the Buddhist
crowds to the demonstration, amidst the waving of thousands of
Buddhist and national flags. Near the statue, which was intended
to become a national shrine, the building of a Buddhist college was
projected. The same magazine added that the inauguration of the
statue came about in the presence of a crowd of Buddhist monks
and faithful that had never been seen before in the history of
Vietnam.[17]

The magazine further points out that during these same months
(May–June 1963), there was a new Buddhist review founded at
Saigon, *Tong Ket,* as well as the inauguration of a great pagoda in
the presence of members of the government.[18]

The political aspect of the Buddhist rebirth. The Buddhist revival also had a political component in the following sense. While
up to thirty or more years ago Buddhism was chiefly the religion
of the poor and the farmers, with Confucianism dominant among
the upper classes and the intellectuals, the cultural and religious
awakening in Buddhism (which also had literary and artistic aspects) gradually brought Buddhism to be the religion of the intellectuals as well, supplanting Confucianism which lacked organization and was not a "church" in the strict sense. During the Diem
period the rapprochement of the upper classes and the educated
population of the cities in general with Buddhism could not avoid
political ramifications. In fact, as we have pointed out, opposition to
Diem did not come chiefly from the country areas but from the
cities, not from the lower classes but from the educated who felt
more strongly the lack of political freedoms.

It is in this way that a renovated Buddhism, in the absence of political parties and associations, found itself in the center of the opposition to Diem, sustained also by people who were not actually Buddhist but who saw in Buddhism the religion of the masses, with international connections and the means to free themselves from the dictator.

Along with this political impetus there was religious frustration. In its task of renewal and modern organization, Buddhism found itself face to face with the Catholic Church which was already well-organized and modernized, with imposing and numerous institutions, an educated clergy, associations of militant laymen, newspapers, upper schools, universities, etc. This was the source of the frustration and the tendency to attribute to the "protection" of Diem the advance of the Catholics in the life of the nation (which, actually, was due more than anything else to the excellent school system which the Catholics had had for some time, and to the centralized organization of the Church which the Buddhists, divided into various sects and currents of opinion, had still not succeeded in acquiring). Undoubtedly, Diem gave the Church prestige and made use principally of the Catholics, who were the chief supporters of his regime, but the fact of the "power" of the Church is explained in quite another way than by Diem's "protection": this is so true that even after Diem, with Buddhist governments, the Catholics continued to occupy the positions of greatest responsibility.

The Buddhist revolt at Hué. The underground opposition of the Vietnamese elite to the Diem regime broke out unexpectedly in May 1963 and concluded in November of the same year with the assassination of Diem and his brother Nhu.

May 8 was the 2,507th. anniversary of the death of the Buddha, and the Buddhist faithful were preparing to celebrate great religious festivals, especially in the city of Hué, the national center of Buddhism and a city of ancient Buddhist tradition. Two days before the festival, on May 6, a government ordinance restated the law forbidding the carrying of religious banners through the streets of Vietnamese cities. This went back to 1957 and was restated by the government in 1958 and 1962 on the justification of the need to give the people of South Vietnam a national awareness—in fact, in religious processions and demonstrations it was obligatory to carry the national flag. The law obtained not only for the Buddhists but also for the Catholics, and the Catholic bishops (for example, the Archbishop of Saigon, Mgr. Binh) had already reminded their priests and laity several times to observe it. However up to May 8, 1963, practically no one knew about it, either in the religious communities or in the government. In the past there had already been some incidents in regard to this government order, which was observed in cases where there was a fear that religious demonstrations might give way to disorder. Especially in the latter years, with the outbreak of the guerrilla war, it had already happened several times that there had been infiltration by guerrilla elements into religious and, especially, Buddhist processions.

A few days before May 8, the archbishop, Mgr. Thuc, President Diem's brother, had celebrated his episcopal jubilee at Hué, and the Catholics had been able to carry their banners through the city. On May 6, however, only two days before the Buddhist festivities, the government ordered the local police to enforce the law on religious flags, and the Hué police notified the Catholics and the Buddhists of the government order. But the order was hateful only to the Buddhists since the Catholics had already celebrated their festival a few days before. Thus, on the day itself of the anniversary of the Buddha's birth, some 10,000 Buddhists clashed with the police, who had requisitioned their flags and were unwilling to allow the Buddhists to use radio Hué for their protest: there were 8 dead and some 20 wounded.

The government, frightened by international reactions, began negotiations with the Buddhists, who presented five demands. The first three concerned the happenings at Hué: permission to carry religious flags of whatever type, acknowledgment by the government that the police had fired on the demonstrators and making compensation to the victims' families. The other two requests were of a more general nature: they sought the abolition of the law on assemblies, going back to 1950 and, therefore, some time before Diem, through which the Buddhist associations were controlled by the government and had to present a written report on their activities, and the acquisition by the Buddhists of the same privileges enjoyed by the Catholics in regard to army military chaplains and the exemption of clerics and priests from military service.

On June 16 the government and the Buddhist leaders stipulated an agreement on the basis of the five requests formulated by the Buddhists which was signed not only by the three Buddhist members of the delegation and three members of the government but also by the Ven. Thich Tinh Kiet, head of the Vietnam Buddhist Association, and Ngo Dinh Diem, who wrote before his signature, "The points of this joint communiqué were approved by me in principle from the very beginning" (i.e., of the talks). The points of the agreement[19] eliminated any discussion and future dissent in the religious field. There was a new and carefully worked out regulation on the public display of religious banners (art. 1); the government's promise to pass at the beginning of 1964 a new law on religious assemblies and associations (art. 2); the setting up of an enquiry commission on the injustices denounced by the Buddhists and the act of presidential clemency for all who in the Buddhist demonstrations had broken the law (art. 3); the renewal of the guarantees for more ample religious freedom in all its aspects (art. 4) and, finally, the punishment of the members of the police who were proven guilty in the clash with the Buddhists and the agreement to give aid to the families of the victims (art. 5).

Public immolation of the Bonzes and martial law. At this point, the conflict seemed healed, since the major Buddhist leaders had acknowledged the government's good faith and signed an agreement based on their own demands.[20]

Unfortunately the peace between the government and the Buddhists lasted only a few days, since on June 18, this time in Saigon, a new Buddhist revolt broke out which was put down by the police and resulted in one death and many wounded. The day had been set for the funeral and cremation of the monk, Thich Quang Duc, who had burned himself on June 11, but at the request of the government the Buddhist leaders had agreed to postpone the public ceremonies in order to avoid new tensions in the city and possible incidents. But when the bonzes announced over the loud-speakers to a crowd of 10,000 people that the ceremonies had been postponed, the crowd began to shout and call them "traitors" and "sell-outs to the government"; led by students, the demonstrators proceeded towards the center of the city where they clashed with the police.

From this moment on, the two sides no longer got along.[21] The government continually recalled the accord signed on June 16, claiming its strict observance, and it began to accuse the Buddhists of allowing themselves to be drawn into political demonstrations against the regime, while the Buddhists in turn reproached the government for new acts of violence against the faithful and the pagodas.

Nevertheless, President Diem strove to resume contacts with the Buddhists, declaring himself disposed to discuss all their proposals with a view toward other agreements signed by both sides. But in July and August there was a noticeable hardening of attitudes both on the Buddhists' and government's parts.

In August three more bonzes and one nun burned themselves in the squares of Saigon to protest against the government, although since the middle of June, the Buddhist leaders no longer accepted Diem's numerous invitations to dialogue and negotiations. However, if Diem had a responsible and moderate attitude, this was not the case with other persons of the regime, for example, Mme Nhu, whose contemptuous statements against the bonzes went round the world, arousing indignation everywhere.[22] At this juncture we cannot follow step by step the events of this "hot summer," which have already been reported in full by various authors,[23] but it is interesting to note how, out of an almost ludicrous conflict on a question of flags in a religious procession, both sides reached a state of escalation, going from dialogue to protest, from demonstrations to invectives, and finally arriving at repression on one side and open antigovernment revolt on the other.

And we can say that neither of the two sides wanted to go to such extremes. It was certainly not Diem's or the government's intention to reach the point of an open encounter with the Buddhists; nor, on the other hand, did the Buddhist leaders want the question to degenerate into politics and provoke the fall of the dictator (or at least, as we said in the preceding chapter, this is what the Vietnamese leaders say today. They wanted Diem to get rid of any discrimination against the Buddhists, but they did not think it was necessary to overthrow him for that reason since they acknowledged in him other gifts that were very useful to the country).

However, whether it was wanted or not, the conflict degenerated into an open public struggle, even by intervention, on the side of the Buddhists, of all the people who were dissatisfied with the Diem regime. In August tension grew throughout the country, with clearly anti-government political demonstrations, like that of August 18 at the Xa Loi pagoda, in which addresses were delivered calling for Diem's end and thousands of copies of a declaration against Diem were distributed. According to a statement by an observer, (an anonymous correspondent of a news service from Saigon, published in the Hong Kong *Sunday Examiner* of September 6, 1963, p. 1), the declaration contained exaggerations and was most offensive since up to then the Buddhist representatives had never revolted against the government.

But now it was not a question of simple religious claims or of permission to carry Buddhist flags in procession (which was granted two months before). On August 20, Diem proclaimed martial law throughout the country, while the army and police initiated a massive campaign of repression with the occupation of the principal pagodas and the arrest of some bonzes. Tri Quang took refuge in the American embassy as a guest of the new ambassador, Henry Cabot Lodge, who had just arrived in Vietnam as a replacement for Nolting; he was more open than his predecessor to the Buddhist claims. The reaction of international public opinion to the government's act of force was very widespread, and the situation in Vietnam continued to degenerate into open revolt against the regime, whose position became almost intolerable both at home and in relations abroad, especially with the protective power, the United States. The military coup d'etat of November 1 was the consequence of the whole lengthy crisis, even if the precise and documented history of what happened still has to be written, and it is still unsure who was responsible for it.

Not religious persecution but political conflict. Before examining the Church's position throughout the crisis, it is necessary to delve more deeply into a few more important aspects of the question. First of all, it may be easily affirmed as a now universally accepted truth that Diem and his government never persecuted the Buddhists either before or during the "hot summer" of 1963. The "religious persecution of the Buddhists" is a fiction of the Western press, and today, at some distance of years, neither Diem's severest critics nor the Buddhist leaders of Vietnam are disposed to uphold it. That there were discriminations in favor of the Catholics (not *qua* Catholics but as certain foes of Communism) is undeniable, but that Diem "declared a religious war against four-fifths of the population, who were Buddhists"[24] passed for the truth only with a certain kind of Western press which never raised the least protest about the absolutely authentic persecutions suffered by Buddhism in North Vietnam.[25]

The conflict between the Buddhists and the government, even if it orginated as something religious, namely, the prohibition against carrying religious flags, immediately developed into something clearly political. This was especially true when, with the agreement signed on June 16 between the government and the greatest representatives of Buddhism (among whom was also Thich Tam Chau, then part of the most extreme wing of Buddhism, that of Tri Quang), the religious questions were resolved with the Buddhist demands fully satisfied. It subsequently became clear that behind Buddhism were marshalled all the political opponents of the government—especially at Saigon and Hué, the two major cities, where they were quite numerous—who understood that this was a good opportunity to cause a crisis for the regime.

The international news agencies, already quite critical of Diem, gave ample coverage to the "Buddhist question," especially after some bonzes (6 in all: one in June, 4 in August, among whom was one nun, and one in September) burned themselves in public —events covered by photographers and television cameramen who were advised in advance.[26] The Western European and American press unanimously condemned the persecution of the Buddhists, arousing public opinion against Diem and his regime and making untenable the position of the American government which officially supported Saigon.

It is hard to say whether and to what extent the leaders of Vietnamese Buddhism were aware of the fact that the protests of the Buddhist masses against Diem were taking a dangerous turn and would lead to the violent end of the regime. At the beginning of September, various Buddhist leaders subscribed to a declaration of fidelity to the government, along with the leaders of the Cao-Dai and the Hoa-Hao. Others assert that the political outcome was completely extraneous to the Buddhist demonstrations, which were understood only as a safeguard of religious freedoms.

Nevertheless it is certain that the repression of the demonstrations of the Buddhists was ordered by the government for solely political reasons, i.e., out of the conviction that they were maneuvered by antigovernment elements infiltrated by the Communists.

Certainly, the government did not wield a light hand. Although before August 20 the regime, and Diem himself, had showed much good-will in reaching an agreement with the Buddhists (in the month of July alone there were six radio appeals by the president and about ten official missions sent to the Buddhist leaders), after the decision to impose martial law on August 20, the policy of the iron fist was begun, without even the velvet glove, which was a sign of the total decadence of Diemism in the eyes of international public opinion. If before August 20 the regime could have been reproached almost solely for the inopportune prohibition of May 6 and the outbursts of Mme Nhu at the beginning of August, after that date there was the beginning of a "Buddhist hunt" (occupation of the pagodas, imprisonment of the bonzes, brutal repression of the demonstrations, etc.) which by the middle of September rapidly achieved an almost total calm. But in the meanwhile world public opinion rose against Diem, and even within Vietnam it seemed impossible to continue with such an unpopular government; this resulted in the military coup d'etat of November 1.

We must also add that if it is true that Diem never persecuted the Buddhists, reasons were not lacking for them to be unhappy with the regime, either from a religious or civic point of view. Although the Buddhists never said they were persecuted,[27] they had in the past, for various reasons, protested against the government. For example, in 1960 the Vietnam Buddhist Association had presented to the government a voluminous dossier with detailed accusations against the government and especially against lesser functionaries; the essential element of these complaints was the position of favor enjoyed by the Catholics and, as a consequence, the discriminations to which the Buddhists were subjected.

A misunderstanding that must be clarified. Another misunderstanding that must be cleared up, which is still current today with not a few commentators on Vietnamese problems, is that which attributes to Buddhism some 80 percent of the South Vietnamese population, which then leads to the conclusion that all the Buddhists were against Diem. Both assertions are false, and we point this out especially because this will aid the reader in understanding the present position of Buddhism in South Vietnamese society.

According to data furnished by the Vietnam Buddhist Association in July 1962, the Buddhists, who were members of one of the three communities (*samgha*) recognized by the association, were one million, while those who had not signed up but who sympathized were calculated at 3 million. Therefore, the Buddhist faithful were somewhere around 4 million, i.e., less than 30 percent of the 15 million Vietnamese.[28] Even if many of Diem's opponents in the cities aligned themselves at the side of the Buddhists, in order to oppose the dictator although they were not Buddhists themselves, it is beyond any doubt that the Buddhists never represented, as they do not today, the majority of the Vietnamese people.

Once again, we must point out that one part of the Buddhists were not in agreement with the protests against Diem. The Western journalists always simplified, and spoke of Buddhism as a kind of hierarchized and organized Church. Actually, every pagoda and every monastery is independent and does not recognize, in the strict sense, any authority other than its own. After 1950, as we have already said, the leaders of the Buddhist renewal, young people who had studied abroad and who were under the influence of the World Congresses of Buddhism and the World Buddhist Association of Colombo, Ceylon, sought to organize the Buddhist institutions with the Vietnam Buddhist Association by advocating a Buddhism that was active, missionary and committed to social and cultural works as well as to politics. These were all marshalled against Diem, although with different shades of dissent. But the leaders of traditional Buddhism (which according to some estimates numbered about 800,000 members in the South), who were also members of the Buddhist Association, always criticized the "new wave," claiming that it was against all the principles left by the Buddha and against all traditions. For this reason, even in the conflict with Diem there were some bonzes who defended the dictator, stating that there was no persecution of the Buddhists and even accusing some Buddhist organizations of having introduced into their ranks political intriguers and Communists.

The basic accusation that the Diem government made against the Buddhists in the summer of 1963 in order to justify martial law and the occupation of the chief pagodas was that not only did the anti-government demonstrations have a political and not a religious character, but that they were partially at least led by Communist elements that had infiltrated into the pagodas and Buddhist organizations. What value is there to this accusation, which still burdens the Buddhist movement today?

Buddhist neutralism in regard to Communism. First of all, some students of Buddhism agree to the doctrinal nonopposition of Buddhism to Communism. The English expert on Buddhism, E. Conze, states that the doctrinal similarities between Mahayana Buddhism and dialectical materialism are surprisingly close and a reciprocal influence of ideas is destined to be verified, producing long-range consequences for both. And Conze is not the only one who has this opinion. Migot sees close connections between Communism and Buddhism, since the latter has the great merit of substituting rational notions for the metaphysical thought of its time and of having created a real spiritual materialism based upon dialectics.[29]

The magazine, *Croissance des jeunes nations,* recently dedicated an article to the theme, "The Buddha opens the way for Karl Marx" (May 1965), in which there is a synthesis of the doctrinal collusions between Buddhism and Communism which, without making the Buddha a precursor of Communism, would be numerous and surprising: "Many observers ask themselves [says the magazine] whether Buddhism, which had so much said about it in Saigon after the fall of Diem, constitutes an obstacle to Marxism, or whether, on the contrary, it prepares the way for a Marxist regime."

On the concrete level, beyond any possible similarity of doctrine and philosophy, it is quite curious that, although Communism is one of the chief problems in Asia and has almost eliminated any trace of Buddhism in China, North Vietnam, Mongolia, Tibet, central Asia, and North Korea, the Buddhists of the so-called "free world" have never strongly denounced this massive and systematic persecution. Not only this, but they have never even put the Buddhist faithful of Asian countries on guard against the danger represented by Communism. In paging through Buddhist books and periodicals I have rarely come across references to Communism; the problem is simply ignored. When these periodicals and books treat of Buddhism in China in our time, for example, they point out some ancient pagoda—a national monument—restored by the government and the trips abroad made by some Buddhist leaders subjected to the wishes of the dominant regime. They never mention the thousands of closed pagodas, the scattered bonzes and nuns, the antireligious and anti-Buddhist campaigns of the Communist press, the people's trials and the condemnations of Buddhist personalities who were unwilling to submit, etc. It is difficult to understand why. And then, when Tibet is mentioned—a case of outrageous racial and religious persecution—they mention nothing more than some "conflicts between the religious leaders and the local government," as if it were a question of some ordinary administrational procedure.

In general, it can be said that in Asia, Buddhism's position as regards Communism[30] and the Communist regimes is one of absolute neutralism: neither praise nor condemnation but rather a problem that is almost completely ignored. This does not mean that the Buddhist communities are not opposed to Communism, especially those of the Hinayana group (the "little vehicle") who have opposed and do oppose considerable resistance to Communist infiltration in their countries, as has been demonstrated in Ceylon, Burma, Thailand and Cambodia. This is attributed to the fact that Hinayana Buddhism is well organized and quite rigid from the doctrinal point of view, constituting in the countries of South-East Asia a considerably weighty national force.

On the other hand, Mahayana Buddhism is a much more elastic and syncretistic religion. Its community (*samgha*) is not organized, nor is it in the majority on the national level in the various countries to which this type of Buddhism has spread (China, Central Asia, etc.), but rather it is dispersed and dependent upon the various pagodas. This is why Mahayana Buddhism (the "great vehicle") is easily adapted to Communism and has never showed resistance to its infiltration and spread among the faithful, as was the case in China and Central Asia and as we have seen in Vietnam[31] (there is the exception of Tibet, on account of the special social and cultural organization that the majority religion, Lamaist Buddhism, implanted many centuries ago).

With this in mind, it is no wonder then that among the Buddhists and bonzes of Vietnam—under Diem but also afterward—there was a specially prepared infiltration of Communist elements. Suffice it to say that Communist troublemaking elements, well prepared for their job, also infiltrated Catholic organizations![32] And we must point out that it is much easier to become a bonze than to pass for a young member of Catholic Action. Actually, to become a bonze, all one had to do was to put on the saffron or black robe of the bonzes and fulfill their outward acts of worship; many men and youths spend a month or a year in a pagoda or a monastery, without any control or supervision.

It is certain, however, that in South Vietnam, at least up to 1963, Buddhism never took any official position in regard to Communism. When Diem was striving to involve the Buddhist leaders in an action of containment of Communist infiltrations into the country, the bonze, Thich Thien Hoa, chief of the inter-sect committee for the defense of Buddhism in Vietnam, answered Diem's request clearly in a letter with these words: "we absolutely do not involve ourselves in politics, nor are we under anyone's influence just as we allow no one to take advantage of us."

This is undoubtedly a respectable and even admirable position—and it has more than once been reaffirmed by various Buddhist personalities—if it corresponds with reality. In practice, however, by opposing the Diem government and completely ignoring the rival force (i.e., Communism), the Buddhists in South Vietnam certainly did not take an impartial position. And this is all the more noticeable if, as people say, the opposition to Diem was of a purely religious character (granting the regime's "persecution" of the Buddhists) since it is hard to understand why the much more totalitarian and bloody persecutions by the Communists were never denounced.[33]

The clear position of the Archbishop of Saigon. We have now reached the point of looking at the position taken by the Church and by Catholics during the struggles between the Buddhists and Diem in the summer of 1963. First of all, we must specify that these same Buddhist leaders always stated that they had nothing against the Catholics: "Let it be very clear [declared a bonze of the Xa Loi pagoda, for example] that we are not against the Catholics; we know very well that we do not have to defend ourselves from a Christian *crusade* but from certain Catholics in power."[34]

But even so, the Church could not remain silent, all the more because both abroad and in Vietnam itself people continued to call Diem's government "Catholic." In this regard we have a few statements of Mgr. Nguyen-Van-Binh, Archbishop of Saigon and Primate of the Vietnamese Church. In his pastoral letter of June 16, 1963, Mgr. Binh recalled the Catholic teaching on the relationship between Church and State and between the state and religion. After having mentioned the separation of Church and State and their respective autonomies, Mgr. Binh states: "Consequently, the Catholic Church acknowledges itself to be without mandate in the field of purely temporal power, just as it cannot allow interference in the field of divine things which is its own."

Then the archbishop recalled the principle of John XXIII in

Pacem in Terris: "Everyone has the right to honor God in accordance with the right ruling of his conscience and to profess his own religion in his private and public life."

The Archbishop of Saigon, Mgr. Binh, then stated that

. . . every Catholic therefore must recognize and respect the principle of freedom of conscience. . . . [The Church] desires only free and sincere conversions. . . . This is the sense of the respect of the human person as professed by the Church, since man is made in God's image. The Church always teaches and practices justice, charity, union and peace toward all, without distinction of race, language or belief. The Church's line of conduct in this matter is manifestly clear. . . . For this reason, I strongly insist that you priests, religious and faithful of my diocese, make the principles mentioned above a matter of study and reflection, as the proper norm of behavior. . . . Let everyone in his own particular position strive loyally for union and peace! Let no one allow himself to be led into wrong actions! Let us not allow ourselves to deviate from our duty, either because of groundless rumors or offensive words against the Catholic community, or rash acts, whatever their source.[35]

Keeping apart from any political judgment, Mgr. Binh recalls the value of freedom of conscience and religion and the impassable limitations that the state must impose upon itself in regard to religion; the last references to "groundless rumors" and "rash acts" refer to the rumors, reported amply also by the Western press, that the Catholics were oppressing the Buddhists in Vietnam and to the anti-Catholic reactions of a small group of Buddhist demonstrators, especially in the villages where the moderating influence of the leaders made itself less felt. In this letter the archbishop took a clear position against state interference and any oppression in regard to the various religions.

As the atmosphere reached fever pitch, Mgr. Binh published another pastoral letter on August 15 which, like the preceding one, was also read in all the churches and published in the Catholic

press. Recalling the recent encyclical, *Pacem in Terris,* the archbishop first of all expresses the desire for peace that animates the
Church and the contribution that the Catholics made to the return
of peace after the recent happenings. After these premises, Mgr.
Binh enters into the argument at hand:

Some therefore have accused the Church of having provoked these
incidents. This is untrue. The Church did not provoke them but rather
deplored them for their intrinsic noxiousness and for the harm they
have caused. Furthermore, as my last letter [of June 16, reported above]
demonstrates, the Church instructed the faithful about their obligations.
. . . We must also answer those apparently more moderate people who
would want it believed that the Christians have oppressed the Buddhists
in these recent times. These calumnies, due often to persons residing
abroad, do not hold up against the truth of the matter, since religious
peace, based on a spirit of tolerance, did reign between Christians and
Buddhists. This peace still reigns between them after the incidents at
Hué and Saigon. This peace, treated so lightly by those who live far
away from the danger and who have some interest in fomenting discord, is too precious for Buddhists and Christians, sincerely attached
to their faiths, to attempt thoughtlessly to destroy it at a moment when
we are all defending ourselves against Communist subversion.

Mgr. Binh goes on to take up the problem of the relations between the Church and the State and recalls the Catholic doctrine
in this regard. Then, returning to the Catholics, he states:

We freely practice our religion in South Vietnam, as the faithful of
other religious confessions do also. Let us rejoice in this freedom, but
let us not try to add to it excessive rights and privileges. Let us not
confuse the spread of the faith with the growth of political influence or
social prestige.[36]

Another interesting document of Mgr. Binh is a "letter to foreign
friends," which was written as an answer to the questions of Cath-

olics throughout the world about the Church's position in the conflict between the Buddhists and the government. Among other things, the Archbishop of Saigon writes:

We are deeply pained to see how the question of the Vietnamese Buddhists has been exploited by the whole world. If the journalists had taken the time to study the situation calmly, they would have been more objective in their reports, people would have become less excited and the Church would not have been calumniated, as has actually happened. Some people have reproached us for not having spoken out boldly in defense of the Buddhists. We should have done so if the Buddhists were being persecuted for their faith and if their activity had remained on the religious plane. There is no persecution of the Buddhists, either on the part of the government or by the Catholics, since they cannot be blamed for certain isolated and individual acts of discrimination. The press has described all the facts in a false perspective of persecution or discrimination.[37]

Catholics and the crisis between the government and the Buddhists. The position of the Catholics in the Buddhist-government conflict is also shown by other documents. For example, in a declaration of the National Catholic Action Committee, published at the beginning of September, reference is made to *Pacem in Terris* and to various interventions of Paul VI in the Vietnamese situation, and the Catholics are reminded of their duty in regard to this situation. It then goes on to state:

(1) Every person has the inviolable right to freedom of faith and worship. We give our support to the just requests to assure this right.

(2) The government has the duty to promote the common good and therefore to make laws to assure this common good.

(3) In every case in which these rights and these duties must be harmonized with one another, we request that this be done in accordance with strict justice and charity, in accord with the natural law, so that these rights may be respected within the limits and according to the words of *Pacem in Terris*.[38]

Seven Vietnamese bishops, at Rome for the preparatory work of the council, published a common declaration which said:

When a head of state takes coercive measures out of political and not religious reasons and for the security of the state, the Church recalls the evangelical precepts that violence and hatred be avoided, and its own charitable institutions be not implicated: this is our case in Vietnam. . . . Buddhists and Catholics are equally adverse to violence and respect the consciences of others, which means they cannot be at odds. In our country, as in the other countries of Asia, and to the extent they are faithful to their principles, people are disposed to collaborate for peace in the world; every man of goodwill should help them dispel the falseness of the intentions that first create tension and then aggravate it. . . . In the face of what is happening at present, it is difficult to have sufficiently impartial news; we must therefore be on our guard against making premature judgments. One cannot understand something that has happened except within the human context in which it takes place; lacking this knowledge and this calmness of judgment one runs the risk of being mistaken.[39]

In the concrete, prescinding from the official documents, what was the attitude of the Church and of Catholics? I was able to cull in Vietnam many direct pieces of evidence in this regard, almost all of which agree. The Catholics and the Church were in a painful situation that summer of 1963. On one side, they were ready to defend the religious freedom even of the Buddhists whenever that was found to be endangered; on the other side, their judgment about the situation disagreed to an extent with the Buddhists (or at least, as we said, with some currents of Buddhism). The Buddhists claimed to be persecuted for their religion,[40] while the Catholics thought that there was no religious persecution but only a political conflict. And the Catholics—this fact hardly needs emphasis— were not in the majority in agreement with the political aims of the rebellions, i.e., the crisis and the downfall of the Diem regime,[41] insofar as they judged that under the pressure of the Communist invasiveness to overthrow the one person who was well-known and well-established throughout the country, would have resolved nothing, and might even have worsened the situation (which is precisely what happened).

The Catholics bewailed the open conflicts, had speeches and demonstrations of sympathy for the victims of police repression, claimed for everyone the most complete religious freedom, worked to obtain moderation from the government and to depoliticize the Buddhist movement, but they went no further. They did not take any part in the antigovernment demonstrations, nor did they go against the Buddhists after the proclamation of martial law in August. After this measure, obviously too severe, which was followed by the occupation of pagodas and the arrests of the bonzes, there were a few isolated gestures of greater participation by the Catholics. For example, in addition to the communiqué of the Catholic Action organization already quoted, the rector of the university of Hué, Fr. Cao Van Luan, was released from his post for having sided with the Buddhists; with him some 15 university professors resigned, among whom were 2 priests and one Catholic layman. At Saigon, about 20 young Catholics passed a night in jail for having demonstrated against the occupation of the national pagoda of Xa Loi by the police. Two Catholic newspapers, the *Song Dao* (rather neutralist and progressive) and the daily *Tu-Do* (*Freedom,* strongly anti-Communist) were censored and prevented from publishing. Even the publisher of *Tu-Do,* Pham Viet Tuyen, and the editor, Kieu Van Lan, both Catholics, were arrested on September 4 by orders of the military governor of Saigon, and their paper was closed down.[42]

These were isolated acts, as we said, and we could mention more. But the Buddhists were not insensible to them, and this contributed toward bettering the relations between Catholics and Buddhists, or at least toward preventing the Buddhists, in their argument with the "Catholic" government, from being able to think that the Catholics were more on the side of the government than on their own. For example, for the communiqué of the Catholic Action group on August 26 (quoted above), the Vietnamese Buddhist Students' Association sent a letter of thanks in which, after having expressed gratitude for the defense of religious freedom taken up by the young people and the members of Catholic Action, we read:

Our efforts are not directed towards creating a division between Christians and Buddhists. . . . The spirit of the encyclical of the late Pope John XXIII, like the message of the new Pope Paul VI[43] were both greeted with enthusiasm in all of the Buddhist circles, which found them in agreement with Buddhist doctrine and the aspirations of humanity. We hope to see the bonds of charity and harmony become increasingly close between our two religions.[44]

Thus, when Fr. Cao Van Luan was reinstated in his position as rector of the university of Hué in November, after Diem's fall, a thousand Buddhists went to receive him at the airport in acclamation. When he came into the city, he was fêted by Catholics, Buddhists and Confucianists.

The "settling of accounts" with the Catholics. With Diem's fall, the Church ultimately derived great benefits, as we shall see in the next chapter. But in the first months, indeed, in the first year after the assassination of the Catholic president, the Church spent some difficult moments. From one day to the next the Catholics went from being "privileged" citizens to being calumniated and oppressed. The national press, directed now by Diem's adversaries, who came out of hiding or from prison, raised a violent campaign against them, claiming that they were responsible for all the misdeeds of the previous regime.

The Buddhist leaders, it must be said to their honor, behaved almost everywhere with great moderation and good sense, stating frequently that the fight was not with the Church and the Catholics but only with the Diem regime, and they invited the Buddhists to collaborate with the Catholics for the good of the country.

The reaction to the death of the dictator, however, produced a "settling of accounts" with the Catholics, especially in the north and central regions of South Vietnam, which raised the fear for some time of the unleashing of a real "organized persecution." Actually, there was no question of this but only of an instinctive reaction towards the Catholics who had supported the Diem regime, especially in the Hué region, where the archbishop was the president's brother, and in Danang, where there were more mass conversions than anywhere else.

The bulletin of the Diocese of Hué reports many cases of harassment of Catholics. We cite only a few as an example:

At Vinh-An and Trach-Pho, the crowd maltreated members of the parish council, smashed statues in the churches, enjoined the faithful to no longer practise (their religion). . . . At Mai-Xa, another parish of Hué, fifteen Catholics were illegally arrested . . . the houses of the faithful were searched, and anti-Catholic demonstrations organized. . . . At Gio-Linh, without government authorization, the church and the convent were searched. The parishioners, in a panic, no longer dared go to the church. . . . At Dong-Ha, there was a campaign of slander: the Christians were accused of having fomented anti-Buddhist plots, prepared trenches to "bury the bonzes alive," hidden arms in the churches, poisoned the wells. . . .

Facts of this kind were reported by *Fides* up to almost the end of 1964,[45] and in Saigon, the *Song-Dao* had a half-page weekly column for recording the acts of anti-Catholic "persecution." But, generally, in the Catholic newspapers of Vietnam little was said about these harassments of the faithful, priests and religious buildings, either so as not to alarm the Catholic people or to put no obstacles in the way of religious and civil peace, which was sincerely wished by the governments succeeding Diem and the Buddhist leaders as well as by the leaders of the Catholics and the other religions.

At the beginning of January, 1964, *Fides* wrote:

People speak of persecutions of Christians. The word seems too strong; yet one should not minimize certain verified incidents here and there, such as threats that in certain cases even resulted in apostasy and at times also the sacking of churches. It would be wrong however to dramatize matters and maintain that this is a kind of Buddhist vendetta. They have admitted to having elements in their ranks who have been corrupted by Communist propaganda, which seems at present to have free rein. Strange rumors are bruited about, analogous to those of a not too distant past: poisoned wells, harmful medicines distributed by Catholic health stations, bonzes or Buddhists buried alive by the Christians, etc. All this is known to the new government and it is making an effort to react fairly, since it does not want nor would it tolerate a religious war which would diminish the moral potential of the nation towards the Communist peril. The same thing is happening with the denunciations that abound against those who had, or were presumed to have had, links with the previous regime. Communist tactics are always the same: under the pretext of a purge they eliminate everyone who would be useful under the present circumstances.[46]

One very serious episode was the condemnation of the Catholic commander, Dang-Sy, against whom there was leveled a dishonorable press campaign. Dang-Sy was the commander of one of the groups of police who clashed with the Hué Buddhists on May 8, 1963. After his arrest, they sought with every means to make him "confess" that the Archbishop of Hué, Mgr. Thuc, the brother of President Diem, had personally ordered the police to fire on the Buddhists. They wanted in this way to accuse the Church directly of having oppressed the Buddhists, and the press, even before the trial, took it for granted that Mgr. Thuc had ordered the shooting and the oppression of the Buddhists of Hué. If this ploy had succeeded and if it had been swallowed by the Vietnamese and foreign public opinion, the Catholics and the Church itself would really have gone through a difficult time! At the trial no one could prove the accusations, and Dang-Sy made no "confession" but was still condemned to forced labor for life by an unjust sentence which was criticized by many non-Catholics as well.

The Catholics rose up with protest demonstrations because the trial also had an anti-Catholic tenor. In fact, instead of arresting and

trying all who had been implicated in the Hué affair, almost all
of whom were Buddhists, only the Catholic commander was tried,
and the others still lived in freedom. At the end of May 1964, the
Archbishop of Saigon, Mgr. Binh, addressed a letter to generals
Minh and Khanh, head of state and head of the government re-
spectively, in which in the name of the episcopal conference (of
which he was the elected president) he protested against the injustices of which the Catholics were victims after the coup d'etat of
November 1, 1963.[47] After having stated that he had remained silent
up to that time in order not to aggravate the difficult position of
the government and not to harm the national spirit of unity, the
bishop said that to continue to keep silent at the present moment
would be to fail seriously in his duty to the nation. He continued:

A good number of Catholic functionaries and military men have been
victims of completely unjustified measures. Many are imprisoned for
the sole reason that they are Catholics. . . . To make a revolution means
to put an end to what is bad in order to build a better future and a
better present. Therefore the Revolution ought not to be built on
prejudices against individuals or communities. . . .

It is inadmissible that the government dare sacrifice us, we who
are the most recalcitrant anti-Communists! We think that to condemn
Dang-Sy is to condemn indirectly all Catholics en bloc. Before November 1, 1963, we had clearly made it known to the authorities what our
position was, and we do the same today. If we raise our voice it is only
with the intention of saving the fatherland and of working for its
reconstruction.[48]

The "settling of accounts" came to an end towards the end of
1964, either because the remembrance of the Diem regime was
blotted out by the bad example given by the subsequent governments, or because at a certain point, despite the bishops' repeated
requests to calm the situation and to forgive the wrongs suffered
in the regions that were most troubled, the Catholics began to
organize themselves into autonomous groups for self-defense, which

no longer left Christians or small isolated communities at the mercy of ill-intentioned people. When the Christians began to defend themselves independently and to retaliate blow for blow against their provokers, the serious threat of a "war of religion" drove the religious leaders to agree to form unitary organizations.

At Saigon and in many of the provinces [*Fides* reports, September 26, 1964] committees were formed to avoid misunderstandings and the exploitation of the religious war by the fomenters of disorder. These committees were composed of Catholics and Buddhists, including priests and bonzes as well. This is an excellent thing, especially since they have issued joint communiqués. Even the Caodaists and the Hoa-Hao have asked to belong to these committees in order better to assert that at this critical moment all religions ought to unite as a sign of the love preached by their ethic.

It was at this time that there was a concrete beginning to a dialogue between the religions in Vietnam, which had already been begun by restricted groups in the preceding period. As we shall see more clearly in the following chapters, this constitutes today one of the best hopes for the future and for peace in Vietnam.

Notes

1. L. Cadière, *Croyances et pratiques religieuses des Vietnamiens,* vol. I (Saigon: Publications de la Société des Études indochinoises, 1958), p. 1.

2. Mai-Tho-Truyen, "Le Bouddhisme au Vietnam," *Présence du Bouddhisme,* the only issue of the review *France-Asie,* Saigon, 1959, pp. 808–809.

3. On Confucianism, which up to the last century had been the principal religion of the imperial courts and the intellectual and mandarin elite, see Nguyen Van Phong, *"La diffusion du confucianisme au Vietnam," France-Asie,* no. 188, Paris, 1966–1967, pp. 179–196. With the rebirth of Buddhism in the last fifty years and the decadence of the imperial courts, Confucianism, a religion that was not organized as a Church but only into a few associations, lost much of its importance.

4. Fr. Louvet, of the Paris foreign missions, wrote in the last century, *La Cochinchine religieuse,* vol. I (Paris: Leroux, 1885), pp. 144–145 and 181:

"The Annamese have a temperament that is quite unmystical and little given to speculations of a supernatural order. They are quite different in this respect from the Indians or the peoples of Central Asia, and they in some way concentrate their preoccupations on the present life, having very little interest about what will happen to them after death. . . . By nature they are not at all fanatical, and they would have no propensity to persecute the Christian religion if the latter, as Buddhism did, could adapt itself to the rites of the country and the local superstitions." And after having given an account of the various local religions, he writes: "All these religions and superstitious practices are intertwined and superimposed on one another; they form an amalgam of contradictory formulas from which it is impossible to become extricated. Everyone observes all of them not out of conviction but because it is the custom and because each person wants to do what everyone else does."

5. Thich Nhat Hanh, *op. cit.,* p. 68. It is untrue therefore to write, as is still often done today, that under the colonial regime the Catholic religion had "positions of privilege" in Vietnam, or that it was aided in a special way by the colonial power. The contrary, rather, is true. As in Africa with Islam, the colonial authorities in Vietnam favored and financed Buddhism, naturally, for political motives. The only thing they assured the Church was the great boon of religious freedom and the only financial help they gave it was for social institutions that benefited the entire people (schools, hospitals, leprosaria, etc.), while with Buddhism they also aided cultural and religious institutions. However, it must be added that while Catholicism enjoyed unrestricted freedom—insofar as there was no reason at the time to suspect that the Church, led by French bishops and priests, would be against the colonial domination—Buddhism was supported in its cultural and religious activities but was also strictly controlled in order that it would not become a support and a center for anticolonial activities.

6. Cadière, *op. cit.,* p. 31.

7. On the secret sects and societies of Vietnam, see G. Coulet, *Les Societés secrètes en terre d'Annam,* Saigon, 1926; A. M. Savani, *Visages et images du Sud Vietnam* (Saigon: Imprimerie d'Outre-Mer, 1955), chap. IV; *Des féodalités . . . et autres groupements armés,* pp. 69–105; A. Bareau, *Les sectes bouddhiques du petit véhicule* (Saigon: Ecole française d'Extrême-Orient, 1955).

8. M. Dufeil, "Les sectes du Sud Viet-Nam," *La Vie intellectuelle,* Paris, December 1956, p. 68.

9. Dufeil, *art. cit.,* p. 67.

10. M. Dufeil, *art. cit.,* p. 72; Buttinger, vol. I, *op. cit.,* pp. 410–412. (The author, referring to the bloody struggle between the Viet Minh and the

Buddhist sects—especially the Hoa-Hao and the Cao Dai—asserts that this was one of the most horrible and scandalous chapters in the history of the anticolonial movement.)

11. M. Dufeil, *art. cit.,* p. 81.

12. For a fuller study, see P. Rondot, "Der Caodaismus," *Kairos,* no. 3, Salzburg, 1967, pp. 205–217.

13. Mai Tho Truyen, *Le Bouddhisme au Vietnam* (Saigon: Xa Loi Pagoda, 1962).

14. As in various other Buddhist countries—especially Burma which has important animistic minorities—in Vietnam after 1954 the Buddhists organized "missions to the pagans" on the Christian model, among the Montagnard tribes of the central plateaus, with charitable, scholastic and welfare institutions, etc.

15. *World Buddhism,* Colombo, January, 1963, p. 20.

16. *Ibid.,* September, 1962, p. 19.

17. *Ibid.,* April, 1963, p. 7.

18. *Ibid.,* May, 1963, p. 9 and June, 1963, p. 14 (the news of the inauguration of the pagoda with the participation of members of the government was published in the first article in which the persecution of the Buddhists by the Diem government was denounced . . .).

19. The documents of the conflict between the Buddhists and the government were published in Saigon in 1963 by the review *Documents* in several numbers and special fascicles in French and English. Other documents on the question, in loose pamphlet form, I found at the Xa Loi pagoda.

20. Following the signing of the agreement, the Ven. Thich Tinh Khiet, supreme leader of Vietnamese Buddhism, wrote a letter to Diem on June 26, 1963, in which he thanked the president for having paid attention to the wishes of the Buddhists and for "having approved the joint communiqué which public opinion had accepted as a satisfactory settlement of the problems that had arisen after Buddha's anniversary and which had been concluded in a spirit of liberty and fairness."

21. One fact of a religious nature that kept the crisis alive and gave the Buddhists courage was this: at the cremation of the bonze Thich Quang Duc, the first to burn himself, on June 11, the monk's heart was not burned by the flames—it is said—but remained intact in the midst of the fire. Placed in a silver urn and surmounted by a photograph of the bonze to whom it had belonged, the heart was exhibited at the Xa Loi pagoda and became the object of many pilgrimages and acts of veneration. From then on the bonze was considered to be the saint-protector of the demonstrations against the Diem government.

22. Mme Nhu said, for example, "They can't even be autonomous when

they burn themselves. They use American gasoline!"; or "If another bonze barbecues himself in the square, I shall be the first to clap my hands . . ." etc.

23. See the full and thorough report, an almost day by day account, made by J. Schechter *The New Face of Buddha: The Fusion of Religion and Politics in Contemporary Buddhism* (New York: Coward McCann, 1967), chaps. VIII to XI, and the chronicles already cited by Fr. P. O'Connor, correspondent of the NCWC News Service, published by the Hong Kong *Sunday Examiner* and reprinted in *Herder Korrespondenz* (*Rückschau auf die Erreignisse in Südvietnam*, Freiburg, December, 1963, pp. 115–122; February, 1964, pp. 235–244. For the Buddhist version of the facts, see the review *World Buddhism*, which we have already mentioned.

24. This was stated in an editorial by an eminent Catholic Italian journalist, but he was not the only one to write in this way. If we reread certain magazines and newspapers (Catholic ones as well) published in the summer of 1963, we get the impression that at that time there was mass slaughtering of the Buddhists. . . . Some of the Catholic press of the time, for fear of not appearing "far enough Left," committed itself to the systematic, unjust denigration of the Diem regime and the Vietnamese Catholic Church (did they not also write of the "persecution of the Buddhists by the Catholic faithful?"). With Diem's death, the denigration continued in regard to the Church and Vietnamese Catholics.

25. It is enough to say that the two largest Buddhist organizations of North Vietnam (North Vietnam Buddhist Association and the North Vietnam Sangha) have, and had even in Diem's time, settled in Saigon, after having fled from the North, (*World Buddhism*, January, 1963, p. 20).

26. On the suicide of the bonzes who burned themselves, the most varied moral judgments were intertwined, according to Buddhist tradition. Some asserted that this way of killing oneself was an ancient Buddhist custom (especially in the Chinese tradition) that had become extinct in the last centuries (see, for example, W. Rahula Thera, "Self Immolation, an Ancient Buddhist Custom," *World Buddhism*, December, 1963, pp. 6–7); Thich Nhat Hanh, in the volume we have cited several times, *Vietnam, pace proibita,* pp. 143–145, explains the bonzes' burning of themselves as a witness that they were giving to the sufferings of the Vietnamese people and as an action aimed at moving the oppressors and converting them: "To express one's own will by burning oneself does not mean committing an act of destruction," writes Nhat Hanh, "but to perform a constructive act, i.e., to suffer and die for one's people. This is not suicide. . . . The monk who burns himself . . . does not believe he is destroying himself; he believes that the sacrifice of

himself can be useful for the salvation of others. . . . I believe with all my heart that the monks who burned themselves were not aiming at the death of the oppressors but only at a change in their politics." On the other hand, there are others who decisively deny that this is a Buddhist tradition. The scholar, M. Percheron, author of valuable books on Asian religions, wrote in *La Croix,* June 14, 1963: "Buddhism is an attitude of wisdom which has at its base respect for the life and the opinions of others. . . . Nonviolence and the refusal to attempt the life of another are the cornerstone of the Buddhist spirit. . . . It is totally alien to Buddhism to have a public and spectacular suicide with the self-immolation in flames of a protesting bonze, since the respect for life extends also to one's own." We cannot disagree with this judgment when we think that with Buddhism the absolute respect for life is even stricter than that of the Christians (the Buddhists are vegetarians and, according to the rules, the bonzes drink only filtered river water in order not to swallow involuntarily midges or other living beings). How this total respect for every form of life can be morally in accord with the suicide of the bonzes is hard to explain. Some see in it an indication of the presence of Communists among the Vietnamese Buddhists, i.e., that their revolt against Diem was instigated and led by alien elements and not by Buddhists who were fighting for religious freedom. It is certain that in no other country of the Orient where the Buddhists had severe conflicts with the local government (e.g., in Burma and Ceylon), was a similar method of pressure like the bonzes' suicide ever used.

27. We have carefully gone through the collection of two international Buddhist magazines, *World Buddhism,* of Colombo and *Young East,* of Tokyo, and in the many accounts of Vietnamese Buddhism we never found the slightest reference against the government before June 1963. On the contrary, there were various acknowledgments of the development of Buddhism in South Vietnam, and also words of praise for the government (for example, in the article "Buddhist Revival in Vietnam," *World Buddhism,* November 1960, the author, a bonze, writes expressly: "I express my gratitude to the government of Vietnam for having given me every possibility for developing my Buddhist activities without any restriction; I was given assistance by the army and the police. With the encouragement of the government, for the first time in history *Vesak* was celebrated in perfect harmony between Mahayanists and Theravadists to an unprecedented extent in the most important cities. Today there is a great Buddhist renaissance in Vietnam . . ."

28. This is the estimate also of students of Buddhism who wrote before 1963. For example, M. Delahoutre, in his *Le Bouddha et son message* (Paris:

Fleurus, 1962), pp. 89–90, asserts that Buddhism in South Vietnam numbered about 2 million faithful. It would seem clear then that of the 15 million South Vietnamese, more than one million and a half were Catholics in 1963 (we shall see later that today they are about two million), one million Hoa-Hao, two million Cao-Dai, one and a half million animistic Montagnards. To these we must add the Confucianists, the Taoists, the Moslem and Protestant minorities and, finally, the great mass of those who practice only ancestor worship as a family religion, even if they sometimes go to the pagoda (just as it happens that many non-Christians enter Christian Churches to pray or participate in Christian religious processions and demonstrations: and this is not only in Vietnam).

29. The two authors are quoted in A. Rizza, *Buddhismo in risveglio* (Milan: P.I.M.E., 1964), pp. 106–107.

30. On the complex theoretico-practical connections between Buddhism and Communism, see E. Benz, *Buddhism or Communism: Which Holds the Future of Asia?* (London: Allen and Unwin, 1966); see also the book of Schechter already mentioned in the second chapter. In the Asian Buddhist magazines we read disconcerting articles and contradictory positions taken in regard to Communism. For example, in the Japanese Buddhist quarterly, the principal magazine of Japanese Buddhism, *Young East,* no. 56, Tokyo, 1965, pp. 18–24, in an article entitled "World Coexistence of Buddhism and Communism," there is the desire to show that the oppression in Asia comes from Christianity and white people, while salvation comes from Buddhism united with Communism since both complement one another and have the same aspirations and the same goals: "Between Buddhism and Communism, there is more that unites than divides," we read. "It is very doubtful that Communism has infiltrated into Buddhism in Vietnam, since Buddhism and Communism are everywhere united for the common cause." In Vietnam, where the Buddhist leaders always forcefully denied any Communist infiltration, we believe that an article such as this would certainly not be approved. (Tri Quang asserted in his rare interviews and articles that there were no Communists in Vietnamese Buddhism. See, for example, the interview given to *Life-International,* May 2, 1966, p. 20 ff., in which Tri Quang responded to the question whether Vietnamese Buddhism had been infiltrated by Communists: "This is a pure lie, and we give no weight to it.")

31. In North Vietnam Buddhism gave not the least resistance to Communism and to its own elimination by a dictatorial regime: either they lacked a preparation of the faithful for the defense of religion and for resistance against materialism, or else a national organization which coordinated the action of the faithful and of the various groups or pagodas.

The Catholics in the North are still alive and organized, notwithstanding the many years of persecution and pressure of every type, while it seems that Buddhism has been completely extinguished, at least as an external cult and as an organized religious life.

32. One bishop of Vietnam—although I had heard this from others as well—told me that he discovered among his young members of the Legion of Mary or Catholic Action or catechists some Communists that had come from the North and were deliberately prepared for this task of infiltration and subversion from inside the Catholic community. The bishop succeeded in gaining the confidence of some of them after promising not to denounce them to the police. From evidence gathered from various dioceses, it was discovered that near Hanoi there was a school for the training of young men and girls coming to the South who were to pass for Catholics and penetrate the Christian communities, where they were to spread rumors and suspicions, keep an eye on certain clergymen and bishops, etc. These young people learned catechism, the liturgical ceremonies, the organization of the Church, and lived for some periods of time as exemplary Catholics, etc.

33. This was the position at Diem's time, since afterwards, as we shall see, the greater part of the Vietnamese Buddhist organizations took rather clear positions against Communism, particularly after the intensification of the guerrilla war in the South, and the real threat of a Communist dictatorship.

34. Quoted in *Études*, Paris, October 1963, p. 65. An authoritative exponent of the Inter-sect Committee, Thich Duc Ngiep, declared on August 25: "We have no problem with the Catholics: the conflict is only between the government and the Buddhists," and other Buddhist personalities expressed the same thought at different times: see *Sunday Examiner*, Hong Kong, August 30, 1963, p. 1.

35. Text in *Fides*, June 29, 1963, pp. 429–430; and in *La Documentation catholique*, coll. 1093–1096, 1963.

36. Text in *Fides*, September 4, 1963, pp. 521–522; and in *La Documentation catholique*, coll. 1135–1140, 1963.

37. Original text, in French in *La Documentation catholique*, coll. 1375–1377, 1963.

38. Text in *Sunday Examiner*, Hong Kong, September 13, 1963, p. 7.

39. Declaration published in *L'Osservatore Romano*, September 26, 1963, p. 2.

40. We must remember that if the Buddhist leaders in Vietnam generally held a moderate attitude and never openly stated that they were suffering religious persecution, other Buddhist representatives living abroad made dramatic statements to the press—reproduced in the newspapers with ample

space—as if there were under way in Vietnam a preordained plan for the extermination of Buddhism.

41. The most active and convinced representative of the mentality common among Catholics, i.e., the defense of the government and the accusation of the Buddhists for having allowed themselves to be politically exploited by the enemies of the Diem regime, was the Archbishop of Hué, Mgr. Ngo Dinh Thuc, brother of President Ngo Dinh Diem. He made a few statements over the Vietnamese radio, granted interviews to foreign newspapers and also made a few trips to Europe and America in order to clarify the situation from the government point of view. According to *Informations catholiques internationales,* October 1, 1963, p. 42, this activism of his displeased the Vatican at a moment in which the Church was seeking to show the world and the Vietnamese Buddhists that it was not involved in the excesses of the Saigon government in the repressions of the Buddhist demonstrations.

42. *Tu-Do* is the most representative newspaper among these Catholics in Vietnam and perhaps the most prestigious daily in the country. Founded in 1954 by a group of Catholic intellectuals who had fled from North Vietnam during the Diem period, it had a clearly anti-Communistic tone, but it was also able to keep itself independent from the government by criticizing its corruption and dictatorial methods.

43. During the Vietnamese crisis, Paul VI made three pronouncements: the first in a discourse to Vietnamese students on August 3, *Osservatore Romano,* August 4; the second in a "message to the Vietnamese people" on August 30, *Osservatore Romano,* August 31; and the third in a letter to the Archbishop of Saigon, about whom the Vatican newspaper had spoken in the September 20 issue (the letter bore the date August 20: the full text is in *La Documentation catholique,* col. 1375 1963). Let us point out that the message of August 30 was censored by the Saigon government and was not permitted to be published in its entirety; in this document the pope expressed his "painful worry about the hardships afflicting the dear people of Vietnam. The anguish becomes day by day more deep and excruciating . . ."; and he was looking forward to the time when "all, in a generous collaboration and in mutual respect of legitimate freedoms, would agree on reestablishing reciprocal concord and fraternity." According to *Informations catholiques internationales,* September 1, 1963, Paul VI intervened at the beginning of August, by diplomatic means, with the Saigon authorities, inviting them to use moderation. The bonze Thich Tinh Nhiet, supreme head of the Buddhist Association thanked Paul VI "for his intervention in favor of a just solution of the Buddhist problem."

After Diem's fall, the Inter-sect Committee for the Defense of Buddhism, which was the most warlike organization against Diem, addressed this telegram to Paul VI: "Vietnamese Buddhism, freed by means of the revolution from an oppression unprecedented in national history, begs you to accept its gratitude for your exalted intervention in favor of its fight. We hope that your noble gesture will be understood by our Catholic brethren here, whom we assure of our religious good-feeling" (quoted in *Informations catholiques internationales*, December 1, 1963, p. 23).

45. See *Fides,* December 4, 1963, pp. 733–734; 1964, pp. 46, 73, 221, 465, 481, 517. At Saigon, seven Catholics were killed in August, 1964; at Danang there were assaults on the Catholic refugee camps and on churches which ended up with some deaths and wounded; elsewhere there were burnings of churches, beatings, unjust trials, etc. But these were almost everywhere isolated and sporadic episodes, and not a preordained plan or a general outburst of anti-Catholic fury.

46. *Fides,* January 22, 1964, p. 47.

47. *Informations catholiques internationales,* June 15, 1964, p. 7.

48. If Diem's fall was positive from the point of view of having freed the country from a family dictatorship that had lasted for too long a time, it also had completely negative effects on the military and psychological levels of resistance against Communism. Lacouture writes, *Le Vietnam entre deux paix* (Paris: Ed. du Seuil, 1965), pp. 170–171: "Of all the coups d'etat, that of November 1, 1963, was of great service to the NLF especially. Of course, the majority of the generals were more bound to and faithful to the Americans than the Ngo were [i.e., Diem's family]. But the banner of anti-Communism was associated in the consciousness of the people with Diem's person, and the elimination of the dictator had lowered that banner." The clear worsening of the military situation that began immediately after the killing of Diem was attributed, in addition to the general decadence of the state, to the purge of many Catholic commandments and to the discouragement that affected even the "nonpurged" Catholic military in seeing themselves the object of suspicions and defamatory accusations.

VI

The Church of Vietnam
and the Council

The fall of the Diem regime had many positive effects for Catholics, since it produced a renewal of a more genuine religious spirit, freeing the Church from a political guardianship that was quite at odds with its apostolic goals. In addition to the Church's disinvolvement in politics, there was a notable religious renewal inspired by the Council.

For a more adult and mature faith. The basic characteristic of the religious renewal in the last years has been a deepening of the faith, which has become more personal. Although the biblical movement went back some fifteen years, it was only recently that it gained impetus and became widespread, with the foundation of study centers, the translation of the Bible[1] (the printing of carefully produced editions and pamphlets for wide distribution), and the multiplication of scriptural study groups. Even the texts of Vatican II had several translations and a good distribution. A widespread movement of religious education accompanied this return to the Gospel, in humility and charity, through the courses of religious instruction for the Catholics. Mgr. Nguyen Kim Dien, Archbishop of Hué, expressed to me the bishops' concern to give Catholics an adult and mature faith, in order to avoid their present faith, a very simple one, from being endangered by modern ideas and new situations. Even in Vietnam these new factors were beginning to make themselves felt, especially since the war had overturned all the old traditions and had brought them in contact with modern hedonism and materialism, which the Americans had spread on a vast scale.

Among the conciliar decrees that were applied more quickly in Vietnam was the one on the liturgy, through the translation of the mass, the ritual and the other liturgical texts into Vietnamese. An important date is October 20, 1964, when the pope granted the request of the bishops of Vietnam and allowed them to apply in their country the instruction *Plane compertum est* (December 8, 1939) on the question of the "Chinese rites" and ancestor worship. In the pastoral letter, published on June 14, 1965, the bishops made known the Holy See's permission and explained the way the pontifical decree was to be applied to the faithful.

First of all, recalling the Council and the pontifical texts, the bishops said that the Church does not reject any popular tradition or any culture, just as it seeks dialogue with other religions and wants its faithful to preserve their national values and their history. In Vietnam, many gestures and actions that once had a religious or superstitious significance were now nothing other than acts of courtesy or ways of expressing one's veneration of the great men of the past. Not only does the Church not reject them, but it also desires that its faithful take part in them in accordance with the local traditions.

Thus the gestures [the bishops' letter says] the attitudes and the rites that of themselves or by reason of circumstance clearly have a secular meaning: demonstrations of patriotism, filial piety, veneration or remembrance of ancestors and heroes by displaying a photograph or a picture, erecting a statue, bowing out of respect, placing flowers and candles, organizing anniversary celebrations . . . can be done or can be actively participated in.

Then the bishops recall the duty to protect the integrity of the faith:

Therefore, the faithful do not have the right to officiate at or participate in anything that has a religious character incompatible with Catholic doctrine, for example, any ceremony that shows submission or dependence in regard to a creature as if it were God, or in clearly superstitious acts (like burning votive cards),[2] or, finally, in actions that take place in those areas reserved for sacrifices. In the case where (a Catholic's) presence is unavoidable, only a passive attitude is allowed.[3]

For those acts that do not have a very specific nature, i.e., it is not known whether they are truly religious or superstitious, or which are done out of courtesy or patriotism, the Catholic can decide in the individual case, in the context of the frame of mind of the particular people involved and with the explanation, if necessary, of the fact that the Catholic's participation in certain ceremonies is nonreligious.

More radical attempts at adapting the liturgy to the Vietnamese culture were made with the authorization of the ordinaries in various dioceses and in some Benedictine monasteries, particularly at Thien An, which was very advanced in this area. Some attempts have aroused arguments or criticism on account of the still too conservative mentality of the Christian community and of a great part of the clergy; on the other hand, others were well received, especially those regarding the introduction of local music into the sacred functions and of the temple architecture into the building of churches (we have seen excellent churches built in Vietnamese style), of painting in the style of the country,[4] etc. In a word, the most superficial adaptations (language, art, music) were well received, while there was hesitation about introducing more profound adaptations. And this, moreover, is not only a problem with the Vietnamese Church but reflects the lack of theological preparation in all the "young Churches."

Scant theological maturity. Even though it is still largely incomplete, the religious renewal of the Vietnamese Church presents other interesting aspects. On the catechetical level, we would like to point out a new catechism that has the great virtue of being autonomous from the Western catechisms (the first ones used were mere translations) and it has given up the terminology derived from Latin (or French and Spanish) which made the language of the Christian community quite different from that common to the Vietnamese, and therefore difficult to understand for the non-Christians and the neophytes.

We shall now say something about the still scanty progress made in the area of theology in the Vietnamese Church, the lack of commitment to an autonomous theological research that would answer local needs in accordance with the Council Decree *Ad Gentes* (no. 22). The opening of the first theological faculty in the national pontifical seminary of Dalat on March 7, 1966, has still not produced results of theological inquiry and renewal, and furthermore, in so short a time since its opening and considering the present situation, it would be unrealistic to expect immediate results. The faculty is headed by an Italian Jesuit, Fr. Raviolo, from Piedmont, with a staff of Jesuit teachers (of eight different nationalities) and of priests from the Vietnamese clergy, all highly qualified. It has in these few years one of the best equipped theological libraries in the whole Orient, and there is good hope that it will be able to arouse in the local Church that stimulus of theological renewal it so sorely needs. Even in the case of moral theology, the books in use at present by the clergy are simple "casus conscientiae," imitating Western models.

Other religious orders in which Vietnamese members are in an absolute majority are collaborating in theological and pastoral research: we might mention the Redemptorists, Dominicans, Benedictines, the Brothers of the Christian Schools (with their magnificent Institut Taberd in Saigon), and of course the priests of the Missions Etrangères de Paris, who now specialize in the apostolate to the Chinese and the Montagnards, after having given the Vietnamese Church so many institutions and an unequalled evangelization.[5] Even in the West, the work of Fr. Dournes in adapting the Christian message for the Montagnards[6] is well-known, but other studies and works of lesser international renown have been tried by the MEP Fathers.

For the Vietnamese clergy the monthly *Sacerdos* is published, and it is the only solid theological and pastoral review edited by Vietnamese priests in Saigon. Everything leads one to believe that theological evolution will be slow, which, as time passes, can be an unpardonable error. The bishops' participation in the Council has done them a great deal of good; they are all quite advanced theologically, but their flock is far behind, and there is only a minority of priests and laymen who are open to conciliar innovations.

The ardent faith of a pre-conciliar Christianity. From the point of view of faith and Christian practice, Vietnamese Christianity is certainly exemplary. "Here everyone has the spirit of martyrdom," one bishop told me; "they would be ready to be killed for the faith without blinking an eye." And it must be said that he was not exaggerating: the Vietnamese Christians feel themselves to be descendents of the 300,000 martyrs killed in the persecutions of past centuries; the veneration of the martyrs, the pride of sensing one is a living part of a community that has suffered and continues to suffer for the faith, gives the Christians an extraordinary enthusiasm for the faith that with us today would be unthinkable. The unfortunate thing about this is that they live somewhat too much in the memory and veneration of the past, however glorious it was, without becoming fully part of the contemporary situation with a spirit that is adequate for the times.

A few facts may give a vivid idea of this religious fervor.[7] Attendance at mass is impressive: I have seen in various city parishes great numbers of people attending the evening masses, with hundreds of communions (I am speaking of weekdays, of course). And then the poised concentration of the faithful, mostly young people, who follow the liturgical ceremonies without distraction, without chattering, without trooping to the back of the church.

The faithful still go to mass almost every day, say common prayers at home, take the sacraments with a frequency that among us is reserved only to a very small number, and they have a veneration for the clergy which sometimes borders on servility. Here is how Fr. Gian, rector of the Vietnamese Mission in Paris, describes the life of community piety of these Christians:

Like all Orientals, the Vietnamese Catholics possess a deep religious spirit, demonstrated practically by an acute sense of the sacred. Another characteristic of their piety is traditionalism. Having grown up in Confucianism, the Vietnamese has a natural reverence for the past and for his ancestors. Our Christians, however, are heirs of a particularly glorious and relatively recent past, whose memory is kept very much alive. A great number of families recall with pride their ancestors who gave witness to Christ with their blood. There is great respect for ancient customs, and traditional morality has an important role. . . .

Another aspect of Vietnamese Catholicism is its community character. The Vietnamese are very attached to their village, and their life is only a participation in the collective life of the village. The religious life of the Christians thus becomes a community life based on the Christian group.[8] Consequently their piety is vested in public and spectacular demonstrations: village festivals, neighborhood and family feasts furnish many opportunities to meet around the altar in the house of the leader for common prayers, followed by the drinking of tea. Funerals and religious processions always provide much opportunity for collective prayers, recited along the way.

The religious life of the family shows similar aspects. Walking through a Catholic village between nine and ten o'clock at night, one can hear coming from every house the solemn, if somewhat monotonous, chant of evening prayers. . . . At five in the morning one can hear the lively peal of the Angelus. It is the official signal to rise. Immediately, every Catholic family recites morning prayers in a loud voice for at least a quarter-hour. Then some members of the family, if possible, go to church for mass.[9]

A missionary, Fr. Cussac of the Paris foreign missions, adds a few touches to the picture painted by Fr. Gian:

In the city, the parish communities naturally have a somewhat different aspect, but they are no less alive. Everywhere, in cities or country areas, morning mass brings together a great crowd of people every day. On Sundays and Holy Days the churches are literally crammed and when there is some extraordinary happening, such as a procession of the Blessed Sacrament or the Virgin Mary, the crowd of non-Christians that respectfully joins up with the Christians gives the impression that one is in a Christian country. . . . One of the traits that characterize the Vietnamese Catholics, and by no means the least interesting, is the pride they show in being Christian. They are easily recognized everywhere by the emblems they wear visibly: crosses, medals, rosaries, scapulars. If their small number and the persecutions and calumnies to which they were so long subjected has often obliged them to keep somewhat withdrawn into themselves, this was never the result of a kind of inferiority complex. They understood the value of the faith they received and are proud of this faith for which their ancestors had suffered and died and for which they themselves are ready to suffer.[10]

These two descriptions explain, more than anything else, what a serious thing Christianity is for Vietnamese Catholics, an extremely serious thing that is a truly integral part of their daily life, influencing all their actions, thoughts, behavior and conversations. Thus, for example, the increase in priestly and religious vocations in an exorbitant number, considering the capacity of the seminaries and novitiates.

But unfortunately the Vietnamese Catholic community, despite the beginning of a post-conciliar renewal, is still a community of an old and preconciliar type. We note a marked clericalism, the decisive importance of the priest in solving any sort of a problem, the fear of new ideas coming to disturb the peaceful grasp of the faith (the French progressivist Catholic press is condemned absolutely, and also because of its position on the war in Vietnam), the inability to distinguish between the spiritual and the temporal, the spirit of the ghetto and of intransigence, the closed mind towards other religions, a triumphalist spirit which they are still far from abandoning, etc.

The failure of the Vietnamese Church to evolve is attributed above all to the permanent threat of Communism, which gives the Catholics a defensive spirit and closes them off from many of the new conciliar proposals. But there are other facts and psychological conditioning that we must mention. For example, for someone coming from Europe, the Christian community at first sight seems "triumphalistic": processions, public demonstrations, country people with medals and crucifixes around their necks, houses of Catholics with a cross on the roof or in front, a marian devotion that seems to be the basis of this Christianity, etc. But for the Vietnamese, is this a question of "triumphalism" or is it rather his own way of living Christianity differently from the way we do?

You are a curious person [said an old missionary to me while we were talking of these matters]. First you say that in Vietnam the Christians ought to live Christianity in accordance with the local culture and mentality and not after a European model; and then you call triumphalism everything that is a really local expression of Christian life, and you would like to impose on us all at once a conciliar revision that is not sufficiently mature here and would therefore not be authentic but merely an imitation of what you are doing in the West.

Actually, it is extremely difficult to make a judgment about situations such as these in a country you visit for a few months! Undoubtedly on one side there is the Asian psychology that looks for the spectacular, the institutionalized and the external façade. Therefore, Vietnamese Christianity is perfectly adapted to this aspect of the local culture (indeed, the Vietnamese Buddhists are undoubtedly more "triumphalist" than the Catholics, with their noisy processions, their banners and ensigns and hand-bells, their open involvement in politics, etc.). On the other hand, however, one wonders how long this Asian psychology will be able to perdure if it is not already on the brink of being destroyed by the current of modern ideas. Therefore, would Christianity not do well to anticipate what may happen (at least since the Council has clearly indicated certain routes)?

The local appraisal of "triumphalism." The same thing may be said for another and somewhat irritating aspect of the Vietnamese Christian community: the ostentation of force, power, riches and organization. The Church has to appear to the outsider as an organized, rich and powerful bloc; humility is cultivated as a personal but not a group virtue.

After having praised the formidable Catholic organization, the "real secret" that makes the Christian minority of 13 percent as important as if it were a majority, a Vietnamese Catholic observer writes:

Power and organization, this is the face given by the Church at first sight to non-Christians. . . . The Church is admired for its organization and feared as a power. The majority of Catholics are poor, but the Church appears "rich," and it is thought that it has immense financial means at its disposal. Whether this has any foundation or not, the opinion originated from the Church's appearance of richness which it inherited from the colonial period, is everywhere seen, and which clashes with the surrounding poverty. In the rural areas, it is not rare that the only brick buildings in a village would be the church and the priest's house. Through a strange paradox, the convents in which religious men and women practise asceticism all look like the houses of the rich.[11]

On the "triumphalism" of the Vietnamese Church, a friend who is very open to the importance of the Council sent me from Vietnam, this clear historico-psychological explanation:

Up to today, it is true that the Church of Vietnam, in view of the situation of persecution it had long known, gave priority to a show of power and also to triumphalism, whenever it seemed possible. Such a state of affairs, I might add, is in conformity with the Asian outlook, and it is for this reason that we should not wonder that it is so. The rise to power of a Catholic (Ngo Dinh Diem) merely strengthened this notion of a Christianity that had been victorious over paganism, which was too easily likened in the popular mind to Satan himself.

In fact, the magnificent churches, the monuments, the colleges that were built, the grandiose processions and demonstrations that took place, especially during the Diem period, on the whole did not scandalize local public opinion, even if at times they gave rise to jealousy, especially among the Buddhists, who had less means and a lesser sense of organization. To show the Church's strength and power was also for some people a kind of motive of credibility, capable of attracting the non-Christian masses who are traditionally sensitive to such matters.

We can be quite happy today that triumphalism has become less visible. In the Vietnamese episcopate, in particular, the influence of the council has made itself felt. This is undeniable. The bishops have often put aside their episcopal insignia outside of religious ceremonies, go about in modest automobiles, and are often among the people in all simplicity and modesty. But the clergy and religious have been less marked by the council spirit (although I know many who live in absolute poverty with an admirable spirit of sacrifice).

Triumphalism derives from the concept of "face" (to save face, lose face, face someone straight on, etc.). These notions are rooted in the Confucian culture of the past and are deeply felt by the people. Perhaps, during the period of priestly formation, there was not enough insistence on getting rid of these ideas as opposed to the spirit of Christ. On the contrary, at times great spectacles were advocated and given an essential place in the life of the Church. There is a need to "return to the sources" and especially to the Gospel, the Acts of the Apostles, the Epistles, and Revelation, with its message to the seven Churches. Only then will we succeed in gradually extirpating something that is deeply rooted in local tradition.

On the other hand, we must say that since the Asian does not have the same logic as the Westerner, he rarely distinguishes what is accessory from what is substantial. For him, everything is often put on the same level, and at times the accessory prevails over the essential, since the accidental frequently contains a brilliant side that is pleasant and alluring. . . . From this we can understand that a whole revolution has to be brought about in people's spirits, and this will not happen between today and tomorrow. . . . Even Buddha sought to separate the spiritual from the ritual and to furnish his followers with the bases of an interior life with the aim of bettering man and society. But today there are few bonzes or Buddhist faithful who see the doctrine of the "Enlightened One" in this aspect and strive to live it. Even among them priority is given to the rites, ceremonies, practices, devotions, demonstrations, external display . . . contrary to the teaching of the Master.

Is the Vietnamese Church really rich? However, if we inquire into the "riches" of the Church, we see, as happens at times even with us, that the rumors do not correspond with the facts. It is true that the Church has the appearance of being rich—and this is both harmful and a lack of evangelical poverty—with its brick churches in the main squares of the cities and villages, its modern and spacious seminaries and religious houses, its organized clergy, its flourishing charitable and scholastic institutions, etc. But more than "riches," this is service, a well-done, well-organized, efficient and up-to-date service (even the church and the seminary are a service, not to speak of schools and hospitals). In a poor and even neglected country, the Church has adopted Western methods of organization and efficiency: even the tiny Catholic clinic I visited in the hills near Kontum, made out of wood, newly painted and spotless, looked like a rich man's house![12]

In Vietnam one hears it said that the Church is rich in rice lands —the chief source of riches in the country—and that these riches come especially from fields acquired during the colonial regime. According to an investigation made by Fr. O'Connor,[13] the colonial government did give the missionaries much land in the Mekong delta when this region was unpopulated, but it was salted from sea

water and was given to the missionaries so they would make it
farmable and then set up colonies of farmers. This did happen, but
people continue to believe erroneously that all these lands belong
to the Church. Father O'Connor goes on to say that the missionaries
were accused either of neglecting these tasks (when they were not
involved in an enterprise of this nature) or, again, accused of
exploitation when they were.

According to the same inquiry, the rice lands registered today as
belonging to the Catholic Church are only 5,579 hectares in all of
South Vietnam: Even if we add another 10 or 20 percent for those
rice fields that are not registered under the name of the Church but
under the name of individual priests or bishops, the fact still
remains that such properties constitute less than one percent of all
the rice fields in South Vietnam! With facts and authoritative
citations, Fr. O'Connor disproves that Diem ever gave one hectare
of land to the Church, although he gave unfarmed public soil for
the villages of the refugees (most of whom were Catholic) or for
social institutions that benefited all the people (schools, hospitals,
etc.). He did this for the Buddhists and other religious organizations as well.

The temptation of money is strong today in Vietnam, with the
flood of American dollars and the various possibilities of earning
great sums with little effort. I found bishops and priests most
sensitive to this danger (I remember especially the example of the
Archbishop of Hué, Mgr. Nguyen-Kim-Dien, of the Congregation
of the Little Brothers of Jesus of Charles de Foucauld,[14] who perfectly exuded the spirit of his master in order to make people
understand the Christian notions of poverty, humility and self-
abnegation). The worst aspect of the war, according to many, was
not in what was happening militarily but in the moral order,
especially in the cities which were most infected by the plague of
corruption, from many points of view. In Saigon and in other
cities, the war has become the chief occupation of a great number
of Vietnamese: soldiers in the war supporting families, workers
in the service of the Americans or the government (financed by

the Americans), profiteers, loan sharks, prostitutes, owners who lease property to the Americans. Then there are dealings in surplus goods from the army warehouses, dealings in permits and licences of various kinds, the black market in automobiles and other goods whose importation is highly taxed. It is superfluous to recall the various aspects of corruption in a country at war, whose economy is artificially sustained by American aid and by the half-million Americans who can spend money foolishly (for this country).

Saigon is a motorized city, perhaps no less than some of our lesser Italian cities. There are not so many cars, but there are certainly many more motor scooters, in the type of a Vespa or Lambretta; the people are properly dressed, and few leave the capital, where the refugees from the war zones are amassed, reminding one of the huge areas of huts that I saw in India and in other countries of Asia and Africa, not to mention certain cities in Brazil. It is also curious, for a country of the third world, that one sees almost no one begging for alms. "The moral harm comes precisely from this [a Vietnamese priest told me] that our people are accustomed to a standard of living that is too high for our own resources, to riches artificially produced, as long as this wretched war goes on." In a country devastated by war, luxury, money, pleasures, and the capacity to get rich quickly and easily are among the most common temptations. To make money from the Americans and from more or less illicit trafficking has become in Vietnamese cities today the "national sport," which even some Catholics cannot avoid (and even a priest, unfortunately, although cases of this kind are isolated). The awareness of moral values is gradually being lost, the border between what is licit and illicit has become hazy, even honest working fathers of families and good Catholics are beginning to think of the "commercial value" of their wives and daughters, and even the priests are wondering, at least at times, whether it is lawful or not to build some Catholic institution or embellish a church with moneys obtained from some questionable business, since "everybody is doing it." The family is breaking up, free and provisional unions are appearing, which Vietnam had never known in such numbers, the young boys are organizing into groups to raid the American stores and sell their booty at the "thieves' market."

In the last three or four years, since the military operations have been increasingly disturbing the country [writes an observer who had long experience of living in Vietnam] immorality has burst out like a plague in the cities, giving a harsh blow to traditions, especially to the solidity of the Vietnamese family. In the cities, the family is openly in crisis, even with many Christians; there is a deep gulf of misunderstanding between the generations, which yesterday would have been inconceivable; the parents have lost their authority, as have the old people of the household; marriages are made and unmade with facility; there is promiscuity caused by the war and the destruction, contraceptive pills are distributed, with all the health risks that they imply, especially when they are sold by unscrupulous tradesmen. . . . It is a race for pleasure that sweeps away every moral barrier. . . . I have said that even the Christian milieus are not exempt from these sad developments, which is evidenced by the fact that vocations are becoming more and more rare in the cities, particularly the capital. The majority of the seminarians come from the country areas and from the parishes of Northern refugees, who have preserved a veneration for the traditions.

But my friend goes on to say in his letter:

Given the shocks Vietnam has suffered over the course of more than twenty years of war, it is excusable for being what it is, since no people would be capable of resisting the trials of every sort that this poor Vietnamese people has gone through. The Marxist materialism and the Western materialism it has known and still knows are ruining the moral, spiritual and family life of a people which because of its natural goodness would have deserved a better lot.

The lay apostolate in a still too clerical Church. It is easy to understand how, in a situation such as this, the simple and enthusiastic faith of the majority of Christians risks being swept away in the general loosening of morals and in the overturning of the traditional moral values which in Vietnam, among Catholics and non-Catholics, were and remain most valid, especially within the family circle. Hence, the effort to give Christians a personal and mature faith by involving them in the various movements of Catholic action, which have experienced a strong growth in recent years. In addition to Catholic Action properly so-called, which is present in all dioceses and parishes but often more on paper than in reality, there are other younger movements which are more vital because they are more elite.

For example, the Legion of Mary, whose great growth is due to two factors. First, because it is under the patronage of Mary, for whom the Vietnamese have an exceptional devotion; secondly, because it brings together small groups who meet each week and propose concrete and immediate objectives, with the members required to give a report on their activities. The Legion formula achieved undeniable success, especially in the cities, and there is practically no apostolic activity in which legionaries are not involved.

The YCW was less widespread and had a revival in recent years. After its foundation in 1937 by Fr. Vacquier of the Paris foreign missions and the successive ups and downs that had brought it almost to extinction, the movement, which has two sections, male and female, works fruitfully for the rechristianization of the laboring classes. It also supports the Vietnamese Confederation of Labor by organizing courses of study on social problems and days of Christian formation for the young workers. Many Catholics who were trained in the YCW afterwards became active union leaders.

It would take too much time to record the activities of the various Catholic movements that appeared and grew in the past few years. But we might still mention Pax Romana, for the intellectuals, YCS, for the students, and the AEC (Association of Catholic Educators), which organizes pedagogical sessions for the training of teachers and the professional advancement of every kind of instructor. In the cities, courses preparing people for marriage were worked out under the direction of Fr. Hong Phuc; a few student centers were set up, the best known being one called Alexandre de Rhodes founded by the Jesuits in Saigon, and the Cursillo de cristiandad, recently imported from the Philippines (this involves intense courses in Christian formation in a few days of lessons and discussions). In the rural zones, associations of a traditional type prevail since they are more adapted to the scant evolution of the local people.

One of the major obstacles to the growth of the lay movements is the still excessive "clericalization" of the Vietnamese Church, because of which the laity are still often considered to be minors. One local observer told me:

The priest here is accustomed to give orders everywhere, and to think it normal that every word of his be considered Gospel by the Christians. Even in the cities where there are many educated and capable laymen, the priest thinks he has the duty to make decisions for everyone, to give instructions about everything, to be obeyed blindly in every field. Up to today we still have not seen a movement of "revindication" of the laity's autonomy, with the exception of a personal case or two that received little notice, but things are changing rapidly and the priests too will have to change their mentality; our bishops have already made enormous progress in this direction in a short time. The layman lives in the world, he is sensitive to the most profound changes and problems of society, which the priest often does not succeed in understanding in all their depth and urgency. The layman is in search of solutions, poses problems and demands. At times, he does not have the courage to ask questions of his parish priest because he is afraid of receiving a reproach, and anyway he knows that it would be difficult to discuss on an equal footing, serenely, and without seeming to impose authoritarian means.

Fr. Léopold Cadière, M.E.P., wrote some time ago, but his description is still partly valid today:

At the summit of the parish organization is the pastor, the much listened-to and uncontested leader. He is a leader not only in religious matters but for many others in the civil field, and, so to speak, in the criminal field. Christians come to him, either at first instance or in appeal, with their small arguments of family concern and in their disputes with their neighbors. The village comes to him in the conflicts between family clans, in trials of common concern, in disputes with the neighboring villages, in the relations with the mandarin authorities. Obviously, these are so many delicate circumstances in which the priest must give evidence of great good sense, absolute impartiality, prudence without weakness, and unceasing patience; in one word, he must show great love for his flock. This is the capital virtue, even if he at times makes a mistake, which assures him the respect and the obedience of his Christians.[15]

The "Church of the poor" in Vietnam. On the other hand, on the pastoral level and that of living the Gospel, the Vietnamese priests are above praise, as are also the sisters, catechists and faithful in the war zones. Never will I be able to forget certain concrete cases of real heroism that I was able to observe at close hand for some days in various parts of Vietnam. I remember three young Vietnamese sisters who kept open a school with a medical dispensary just below the border with North Vietnam (who knows where they are today!), with day and night concerts of bombs and machine gun fire, continuously in danger of their lives, yet they were so calm and smiling, amazed at my astonishment at finding them in that place. I remember the priests of Dong-Ha, Gio-Lin, Cam-Lo, and Quang-Tri, who stayed on in the villages that were just a few kilometers from the demilitarized zone of the 17th parallel; with their sisters, they kept open the only schools and the only medical and charitable assistance program in the region, in which the government functionaries were seen only by day, and from where the civil leaders of the communities had fled to the cities. Fr. Pierre Poncet, M.E.P., a missionary at Khe-San, who accompanied me in my visit to the Northern zones, died in

February 1968, shot by the North Vietnamese during the Têt offensive, along with his colleague, Fr. Cressonier.

In the vast rural and mountainous zones of Vietnam, often the only presence of social assistance, education and "protection" among the people is in the person of the Catholic priest or the Church organization (there are very few Buddhist bonzes in the country districts). Many priests told me that they remained at their post because if they left, all the people would follow them to the cities where they would be victims of want more than in the country. (Now, I do not know, after the assault on the Vietnamese cities, begun in February 1968, whether they would be safer in the country or the city!)

Poverty is another characteristic that struck me in the life of the clergy of Vietnam. If the Vietnamese Church is rich, its riches are used to build great schools and social institutions, to embellish churches, but certainly not to give the clergy a soft life. In the city of Saigon I saw priests who were national directors of great institutions and organizations, working under wretched living conditions because of a lack of space or comfort, with tiny offices submerged under tons of paper and work materials. To give an example, I remember the office of Fr. Nguyen-Dui-Vi, editor of the magazine *Sacerdos,* already mentioned, and director of the press and social communications center of the Vietnamese episcopal conference—an office that is also his residence, near the premises of a great secondary Catholic city named after the first Vietnamese bishop, Nguyen-Ba-Tong. The tiny room is piled to bursting point with books, heaps of magnetic tapes for recording the Catholic radio programs, two recorders, rolls of film, card files, a radio, a duplicating machine, a typewriter, personal effects and a television set stored under his bed. ("I only take it out at night to watch the short daily television program," said Fr. Vi.)

In the rural and mountain areas, I remember the example of the Church of Kontum, a real "Church of the poor" in every sense, and I thought, visiting the diocese, that while we in Europe are writing profound theological treatises on the poverty of the Church, here in Vietnam (and in other countries of the third world) there are priests who really live poverty to an extent unimaginable to us. The house in which Fr. Arnould lived at Dak-To—here too there was almost continuous bombing in the midst of the extremely poor Montagnards—is a hut made of straw and bamboo, about ten meters by three in area, divided into three sections: the missionary's kitchen and bed in the first; a table with parish registers, books, and some joiner's tools in the second; storage space in the third. In the whole "house" there was only one "real" piece of furniture, a medicine chest that was locked with a key (the only thing that was actually locked) in which the missionary kept money and reserved documents; the rest of the "furniture" was all made by the missionary himself from the wood of the boxes that had contained cannon ammunition or other American army material. The floor was earthen and the food that of the people of the area.

And the house of Fr. Dujon at Dak-Chu? It is worse than Fr. Arnould's, who at least had a tiny church of masonry that had already been hit twice by bombs. Fr. Dujon had only a straw hut that was used for everything: the larger part for the church, the smaller, separated from the latter by a bamboo trellis, was where he lived. Here, within the space of a few square meters, were piled up books and working tools, medicines and his "bed," a kitchen, and everything that a missionary of these parts might need, from nails to school books for the children. Fr. Dujon, however, had the good fortune to have an old refrigerator, which Fr. Arnould still did not have (here people are most familiar with jet planes and the most perfected bombs, but not yet with electricity).

And the house of Fr. Chastenet? And that of Fr. Creten, who has been in Vietnam for more than forty years? But I would never finish, even were I to speak only of the "houses" lived in by the Paris missionaries in the Dak-To valley! The night I slept in Fr. Dujon's quarters, I was constrained to lie down in his "bed," a wooden table and a bamboo mat, while he slept on the ground.

"I'm used to it," he told me, "I slept on the hard ground for six months when the Vietcong took me prisoner. . . . And I ought not to lose good habits: one never knows!"

These are small examples of cases I saw personally, and I could mention many more. Anyone who has visited the Vietnamese Church, in the cities and out in the country, agrees with this judgment about the local clergy expressed by the Archbishop of Saigon, Mgr. Binh, some years ago:

During the past ten months I made an effort to go and visit both the small and the large parishes of the diocese. . . . In doing so I was able to find out about the life led by the priests both in the cities and in the most remote country areas. Their way of living deeply moved me. The enemies of the Church calumniate the clergy. They are lying when they say that the priests are bourgeois, living aloof from the people, that they do not mingle with the faithful, that they love honors and comforts, prefer the luxury of the cities, shun work and hardship, profit from their position to pile up riches for themselves and their families, live in idleness at the expense of their flock. . . . Let those who say such things take the trouble to see with their own eyes what I saw these past ten months. . . .

The archbishop then enumerated the manifold activities of the priests for the Church and to help the people, praised the altruistic spirit of the more well-off who came spontaneously to the aid of their less fortunate colleagues, and comforted those who live in material poverty and often in misery or who suffer because of their isolation or state of insecurity.

Despite all of this [Mgr. Binh writes] no priest is complaining. On the contrary, I only heard them say decisively: "Whether alive or dead, I shall stay with my Christians!"[16]

Seminaries and Church statistics. Vocations to the priesthood and to the religious life, as we have already mentioned, are abundant,

and the education in the seminaries is good, completed and fortified by a long period of military life that is practically obligatory
for all. This military life opens great gaps in the ranks of the clerics
by causing a strict selectivity, and because of this, the vocations
which were numerous at the beginning of seminary life end up by
being barely sufficient at the end, i.e., the number of priests ordained
each year in Vietnam is enough to maintain the present numerical
level of the clergy or augment it a little. But, for the needs of a
Church in a mission status like the Vietnamese, a rapid increase in
clergy would be necessary. Because of this, perhaps, but also for
other causes, the Vietnamese Church is not sufficiently missionary.
Every priest is committed to the ordinary pastoral needs of his
Christians (cared for very well by the Vietnamese clergy), but he
almost completely neglects "the outsiders," without feeling or
transmitting to the faithful the missionary ardor to bring salvation
to all. I heard this lack of missionary spirit lamented in various
parts of the country, and, furthermore, it is not only a problem of
the Vietnamese Church but of many other churches of the third
world.

The training in the Vietnamese seminaries is still somewhat traditional and not everywhere receptive to the new openness and to
the conciliar trends. At times the structures are fossilized, and
people are living more in the past than in the present or the future,
especially on account of too marked a nationalism, since it is
necessary to open the souls of the young to the *sensus catholicus,*
i.e., universality, which in the context of Vatican II is the only thing
adequate at this time of interdependence in which the world is
living. Fortunately there is a trend toward greater openness of
horizons and methods, and very recently the superiors of the
diocesan and religious seminaries met for the first time on a national level in order to put their experiences together. I was able to
visit rather thoroughly the pontifical seminary of Dalat which, in
miniature, reflects the physiognomy of the most evolved part of the
Vietnamese Church at this moment in its history: a solid, rigid and

somewhat traditionalist training, an openness to social and pastoral problems, a life of poverty and sacrifice.

However, we must not think of an antiquated seminary, with a mind closed to modern experiences. Quite the contrary! All the clerics have their own rooms and are free to read any kind of literature, and are in fact encouraged to do so. The practical initiation into the apostolate and the contacts with the outside world are very advanced.[17] Every cleric interrupts his studies for a year to serve in a parish of his diocese as a catechist, and during his seminary studies there is a lot of outside apostolic work in the Dalat parishes, in prisons, hospitals, visiting of families, especially in the populous quarters and among the refugees. The clerics themselves print a small magazine for prisons and hospitals. The studies are very rigorous. The teaching is still partially done in Latin (for want of theological texts in Vietnamsee) and the examinations are kept on a high level and are difficult. "If they don't succeed in one year," I was told, "they will succeed in two or three, but the priest who leaves the pontifical seminary must be well-trained." At Dalat there are somewhat less than 200 clerics in philosophy and theology, sent from all the dioceses in South Vietnam, the best from each diocese, in order to complete their studies in the theological faculty there. Other than the one at Dalat, there are two major seminaries for the diocesan clergy, at Saigon and Hué, and several others for religious.

The great majority of Vietnamese priests are natives: only 180 foreigners out of a total of almost 2,000, between seculars and religious. Among the bishops, there are 13 natives and only one foreigner, Mgr. Seitz, of Kontum. We are giving here the latest available statistics on the Vietnamese Church (June 30, 1967), and comparing them to those of the same date in 1965:

	1967[18]	1965
Population of South Vietnam	16,067,136	14,764,329
Catholics (estimate)	1,731,989	1,559,077
Catechumens	14,536	52,400

Baptisms (child)	128,240	94,436
Adult baptisms (two years)	11,372	24,659
Diocesan priests	1,476	1,376
Religious and missionary priests	423	395
Brothers	932	884
Sisters (in great majority natives, like the brothers)	5,699	4,826
Clerics in philosophy and theology	795	685
High school seminarians	3,199	2,725
Churches	884	832
Catholic primary schools	1,406	1,158
Primary school pupils	311,000	83,103
Catholic secondary schools	188	178
Secondary school students	112,000	264,801
Students in the Catholic University of Dalat	2,000	1,280
Catholic hospitals	6	5
Hospitals entrusted by the government to Catholic sisters	39	26
Orphanages	79	55
Catholic leprosaria	6	5
Rest homes for the old and infirm	28	19

The statistics were compiled on the basis of data reported by each of the dioceses in the annual report, but, especially for the number of Catholics, they remain approximate. At Saigon in December 1967, the apostolic delegate Mgr. Palmas showed me a report to the Holy See in which it was stated that the Catholics were more than two million.[19] It is easy to understand that the war, the hundreds of thousands of refugees, and a good part of each diocese cut off from any supervision did not permit an accurate census, whether religious or civil. To these same causes may be attributed the notable drop in the baptisms of adult converts, especially with the fear of a Communist victory, which would have had unimaginable consequences for the Catholics. The baptisms of adult converts were as follows over the last ten years (the figures are for two years each, beginning with June 30): 1957–1959: 54,770; 1959–1961: 74,859; 1961–1963: 53,115; 1963–1965: 24,659; 1965–1967: 11,372.[20]

Song Dao, *a "different?" Catholic newspaper.* An important means for spreading Christian ideas and contributing to the formation of the faithful is that of the press, especially in Vietnam where people read a good deal and illiteracy is now practically nonexistent. Saigon is the headquarters of the press and social communications center of the episcopal conference, directed by Fr. Nguyen-Duy-Vi, who is involved with Catholic radio programs (12 in all over the 14 radio stations of the country, all government owned) and cinema criticism: the beginning of TV (February 1966), with one very limited evening program, has brought new work for the center.

Christian news in the Vietnamese press is assured by the weekly information bulletin, *Tong-Tin Cong-Giao* (1,000 copies), published by Fr. Vi's center, and also by another news bulletin, appearing irregularly, called *Veritas* and edited by lay Catholics, while the Catholic press itself numbers 2 dailies out of the 30 in the country: the *Xay Dung* (20,000 copies), one of the most influential in Vietnam, and the *Hoa-Binh* (7,000 copies); there are two other dailies with a Christian inspiration, *Tu-Do* and *Saigon-Bao,* edited by two ex-seminarians, the first with a wide circulation. The most read Catholic weeklies are the *Thang-Tien,* which has a political bent (18,000 copies), the *Nguoi-Moi,* more of a family and popular character (25,000 copies), and the *Duc Me Haang Cuu Giup,* of a religious type (22,000 copies). A very summary list, which is easily understandable since there are many other specialized reviews, devotional and association bulletins, etc.

Fr. Vi spoke to me of the urgent need for a Catholic center for social communication media with more space and more personnel than he had at present, but for the moment the means were not available. In Vietnam the press has great influence, more than in other countries of the third world, especially since the war has awakened everyone, even to the inhabitants of the remotest fishing village, and all are concerned about the country's problems.

One "different" newspaper is the *Song-Dao* (Live the Faith) which enjoys wide fame in Vietnam, although its ideas are not shared by the majority of Catholics. I visited its offices, in makeshift quarters, and met with the lay director, Nguyen-Duc-Phong, and with the editor-in-chief (also a layman), Nguyen-Dinh-Dau; the editorial staff is made up of lay Catholics and a few priests: Truong Ba Can, the national moderator of the YCW, the Dominican Nguyen-Huy-Lich, the Redemptorist, Fr. Lan, etc.

The *Song Dao* [Mr. Dau told me][21] was founded in 1962 with the aim of preparing Christians for the conciliar ideas and with a religious and social program that is nonpolitical. The first issue had 35,000 copies and opened with a letter of good wishes from the Archbishop of Saigon, Mgr. Binh. In the beginning we had enormous success: we published from twenty to thirty thousand copies, which is a great deal for an intellectual weekly like ours. Our basic ideas have always been those of the Council: we want to get Catholics out of their ghetto and the isolation in which they have always lived, to make them open to collaboration with the other religious and social forces, and to get rid of a purely negative anti-Communism. Our themes are of a religious and social nature. We speak of the reforms wanted by the Council, we give great prominence to what the pope says and we treat of the social problems of our country, trade union questions, and finally we talk about peace and collaboration with the Buddhists and the other religions. We were the first to make contacts with the Buddhists.[22]

In addition to the contacts with the Buddhists which are still carried on with intensity by the editors of the *Song-Dao,* the weekly organized debates on the Council, an itinerant display on the Council (which was appreciated also by the non-Christians), conferences and study days on the pontifical documents on peace and social justice (in June 1967 there was a two-day study session on *Populorum Progressio,* under the presidency of Archbishop Binh and the apostolic delegate, Mgr. Palmas; it had great success).

But the life of the *Song-Dao* has not been easy: on one side, there was the political nuisance of government censorship and suspicion (after the Viet Cong Tet offensive in February 1968, the weekly spontaneously and temporarily suspended publication until this most difficult period of disorder was over); on the other side, the majority of the Catholics and the priests looked with suspicion upon a newspaper which, according to them, was too revolutionary and critical toward the Church. Because of this some difficulty resulted in its distribution in Catholic circles, while the interest of the non-Christian elite was on the increase, and there were polemics in the Catholic press, benevolent but firm warnings by the ecclesiastical authorities, etc.

The Confederation of Labor and the Social Secretariat. One last aspect of the Church activities in Vietnam to be put in relief is the contribution made by Catholics to the social progress of their country.

Of necessity we shall have to give a synthesis of such a vast subject. First of all, let us remember that the Vietnamese Confederation of Labor, by far the most important trade union in Vietnam (there are four), was founded in 1950 chiefly by Catholics with the name Vietnamese Confederation of Christian Workers, subsequently changed in 1964 since the majority of the members of the union are non-Catholics. Although the Confederation is still affiliated with the CISC (International Confederation of Christian Trade Unions), which gave it assistance and assured its development for a long time, many of its branches are now affiliated with the international CISL.

The work of the union in Vietnam has been particularly noteworthy in forming a mentality of social vindication among the workers, giving them an efficient national organization even in the rural areas, and, especially, for having succeeded in obtaining a social legislation that is considered among the best on the Asian continent. The union also founded hundreds of cooperatives among the farmers, fishermen and laborers on the plantations (coffee, rubber), which constitute today one of the most solid and resistant structures in the face of Viet Cong terrorism in the country areas, and which freed thousands of families from indigence.

The president of the Labor Confederation, Tran Quoc Buu (a Buddhist), spoke to me about the forming of cadres through union training courses, which were 480 in 1966 and about 550 in 1967, with the participation of more than 30,000 young people. The total membership of the Confederation is some 550,000 workers, a most remarkable number for a country of the third world with 16 million inhabitants. This organized force of workers is today one of the most solid forces in the general decadence of the state structures in South Vietnam, and even though it has never become directly involved in active politics, limiting itself to promoting social claims, it is clear that in the future reorganization of the country it will have a not inconsiderable importance.

Another important initiative in the social field is the "Social Secretariat" founded in 1953 at Dalat by Fr. Parrel, M.E.P., as a center of documentation and training of the Catholic elite and for the purpose of diffusing the social teaching of the Church throughout the country. The Secretariat made a good contribution toward the formation of the first Vietnamese trade union elite, for whom it organized many courses (Fr. Parrel is still today the moral adviser of the Confederation of Labor). Transferred in 1961 to Saigon, the Social Secretariat has continued its activities on the level of study and research into the major problems of Vietnamese society, which were published for some time in the review *Economie humaine,* directed by the secretariat itself; it appeared for two years, 1965–1966, and then in various local newspapers and independent bulletins. The activity of the secretariat, in addition to its investigation of the local social problems, has also developed on the level of the diffusion of the data of its research (through conferences, debates, study days, radio broadcasts, constant collaboration with the local press, pamphlets, forming of Catholic groups interested in these problems), with the purpose of forming in Catholics a mentality that is open to social problems and reforms. Furthermore, we might point out the collaboration given to government organizations and the trade unions, as well as the publication of the pontifical social encyclicals.

The strongest criticism that the young people of the Social Secretariat and their director, Fr. Parrel, make of the Vietnamese Christian community is the lack of social formation among the priests and, consequently, among the lay people. "It tends too much [Fr. Parrel told me] to limit itself to charity taken in the sense of almsgiving and immediate assistance to the suffering, but it also ignores what social justice is. It is true that the Catholics do very good work in the unions, but the great bulk of Christians is not trained to these problems, although, with the organizational strength the Church possesses, very much could be done."

In a document published by Vietnamese Catholic Action in 1965 under the title *Communism and We Christians,* we read:

Let us not forget that Communism declares itself to be the champion of social justice. We know that this social pretense is only an illusion because in reality Communism establishes a very harsh and inhumane regime. However, we should not draw the conclusion from this that their diagnosis of our modern society is mistaken. Our society includes too many social inequities and too much misery; it is no surprise that many of those who are suffering from hunger turn to Communism as their supreme hope. We must become aware of this situation. Eliminate misery and Communism will have fewer adherents. . . .

If, despite everything, Communism arouses such a hope in millions of men, is it not perhaps because of the fact that we have not become sufficiently involved? . . . As Christians we are responsible for this world which is too selfish, unjust and money-centered. . . . Communism reproaches us for a bourgeois spirit. But is it really wrong?

Actually, the Church and the Vietnamese Catholics, caught in the vice of Communist terror after the Diem period, have no longer participated actively in the solution of the country's problems, at least as a group; and this is especially true for social problems, with the exception of the contribution given by the charitable and welfare institutions of the Church. Faced with the Communist peril, everything else has been put absolutely in second place, and there is a lack of courage to confront contemporary society with its many social injustices almost as if there were a fear of promoting "subversion." For example, we were astounded that encyclicals like *Pacem in Terris, Mater et Magistra* and *Populorum Progressio* were not only not given to the non-Christians and discussed on a national level but also not even distributed to Christians and made the center of Church teaching.

The Church's contribution to the development of the country. First of all, we must say that the Church has always made its contribution to the solving of social problems and to the country's development not only with the traditional means of schools and health stations but also with a direct intervention in the field of agriculture, introducing new methods of cultivation, reclaiming untilled lands, founding model factories and farm colonies, opening low interest credit unions for the farmers, etc.[23]

Today, then, the Church is beyond any doubt the organization giving the major impetus to progress and to the aid of the Vietnamese people, apart from the government. Above all, there is the complex of institutions about which we have already given some statistics: schools, medical dispensaries, leprosaria, etc. In order to understand the importance of these statistics, we must remember that although the Catholics represent only some 13 percent of the South Vietnamese population, the welfare and educational institutions of the Church represent about 20–25 percent of the country's total, including those set up by the state or other private and religious organizations. For example, the Church's primary schools are one-fifth of all primary schools in South Vietnam, the secondary schools one quarter; of 3 universities, one is Catholic and the other 2 have a good number of Catholic professors; the 6,567 beds in Catholic hospitals or hospitals under the care of Catholic sisters are one-fourth of the 22,000 beds in all the country's hospitals; the 2,900 lepers of the 6 Catholic leprosaria are almost the totality of lepers cared for in the country; one-third of the alumni of the technical schools in the country were trained in the 2 Catholic technical schools, one at Govap, on the outskirts of Saigon (conducted by the Salesians), and the other at Dalat (founded by Fr. Parrel and now run by the Brothers of the Christian Schools).

On the contribution of the Church to the progress of the country much could be written, for example, in regard to work with the tribal population in the mountains (about 2 million persons as against 16 million Vietnamese). But here I should like to mention the work of Caritas-Vietnam, the chief institution in the social field in the Vietnamese Church of today, founded at the beginning of 1966, when it absorbed various other charitable and welfare organizations.

There are two aspects to the work of Caritas-Vietnam: immediate aid for the poor and the refugees (a short-term program), and the training of social workers and the formation of professional centers (long-term). Its organization is spread through all 14 dioceses of South Vietnam, with 4 principal centers (2 in Saigon, one at Hué and one at Qui-Nhon) in addition to the individual diocesan centers. It is now in the process of establishing centers in all 33 provinces of the country. The operative principle of Caritas—as in all the other Catholic institutions—is to help all who are in need, prescinding from religious faith or politics; in the Caritas teams there are also young non-Christians.

Some concrete data:[24] for aid to the refugees (as we know, in South Vietnam there are some three million refugees in the war zones on the outskirts of the large cities), Caritas-Vietnam last year distributed 50,000 tons of food and clothing and gave financial aid amounting to $100,000; in addition, it has built small houses for the refugees and for the flood victims and has supplied medical assistance to various camps where these poor people are.

The long-term programs include courses of professional qualification for young men and women (typists, masons, mechanics, tailors, typographers, nurses, etc.) in the various Caritas centers, the setting up of social agencies for the poor and the refugees (homes for children, houses for the blind, dormitories for young men and workers, medical dispensaries, etc.), and, especially, the training of social workers. At the end of 1967, there were already 118 social workers at work, trained entirely by Caritas in three-month sessions and working full time, along with some thousands of other young people who give their time one day a week, or one month a year, without pay and in the spirit of service.

Following the route outlined by the Council. At the conclusion of this chapter on the Vietnamese Church, after having looked at its internal state, its institutions and its problems, we should like to take a conclusive look at the balance sheet of the Church and of the missionary work that has been done to date in order to see what goals have been reached and what are still quite remote.

The missionary activity which for less than a century has been able to develop in freedom can boast concrete results of considerable importance. First of all, the solid foundation of the local Church, a goal that was reached here more than in any other "mission" country, with bishops, clergy, sisters, catechists, churches and all the normal structures of a now adult and self-sufficient Church, at least in regard to the ordinary pastoral care of Christians. Alongside this can be placed the fact, exceptional for Asia, of a Christian community that represents, in South Vietnam, 13 percent of the total population, a percentage that is exceeded in Asia by the Philippines alone, and in Africa by only a few countries. Finally, let us mention the exceptional faith and devotion of these Christians, the spirit of sacrifice of the priests, the attachment of everyone to the Church and the pope, the blood of so many old and recent martyrs, etc.

These are no minor results for some eighty years of free missionary preaching and for the scarcity of personnel and money which has always afflicted this Church, as all mission churches. But if we look at the unachieved goals, the unattained results, not out of a spirit of criticism but as a stimulus to complete the work that has been done up to now, we see that much remains to be done in order to make the Church truly a sign of God's presence among the Vietnamese. There are two essential points here: the Church is little known in its true, spiritual goals, and it has hardly incarnated itself in the local culture. "The Church in Vietnam [writes a Vietnamese] as in other countries of the Far East, still looks too European. This has produced the effect of keeping many intellectuals from the Church, because they look at it as a foreign import. But their attitude is not always due to religious feeling (since they are generally skeptics) but is inspired by a strict nationalism and confined to the cultural plane."[25]

Up to now, few efforts have been made to study Vietnamese culture in depth and to train the priests and lay people in a love of their national culture, which at times is still seen more as an obstacle to Christianity than as a human basis which Christianity need only complete through revelation. For this reason, Christians, although they love their country deeply, find themselves in an ambiguous position, not so noticeable on the popular level but suffered by the Christian elite. On one side, they have absorbed a Christian culture that carries with it a clearly Western tone, and on the other, they do not know concretely how to adapt Christianity to the local culture or what in the local culture is compatible with Christianity. The Church does not participate fully in the cultural life of the country because it has never acknowledged the value of this culture; consequently it finds itself in a position only of giving and not of receiving, which is contrary to the spirit of the Gospel and to the recent conciliar and papal directives.

In an "open letter" that a group of Vietnamese wrote in 1963 to the American ambassador, Nolting, we read:

For us Vietnamese, to embrace Christianity means that we would be forbidden to worship our Ancestors, our deceased Parents, when this has been the most important thing in our style of life for thousands of years. . . . The Christians are hybrids, they are eccentric to Vietnamese society, they are absurd with regard to Vietnamese thought. Nor is their language even Vietnamese. . . . The young Vietnamese want to know why there are so many differences between Christianity and their culture, why this religion is so contrary to their *Volksgeist,* why so many monstrous contradictions, why so many absurd superstitions, why this severity and cruelty of the Almighty God who unceasingly curses and threatens men with such horrible words while he ought to be saving them.[26]

We must realize that this letter was written during the hottest months of the 1963 "hot summer," when opposition to Diem had become for many intellectuals opposition to Christianity; the document, therefore, is certainly not indicative of how the majority of Vietnamese look upon Christianity and the Church, but it is still a dangerous indication of a frame of mind that is present at least in a minority of the local elite. Even if today no one any longer questions the patriotism of Vietnamese Catholics, the Church still experiences the burden of Christianity as alien to the local culture, and also the fact that the Church itself is little known in its true nature and in its spiritual goals. Recently, a Catholic university professor, Tran-Thien-Tam, acknowledged this:

Even though it has been present in Vietnam for three centuries, Catholicism remains a mystery to non-Christians, both in its doctrine and in its organization, and no effort is made in the direction of better understanding. People do not even know whether it is a religion or a state. The existence of the Vatican State (of course, non-Christians do not know its origin or significance), the current name for the pope, emphasizing his royal dignity (*Gia-Hoang,* literally, "Religious King"), the administrative character of the ecclesiastical organization, which in some way duplicates the civil administration, the presence of an "apostolic delegation" with the rank of ambassador, etc., all do nothing to clarify matters.[27]

When I went to interview the Ven. Tri Quang, before allowing me to ask him questions, he himself interrogated me for almost two hours: how was the Church organized, what studies were made before becoming a priest (and . . . what studies to become a bishop), why the Council was so important, whether the Vatican had military defense pacts with Western countries or at least with Italy, and a quantity of other questions, some of which appeared decidedly naive in a person of his quality. In the end, at a certain point I found myself thinking that Tri Quang was probably more interested in speaking with a Catholic priest, than I was in speaking with him!

All of this is a sign of an undeniable fact: that the majority of the Vietnamese—even those who are most concerned with religious questions and interested in the Church, like the Buddhist bonzes—although they live side-by-side with two million Catholics, know very little about the Church and Christianity either because of lack of contact or lack of simple written sources that are adapted to them.

And this seems to me to be the basic criticism that can be made of Vietnamese Christianity—of being isolated in a ghetto during the period of persecutions, then of having accentuated this isolation during the colonial era and the Diem period, and finally, for having done very little to break down the ghetto walls and to become fully integrated in the national community.

It is necessary to take literally these words that the Archbishop of Saigon, Mgr. Binh, addressed to his people in a letter from the council:

When we consider Vietnam, we see that barely 10 percent of the population is Christian. How many Vietnamese still remain outside the Church! With the same spirit that animates the Fathers of the Council, I ask everyone, my dear brothers, priests and laymen, to make an effort toward a revision of life and a self-criticism, in order to discover the reason why the Church of Christ is still not very well-known in Vietnam. . . . To make a revision of our lives, to impose self-criticism upon ourselves, to have the courage to reform ourselves in order to permit the work of salvation to be propagated everywhere, this is how all of us will participate, realistically and genuinely, in the life of Vatican Council II.[28]

Notes

1. On the translation of the Bible into Vietnamese, see J. Metzler, "Vietnamesische Bibelübersetzung," *Neue Zeitschrift für Missionswissenschaft,* no. 3, Schöneck-Beckenried, 1964, pp. 195–202.

2. In the Orient it is the custom when one wants to ask a favor of the divinity to write the favor on a piece of paper that is then burned before the divinity, thinking that in that way the favor will be granted.

3. Text in *Missions Etrangères de Paris,* May–June 196, pp. 7–10. On the question of the "Chinese rites" see the first chapter of this book.

4. On Christian art in Vietnam a good essay could be written, but we would be straying too far from our subject. In 1966, the founder of Vietnamese Christian art, Celsus Le-Van-De, died. He was baptized in Rome in 1934 by Mgr. Celso Costantini, the apostolic delegate to China, and he left behind him many works (his Madonnas are most famous) and a school of Christian painters.

5. In 1964 there was a celebration in Vietnam of the 300th anniversary of the arrival of the Paris missionaries in the country. They belonged to an institute of the secular and not religious clergy. These missionaries still number some eighty priests in Vietnam and work in the service of the local bishops in a perfect diocesan spirit, although they remain under one of their own bishops, Mgr. Seitz of Kontum; this is the only diocese in their hands.

6. J. Dournes, *Le Père m'a envoyé,* 1966; "L'offrande des peuples," *Missions Etrangères de Paris,* December, 1966, pp. 25–31; another article on the non-Christian rites and Christianity; J. Moriceau, "Au Vietnam des villages entiers entrent en chrétienté" *Missions Etrangères de Paris,* September–October, 1963, pp. 15–21.

7. The exceptional religious fervor of Vietnamese Catholics is proved, among other things, by the flourishing life of the contemplative orders, which in South Vietnam include 4 Cistercian monasteries, 2 Benedictine monasteries, 3 Carmelite, one for the Poor Clares and one of Benedictine nuns, in addition to many in North Vietnam which are closed for the time being. The activity of the cloister is dedicated to study, land reclamation and also to the missionary apostolate, see E. Parrel, "Missions et monachisme au Vietnam," *Missions Etrangères de Paris,* September–October 1964, pp. 33–38.

8. This fact of a community life of prayer and the organization of a whole village in keeping with a Christian rhythm explains why the Catholics always preferred to live in their own villages, instead of mingling with non-Christians in mixed villages. There are also other reasons: the persecutions, the desire to avoid religious syncretism, etc., but perhaps the dominant motive is that of being able to organize Christian life in a community fashion on the level of the entire village.

9. F. Gian, "Il travaglio di un popolo—La Chiesa nel Vietnam," *Le missioni cattoliche,* Milan, 1956, pp. 26–29.

10. G. Cussac, *Les Missions catholiques,* May, 1955, p. 86.

11. Tran-Thien-Tam, "Les deux visages de l'Eglise au Vietnam," *Eglise vivante,* 1967, pp. 26–33.

12. Certain criticisms of the missionary methods are unjust: at times people write that the churches of the "third world" ought to have institutions of the poor, and not of the rich, adapted to the poverty of the area. This was the idea of Dr. Albert Schweitzer who built a "primitive" hospital at Lambaréné to cure the "primitive peoples" of Africa. He did not want a telephone, running water, a refrigerator, brick houses . . . One Protestant student of African problems, Jan Hermelinck, wrote: "Schweitzer is a man who has great meaning for Europe and America, but he has none for Africa. In reality this is the case, and it must be said with all clarity: Schweitzer has no meaning for Africa, unless an indirect one at the most, namely, that in Europe and America he keeps alive a false view of Africa" (quoted from "Albert Schweitzer, il tramonto di un mito?" *Le Missioni cattoliche,* Milan, October, 1963, pp. 450–451). The cases then are twofold: either the Catholic missions give an example of modern, efficient buildings, of scholastic and religious organizations that could also exist in Europe and therefore bring an exemplary contribution to local society and a stimulus to go further, but they are accused of being rich and of having no spirit of poverty. Or else, they adapt themselves to the local poverty and build poor buildings, ill-equipped schools, mud churches, etc., and then they will have the merit of poverty but not the merit of moving the local society which is still asleep, and, sooner or later, as happened to Schweitzer before he died, they will experience scorn on the part of the very people whom they wanted to benefit and help evolve. In summation, the thought on the "poverty" of the missions is still in its stammering stage, and I have met, around the world, some open-minded and well-intentioned bishops who did not know what to do or what directives to give in the concrete. . . . I could point out, for example, the case of the holy bishop of a great diocese in the Orient, but also one of great poverty. The diocese has charitable, scholastic and social institu-

tions that are elaborate, modern and open to everyone, and more than $50,000 a year in assistance and development aid; but the bishop had for himself a very poor chancery without conveniences and buried in masses of papers for want of space, etc. Everyone praised the bishop's poverty, but everyone said that with such a diocese the only thing that did not function was the episcopal curia, old in its surroundings and poor in comfort.

13. *Sunday Examiner,* Hong Kong, September 1, 1967, p. 11.

14. *Sunday Examiner,* Hong Kong, July 12, 1968, we find an account of the life of this bishop who is one of the key bishops in Vietnam and who seems to illustrate our point so well. Born forty-seven years ago in Saigon, Mgr. Nguyen-Kim-Dien was still quite young when he joined the Congregation of de Foucauld, making his studies and novitiate in France and then in the Sahara, where he remained for some years. After being ordained a priest, he returned to Vietnam and with three companions began his apostolate near the city of Cantho in the Mekong delta, living in a straw hut and working as a taxi driver to earn his living. In 1960 he was named bishop of Cantho, and in 1964 apostolic administrator of Hué in the absence of Mgr. Thuc; in June 1968 he became the archbishop.

15. L. Cadière, "Organisation et fonctionnement d'une chrétienté vietnamienne," *Bulletin M.E.P.,* Hong Kong, 1955, p. 311. This study by Fr. Cadière, who has a deep knowledge of the Vietnamese psychology and culture (we have already mentioned him as the author of the most profound book on religions in Vietnam) deserves to be read in its entirety by anyone who wants to have a more precise idea about Vietnamese Christianity: it is the best study of religious sociology on Vietnamese Christians that we have found.

16. In *Fides,* March 31, 1962, pp. 204–205.

17. See a report on the pastoral activities of the clerics of Dalat in "Un apostolat de premier contact dans un séminaire," in *Le Christ au monde,* no. 3, Rome, 1967, pp. 223–229.

18. Published by Fr. O'Connor, *Sunday Examiner,* June 14, 1968, p. 15.

19. To the statistics quoted, the apostolic delegate added the following: 286 Catholic medical dispensaries, with 3,286,774 consultations in a year (1966); 33 maternity stations with 18,544 births in the year, in addition to social and aid centers under the direction of Caritas-Vietnam, about which we shall speak presently.

20. Statistics taken from *Documents UMC—Omnis Terra,* Rome, December 1966, where one can find other interesting data on the Vietnamese Church.

21. The interview with the editor of the *Song-Dao* was published in *L'Italia*, Milan, December 30, 1967.

22. The long interview with the Ven. Tri Quang was obtained for me by the good offices of the editors of the *Song-Dao*, one of whom acted as my interpreter (since Tri Quang not only very rarely gave interviews—mine was the first granted to a Catholic priest—but also spoken neither French nor English).

23. On this theme of the Church's contribution to the social progress of Vietnam, see Parrel-Marillier, "L'Eglise et la population rurale au Vietnam," *L'Eglise et les masses rurales*, XXXII Mission Week (Louvain: Desclée de Brouwer, 1962), pp. 248–258; F. Parrel "L'Eglise et l'action sociale au Vietnam," *Les Missions catholiques*, 1952, pp. 274–276; Vo-Tran-Loc, "Les Chrétiens dans la reconstruction du Vietnam," *Les Missions catholiques*, 1955, pp. 177–182, 199–203.

24. Caritas-Vietnam received help in money and kind from the various branches of national Caritas organizations in many countries, and from Caritas-International, which has its seat in Rome, but above all it was helped by the American Catholic Relief Service. This service is still present and active in Vietnam: in the year from July 1, 1966, to June 30, 1967, the CRS helped in various ways 200 schools, 30 hospitals and 8 leprosaria, 41 first-aid stations, 87 hostels, 23 kindergartens, 77 orphanages and 10 old people's homes, in addition to food and clothing distributed from 284 aid centers. Even the CRS has as its basic rule the motto *Need not creed*.

25. Nguyen-Hong-Giao, "The Church in Vietnam," *The Tablet*, London, September 11, 1965, p. 999.

26. *Lumen Vitae*, Brussels, 1965, p. 530.

27. Tran-Thien-Tam, "Les deux visages de l'Eglise," *Eglise vivante*, Louvain, 1967, pp. 26–33.

28. *Informations catholiques internationales*, September 15, 1963.

VII

Catholics and the Political Struggle in South Vietnam

The "new course" of the Vietnamese Church,[1] begun after Diem's fall and following the Council, is characterized by the withdrawal of the religious authorities from militant politics and by the attempt at breaking the barriers of the "secret clan" spirit of Catholics, which harmed the Catholics themselves and was of no use to the country. In these years the bishops succeeded in preventing the creation of a Christian Democratic party, which would have done even more to accentuate the spirit of the Catholics' isolation.

The political withdrawal of the Church. When Diem was killed, the Vietnamese bishops were in Rome for the second session of the council. Some quickly returned to Vietnam, and on November 13, the Archbishop of Saigon, Mgr. Nguyen-Van-Binh, paid a visit to the new head of state: the photo of the handshake between Mgr. Binh and General Duong Van Minh, the new head of state, was reproduced prominently by all the newspapers and contributed toward showing Catholics the way to make peace with Diem's adversaries and the non-Catholics that the Church accepted the new government with full patriotic loyalty. On November 14, the apostolic delegation sent a letter to the minister of foreign affairs in which he transmitted the pope's wishes for peace and prosperity for the country, and on November 17 there was read in all the churches of Vietnam the collective pastoral letter that the bishops had compiled together in Rome before any of them returned to Vietnam. It was dated November 7, and in it we read:

While we were preparing this letter, we received news of the serious happenings in our country. For this reason we remind you of the Church's position. Toward any government, the Church teaches its sons to be faithful to their homeland, to love it, to respect the public authority, and faithfully to cooperate with it in all that is necessary for the good of the country and for the well-being of its citizens.

On November 5, a few days after the coup d'etat, the national committee of Catholic Action reminded Catholics, in a communiqué, of their duties "in the face of the new situation":

(1) Catholics must live in union with their fellow countrymen and share in the feelings of the nation.

(2) In an atmosphere of understanding and harmony with everyone, Catholics have the duty to obtain for themselves and to respect in others the basic rights of the human person, like freedom of thought, faith and worship.

(3) Although the Church is absolutely outside any form of government, the Catholics have the duty of working for the common good and of giving a positive contribution to the building up of the country, in conformity with the social teachings of the Church.

About one month after the coup d'etat, the three bishops who had prematurely returned to Vietnam from Rome[2] published a common pastoral letter "in union of spirit and heart with our absent brothers of the episcopate," in which they clearly explained the position of the Church and the duties of Catholics in the "present complex situation." The document is very important because it indicates the road the Vietnamese Church was prepared to follow and indicate to its people:

(1) Because of its spiritual nature, the Church is not bound to any political regime. But since it has flesh and blood members, it maintains good relations with every government that attempts to promote the welfare of the country. As for the faithful, they have the right freely to choose the political regime that most pleases them, provided that it gives evidence of respecting the basic rights of the human person.

In regard to the public authorities, the letter recalls the function of authority and says:

(2) The duty of the faithful, then, is to obey those authorities that faithfully serve the common good of the nation. . . . The Christian must not only be a passive object, but he must take an active part in the work of formation . . .

(3) With regard to the new chapter in the history of our country, we think it important to recall this exhortation of the late Pope John XXIII: "It would be useless to complain and recriminate. We must build up, my dear sons; we must go forward, and lay the foundations of a new age, a more sane, more generous, more just age. . . ." Therefore, we remind the priests of their duty to make the faithful understand the importance of this hour . . . the courage needed to assume their temporal responsibilities . . . and that they must work together for the reestablishment of . . . good relations between individuals and the public authorities.

(4) There remains one very important point: the relations between Catholics and their non-Catholic fellow countrymen. If we carefully call your attention to this particular problem, it is certainly not because of the current difficulties, but chiefly because this is one of the basic requisites of the Gospel and the guiding force of the Council. . . . But Christian charity asks much more of us, a positive attitude: the respect, understanding and concrete love of our fellow countrymen must lead us to have contacts with our brothers and to work loyally together with all men of goodwill in the various areas of human endeavor, as long as they are in accord with the principles of the Church.[3]

Summing up, the bishops endeavored to lead Catholics, immediately after the coup d'etat against Diem, on a new path that had been only rarely trodden in the past: the patient acceptance of the humiliations and harm that came to the Catholic community after Diem's fall (see the last paragraph of Chapter V), obedience to a government that allowed the Catholics to be accused and calumniated, collaboration with all men of goodwill for the welfare of the country, openness to the members of other religions, etc. It is remarkable that while the Catholics were suffering the reaction and even the revenge of the adversaries of the Diem regime, the bishops do not say one word about this but instead invite the faithful to look ahead and to work together for the common good. As an editorial in the *Song-Dao* said in December 1963: "A regime has fallen: let us leave to history any judgment about its worth. We Catholics do not live in the past but in the present and for the future. But the past has taught us something that we cannot forget . . .

The clear words of the bishops in Lent 1964. The basic document of the "new course" taken by the Vietnamese Church is the collective pastoral letter that the bishops published for Lent 1964, dated January 22. We shall report some full excerpts from it even though they may repeat a few ideas expressed by documents quoted in the foregoing pages:

(1) *Above all unity is necessary.* Our first thought is to remind you of the irresistible need for unity. . . . In every parish, therefore, all the members must be united among themselves and with their priests, and they in turn must be united among themselves in union with their bishop.

In these difficult times we want to encourage you to make a special effort toward unity on the level of the national community. The Catholic never constituted a "class" apart from society. He is a Vietnamese among the Vietnamese and considers his fellow countrymen, whatever they may be, as his blood brothers. Various circumstances or influences have created in these last months a tension or even a conflict between Catholics and Buddhists. Painful incidents have taken place.

We do not question anyone's goodwill, but we see a real danger for our country in the spread of a spirit of rancor, division and fighting among the citizenry. We must therefore work with all of our strength, at whatever cost, for the unity of the great national family.

(2) *Discipline in action.* This unity in confidence, mutual respect and charity automatically contains or, better, requires discipline at every moment! This seems so obvious that at first sight it appears useless to insist upon it. However, we must do so because every man is tempted to follow his own point of view. . . . If pride is involved, people will not want to give up their own personal views. This is how dissensions arise, and our action ceases to be strong and effective. It is individualism with all its inauspicious consequences. . . . For this reason, then, we recommend to everyone today a strict discipline.

(3) *Renew in us the evangelical spirit.* The bishops of South Vietnam recall here the example given by the Council Fathers who first listened to and delved deep into the teachings of Jesus, especially those relative to reciprocal love, the spirit of service, and the forgiving of wrongs; then they decided upon a "revision of life" in order to bring about the *aggiornamento* called for by Pope John XXIII.

We urge you, in turn, priests, religious and faithful to dedicate yourselves to this revision of life. Do it in the privacy of your own rooms, but do it also in common among your brothers, after the example of the Council Fathers themselves. For only in this way will the Council truly become the work of all. . . . Times change, and at times we are tempted to go on thinking and acting as we did in the past. . . . If someone among us wants to continue to think, judge and live as he once did, he should not wonder if people will not understand him.

(4) *A Catholic political party?* If the Catholic Church, as such, ought not to create political parties, it is an absolute duty for every Catholic—as a citizen of this earthly city—to take part courageously, intelligently and impartially in the political activity of the country. He therefore may join a political party, found one, etc., provided that its doctrine and aims are not contrary to his religion and its means of action are not condemned by Christian morality. In brief, a Catholic must be a witness to Christ in all his political activities.

Therefore, the Catholic hierarchy of Vietnam expressly declares that, taking into account the historical, political, sociological and religious

situation of our country today, it does not authorize any party to define
itself as "Catholic" or "Christian" in the sense that it might seem to be
the party of the Catholic Church in Vietnam.

The Catholic hierarchy in Vietnam expressly declares that no Catholic
newspaper or Catholic-minded newspaper is actually accredited to be
the official expression of the thought of the hierarchy. Only for communiqués or declarations signed by all the bishops or their authorized
spokesmen does the hierarchy of Vietnam take responsibility. Everything else is the author's responsibility alone.

(5) *The civic behavior of Christians.* The bishops of Vietnam remind
you that truly constructive civic virtue or activity does not exist outside
of the following three basic principles: have a sense of one's neighbor,
think about him, respect him and will what is truly good for him;
have a sense of the common good, i.e., the collective whole, whereby
every individual must sacrifice himself in order to promote it; be
tolerant, which means understanding and accepting that we are different from one another. Then everyone will try humbly and patiently
to make himself as bearable as possible to his neighbor.

In the religious matters tolerance is of the greatest importance for
the peace of the citizenry. Every Christian is obliged in conscience to
respect every religion in addition to his own.

Priests and faithful, if despite your sincere efforts unpleasant incidents
still happen, remember that the keeping of public order is the job of
the state and not of individuals. In case of necessity, it is necessary
therefore to have recourse to the judgment and the arbitration of the
responsible authorities.[4]

A fighting priest: Fr. Hoang Quynh. How did the Christian
community take to the bishop's directives? The counsels to moderation and commitment to the common good were accepted by the
majority of the faithful, but this does not mean that a part of the
Catholics and even the priests had not continued along the road of
political intransigence. The most able exponent of this line among
Catholics, which brought together especially the refugees from the
North, is Fr. Hoang Quynh, who represents (or rather represented
up to two years ago) on one side a fanatical and at times blind anti-
Communism and, on the other, the revolutionary impetus for social

justice in favor of the most miserable classes. This priest was a refugee from the North, small in stature and a fighter. He had a distinct vocation for political and social struggle, and even under Diem he fought against the great landowners in order to extract from them more humane living conditions for the farmhands and tenants who lived the day long in the muck of the rice fields.

Fr. Quynh, and for that matter the majority of politically "committed" Catholics, championed the carrying out of a "Christian socialism" on the basis of agrarian reform, the strengthening of the trade unions and the farm cooperatives, abolition of caste privileges, nationalization of the principal sources of production, etc. This was a revolutionary program for Vietnam supported by the refugees from the North, uprooted from their land, "poor people with nothing to lose" and, therefore, ready to pay personally for the carrying out of their ideals of social justice.

But Fr. Quynh wanted to carry out this socially open program following a politically integralist line, i.e., one that excluded dialogue with the Communists and with anyone suspected of favoring Communism, for example, the neutralist currents of the Buddhists. Militant anti-Communism was the first point of Fr. Quynh's political commitment, and we shall see later that this intransigence of the priest, who was considered to be the chief political spokesman of the Catholic refugees from the North, became somewhat lessened in later years.

Fr. Quynh was one of the chief characters on the Vietnamese political stage from 1964 to 1967. In 1964 he founded the Catholic Committee for the Struggle, which had the principal aim of protesting against the discrimination used against Catholics following Diem's fall and organizing the Catholics to defend themselves against the armed attacks of which they were the object during that year (see chapter V). Afterwards, in 1965, the movement was called Dai Doan Ket (Movement for the Great Solidarity), with the same political aims: the fight against Communism and the pursuit of the objectives of social justice.

The Dai Doan Ket was representative not only of the most committed Catholics, especially the Northern refugees, but also of non-Catholics who found themselves in the same position, and in 1965–1966 it constituted not only a stimulus for social progress but also an element of disorder in the growing political chaos, insofar as its members were always ready to go out into the public square for antigovernment demonstrations when it seemed that the government was too weak in the fight against Viet Cong subversion or seeemed on the way to a neutralist solution.

Fr. Quynh's movement was disavowed several times by the Catholic episcopate. For example, twice, in June and July 1965, Mgr. Binh, Archbishop of Saigon, repudiated Fr. Quynh, who was presenting himself as the representative of the Catholic community; a declaration by the same priest was condemned by four bishops in June 1966; Catholics were admonished not to join demonstrations in the public squares, which would have increased the already considerable political confusion of the country, etc.

In the last two years, Fr. Quynh has effected a considerable revision of his political perspectives. As early as the time of the elections to the constituent assembly, held in September 1966, the North Vietnamese priest came closer to the political policy of Buddhism, fighting against compulsion and asking for a civil and nonmilitary government based on the agreement among the various religions. At that time he founded and was the head of the Front of Citizens of All Faiths, including representatives from the Catholics, Buddhists, and the other religions, and was once again disavowed by the ecclesiastical hierarchy, who were relying on the voting (which in fact was an undeniable success as a popular manifestation, even though it was opposed by the Viet Cong).

On April 12 1967, in an appeal to Vietnamese Christians, Fr. Hoang Quynh expressed his political position and his plans for the solution of the Vietnamese crisis, considerably different from those stated up to the previous year. In his first point, Fr. Quynh states:

We (Christians) are Vietnamese and, therefore, an integral part of the Vietnamese people, but we are only one part of this people and we cannot solve all the problems by ourselves. For this reason, we must unite with the other elements of the community to seek a reasonable solution to the thorny problems that are posed to the country. Being Christians . . . we want a solution that conforms with Christianity's criteria of justice and brotherhood, and for this reason we strongly protest against any solution that goes against Christian moral values. . . . We are faithful to Vietnam and to the Church, and the Church's interests are never contrary to those of the people.

In his second point, Fr. Quynh speaks of peace:

It is the concern of the people to put an end to the war and to obtain a true peace, with respect for law and order. All Vietnamese agree on this point. Peace is also in the interest of the Church since brotherhood is the *raison d'être* of Christianity, and that can only come about in peace. It is in the interest of the Vietnamese people that Pope Paul VI and the dignitaries of the Vietnamese Catholic Church have appealed to both sides, asking them to study the peace proposals.

To obtain this peace, not only must South Vietnam have a normal political life that will allow a juridically-based government supported by the people, but also the nationalists and more especially the faithful of the various religions must unite into more efficacious and courageous organizations for the purpose of being able to contribute to the creation and safeguard of the peace.[5]

Finally, in the third point of his appeal, Fr. Quynh states that he was directly involved in politics and in social action at a time when the Catholics were not organized and lacked lay personalities capable of being their leaders. Today, however, these laymen are not lacking (the priest says), and by this he announced that he no longer wished to be the political leader of one part of the Catholics but appealed to all lay Catholics to unite in order to determine a common political policy, open their movements to persons of all religions, and collaborate with all sound forces in order to restore peace to the country.

After the declaration we reported, Fr. Quynh, for all practical purposes, abandoned active politics and dedicated himself to his mission as pastor in a parish of the poor on the outskirts of Saigon, where he cultivated good relations with the Buddhist bonzes, especially with those who followed Tri Quang. For this reason, perhaps, his generous gesture did not have much of a following among Catholics who were in a position of overt criticism of Tri Quang and his "political Buddhism."

Catholics' presence in the government. Fr. Quynh always represented a minority in the Vietnamese Christian community. We have spoken at length about this on account of the singularity of his change of opinion and on account of the fact that he represents today one of the more prominent "neutralist" and antigovernment figures.[6]

The majority of the Catholics, however, as well as the episcopal hierarchy, have always supported the successive governments after Diem's fall, although with various nuances and maintaining a proper aloofness. For example, in November 1965 the liaison committee of the archbishopric of Saigon published an open letter to the government inviting it to "assure itself of the concurrence, approval and criticism of the people. To achieve this a basic democratic organization should be created on a national scale, and the fundamental freedoms, particularly freedom of the press, should be respected, within the limitations imposed by the war. The acceptance of criticism is the first step toward democracy."[7]

Following the publication of this letter, one Catholic newspaper was confiscated and another suspended. On April 9 1966 a communiqué of the Saigon archdiocese's liaison committee, after having reemphasized the necessity for government stability, said:

Stability, however, does not mean a static or immobile state. In a country that is undergoing apprenticeship in democracy, all the elements of the population have the right and the duty to explain their own points of view on the questions of common concern and to fight for the putting into effect of their legitimate aspirations. On the government's part, "stability" cannot be considered as an end in itself. On the contrary, it is the essential condition for the application of realistic measures aimed at solving the urgent problems of the country. If it only succeeds in maintaining stability, without the courage to adopt the measures called for, this stability would have no effect other than consolidating power and would be of no use for the general situation. . . . The political scene in the South is still beset with some obscure inertia. The government is still unable to create for itself a solid, legal basis by assuring itself of a wide support on the part of the people; the masses remain indifferent to the problems that mean life or death for the country, while in the cities, increasing every day, there is a reign of rottenness, injustice and degeneration due to money (or a thirst for money) and the war.[8]

Following the elections of September 1966 and September 1967, while the military situation became ever more difficult, the Catholics and the hierarchy gave increasingly cordial support to the government, collaborating from within it, as the one means that would prevent the country from sinking into a chaos from which only the Communists would profit.[9]

Catholics took part as candidates of various parties in the elections of September 1966 for the Constituent Assembly. Out of 117 seats in the Assembly, 35 were won by Catholic candidates (the candidates numbered 542, of whom only 19 percent were Catholics), and in the voting for the Senate of the Republic in September 1967, of the 60 elected, 27 were Catholics. In the same month of September 1967, a Catholic, Van Thieu, was elected president of the Republic (with a Buddhist, Cao Ky, as vice-president), from eight lists of candidates for the presidency and vice-presidency.

For these two elections (1966, 1967), which up to then represented the most important demonstration of democracy in the political life of South Vietnam, the bishops urged Catholics to vote, and to give their votes to those candidates who seemed most determined to work for the good of the country, without religious or political discrimination. For example, Mgr. Binh, in an interview given to Saigon newspapers in September 1966, in reference to the vote, stated:

When Catholics go to vote, they do so as citizens, not as Catholics. And they must remember that it is necessary to vote for the most worthy candidates rather than to promote their own coreligionists. . . .

Then, speaking to the candidates, he said:

If a Catholic is elected, that is his own personal affair and he must not profit from his election to the Assembly in order to affirm that he is assuring the presence of Catholicism in this organization. . . . The Catholic candidates elected to the National Assembly must work for the nation and not for the Catholic Church or for their own interests.[10]

Why so many votes for Catholic candidates? These attitudes on the part of the bishops and Catholic organizations were stated very frequently during the last two years in regard to the elections and to the work of the deputees and senators. The fact still remains, however, that the Catholics were elected in a proportion much higher than their numerical standing in the country, and for easily understandable reasons. First of all, the very efficient Catholic school system had for a long time produced a Catholic elite that was well prepared to emerge in all sectors of civil life and not only in politics, even though throughout the whole history of the Vietnamese Church, conversions came almost exclusively from the poorest classes.

In the second place, although the bishops had exhorted the faithful to vote for the worthiest candidates without regard for their religious preference, the Catholics were easily convinced, out of a spirit of solidarity and on account of the great confusion reigning in the country, that the "worthiest candidates" were precisely their coreligionists. Therefore, they voted for them en masse, even though they were not presented in a "Catholic party" but divided over many lists and parties.

In the third place, since the danger most feared in Vietnam today is a Communist victory, even many non-Catholics chose Catholic candidates whom they considered the most secure defenders of the country's freedom. Finally, we must recall that the slight experience in democratic living and the marked individualism of the South Vietnamese elite resulted in an infinity of small political groups that acted as opponents of the government in the cities, presented candidates for the elections, published pamphlets and small newspapers, but who were without the least following in the country areas where the majority of the population lives. The president of the Senate, the Catholic, Nguyen-Van-Huyen, who was already president of Catholic Action, in an interview granted me in Saigon in November 1967, told me:

Our Constitution permits various political parties, with the exception of the Communist party and others that share the same ideas. There is freedom for all, but not for those who use freedom to take power and suppress it! Actually, there are various political parties which during the electoral campaign supported various candidates or lists, but they are too numerous and poorly organized. . . . We have little experience of real democracy. We went from colonialism to the Diem dictatorship and then into the war. . . . So many political parties exist, too many I would say, and new ones are free to be organized. But we do not have a solid political tradition and are too individualistic; if a new party arises today, you can be sure that in a few months there will be two or three more parties arising from it.[11]

In addition to the political sides and parties, the Catholics did have a civic organization that represented them, the Bloc of Catholic Citizens, which expresses Catholic opinion on problems of national concern without being a political party and without presenting or supporting candidates for election (even the Buddhists and the other religious forces have similar representative organizations).

To mention a few concrete cases, in September 1966 the Bloc

officially asked the government to free the prisoners who had been condemned for political reasons after the fall of Diem, i.e., because they had been faithful to the dictator up to the last (the majority of these were Catholics). In June 1967 the Bloc protested publicly before the opinion of the country against a few clauses that limited the freedom of the presidential voting (September 1967), i.e., they made it difficult for a person to be a candidate (a cash deposit of some $1,500 was required, the candidate had to be presented by thirty members of the parliament or regional councils, etc.). On other occasions the Bloc took a position on local social problems, urged the Catholics to remain calm during the period of the Buddhist difficulties in the course of 1966, published statements on the elections, denying that any candidate could present himself as a Catholic,[12] etc.

Notes

1. On the "new course" of the Vietnamese Church after Diem, see the excellent study by Fr. Nguyen-Ngoc-Lan, a Redemptorist and one of the eleven priests who signed the appeal for peace, "L'Eglise du Sud Vietnam à l'heure de la vérité," *Frères du Monde,* Bordeaux, 1964, pp. 23–41.

2. The three bishops were: Mgr. Nguyen-Van-Binh, Archbishop of Saigon, Mgr. Nguyen-Khac-Ngu, Bishop of Long-Xuyen, and Mgr. Seitz, Bishop of Kontum.

3. The text of the document was published in *Sunday Examiner,* Hong Kong, December 13, 1963, p. 15.

4. Text of the letter in *Fides,* February 19, 1964, pp. 104–107.

5. The text of this appeal was published by *Kipa-Konzil* in the communiqué of May 5, 1967.

6. We have spoken at length about Fr. Quynh, but other Catholic priests were tempted by political activity and are still today figures of prominence on the Vietnamese scene. We recall Fr. Cao Van Luan, the founder and for many years the rector of the state University of Hué, who was forced to resign in 1963 because he had taken sides against Diem. After the dictator's fall, he was restored to his post with many honors, only to be forced again to resign in September 1964, partly because of his protest against the discriminations to which the Catholics were subjected, and partly because he

was unwilling to follow the political currents of Buddhism (Tri Quang) in their antigovernment demonstrations. Fr. Cao Van Luan is teaching philosophy today at the University of Saigon. Fr. Nguyen Lac Hoa was the founder of the "Sea Swallows," Catholic paramilitary groups for the defense of the Catholic villages against Viet Cong terrorism. Fr. Joseph Tran Du, secretary-general of the Bloc of Catholics, was disavowed under certain circumstances by the Archbishop of Saigon for his autonomous statements or initiatives, etc.

7. The Liaison committee was set up in 1955 in the archbishopric of Saigon and includes 10 priests and 10 lay Catholics who discuss the country's problems and publish semi-official communiqués and statements as its qualified representatives, not in the name of the archbishop or the bishops nor even of the whole Christian community. From the time it was set up, the Committee has always been thought of as the most authoritative voice of the Christian community in the political field, and its directives are generally followed by the majority of priests and Christians.

8. *Il Regno-Attualità,* Bologna, June 15, 1966, pp. 294–295.

9. In these last years, criticism by the bishops of the work of the government were also not lacking. For example, in the collective pastoral letter of January 5, 1968, the bishops gave a rather sorry description of the country, condemning the lack of freedom, justice, and truth in South Vietnamese society and stating, among other things: "How is peace possible if those on any level who have the responsibility are content with a 'false rhetoric of words,' and if in the way they act we find indolence, lying, cupidity, extortion and thievery?" *La Documentation Catholique,* coll. 267–269, February 4, 1968. Catholic criticism of the government, however, never assumed the character of an overt opposition, as happened in the "revolt" of some Buddhist groups in the spring and summer of 1966 (see the following chapter); on the contrary, as we shall see, the bishops and the Catholics always openly supported the Saigon governments and, moreover, the Catholics were deeply committed to the resistance against the Communist takeover (it is said in South Vietnam—I do not know on what statistical basis —that the Catholics are about 25 percent of the militia in the national army and 40 percent of the officers. Let us recall that the percentage of Catholics in the total population is from about 13 to 14 percent).

10. The voting of 1966 and 1967 was "the most democratic possible for a country overwhelmed by war," as was acknowledged by an authoritative American who is a critic of the American policy in Vietnam. Despite the opposition of the Viet Cong and a few Buddhist groups, 4,900,000 persons voted, which was about 80 percent of those who had the right to vote in

South Vietnam. On the occasion of the voting, in the three previous months, press censorship was abolished and there was the possibility of forming movements and setting up political lists, with the exclusion of the Communists or "neutralists." This certainly did much to limit the effective freedom of the voting. However, in all, there were 48 lists presented with about 4,500 candidates, from whom were chosen the 131 deputies and the 60 senators. For the presidential elections, the government list (Thieu-Ky) took only 34 percent of the vote, while their chief opponent, the attorney Dzu, who presented himself as a decided promoter of peace and negotiations with the Viet Cong, had 27 percent. This is rather convincing proof of a democratic voting process; (it is useless to recall that Ho Chi Minh's one list in the voting in North Vietnam obtains always more than 99 percent of the votes).

11. The interview with Senator Nguyen-Van-Huyen was published in two installments in *L'Italia,* December 31, 1967, and January 2, 1968.

12. On the occasion of the senatorial elections (September, 1967), Mgr. Nguyen-Van-Binh, Archbishop of Saigon, stated that "without a statement by the episcopal conference, no Catholic has the right to present himself as a representative of the Catholics of Vietnam. Likewise, no one can assert that he represents the Catholics of a given diocese if the bishop of that diocese has not given him a written statement to that effect." To our knowledge, no statement of this kind was given to the candidates either by the episcopal conference or by individual bishops.

VIII

The Political Roads of Buddhism and the Religious Confrontation

After Diem's fall, brought about chiefly by the antigovernment demonstrations of some Buddhist groups, Buddhism entered triumphantly into the national political arena. In this chapter we shall see its consequences, and we shall conclude with the new perspectives that the collaboration between the various religious forces of South Vietnam is promising to the country's future.

Detachment from the world or political commitment? First of all it is necessary to study the present internal organization of Vietnamese Buddhism, and to do this is not easy, since the Buddhist leaders themselves are not very clear on this point, at least from what I was able to gather through personal contacts and from consulting various writings and documents.

Leaving aside the two sects of Buddhist origin (Cao-Dai and Hoa-Hao), which are now completely separate and independent from national Buddhism, it is divided into two large groups: the Mahayana (Great Vehicle), of Chinese origin, prevalent in North and Central Vietnam (the Hué region); and the Hinayana (or Theravada, the Little Vehicle), coming from Cambodia, and prevalent in South Vietnam (the old Cochin China, i.e., the Saigon region). Between the two Buddhist currents there are irreconcilable religious differences in worship, in the attitude towards the world, etc. (not only in Vietnam, of course). For example Mahayana Buddhism (also called "broad" and nonorthodox" has deified the historical Buddha, while the Theravada (strict, and orthodox) considers Buddha to be only a man, a prophet who taught other men the way of purification and salvation.

The renewal of Vietnamese Buddhism (which we treated in Chapter V) came principally from the Mahayana current, whose bonzes (dressed in black, brown or white) became involved in social, cultural and political problems, giving rise to almost all the vital organizations of Vietnamese Buddhism in our day. On the other hand, the bonzes of the Theravada current—prevalent in Saigon and in the South—are completely detached from the world, dedicating themselves to meditation and asceticism in accordance with the ancient Buddhist tradition (these bonzes dress in yellow or orange). Naturally, behind this difference in behavior, there is a whole philosophical and religious substratum that would be too long to go into here. We are not dealing merely with contingent differences that could be swiftly overcome. The difference is profound and concerns the very way Buddhism conceives nature. For one group, the more religious, this is a doctrine of detachment from the world, of the abnegation of desires and of purification; for them, as Buddhists, the involvement in the external world is absurd. For the other group, however, Buddhism is a doctrine of justice and brotherhood that can regulate relations between men; it therefore requires a commitment to live in society and be of service to man. For the first group, the true Buddhist is one who follows the Buddha's example and leaves everything in order to go and live as an ascetic in the forest or the mountains; for the second, however, he is one who commits himself to the triumph among men of the Buddhist ideals of peace and tolerance.

In order to overcome these divergences, there have been congresses and unitary organizations since 1930, but with little success. Although at the top level there is a common coordinating organization, on the root level, i.e., among bonzes and the faithful, every one follows his own path; on one side, the Theravada Buddhists keep aloof from every political or social dispute, support the government thoroughly in its anti-Communist activities and accuse their brothers of the other current of having betrayed the spirit of Buddhism and of being Communists in bonzes' clothing; on the other side, the Mahayana Buddhists make the opposite accusations. Thus, we can understand why, either in the action against Diem in 1963, or in that against Cao Ky in 1966, the Buddhists of Hué and Danang (the Mahayana region) rose up, while the Buddhists of Saigon and Cochin China remained calm and supported the government (at Saigon there were also bonzes who burned themselves, but they were from the Mahayana pagodas).

An attempt to organize Buddhism on a national scale. The most serious obstacle to the affirmation of modern Buddhism and its ideas on the national plane is division and disorganization: the pagodas, monasteries, isolated bonzes, the various study or action organizations, all are independent from one another and owe obedience only to the local leader.

However, there do exist important organizations on the national level, although we could not say what effective juridical authority they have, since it was not possible for me to find this out precisely even from the parties concerned themselves.[1] We shall mention the principal organizations.

From December 21, 1963 to January 3, 1964 there was held in Saigon, near the Xa Loi pagoda, the most important modern congress of Vietnamese Buddhists that once again proposed the unification of all the Buddhist currents in the country. For the first time the Buddhists assumed the term "church" and founded the United Church of Vietnamese Buddhism (also called the Association of Unified Buddhism), to which in principle belong many currents and pagodas both of the Mahayana and Theravada groups.[2]

The Congress created a Supreme Patriarch (Tang Thong), an office still held today by the Ven. Thich Minh Khiet, assisted by a secretary, both very old men (Khiet is 84). Depending on the patriarch is a series of active and upright institutions of dynamic and modern bonzes: The Higher Institute of the Clergy (or Institute of Religious affairs, Vien Tang Thong) is a doctrinal-religious assembly composed exclusively of "venerable" bonzes (i.e., those who have had at least thirty years of religious life) who are to concern themselves solely with the problems of faith and customs. In practice, under the impetus of its secretary, Thich Tri Quang, it became an organization of clearly political tendencies until Tri Quang was forced to resign from the office (after the disturbances of 1966) and was replaced by Thich Du Nhuan, a refugee from North Vietnam.

The Institute for the Propagation of the Faith (Vien Hoa Dao) is an assembly representative of all the chief Buddhist sects and currents. It is composed of bonzes and laymen elected by provincial committees who in turn are elected by district committees, themselves elected by village committees elected by the local Buddhists. The Institute, whose secretary was Thich Tam Chau, until 1967, is a kind of assembly of Vietnamese Buddhism whose aim is to organize Buddhist forces unitarily throughout the country; it includes six commissions, each of which has an influential Buddhist bonze as its head (religious personnel, cultural affairs, rites, secular affairs, youth and finance) and on these commissions depend other lesser organizations which act in special fields (youth associations, Buddhist press, military chaplains, relations with the foreign press, etc.).

In this organization of Unified Buddhism (this is how the Church's title has come to be abbreviated) an attempt has been made to integrate the two great currents of Mahayana and Theravada through high-level contacts and discussions between bonzes and laymen of both currents. Even if this goal has not yet been reached, it has succeeded in giving Buddhism a certain appearance of unity in the eyes of the world.

Unified Buddhism has shown a special vitality during these years. In June 1964 at Saigon, the first stone was laid for the Buddhist university of Van-Hunh, which was completed in 1966. It is a large building of four floors, with a great amphitheater seat-ing 1,000, twenty classrooms, two conference halls and a library, which has become the most important center of Buddhist studies, especially in the training of the bonzes. In addition they have built youth centers in a few chief cities and, especially, many modern pagodas in the cities. They are grandiose and also luxurious and represent symbolically in the eyes of the people the rebirth of Vietnamese Buddhism and its growing importance in the society of the nation (a large number of these pagodas were built with government aid).

What do the Vietnamese Buddhists want? The intervention of Buddhism in Vietnamese politics, after the fall of Diem, was one of the main preoccupations of the Vietnamese press for at least a year after the killing of the dictator. A journalist wrote in June 1964:

Since the revolution of November 1, 1963, Unified Buddhism, whose action against the Ngo Ninh Diem government had such an important role in the fall of this regime, lives in a period of real fever. Buddhism had never been so spoken about as during these months. It is on the first page of every paper, reference is made to what it is doing, its messages are transmitted as well as its interventions, while photographs, as well as the movie-makers' screens reproduce its demonstrations everywhere. Everybody has the clear impression that at any cost Buddhism wants to sensitize public opinion and attribute to itself the entire merit of having eliminated the Ngo family, imitating with even greater fanfare that "triumphalism" which the Catholic Church has often manifested during the nine years of the Diem regime.

Not only is Buddhism considered the first religion of Vietnam, but it does everything to prove that whatever is not Christian in Vietnam is necessarily Buddhist. In the last analysis, the aim they pursue is undoubtedly to have Buddhism proclaimed the "national religion." This was practically stated by the Ven. Thich Minh Khiet, supreme leader of the Buddhists—an old man of some 80 years who serves as a front—in the last message he addressed to the Vietnamese people on the occasion of the anniversary festivals of the birth of the Buddha.[3]

In the years 1964–1965, Unified Buddhism (or the United Church of Vietnamese Buddhism) played an important role in South Vietnamese politics under the impulse and the inspiration of its two most prestigious leaders, Tri Quang and Tam Chau (in 1966, the break between these two leaders and other factors about which we shall be speaking were signs of the political decadence of Buddhism).

At the beginning of 1964, Buddhism had remarkable strength and influence in the country, and the government of General Khanh openly supported the Buddhist leaders in many of their requests. But at the same time, the government stood properly aloof from the Buddhist militants' movement when it was perceived that their political aims and pretenses in no way conformed with the public welfare. The Buddhist leaders began to accuse the government "with the same accusations they used one year before against Diem," as a newspaperman wrote. In the summer and autumn of 1964, the Buddhist disturbances grew in intensity, and at the end of October, General Khanh was forced to resign and to hand over the power to a civilian government, with Pham Khac Suu as head of state and Tran Van Huong as leader of the government. Both were Buddhists, and they introduced into the high counsel of the state representatives of the Unified Buddhist Church.

As J. Lacouture mentions, at this point the attitude of the Buddhist hierarchy became disconcerting since, according to the French journalist, the new civil government was not only composed in major part of Buddhists and took very much into account what the Buddhist authorities said, but it was also a government of civilians that was "the most democratic possible" in the situation in which Vietnam found itself. Therefore, we do not understand why this government as well, the fourth since Diem's, was not pleasing to the Buddhist leaders and was attacked by demonstrations in the public square led by the Unified Buddhist Church.

In the article cited, Lacouture writes:

What now is the question is what are the real aims of the Buddhist community and whether what it wants is the development of freedom and the return to peace or an increasing part of the exercize of power, or complete power. People may remember a statement of Huong [leader of the government] according to which the religious movements had to limit themselves to the religious field; it gave rise to the anger of the monks and especially to that of the bonze superior, Thich Tam Chau, while for months his spokesmen never ceased reminding people that the community's objectives were purely religious . . .

Then Lacouture tries to explain what the aims of Buddhist activity are:

. . . the monks consider themselves to be the most authentic spokesmen of the country, and especially of the peasants, and they think that the politico-religious ideology they have fashioned on the basis of pacifism, nationalism and appeals for social justice gives them the right to claim a position of power. It seems also always clearer that their aim is to have Buddhism proclaimed the state religion and to make the religious leaders either the cadres or at least the "consciences" of the future State of South Vietnam. In this they are opposed to the Liberation Front which is prevailingly Marxist. But, in midstream, it seems that for them [i.e., the Buddhists] it is of little importance to serve the guerrillas and, more proximately, to supply pretexts for the intervention of the "extremist" military and of those who are in the employ of the Americans supporting them.[4]

The correctness of this analysis is confirmed by a series of articles published during 1964 in the Buddhist weekly *Hai Trieu Ham* ("The Rising Tide"), in which the Ven. Tri Quang specified the aims of the militant Buddhist movement after having asserted that Buddhism for many centuries was the only national religion in Vietnam which gave the country its unity and fought against French colonialism. Tri Quang maintains that today Buddhism inspires some 80 percent of the Vietnamese and represents the perfect expression of the Vietnamese spirit, since it is the reflection and the idealization of all the best qualities of the people. Tri Quang thinks it is "absolutely necessary in the face of foreign ideologies that have invaded the country" to create a national spirit of Buddhist inspiration, and he reaches the conclusion that Buddhism, in which the Vietnamese people recognizes itself, must be recognized as the national religion, as it was in "the most glorious epochs of the history of Vietnam." "Thus, [as Lacouture writes (and we have given his resume of the bonze's thought)] we can qualify Tri Quang's elaborately worked out system as a 'national Buddhism,' a religion of the people that wants to be the ideology of the state."[5]

The Buddhist revolt of 1966. From the Diem days and in the following years up to today, the militant Buddhist movement has been involved in the dispute over the military and civilian governments, but we must also acknowledge its merit as an impetus for nationalism, democracy and peace, ideals shared by the whole Vietnamese people. "The Buddhist political leaders [Nhat Hanh states in the book mentioned, p. 103] made an effort to find a formula that would be able to express both the patriotism and the yearning for peace of their people; it was for this that they continued to fight. It was for this reason that they sought the aid of a constituent assembly and an elective government, not for personal greed.

Apart from every possible deviation of religious triumphalism and personal ambition, there is no doubt that the militant Buddhist movement has represented and still represents today a basically sound element in the conflicting political scene of the country, which is pursuing goals of national interest. Its mistakes and its limitations were in not taking sufficiently into account the real danger that the "Communist peril" presents for Vietnam; for this reason, during 1966, it lost almost all the support of the city elite and the masses and experienced a serious split between its two prestigious leaders, Tri Quang and Tam Chau. It saw its political importance decline, which today is infinitely less than what it was not only in 1963 but even in 1965.

The coup de grace was given to the political fortunes of Buddhism by the Constituent Assembly elections of 1966. These elections were requested by the Buddhists right after Diem's fall in order to open the way for a democratic constitution and a truly representative government. They remained one of the chief points of contention with the various governments who never wanted to or never could comply with the request.

On May 12, 1966, the United Church of Buddhism in Vietnam officially requested the government to call for national elections for the Constituent Assembly and a civil government, with the exclusion of the military.

In the book by Schlechter already mentioned,[6] the author says that from this point the Buddhists began to apply strong pressure, first with the generals and later in street demonstrations with continual waves of violence. From May to June they brought the country to the brink of total civil war with the 1966 Buddhist crisis. By comparison, according to Schlechter, the 1963 crisis was merely a meek prologue, since at that time the Buddhists had only begun to become aware of their power through the disturbances.

On April 14, the Buddhists got the head of state, Thieu, to sign a presidential decree in which the general elections for the Constituent Assembly were set for within five months. But on the following May 7, Cao Ky declared that the coming Constituent Assembly would in no way be a government: that would have to be elected in further general elections, and therefore his government would still remain in power for at least one year. In addition he stated that he would not have allowed a pro-Communist and neutralist government to come to power since the people did not wish to be "sold" to the Communists.

The Buddhists felt betrayed. They had thought that the Cao Ky government would have yielded power to an Assembly elected by all the people, hoping to control this representative organization. Now, however, they understood that it would be hard to get rid of Ky without a fight. In May and June 1966, a new civil war seemed on the verge of breaking out in South Vietnam. There were violent clashes between the Buddhists and the police at Hué, Danang, Saigon, Nhatrang, and in other cities, with dozens of fatal casualties and hundreds of wounded, the unexpected dropping of parachutists at Danang to recapture some public buildings in the city, the long "hunger strike" of Tri Quang, eleven bonzes immolating themselves by fire within a few days, harsh repression by the army, etc.

The reaction to Cao Ky's statements was understandable but undoubtedly excessive. The Buddhists, who had succeeded in having the promise of the general elections in answer to their requests, now did not want to work together for the successful outcome of the popular vote. In June they rejected a compromise with Ky (accepted by Tam Chau) and demanded not only the elections and the future civilian government but also the immediate resignation of the Cao Ky government. Government repression was ferocious and much more oppressive than Diem's in 1963, but by this time no one, either in Vietnam or in the world at large, was any longer disposed to support the Buddhists.

The political decline of Buddhism. From the middle of June on, the protests of the militant Buddhists lessened in intensity and the military's victory was complete. In September the general elections were held, and were boycotted to no avail by the Viet Cong and the Buddhists of Tri Quang's group (he had by now lost a great deal of his political credibility and influence in the country).

This failure of the Buddhist protests that signaled at least the temporary end of "political Buddhism" (as Tri Quang's group was defined) was explained in many ways and, actually, several factors contributed to bringing it about. The chief factor was the absence of popular support. At the time a lay director of the Buddhist movement stated that in 1963 the whole people became aroused when the monks burned themselves, but that now even if one hundred monks burned themselves the people would look the other way. In 1963 the monks were supporting a good cause, but this is no longer true today.[7]

It is difficult to determine the sentiment of the people in general, and especially the country people who constitute the very large majority of the Vietnamese population. Actually, politically speaking, this people does not "count for much," insofar as it does not have the capacity to express itself or to organize revolts. But in the cities, while the intellectual elite from among the students, workers and trade unions were clearly against Diem in the Buddhist revolt of 1963, they were no longer with the Buddhists in 1966, not because they supported Cao Ky positively but because they realized that the militant Buddhists' systematic overthrow of one government after another (there were about ten between Diem and 1966!) was certainly not the best way to strengthen the country and bring peace. If the 1966 Buddhist revolt had had even the smallest part of the popular support it enjoyed in 1963, it is likely that the Americans, who were anything but satisfied with the autonomy Ky was showing in their regard, would not have hesitated to intervene, as they did in 1963. However, they kept prudently aloof.

The second reason for the failure was the division within the ranks of militant Buddhism itself. In addition to the fact that the other religious groups (the Catholics,[8] Hoa-Hao and Cao-Dai), along with the more moderate Buddhist leaders (generally from the Theravada current), deplored the rebellions and decisively sided with the government, even among the politically committed Buddhist leaders there was a serious split. On June 1, Tam Chau reached a compromise with the government which agreed to add ten civilians to the military junta which was composed of ten generals; Tam Chau exhorted the Buddhists to end the antigovernment demonstrations and to work together for the September elections. Two days later, under pressure from the bonzes of Tri Quang's group, he gave his resignation to the United Church, but on June 7 he changed his mind, resumed his post within this largest of Buddhist organizations and succeeded with the help of the Saigon monks in ousting the bonzes from central Vietnam (i.e., Hué) who represented the extremist current. From that day, within the heart of modern political Buddhism (i.e., chiefly the Mahayana group) the split has never been healed.

The third cause of the political defeat of militant Buddhism was that it underestimated the tenacity and strength of Cao Ky, a factor not present in the Diem situation of 1963. Diem had nine years of dictatorship behind him (the people therefore wanted a change and hoped for the best), while Ky came after three years of continual coups d'etat, and everyone was now convinced that these continual changes of government helped no one. Diem was a Catholic, and the Buddhists had good reason to be unhappy with him, while Ky is a Buddhist and could not be accused of persecuting the Buddhists or showing favoritism to the Catholics; finally, Diem's dictatorship had displeased many people in the cities, while Ky's was still in its infancy and was tempered by controls that prevented him from assuming personal power.

After the 1966 voting, in a conference given to the foreign press, Cao Ky stated that "as a political force in Vietnam, Buddhism can be considered to be liquidated for all time. It is not possible to make all the mistakes the Buddhists made during all these years and then think that one can still fulfill a positive role in the country. Although they have been disoriented by the war, our people have always had a very good sense of judgment and have already drawn their conclusions."

This is an excessively severe judgment and we do not share it. Actually, militant Buddhism experienced the same defeat and political humiliation in 1966 as the militant Catholics did three years previously with Diem's fall, but this does not mean that Buddhism no longer has anything to say in the Vietnamese crisis, nor that it has lost any strength or popular support. Perhaps the period of monks burning themselves and leading revolts in the streets of the cities is over, but aside from this extremism, the importance of Buddhism in the political and social life of Vietnam cannot be questioned.

How the "Council of Religions" works. Many in Vietnam express the conviction that peace will be possible only when a popular and nationalist "third force" asserts itself in the country, a force that would be really independent of the Americans but which would also know how to treat with the Communists on an equal footing, working with them in a coalition government without allowing themselves to be overwhelmed. The tragedy of the Vietnamese situation is precisely this: such a "third force," independent from either side in the conflict (the NLF and North Vietnam on the one hand, the military and the Americans on the other) still does not exist. After Diem's death the country has not found a leader capable of opposing the American intrusion and giving the people a hope in the future. Diem would have been able to deal and make agreements with the Viet Cong (as he was in the process of doing in the last six months of his life), certain of having behind him a good part of the people and therefore also sure of being able to admit the Communists and divide the power without necessarily allowing himself to be overwhelmed.

The government leaders today are under no illusion. If the Viet Cong joined a coalition government and the Americans left, the paramilitary organization of the Communists would win out over any opposition and in all likelihood the people would remain passive, as they do today in the jaws of terror. The political parties existing today in Vietnam involve only a few of the intellectuals from the cities and have no following among the masses of the people who for the most part live in the country areas; and furthermore, as long as the war lasts, it is almost impossible for these political movements to assert themselves on a national level.

In this truly discouraging situation, the only hope seems to reside in the union of religious forces which together could constitute a bloc capable of controlling the country and of coming to terms with the Viet Cong. Unfortunately this is only a vague hope that is still far from being realized in the concrete, although in recent years some progress has been made in this direction with the various religious groups meeting together and collaborating.

The major step in this direction was the founding of the Council of Religions in 1964, as a result of the concern of the apostolic delegate Mgr. Palmas and the Vietnamese bishops. This organization originated during the most fevered months of the "settling of accounts" by the Buddhist extremists from various regions and groups with the Catholics (whom they held responsible for the excesses of the Diem regime). The immediate and initial goal of the new organization proposed by the Catholic bishops but immediately accepted by the leaders of the other religions was to reestablish peace among the faithful of the various religions, avoiding bloody encounters especially between Catholics and Buddhists by creating a climate of understanding and collaboration.

The initial aim was attained, and today the interreligious relations are undoubtedly much better than in 1963–1964. But the old mistrust and rivalries are still very much alive and are aggravated by the differing opinions about the present situation in Vietnam and the methods to achieve peace.

In Saigon I had a long meeting with Fr. Vui, the Catholic priest who is president of Caritas-Vietnam and the Church's representative in the Council of Religions, and I was also able to take part in a meeting of religious leaders at the Council's headquarters in one of the main streets of Saigon, when Mgr. Palmas presented Paul VI's peace message of December 8, 1967. The atmosphere of the meeting, at which the chief representatives of the various religions were present, seemed calm and even fraternal to me; the meeting lasted for more than two hours, and the papal message was discussed and applied to the concrete situation in Vietnam.

Fr. Vui explained to me how the Council of Religions works. These are the priest's own words:

Every Tuesday afternoon we meet for discussion for two or three hours, two or three members of each religion, at the Council's own headquarters, which has an office open every day. In these meetings, which take place in a serene atmosphere of friendship, the various religions inform the others about their problems and latest news, and then we discuss together the social, moral, and political situations in our country. . . . At times, during the week, representatives of the various religions visit religious institutions; for example, we recently visited our seminary in Saigon and ate with the clerics. . . . In the Council we are all on an equal level and the president changes each month. . . . The religions represented in the Council are the Catholic Church, Baha'i, Hoa-Hao, Cao-Dai, Confucianism and the Vietnam Buddhist Association. The Protestants, who are very few in Vietnam, have not yet agreed among their various Church bodies upon a common representative.

After having stated that the Council of Religions already represents the majority of the South Vietnamese population, Fr. Vui regretted the absence of the United Buddhist Church (Unified Buddhism):

This is also the major difficulty opposing a common action in favor of peace. Vietnamese Buddhism is now profoundly divided precisely about the problem of peace. In 1964, at the beginning of the activity of the Council of Religions, the two major Buddhist organizations were represented; the Buddhist Association and Unified Buddhism. The first represents the majority of the Buddhist faithful, but it has never been involved in political problems; the second, on the other hand, is a minority but every active and political. In 1966, Unified Buddhism divided into two currents: the first is directed by Tam Chau, originally from North Vietnam, favorable to the government and an anti-Communist; the second was led by Tri Quang, originally from Hué in central Vietnam, an opponent of the presence of the Americans and of the government of the South, with a rather neutralist tendency. The two currents which both continue to call themselves Unified Buddhism are not represented on the Council since neither is willing to join if the other side also joins.[9]

Common activities and positions of the various religions. The activities of the Council of Religions have first of all the goal of starting collaboration among the religions on a charitable and social plane in order to take common positions later on. Good results have been accomplished: common distribution of material aid to the refugees, war and flood victims; the establishment of a common financial fund for this charitable aid; mutual assistance for social and charitable institutions sponsored by the various religions; the first nursery schools built and sponsored by all the religions in common, etc. Such practical collaborations are intended to create a spirit of fraternity and help to overcome mutual jealousies.

The Council has also taken a position on the moral[10] and social problems of the country, has initiated inquiries into certain problems, published their results, and involved the faithful from the various religions in working together to solve the difficulties encountered by the country; finally, it has published documents and appeals in the direction of morality, justice, the need for working together, etc.

The difficulties arise in respect to agreeing upon common positions and common action in favor of peace, which are directly involved with politics. In the interview mentioned, Fr. Vui told me:

As long as it is a question of making general statements in favor of peace, the matter presents no difficulty and is even superfluous since statements of this kind abound either by the Catholic bishops or by the heads of the other religions. But when it is a question of getting down to the concrete and of proposing together a precise goal to be reached, it is a horse of a different color. First of all, the religions represented, with the exception of the Catholic Church, do not want to commit themselves to statements of a political character since this is not part of their traditions and mentality. But then, once this difficulty is overcome, there is the problem of knowing what influence the position of their leader would have on the faithful of the various religions. This is certainly not true for the Church, which is a very united and organized body; but the other religions do not have a centralized organization and universally recognized leaders who can give an order and be obeyed, or even a discourse and be followed by all their faithful. Religion here in the orient is more of a sentiment than a faith and more of a tradition than an organized Church. Hence there is a certain complex that the others have towards us Catholics: we have discussions and reach an agreement, but as for performing a common action for peace, they are afraid that we Catholics who are more organized and able will then gain control of the situation and be dominant . . .

The Council of Religions has, however, published common statements on the problem of peace, and on other political problems, but it has not yet bound its faithful to one directive and to political action. For example, in January 1965, a common five point statement was published in which it requested the government for a democratic and nonmilitary regime, for a guarantee of religious freedom, the maintenance of unity among the South Vietnamese peoples, the forbidding of illegal demonstrations and the saving of the country from Communist subversion. In addition to the representatives of the other religions, the document was also signed by Thich Thien Minh, leader of the youth movement of the United Buddhist Church.

Very important was the position taken by the Council of Religions in February 1967 in answer to a Vietnam peace demonstration arranged in Brussels for March 4, in which people demanded the immediate withdrawal of American troups from Vietnam to allow Vietnamese to decide their own problems on their own (which has always been the thesis of North Vietnam and the Viet Cong, and is tantamount to the opinion of those who during the Second World War demanded the withdrawal of Americans from Europe in order to let the Europeans decide for themselves about their own problems, all the more since the Nazis never bombed American cities, just as the Viet Cong and the North Vietnamese have not done in this war). Since the demonstration seemed also to have implicated Cardinal Cardijn, the Council of Religions sent him this message:

The Council of Religions in Vietnam is in unanimous agreement with the demonstrations for peace in Vietnam. In all sincerity we ask you, in the name of freedom and clarity, to adopt these principles:

(1) Put an end to political assassinations, to the "scorched earth" tactics, to the Communist invasion of South Vietnam, and at the same time stop the allied bombings of North Vietnam.

(2) To give the Vietnamese people self-determination it is necessary to bring a planned and effectively controlled halt to any military aid, whether from the Communists or the allies.

(3) We solemnly request the people of Belgium to avoid any decision that may signify material or moral harm for the Vietnamese people, who find themselves today in the same situation as the Belgian people in 1940–1944.

(4) Since we have confidence in the heroic past of Belgium which has barred the way to dictatorship in the defense of freedom, we request your country to give fraternal assistance to the Vietnamese people who are fighting against the Communist dictatorship, just as the free world aided Belgium in the fight against Nazism.[11]

Other common actions and statements were made during these years by the Council of Religions,[12] but we think that what has been said is enough to give an idea about this very important organization, which is still developing.

The pontifical mission of Mgr. Pignedoli. An event of great importance, with the purpose of achieving better understanding and collaboration between religions, was the "mission" of Mgr. Pignedoli who visited Vietnam from September 28 through October 5 bearing a message from Paul VI to the Council of Religions. Here are some excerpts:

It has been for us a source of comfort and satisfaction to learn that qualified representatives of the various religious communities in Vietnam have founded an organization, the Council of Religions, with the aim of promoting an ever more effective collaboration among the citizens. To such a generous initiative the Catholic Church cannot not belong, she who, by divine mandate, favors and stimulates the union and the charity of all men and of all peoples, since they have in common the same origin and the same end.

The Catholic Church in no way rejects what is true and good in different religions. She respects the modes of living and acting, the doctrines and the teachings that point the way whereby men, acknowledging their radical insufficiency, seek with a trusting and submissive heart to arrive at the stage of perfect illumination by their own efforts and with the help that comes from on high. It is for this reason that we desire to express to the delegations of the Council of Religions our congratulations for the happy success of their arduous enterprise and to witness to them that sympathy which, by virtue of the principles of universal brotherhood, we harbor toward all, and particularly toward the generous people of this country in this difficult and resolute hour for their fatherland.

We like to think that the Council of Religions—in the spirit aroused by Vatican Council II—will be able to contribute toward extending this dialogue begun under such promising auspices. It will undoubtedly contribute toward dissipating misunderstandings, preventing unjustified barriers from separating the sons of one and the same fatherland, promoting mutual respect, uniting all in the defense of spiritual, moral, social and cultural values that constitute the solid bases upon which human society rests.[13]

On October 5, Mgr. Pignedoli met the members of the Council of Religions, who had come together in an extraordinary session.[14] and presented them with the papal message, with short words of commentary, followed by a lengthy exchange of ideas in an atmosphere of sincere friendship. I can state personally, having gone to Vietnam more than one year after Mgr. Pignedoli's visit, how opportune his mission was, and it is still remembered by the non-Christian members of the Council of Religions (in addition to the Christians, of course).

An extraordinary assembly of Vietnamese bishops. Mgr. Pignedoli's mission, even before his personal meeting with the leaders of the other religions, was a stimulus to the Christian community in general to work with greater concord and decisiveness for peace, putting themselves unconditionally at the service of the country. This is proved by the message of Paul VI to the Vietnamese bishops and the final communiqué of the bishops' extraordinary conference, presided over by Mgr. Pignedoli. In his message to the bishops of Vietnam, the Pope wrote, among other things, after have praised "the admirable attachment to the faith of the fathers" of the Catholics and "the apostolic impetus" of the bishops: "At this point we should like to recommend warmly to them [i.e., to the Catholics] to cling always in their activity to that enlightened prudence and that common discipline imposed by the present situation . . . [and to] work for a meeting of minds and an understanding of spirits: these are the two indispensable factors for a return to peaceful and tranquil work in all fields and for the putting into effect of the so desired social and political reforms.[15]

After the extraordinary episcopal conference, which lasted from September 28 to October 7, 1966, a communiqué was issued, signed by all the bishops of Vietnam, the apostolic delegate, Mgr. Palmas, and the papal legate, Mgr. Pignedoli. It is a very important and clear document which continues to inspire the action of Christians and the Vietnamese Church throughout the last two years. In it, the bishops, after recalling the Pope's work for peace in Vietnam and joining their voice to that of Paul VI in the resquest for peace, and after greeting the Christian people, reminding them of their duties toward their neighbor, wrote:

We desire to address our fraternal greeting to all the faithful of the other religious denominations. We declare ourselves universal brothers of all men. We want only mutual respect, concord, fraternal dialogue. We are very much aware that in such sentiments and in the cordial and respectful union of each and everyone the Nation will be restored, and it will build a better world for itself. We warmly urge our Catholic faithful to participate in this constant and sincere effort.

But to our faithful, we should also like to give some valuable and urgent advice:

(1) It is well-known that, as a whole, the faithful are fervent and animated by the spirit of sacrifice. However, there are some who have reactions that are more sentimental than reasonable, who cling more to the letter of the law than its spirit, who live an insufficiently deepened Christianity to the point that their judgment risks confusion and their activity risks being considered rash, especially in the difficult moments in which we are living. We particularly notice the fact that private and public morality is being compromised, justice is not respected, the rush for pleasure and money is unbridled, and in this way our society is allowing itself to be seduced into a state of affairs that is completely contrary to our best national traditions and to the evangelical spirit.

After having urged the faithful to deepen their faith and to live in accordance with the Christian spirit, the bishops continue:

(2) The hour has come, dear brethren, in which the Christian must become more aware of his own responsibilities. . . . We stress this with you so that you are not afraid to assume your responsibilities as laymen in the areas that belong to you; in this way your priests can better devote themselves to the pastoral and spiritual tasks that are theirs . . .

(3) Let the Catholic never forget that he is a full-fledged citizen in his common fatherland. . . . In order for justice and the common good to be respected in all activities, the Catholic citizenry must preserve calm and concord, avoiding everything that can be a reason for hatred or revenge. At times, they prefer to suffer harm, although asserting their rights in justice, rather than create a climate of discord.

In the specifically political camp, let the Christian become involved not out of personal interest but for the good of the national community. He will not hesitate, if it so happens, to join a particular and upright political party which, whatever its aims, is concerned for the country and respects religion.

The bishops requested greater instruction and discussion about political and social problems in order to make the people more staunchly mature, and they went on:

(4) Finally, with joy and with special friendship, we say to all the young people that we have great confidence in them. You are, friends, at an age of searching, at an age of generosity. . . . Never let yourselves be discouraged by the difficulty of the times. . . . Shun every hypocrisy and every selfishness. . . . Be men of honor, upright in all things and always loving loyalty and justice. Therefore, from now on, you are builders of the future . . .

Dearest brethren, this is the practical way for us all to work ardently for the building of the peace that we all desire; this is the way that we shall bring to the world the witness of love and faith that it expects from Christians.[16]

Commenting upon the assembly of bishops and the final communiqué, Mgr. Pignedoli stated that the convergence and the understanding between the various religious forces was

stabilized after the extraordinary assembly of the Vietnamese episcopate, over which I presided in the pope's name; a most important assembly, either because it was the first one since the Council or because it was held in a very special situation and at a very particular historical moment. It issued a document, three points of which I would like to underline: the exhortation of the Catholics to unity; the attitude the churchmen have to keep aloof from politics, and to leave political involvement to a laity we consider mature; the freedom acknowledged Catholics to belong even to non-Catholic parties that guarantee respect for religion and the human person—a daring concession.[17]

The Church must be the first to move. What are the concrete possibilities of unity and common action on the part of the different religions, especially in regard to peace? At present they seem in all sincerity very rare, especially on account of the mutual distrust and misunderstandings that continue to subsist very strongly. Religious dialogue between the religious communities has still not begun, except for the rare exceptions of the elite and the work of the Council of Religions. On the part of the Christians—who are of more concern to us here—they are still lacking the basic dispositions for this dialogue.

A Vietnamese religious writes:

We must acknowledge that the current attitude with Christians is to think that they already possess all the Truth and, consequently, that they have nothing to learn from the others. Since Christianity is the definitive and perfect religion, it no longer has anything to receive, no problem to solve, no progress to effect. This attitude is clearly contrary to the spirit of dialogue. Christians need to realize . . . that they have the duty to pay attention to their brothers, to seek to understand them, to become informed about their beliefs, to enter into contact with them; and all this must be done with the greatest respect for their freedom, without the intention to win them over or to proselytize.[18]

And a missionary with long experience in Vietnam, Fr. Parrel, writes:

What is certain is that few among our Christians and even among the priests know Buddhism, and this is too bad, since to dialogue it is necessary to know one another, to be friends, to have mutual esteem instead of ignorance of one another, and not knowing what the other person thinks. We must therefore hope that the contacts which have already begun will be widened.

Certainly, the Buddhists generally do not have an instinctive fear of Communism like the Catholics. Their doctrine, moreover, recommends nonviolence, while the Christians, particularly the refugees from the North who have known Communism through personal experience, show themselves to be intractable on this point and are always ready to lead a real crusade. We think that many misunderstandings come from this diversity of outlook.[19]

Despite the bishops' urgings to collaborate with all the Vietnamese for the building of peace and the stabilizing of relations of real friendship with the faithful of other religions, the Catholics still have the tendency to be self-inclosed, to ignore the "others" and at times even to flee contacts with them as a danger to the faith. We must naturally take into account, in order to make an objective judgment, the fact that this mentality arose and is maintained with one specific motivation, incorrect but still understandable, of the defense of the faith. In the Orient, the common frame of mind and the religious relativism and, especially in Vietnam, the religious syncretism, have had their greatest expression, as we have already seen.

The Christian brother whom we have already mentioned writes:

Relativism is an aspect of the Vietnamese mentality. The Vietnamese religious spirit is characterized by a basis of animism on which has been grafted a syncretism that includes Confucianism, Buddhism and Taoism. A Vietnamese finds no contradiction in honoring Confucius, going to the pagoda and occasionally practising sorcery. It is not rare to find in the pagodas altars dedicated to Taoist divinities, to spirits or to heroes of the country. The fact is very significant that Caodaism, the only religious sect to be born in Vietnam, is an amalgam of Christianity, Buddhism, etc. . . .

One Vietnamese priest had me read the "Open letter to Mr. Nolting" addressed in 1963 by some Vietnamese figures to the American Ambassador, a document about which we have already spoken; among other things we read the following: "Confucianism, Caodaism and Buddhism have fused to become 'The Union of the Three Religions in Vietnam.' Caodaism honors both the Buddha and Jesus Christ. Why, then, can Christianity not meld with the Three Religions to make a Union of the Four Religions, as the Vietnamese have always done for centuries?"

The dialogue with the other religions, this priest told me, is desirable for us, but only on the social and political levels in the areas of understanding and fraternal collaboration and not on the level of religious syncretism, since this would mean the end of our minority Christianity, with its simple faith and lack of familiarity with theological subtleties. Ours is primarily a peasant people, a people of fishermen and simple workers. They do not have the culture you have in Europe.

But this is precisely the problem: for fear of contaminating the purity of the faith, the dialogue with the faithful of other religions never comes about in the social, cultural or political level! We think that the Vietnamese Church has not yet done what it could to establish dialogue with the non-Christians, to emphasize "more what unites us than what divides us," according to the principle given by John XXIII for ecumenism.

What unites the various religions in Vietnam is of particular importance for the future of the country, and all the faithful in the various religions, just like the organizations and the representative figures of these religions, must be ready for a concerted action in this direction. On the social level, solidarity among all the Vietnamese, charity toward the poor and the refugees, social justice; on the moral plane, detachment from money and pleasures, respect for the human person, the unity of families, the condemnation of immorality in all of its aspects; on the political level, democracy, freedom of the press and of thought, popular representation in the government, the refusal to use political means to further the interests of particular religious denominations, the defense of religious freedom. . . . All of these things, which unite the various Vietnamese religions, seem more than sufficient to undertake courageously an action in common.

But this is still not enough: what principally unites all the Vietnamese is the search for peace, the creation of a spirit of peace, and the removal of reasons for division and struggle. On the peace theme all the religions agree, even if there is some diversity in the concrete way of willing peace and the means that must be taken to achieve it (but we shall be speaking of this in the next chapter).

Notes

1. The interesting book of the bonze, Nhat Hanh, *Vietnam pace proibita,* Florence, 1967, completely passes over the internal organization of Vietnamese Buddhism.

2. Alongside the official Church, the Vietnam Buddhist Association,

headed by the same Ven. Thich Minh Khiet, Supreme Patriarch of the Unified Church, continues to exist. However, the two Buddhist currents have their national association: the Association of Vietnamese Theravada Buddhists, with their leader, the bonze Nguyen Van Hieu, and the Mahayana Association of Vietnam, with Mai-Tho-Truyen as its head.

3. *Le Monde,* June 17, 1964, p. 4.

4. J. Lacouture, "Mais que veulent les bouddhistes sud-vietnamiens?" *Le Monde,* December 18, 1964 (in 1963, Lacouture supported the Buddhist thesis against the Diem regime).

5. Lacouture sums up Tri Quang's articles in *Le Vietnam entre deux paix* (Paris: Ed. du Seuil, 1965), pp. 213–214. Tri Quang expressed the same ideas in a study entitled "Bouddhisme: 'religion nationale' "? published in a mimeographed work *Vietnam, relations entre le Bouddhisme et le Catholicisme,* published in 1964 by the OSCO (Overseas Students Coordination Organization) of Bonn (pp. 1–7). On the question of a "national" or "state" religion, the bonze Nhat Hanh, a disciple of Tri Quang, denied in the West that this was the aim of militant Buddhism in Vietnam, see *Vietnam, la pace proibita,* p. 58, and "Où en est le bouddhisme au Vietnam?" *Frères du Monde,* no. 2, 1964, pp. 62–63.

6. J. Schechter, *The New Face of Buddha* (New York: Coward-McCann, 1967), p. 212.

7. Schechter, *op. cit.,* p. 236. Even international public opinion was no longer with the Buddhists in 1966, although it had strongly supported them in 1963. The six Buddhist monks who burned themselves in 1963 were enough to spread throughout the world—and not only in the Communist or neutralist world—a violent campaign against the Diem regime which ended with his fall; in 1966, eleven bonzes and nuns burned themselves in all and several others voluntarily mutilated themselves, but their singular protests passed almost unnoticed in the international press, even in that part of it that had always taken sides with the Buddhists.

8. In the "Buddhist crisis" of the spring of 1966, the Catholic bishops published various invitations to remain calm, forbidding the Catholics to make counterdemonstrations against the Buddhists (which in fact was done by a few groups), and supporting the government, although they urged it to put into practice democratic institutions, grant greater freedom of the press, actuate reforms, etc., see *Fides,* April 20, 1966, the communiqué of March 29 of the Archbishop of Saigon's "Liaison Committee," and *Sunday Examiner,* Hong Kong, June 17, 1966, p. 7, the communiqué of the Catholic information center, which launched an appeal for calm and moderation).

9. The complete interview with Fr. Vui was published in *L'Italia,* Milan, January 19, 1968.

10. To give a concrete example, let us report the intervention of the Council of Religions in the question about the term God in the Vietnamese Constitution. This was discussed and approved during the course of 1967 by the Constituent Assembly, elected on September 11, 1966. In the projected constitution the preamble contained these words: "The Vietnamese people assumes the responsibility before Almighty God and before history to renew its tradition of independence and to accept new ideas." These words of a spiritual tone were taken out of the text at the last moment despite numerous protests from newspapers and prominent figures.

On March 20, 1967, two days before the constitution was promulgated, the Council of Religions wrote the following letter to the president of the Constituent Assembly: "The Council of Religions intends to affirm before our fellow countrymen and the constituent assembly that: (1) The Vietnamese are a religious and believing people. (2) The refusal of the Constituent Assembly to accept its responsibility before Almighty God is contrary to the faith of the whole Vietnamese people and, by doing so, in accordance with the tradition of the people, the Assembly rejects every moral grounds guaranteeing authority."

It was later found out that the phrase referring to Almighty God was removed after pressure from the Buddhist groups detached from the Vietnam Buddhist Association (which was a member of the Council of Religions); the protesting groups with their two leaders, Tri Quang and Tam Chau, could not accept the reference to God because the same expression was used as in the Catholic creed, Dang Toi Cao (Almighty God or Supreme Being).

On the day the constitution was promulgated (April 1, 1967), the president of the Constituent Assembly promised that a compromise would be sought in the reference to God. Following many contacts with the Council of Religions, the compromise was reached some weeks afterward, with the approval of a codicil added to the constitution: "The National Assembly, elected on September 11, 1966, stated solemnly before all the people: the Constitution of the Republic of Vietnam, approved last March 8 and promulgated on April 1, is based on religious faith, respects religious freedom and is opposed to atheistic Communism. The National Assembly proclaims deep trust in the Divine Being of all religions." Naturally, the Vietnamese word for Divine Being was different from what was used in the first project and was then discarded (*Thieng Lieng* was the term used).

One other example. On January 23, 1967, the National Assembly voted a law, established afterwards by contacts with the Council of Religions, which guaranteed freedom for all religions and forbade the government to declare a state religion; the same law established the equality of all religions before the state and the equality of all citizens, irrespective of sex, religion, political opinions, etc.

11. The text was published in its entirety in *Sunday Examiner*, March 3, 1967, p. 15. On February 19, Cardinal Cardijn published a responding communiqué to the message of the Council of Religions (see the same issue and the same page of the *Sunday Examiner*) in which he stated that he was not the organizer of the demonstration but that he had given it his support out of a love of peace and of all the Vietnamese, after the example of Paul VI. Finally, the Cardinal specified that his support was solely for peace, with the exclusion of any political significance.

12. Let us cite some other facts. From January 1965 and in the years after the World Day of Religions was celebrated in conjunction with the Unity Week, celebrated by the Christians, the aim was to create fraternity among the faithful of the various religions, involving them all in the struggle against materialism of whatever kind that was threatening the spiritual life of the people. On April 28, 1968, for the first time, Catholics and Buddhists in Saigon celebrated a religious service together in memory of the victims of the Viet Cong Tet offensive (February, 1968); the service was presided over by Fr. Hoang Quynh and by a venerable bonze. In June 1968 the Council of Religions published a declaration in which they condemned the indiscriminate attacks against the cities of South Vietnam, especially Saigon, which had almost never stopped from February to June 1968. The document attributes a terroristic character to these ruthless acts of war and asks for an end to these inhumane methods of extermination, see *L'Osservatore Romano,* June 28, 1968, p. 1.

13. *L'Osservatore Romano,* October 5, 1966 (the document is dated September 15, 1966, the very day of the publication of the peace encyclical, *Christi Matri*).

14. In which also the members of the United Church of Buddhism participated.

15. *La Documentation catholique,* coll. 1741–1746, 1966.

16. *L'Osservatore Romano,* October 17–18, 1966.

17. *La Civilità Cattolica,* November 5, 1966.

18. Hoang Gia Quang, "Une Eglise cherche à adapter son message: évolution du Vietnam et catéchèse," *Lumen Vitae,* no. 3, Brussels, 1965, pp. 549–550.

19. F. Parrel, "L'Eglise et les religions non-chrétiennes au Vietnam," *Missions Etrangères de Paris,* March–April, 1966, p. 30.

IX

War or Peace? The Choice
of Vietnamese Catholics

"Father, tell us something about peace! Describe to us how people live in a country at peace!" This is the strange and moving question I was asked by a girl student during the course of a meeting with students I had in Hué. I had asked them for their opinion on the war in Vietnam. But rather than speak of war, these young people wanted to hear from me, coming from Italy, the description of life in a country at peace. It was the most beautiful and most complete answer to all my queries about what Vietnam's youth thought, and what were their greatest aspirations.

Each year 600,000 babies are born in Vietnam, and the population under thirty represents from 70 to 75 percent of the whole South Vietnamese people (about 16,000,000). These young people under thirty have known nothing but war in their lives, a war which in Vietnam has lasted, more or less, since 1941, a year that for them is far in the past.

A detestable war. For one who does not sufficiently detest war as a means of resolving political and ideological conflicts, a visit to Vietnam is advisable: not an airplane trip with the American forces or a short stay in the air-conditioned hotels, but living in the terrorized villages among the refugees who have lost everything, in the cities and country areas where people spend their days and nights in a slow agony.

The Bishop of Dalat—one of the more fortunate areas of South Vietnam since it has been hit less hard by the guerrilla war—Mgr. Nguyen-Van-Hien, wrote a letter in the autumn of 1966 to the pope to thank him for his concern for peace. In the document, we read the following:

The war has caused enormous damage in our villages, created many gaps in our families, and reduced many persons to the most wretched misery. In our diocese alone, according to official statistics, there live 22,000, but who knows their real number? One mother, holding her two little children to her breast, told me one day: "I had seven children. Bullets struck five of them down. My husband and I, with these little creatures in our arms, walked more than 37 kilometers to save ourselves."

If I should want to tell all of the bloody sights I witnessed, even though mine was a short stay in Vietnam, I would have to write another book: a civilian railroad car, blown up by a mine, with seven dead and some ten seriously wounded; a village destroyed "by mistake" by American cannons in the mountains; shootings along the country roads, people killed in the night by Viet Cong terrorists. . . . I still have before my eyes the last dead person seen in the city of Nha-Trang, a floating corpse, black and swollen like a wineskin, which the river current had brought along to a bridge-support where it became anchored. . . . And then the wretched refugee villages on the outskirts of the cities and just below the demilitarized line:[1] poor people uprooted from their fields and villages, the most heart-rending victims of the war, without steady work, supported in great part by government aid and the charitable assistance of the whole world.

Thirty billion dollars a year! And then there is the moral damage of the war. Even more than prostitution, which is undoubtedly very widespread but almost solely in a few large cities, what is most horrifying morally is the fact that people have become used to war, bloodshed and cruelty. Before becoming a military and political condition, peace is a state of mind with respect for one's neighbor, an inclination to come to an accord with one's adversaries and not to resolve the eventual divergences with force but with sincere dialogue and understanding. How is education for peace possible when the majority of the Vietnamese know only war? The use of arms is the chief occupation of men and youths, whether they are in the government army or with the Viet Cong. The term of service in the army is practically unlimited. In the Viet Cong training it is the same: whoever joins up, willingly or otherwise, no longer has any possibility of getting out. Once there is military and political peace, how will these thousands of young peasants, trained only to kill, adapt to civilian life?

Then there is economic damage. There is not only visible damage, abandoned country areas, (South Vietnam which used to be a great exporter of rice now lives partially from American rice!) streets, bridges, railways destroyed, etc., but also the damage created by an artificial war economy which tomorrow, in peacetime, will cause the country to be faced with the difficult problem of reconversion. In the country areas the war has brought hunger and poverty. In the cities or near the military bases it has created, on the other hand, a high but completely artificial standard of living. Tomorrow, if there is no massive foreign aid to help create peacetime industry, the awakening will be most difficult.

Finally, on the negative balance sheet of this war—although I make no claim to completeness—we must put its scandalous financial cost, when half the men in the world do not even have enough to eat. I was able to visit the American military base of Cam Ranh, the largest in the Orient and possibly in the whole world, some 60 kilometers south of Nha-Trang. It was a thorough visit of one whole day, and I used the jeep of a Catholic military chaplain, Fr. Joseph Cusma, whose family came originally from the Abruzzi. I shall not try to describe what I saw, since I have neither the com-

petence nor the space: mountains of barrels and cases, long kilometers of jeeps and small trucks, hundreds of airplanes and heli-
copters, stocks of bombs, bullets and arms that would make one
dizzy. . . . The base is some 50 kilometers long and 5 to 10
kilometers wide and stands on the Cam Ranh peninsula and the
surrounding land. It is actually only a succession of military camps,
offices, hospitals, depots and airfields, with a port which, when it
is completed, will be one of the largest in the whole Orient.

Certainly, when one thinks that America is spending for the
Vietnam War in one year almost twice the annual budget of Italy
(i.e., about 30 billion dollars), we cannot help thinking what such
a colossal financial effort could do in relieving so much misery if it
were used for peaceful aims and not for war.

Is it true that the Catholics do not want peace? The problem of
peace in Vietnam torments the conscience of the peoples of the
whole world, especially the young. But, we must ask ourselves,
what is the position of the Vietnamese Church in regard to the
war? What is the Vietnamese Church doing for peace?

The greatest calumny that causes Vietnamese Catholics (and
their priests and bishops) to suffer is what we read from time to
time in some newspaper or magazine of the West, namely, that the
Catholics of Vietnam do not want peace but the continuation of the
war.

There is an enormous difference between us in the West and the
Vietnamese. While we are demanding peace without worrying
about "afterwards," the Vietnamese Catholics and the whole people
in general seek a peace that would guarantee freedom and not
"peace at any cost" which would then become a "Communist
peace." Catholics do want peace but not just any peace; they
want a just peace, in freedom, fraternity and justice.

Coming back from a trip to the Orient, after having visited not
only Vietnam but also the neighboring countries, Thailand,
Cambodia, Hong Kong, the Philippines and India, I was struck by

the fact that while we in Italy and the West are demanding peace in Vietnam, and a peace without adjectives (I would say "peace at any cost"), and while what is important for us is that the shooting and killing stop, so that we might be at peace with our own consciences, for the people of Vietnam and the neighboring countries, i.e., for those living in the area directly involved by the war, the most important thing is that the cessation of hostilities really bring peace, in fraternity, justice and liberty for all. For what kind of a peace would it be if it produced dictatorship, suppression of adversaries, the loss of religious and civil freedom, and the revival of hatreds and vendettas?

The thought of Vietnamese Catholics is summed up very well by the Bishop of Dalat, Mgr. Nguyen-Van-Hien, in a recent interview:

Today, the word "peace" has become an ambiguous word. . . . We Catholics desire a true peace, the peace called for so often by the pope and by us, the bishops of Vietnam, i.e., peace among brothers, which we all are in Vietnam, in justice, freedom and charity. The Communists, however, are using the word "peace" in an ambiguous sense. They may desire a peace that is not a true peace, which is merely the cessation of hostilities and not a general reconciliation in justice, freedom and charity of all the Vietnamese. This peace is not very agreeable to us Catholics because it conceals a terrible trap, and since many of us have been under the Communist yoke and have still today many of our brothers in North Vietnam who write to us of their very grave sufferings, we see this trap clearly. The young especially are well aware of the danger, both the Catholics and the Buddhists as well as the young people of the other religions, and they are asking for a real peace. But we can also say that the majority of the people of South Vietnam, and therefore the majority of the Buddhists, agree with us in this . . .

We who have been suffering war for 27 years are the first to be happy with these appeals [for peace], and all of us are asking, praying and wishing for peace, a most precious possession. We have had more than enough of this war that massacres the people, burns villages, and de-

bases the humane and moral sense of the people. But we want the peace
requested by the pope, a peace in justice, freedom and mutual love, not
hatred. Other appeals for peace, however, are aimed solely at the military aspect, at the cessation of hostilities, without concern for the rest:
we ask for the freedom to choose our future, and we do not want the
Communist yoke to be imposed on us. The appeals of the pope and of
all who are wishing for a true peace were very much welcomed by our
people, and we are thankful for this deep concern for our sufferings.
Peace in slavery, however, would be a betrayal of our hopes and no one
wants it.[2]

Therefore, to maintain that the Vietnamese Catholics do not
want peace is a pure calumny. We can say, however, that they do
not want just any peace but a true peace that unites and does not
divide the Vietnamese. This, it seems to me, is also the peace that
Pope Paul VI has been requesting for several years.

The peace desired by Paul VI for Vietnam. The activity of Paul
VI for peace in Vietnam is a subject on which one could write at
length, examining its various aspects, words and actions, diplomatic
contacts, prayers, moral directives, political efforts, etc. But all this
does not enter into the scope of our book. We only want to emphasize how the pope, placing himself on the moral level of an
"expert in humanity" (according to the definition he gave of
himself in his speech to the UN), was not pursuing political aims,
nor did he want to serve political interests. All he intended was to
put himself at the service of the Vietnamese people, for whom he
demanded true peace in justice and freedom, not in a dictatorship.

In a discourse of January 29, 1966, Paul VI explained the reasons
for his intervention in the question of peace in Vietnam:

This action was not motivated by any claim to investigate and judge
political questions and temporal interests which are foreign to our com-
petence; still less was it suggested to us out of a desire for publicity;
but it seemed our duty because of the gravity of the situation and the
requirements of our ministry. . . . We have spoken from the heart with-

out any advantage of ours to be gained but with the charity of Christ which impels us to dare to intervene and to make contacts that are quite foreign to common procedures and, even more so, to the procedures of protocol. . . . We have spoken with the heart of one who has no preconceived preferences to follow but only love for all men.

But the pope immediately adds that love for all men must not lose sight of justice:

We have not, however, lost the sense of justice by which the events must be judged, but we have not wished to claim to make judgments about concrete situations; we have, nevertheless, strongly desired that justice never be forgotten or betrayed. Our service in the cause of peace is not intended as pacifism which ignores the rights and duties relative to the conflict in question and neglects to see the negative consequences that its unjust and unfair solution could bring about. *Opus iustitiae pax.*

What kind of peace does the pope want for Vietnam? Above all, a peace that is the outcome of negotiations and not the result of a victory of one of the sides. On January 29, 1966, Paul VI said:

. . . It is regrettable that up to now [the peace offensive] . . . has not had a positive acceptance; it is a grave, a very grave responsibility to reject negotiation, which is the only way now to put an end to the conflict . . . without leaving the decision up to arms, the increasingly more terrible arms. . . . We must again wish and hope that the invitations to a negotiated peace will not be refused, and that the solution to the quarrel will not be sought by means of force and destruction, whose consequences are always unforeseeable . . .

And in the allocution to the Sacred College of December 22, 1967, Paul VI said: "Let violence of every form cease. We are certain that as a final goal an oppressive victory must not be pursued but rather security, peace and freedom for all. Frank and loyal negotiation, in fact, is the only constructive road to a true peace."

What kind of peace should come out of the negotiations? Still remaining on the moral plane and without pronouncing himself on the political aspects of the problem, the pope asserts (in the encyclical *Christi Matri* of September 15, 1966) that "it is necessary to establish a peace based on justice and on the liberty of men, which therefore takes account of the rights of persons and communities. Otherwise it will be weak and unstable."

One more quote from the many that could be made. In his *Message for Peace* of December 8, 1967, Paul VI wrote:

Peace cannot be based upon a rhetorical force of words, which are well received because they correspond to the profound and genuine aspirations of men, but which can also serve, and have at times unfortunately served, to hide the lack of a real spirit and real intentions of peace if it does not really serve to cover sentiments and actions aimed at overpowering adversaries or partisan interests. Nor can one legitimately speak of peace where the solid bases of peace are not respected, i.e., the freedom of individuals and peoples in all its expressions, civic, cultural, moral and religious. Otherwise, there will not be peace—even if, by chance, oppression is able to create an outward appearance of order and legality—but the continual and indomitable germination of revolts and wars.

Is it possible to collaborate with the Communists in a free regime? On the problem of peace in Vietnam, the Vietnamese Catholics are exactly in the position of Paul VI even if, as we shall see, there are various opinions on the concrete means to be used in order to achieve the same result, a true and just peace.

The bishops have several times expressed the peace hopes of the Christian community. For example, in a common letter of January 29, 1966 to the Vietnamese Catholics, the episcopate condemned the war, recalling the many exhortations to peace of Paul VI, and then added:

But this is not peace at any cost. There is no real peace in slavery, in injustice, in oppression, in hatred and in vengeance. There is no peace between the conquerors and the conquered. True peace consists only in justice and truth, in freedom and charity, in forgiveness and mutual understanding. . . . In the face of the prospects of an ever more destructive war we, the bishops of South Vietnam, ask our brother Catholics with insistency to pray that everyone will redouble efforts to put aside obstacles and to seek a moderate, fair and efficacious solution aimed at a just and durable peace for our country.

The public documents of the Vietnamese bishops, although they often mention peace, are very prudent, more prudent than those of Paul VI, for example, in indicating the terms of a true peace, which could be interpreted as taking a position against the "Communist peace." The reason is very simple: Vietnamese Christianity is subjected to the terror of reprisals by the Viet Cong, who generally respect the churches, priests and sisters in their zones but inexorably eliminate those priests (about fifteen to date) who openly pronounce themselves against Communism in public speeches. The Archbishop of Hué, Mgr. Kim-Dien, told me: "If I said one word of condemnation of Communism and its fighting methods, my priests and my Christians living in the country areas would pay for it, and I, who up to now have always been able to visit them, could no longer leave the city."

This fact also prevents the bishops from condemning certain aspects of the war, like the American bombardment of North Vietnam. In private they declare themselves against it and perhaps have privately intervened with the national government and the American command to make them stop, but in public they are forced to remain silent. If they did speak out in this sense only, their position would be interpreted in Vietnam, and especially abroad, as siding with the Viet Cong and North Vietnamese positions (on the other hand, they are unable to say anything against Communism).

However, even apart from the public statements, there is no doubt that the Catholics, almost to a man, are clearly anti-

Communist, i.e., they do not want to end up under a Communist dictatorship. Indeed, at times I would say they are fanatically anti-Communist: it is almost impossible to speak with them, as I experienced several times, about dialogue with Communism, the possibility of an entente with the Communists, etc. Certainly it is easy, for one coming from Italy and returning there, to criticize a similar attitude, but it is necessary to try to put oneself in their shoes in order to judge.

One Vietnamese priest, who occupies a position of great responsibility in the Church, told me:

A few months ago a French priest came here trying to make me understand that in France the dialogue with the Communists was well under way and that we, too, if we were less intransigent, could do the same. What you don't get to understand is that our Communism is quite different from yours. The French priest told me that we ought to give up the "Anti-Communist crusade mentality." Ridiculous! We do not feel that we are crusaders. We are only those poor people who do not want to be oppressed and massacred. I assure you that in the South, after such a hard war, if the Communists won, there would be a massacre of at least one million persons!

Your Communists in France and Italy are bourgeois fat cats, travelling in automobiles, workers who have every convenience, intellectuals who are Communists because it's fashionable: people who wouldn't hurt a fly, people with Christianity in their background, humanitarians. You with your dialogue with these people risk nothing. Here in Asia the Communists are filled with hate and ready for any kind of violence. They are "Chinese" Communists, elated by the victory of Dien Bien Phu and hardened by the long struggle. In Europe, the Soviets are speaking of peaceful coexistence. In Asia, Mao preaches hate and violence: why don't you want to take these differences into account? Get it out of your heads that we are anti-Communist "Crusaders": we are a people under terror, much more terrorized than you were under Nazism.

The ideal solution for many would be a neutralized Vietnam in which there were no foreign (i.e., American) military forces, with a coalition government that would be truly representative, i.e., one that also included the Viet Cong. But is it possible to cooperate with the Communists in a regime of freedom for everyone?

One leader of the association of Buddhist laymen, a refugee from the North, whose words I heard repeated many times, told me:

No one who has lived in the North with the Communists can think that any democratic collaboration with them is possible. Even in the South, as in the North during the guerrilla war against the French, the Communists eliminated not only every "collaborationist" but also all those who were opposed to the present government, as they once did with those who opposed the French but who did not allow themselves to become regimented by the Communists. Why is there no one from the North who is of the opinion that a coalition government is possible? The only people who think this way are those who have always lived in the South, in the cities, far away from direct contact with the Communists' methods of acting.

One other Catholic figure said in an interview, responding to the interviewer's question about the possibility of conversation with the Communists:

You see, my dear friend, there are certain things that you have to have experienced personally or have lived as the drama of your own country in order to understand them. What if you, during the last world war, had told the Nazi-oppressed people of Europe or the prisoners in Nazi concentration camps that, actually, when all was said and done, they could have reached an accord with the Nazis, made peace, and had a dialogue. . . . Someone who has had the frightening and painful experience of living under a Communist regime will never again forget it: a person who has seen all freedoms abolished, freedom of religion, of expression, of politics, of education, of movement, of speech; a person who has seen people oppressed, imprisoned and even killed for absurd reasons is no longer willing to live under the Communist yoke at any cost, just as a person who was oppressed by Nazism no longer wants to have anything to do with it. We do not want to live under a Communist regime; this we proclaim openly.[3]

The courage to make a peace statement. There are Catholics, however, who think somewhat differently. For example, the staff of the *Song-Dao,* the staff of *Economie et humanisme* and the Social Secretariat of Fr. Parrel, exponents of the YCW, and a few priests known to be "progressives." We must say that these groups, although they are more restricted, are succeeding in causing a more "conciliar" awareness to ripen in the local Christian community by their continual objections to the positions of the majority.

Let us mention a few documents. For example, the "manifesto"[4] of 11 Vietnamese priests of January 1, 1966 (3 Franciscans, 3 Redemptorists, one Dominican and 4 priests of the Archdiocese of Saigon), which gave rise to many polemics within Vietnamese Christianity. The priests described the sufferings of the Vietnamese people, expressed their despair at a war that never ends, condemned the armament race and escalation, called for peace through negotiation and not through a one-sided victory, and launched an appeal to all men of goodwill, especially in Vietnam, to unite and bring an end to the hostilities. Any political reference is positively excluded from this document, because they wanted it to be a Christian witness against the war and the divisions among the Vietnamese.

The letter, however, was much criticized in South Vietnam by Catholics and non-Catholics, especially by the former who felt they were "betrayed" by one of their own! The eleven priests were accused of having put on the same level both the victim (South Vietnam) and the aggressor (North Vietnam), and of not even having mentioned Communism; finally, the eleven were considered as not representative of the Christian community because they were educated in France (which in Vietnam today is little less than a mortal sin, at least in Catholic circles) and because they had come back home only two or three years ago without ever having experienced life in the country areas under the threat of Viet Cong terrorism. Some of the eleven priests fought back in an article, saying that they were not in fact ignorant of the Communist danger and that they were not looking forward at any cost to the

Communist domination of South Vietnam. But, they added, if we continue to maintain solely a position of negative anti-Communism, we shall not make the slightest progress toward ending the war.

We must add, in order to understand the "scandal" provoked by the letter of the eleven priests, that until recently the very word "peace" was almost forbidden in South Vietnam. Not that the Catholics and the South Vietnamese in general did not desire peace, but the term itself was so exploited by international Communist and pacifist propaganda that it ended up by meaning "peace at any cost," i.e., the unconditional withdrawal of the Americans and the domination of the strongest, the Communists. . . . It was Paul VI especially who dispelled this unbelievable psychological complex with his continual appeals for peace, which in the past had been censored by the South Vietnamese press and ignored by the Catholic press.

In an article in the *Song-Dao* of February 2, 1966, there is an exhaustive treatment of the progressive Catholics' view of things. The article states that the *Song-Dao* agrees with Paul VI's position:

(1) The establishment of peace in Vietnam through loyal negotiations is sincerely wished, since this is the only solution that agrees both with the interests of the Vietnamese people and with those of mankind, as well as with the exigencies of the Christian conscience. . . . There can be no military solution to the problem of Vietnam . . .

After having recalled that this was also the position of the Vietnamese bishops, the paper continues with this important specification:

(2) To wish for peace by means of negotiations does not mean to wish for peace without conditions. Now, one of the basic conditions is obviously this: that South Vietnam not fall under the yoke of Communism. Whoever has a modicum of good sense understands the difference between these two positions. If there are Catholics for whom the wish for peace through negotiation is the same as "placing oneself in the

service of Communism," the *Song-Dao* wants no discussion with them, since that would be to lack deference for the Holy Father. We ask simply that these Catholics confront their own consciences and rethink calmly the statements of the pope and the Vietnamese bishops.

One very well known representative of the Vietnamese Catholic progressives, Fr. Cao Van Luan, founder of the universtiy of Hué, and, as we have already mentioned, an opponent of Diem in the hot summer of 1963, held a press conference in Rome in May 1968 for the Italian newspapermen. Here is the most interesting part of his report:

For Fr. Cao-Van-Luan, there is no doubt that the war in Vietnam began with the aggression of the North against the South. He therefore looks upon as legitimate the war of the Vietnamese, faithful to the Saigon government, against those of North Vietnam. Speaking of the city of Hué—where he returned immediately after the reconquest [in the Tet offensive of February, 1968]—he said that he saw personally "innumerable common graves in which were amassed the victims of the Communist reprisals, among whom were mostly young Catholics, belonging to the police and medical forces, as well as European missionaries."

To the many questions of the newspapermen, Fr. Cao-Van-Luan responded by stating that "South Vietnam does indeed aspire to peace, but on the condition that it is a just peace and that it does not compromise the freedom of the people. If the United States forces do not leave Vietnam and if the peace agreed upon with Hanoi does not offer guarantees of freedom," he said, "the war between the Vietnamese of the two states will continue. Even if the desire for peace is profound, even more profound and deeply rooted is the fear of Communism." He then denied that there existed any differences of position between Catholics and Buddhists in regard to the problem of freedom.[5]

The thesis of the progressive Catholics. In the concrete, what are the theses of the "Catholic progressives" in Vietnam? I have discussed them at length with laymen and priests and I think that I can sum them up as follows:

(1) The fear of Communism, which is a real thing and which we would not dream of denying, has made the Catholics and the hierarchy as well, who see only this, lose their heads, while everything else is brushed aside as of secondary importance.

(2) We too fear Communism, and we know that if it came to dominate the South, it would oppress the people and their religions, as it did in the North. However, the problem is, with the war today waged chiefly by the Americans, whether the Communist danger is held in containment or whether the country is not left open to conquest. In this war there are aspects which we Catholics almost completely neglect: the nationalistic aspect, for example, which is most important for a country that suffered Chinese domination for a thousand years, then underwent a century of French domination, and is now under the domination of the Americans. In this situation, the Viet Cong and the North Vietnamese always come out as national heroes, even if their fighting methods and governing methods make them hateful to the people. Then, there is the racial aspect, towards which the Americans, being white, are already quite unsympathetic. . . . Finally, there is the social aspect: the Communists promise land to the peasants, they promise equality for all, they promise a state of well-being, a united and strong fatherland, freedom from every kind of need and exploitation. Even if we know what little worth these promises have, the simple people of the country areas end up by believing at least something of this and by asking themselves if it is worth such a disastrous war to fight people who are making so many promises.

(3) The Church and Catholics ought to involve themselves more in order to become, with the other religious forces, a real "third force" capable of defending the country from Communism without turning to foreign forces. Therefore, in the concrete, we propose: to maintain a position of equidistance (neutralism) between the government and the NLF, sincerely condemning what is damnable (Viet Cong terrorism, the bombings of the North, government corruption, the dogmatism of the other side, etc.); to request more

social justice in our country, involving the Catholics in studying social problems and in actions of social revindication. Today, the Catholics, with the exception of those involved in the trade unions and associations like the YCW, do much charity, but they fight very little for justice. Restore public morality, fight corruption in the state, rebuild the people's trust in the authorities; to promote in Catholics a spirit that is more open in regard to the faithful of other religions, and get to the point of forming a neutralist political movement which would win the confidence of all religious people (i.e., the majority of the population) and in the near future take over the country; therefore it is necessary to fight the military dictatorship, even if today it is disguised in a certain democratic spirit, and form a political consciousness in the people.

(4) We do not ask for the pure and simple withdrawal of the Americans, which in the present circumstances would be the equivalent of handing over the country to the Communists. But we do ask the Americans, if they really wish the good of our country, to withdraw gradually from South Vietnamese politics, allowing the formation of a more representative government made up of civilians which would have power over the armed forces and not put all their trust in the military alone. Once there is a representative civilian government, this will be able to make agreements with the Viet Cong and study their participation in the direction of public affairs and their integration into the country. The Americans should then be ready to withdraw and leave the country in the hands of the Vietnamese. We are confident that in a country at peace and without the pressure of the North Vietnamese forces (which also will have to withdraw), our people and the united religious forces will be able to defend our freedom and induce the Communists to collaborate in the rebuilding of the country and to abandon their plans for a take over. This is a great risk, we realize, but it is the only hope remaining to save the country from total destruction.

Aligned with these positions is the majority of the political representatives of the opposition to the present government and the "Leftist" Buddhist current under the leadership of the Ven. Tri Quang, although with many and varied nuances. On the other hand, there are others, including the majority of Catholics and many politicians opposing the government, who take more intransigent positions, judging as impossible any democratic collaboration with the Communists, who are the only ones to have a paramilitary party organization that is efficient and spread throughout the country.

To better illustrate the primarily moral position of the progressive Catholics, I shall report part of an interview with Fr. Tho, a pastor in a populous quarter of Saigon and one of the eleven priests who signed the appeal I mentioned:

The war started from Hanoi. No one can deny this. But the virulent anticommunism that developed in our country is negative, since it is accompanied by a quantity of factors that favor Communism. The more the war continues, the more it is to the advantage of Communism. Our country is continually losing more and more of its autonomy and becoming a protectorate, a situation which makes any government unpopular. It is for this reason that all our efforts should be directed toward bringing the war to a halt through a solution that safeguards democratic freedoms.

To the interviewer's question as to whether one should fear that the Communists would take power in a country at peace, Fr. Tho answered:

We do not want the Americans to go and leave the field wide open to the Communists! No! Our appeal was for the cessation of hostilities, but the technologists must see to it that the cease-fire is respected and freedoms preserved. We are spokesmen for the masses who want peace and who are in danger of being won over to Communism. If the war is prolonged, the masses will go to the other side. If one looks at the balance sheet of recent years, one can see that the population has been

worked over by means of terrorism or persuasion on the part of the
NLF. Today in Saigon, the Viet Cong are making enormous propaganda and are ably exploiting all the mistakes made by the Americans:
bombings, economic waste, offenses to public morality, the misery of the
poor.[6]

The neutralists want neither war nor Communism. The difference
between the majority of Vietnamese Catholics and the Catholic
"progressives" is in fact only this: for the former, since the impossibility of collaboration with the Communists has been demonstrated historically, a coalition government with the Viet Cong is
unthinkable in South Vietnam, because it would be tantamount to
giving the country into the hands of the most organized and most
violent faction which knows what it wants, while the rest of the
country is divided and does not have a single ideology; for the
other group, since the war is the worst moral and physical evil,
peace must be achieved and collaboration risked even with the
Communists in order to put an end to the carnage that is in
danger of becoming the genocide of the Vietnamese people. Even
the "progressive" Catholics fear Communism as a most serious
calamity for the country and call for international guarantees to
prevent this calamity; they are ready to fight in order not to allow
the imposing of a Marxist dictatorship, as in North Vietnam.

The mistake of much of the Western press, including the Catholic
press, which sincerely wants peace,[7] is to disregard the will of the
very great majority of the South Vietnamese people, which is this:
peace, but not a Communist peace. Many people, however (in the
West, but not in Vietnam or in the Orient, as I have said), are
merely calling for peace without concern for anything else and even
accusing the Americans of being solely or chiefly responsible for the
war. We may or may not take account of what the Vietnamese
themselves think, but we cannot ignore the fact that they have
an indisputable terror of ending up under a Communist regime.

The non-Catholic representatives of the Vietnamese religions agree on this basic point of not wanting a Communist dictatorship which would persecute the religions and oppress the people. Within the Council of Religions this common desire has never been questioned even if, as we have already said, the Council does not want to commit itself to political statements. The anti-Communism of the Hoa-Hao and the Cao-Dai is known, as is that of the Vietnam Buddhist Association, although the unified Buddhist Church takes politically more neutralist positions. However, even the most qualified representatives of this latter group, if they have argument with or are against the present military government and criticize the Americans, are still not supporters of a "Communist peace," despite what some Western commentators seem to maintain (they think that whoever is against the government in Vietnam and against the Americans must then be for the NLF). This opinion is completely false, since within the Vietnamese political array there is a third way, which is that of neutralism and nationalism, but not Communism. Up to now, under pressure from both adversaries in the struggle, it has unfortunately had not any way of expressing itself.

The same bonze, the Ven. Tri Quang, leader of the neutralist current of Buddhism (arrested in February 1968 by the government and released only in the following July), in the interview already mentioned (*L'Italia,* Milan, January 25, 1968), although he is very critical of the Americans and the government, told me precisely:

From the religious and philosophical point of view, my position towards Communism is no different from that of the Catholic Church, since Communism persecutes every religion and strives to take from man's spirit every sentiment of religiousness. I am against the NLF which is an instrument of Communist domination in order to impose a dictatorial and antireligious regime on our country, as in North Vietnam; I do not want the NLF, therefore, to join the government of South Vietnam. But I strongly fear that this will happen on account of the mistakes made in the fight against Communism.

To my question about what these mistakes were, Tri Quang answered:

Two above all: not having understood that this is a political war and therefore wanting to solve everything on the military level, instead of giving the country a truly popular and representative government: and secondly, having allowed the moral and social situation to deteriorate to the point that any moral resistance to communism has become impossible on account of the general corruption.[8]

When asked why he did not commit himself in public statements against Communism, Tri Quang replied: "In South Vietnam everybody is anti-Communist, except for a very few fanatics or a few others impelled by force and terror to serve Communism. However, the official anti-Communism of our governments serves only to disguise interests that are quite shady and which I do not wish to support by declaring myself an anti-Communist."[9]

Finally, my last question on the political problems was the following: Do you think the Americans have valid reasons for staying in Vietnam or should they leave as soon as possible? The monk had me repeat the question, asking me to be more precise. Then he gave me an answer that summed up his political thought:

You put the question badly. I am neither pro- nor anti-American, but I say that the Americans ought not to commit the error of the French, which was to make war in order to defend us from Communism and then leave half the country in Communist hands. If the Americans have decided to stay in order to defend us from Communism, then let them fight with adequate means and not with war and bombardments. If, however, they decide to leave, let them not sell us out to the Communists, as the French did with North Vietnam. I do not question the good faith of the Americans and their desire to save us from Communism: but, for example, their involving themselves in all the country's affairs and taking on all the responsibilities certainly does not help to form a strong nationalism capable of resisting Communism.

The disciple of Tri Quang best known in the West, Thich Nhat Hanh, wrote in the book[10] we have mentioned several times:

> Vietnamese anticommunism originated from the methods that organized Communism employs to achieve its goals: the suppression of every perceptible dissent and debate; the liquidation of even the most loyal opponents, at times by violence; the party's claim to omniscience; a kind of fanaticism that makes meaningless any continued search for truth, such as the one in which the Buddhists are engaged, and the determination to completely sacrifice the existence of a small country like Vietnam to the advantage of the "wider" interests of the Communist party in the cold war between the great powers. We assert this does not favor the theory of the non-Communist nationalist Vietnamese, who were persecuted with the same ruthlessness North and South of the 17th parallel, by the North Vietnam-NLF-China coalition and the Diem-Ky-U.S. group.[11]

As for the other current of the Unified Buddhist Church, that of Tam Chau, it seems superfluous to me to cite many quotes since it is well known that it supports the military government and the American presence in Vietnam. Nevertheless, in order to report a recent statement, here is Tam Chau's message to the World Buddhist Association, of whose council he is the vice-president:

> Precisely on the lunar New Year's day, traditional for the Vietnamese people, the Viet Cong—the Vietnamese Communists—profited from the recent "cease-fire" in order to infiltrate among the populations of the large cities, killing human beings and destroying the property of our fellow citizens. I sincerely hope that all of you will pray for our Vietnamese people that they may soon be free from the Communist yoke, and help them spiritually and materially.[12]

As for the Protestants (who are about 40,000 in South Vietnam), even their pastors express the fear of a Communist victory:

We thank you for your interest in this unfortunate country of Vietnam [writes a Swiss pastor and missionary in Saigon in the Italian *Waldensian Weekly*]. Pray with us that in the event of a Communist regime there may not be too many massacres. My greatest fear is that the example of North Vietnam and the significant happenings on the occasion of the Tet battle allow us to predict the worst. We must not look at yellow communism with European eyes. It is an implacable regime that systematically practises physical elimination.[13]

The position of the Vietnamese people, besides the religious representatives, is well expressed also by the Vietnamese Confederation of Labor, which has more than one million members and, although it is not very much in accord with the present government nor with the preceding military ones,[14] is absolutely against a Communist domination, rejecting the Communist thesis on the Vietnamese war. The president of the Confederation, Tran Quoc Buu, to my question as to whether the Americans should leave Vietnam or not, answered:

Our trade union confederation is neither for nor against the Americans. Undoubtedly the Americans have done some harm in our country, and they are rather inconvenient guests. If we were at peace, we would not hesitate a moment to tell them to go home. But, in the present circumstances, we realize a very obvious truth: if the Americans leave, in less than a month South Vietnam would be in the hands of the Communists, and then would begin one of the greatest massacres in our history, beginning with our unionists. Our people do not want the war, they aspire to peace with all their might, but they also do not want to end up under a regime like the one oppressing our brothers of the North, a ruthless and tyrannical one that takes all freedom away from the people . . .

Mr. President [I asked Tran Quoc Buu] in Europe the idea is very widespread that the guerrilla war in South Vietnam is a movement widely supported by the people for reasons of social order. They say that people are rebelling because they are victims of social injustice. What are your thoughts on this?

. . . That in our country there still are profound social injustices is a reality that we denounce every day and which we are seeking to change with our union action. But that the guerrilla war originated from motives of social order and that it is supported by our people voluntarily is a completely false and absurd idea. The truth is this: the guerrilla war was unleashed by the Communists and sustained by means of the most ruthless terrorism and with the help of North Vietnam. And the reason for the war is neither social justice nor the independence of the country but the triumph of the Communist idea and the enslavement of our country in a Communist regime. No reasonable doubt is possible about this.[15]

Several politicians opposing the government, interviewed by me or simply present in conversations with friends, among whom was, for example, Au Truong Tanh (arrested by the government in February 1968), confirmed to me that the great majority of the Vietnamese people and the elite are in a neutralist but non-Communist position. There was recently held in Paris a meeting of Vietnamese students and workers in France, organized by the *Alliance des travailleurs et étudiants vietnamiens d'Europe.* Despite the influence of the French milieu, the assembly made a pronouncement for peace, but not for a "Communist peace." The president of the assembly, Nguyen Kieng, made this statement in his speech: "The Vietnamese people do not want the peace that the Communists would want to impose on them. They want peace in human dignity. In a parallel way, they want a profound social revolution to assure the future of the Republic of Vietnam."[16]

The resolution, adopted by more than 500 Vietnamese present at the Mutualité, declared that "it resolutely opposed any attempt to 'Communize' Vietnam, and it severely condemns the policy of the Communists who are aiming to take over South Vietnam with arms." The posters carried by the Vietnamese said: "Social revolution, yes! Communism, no!" "Long live free and independent South Vietnam!"[17]

A "Systematic and scientific" terrorism. All the evidence we have given up to now expresses the identical worry (i.e., the fear of a

Communist victory in South Vietnam) which is not very common in the West among those who have a generous interest in peace in Vietnam. Why this unanimity of views among the Vietnamese?

It is unquestionable that the South Vietnamese have good and solid reasons for not wanting a Communist victory and their dictatorship. We have already mentioned the historical reasons: the elimination of the non-Communist patriots during the guerrilla war against the French (1946–1954), the flight of some million North Vietnamese to the South from 1954 and afterward, persecution of the religions, and the suppression of all opposition to the regime in North Vietnam. These factors are often ignored in the West not only by the public at large but also by those who are writing the history of Vietnam with a claim to completeness and impartiality, although in Vietnam they are even known by the young who had not even lived through them.

For the people of the South, however, the most odious aspect of Vietnamese Communism is the terrorism that the Viet Cong use systematically to impose themselves on the population.

It is hard to understand the common mentality of the Vietnamese unless one has lived for some time in the areas infested by the Viet Cong and unless one shares the terror under which the population constantly lives. One begins to penetrate deeply into an understanding of the Vietnamese war when one leaves the relatively secure cities[18] and has the opportunity to visit and live in the country villages and the forest areas, an experience which is not very easy for a white person (I was fortunate to have been able to travel and live, as a priest, with the missionaries and the Vietnamese priests).

What is this terrorism that has been defined as "systematic and scientific"? At night, the South Vietnamese and American troops cannot defend all the small and dispersed villages; instead they retreat to their camps or defend the public facilities and institutions —bridges, dikes, electrical power centers, irrigation canals, etc. The undefended villages are systematically visited, one by one, by the

Viet Cong, who eliminate all those who are pointed out as opponents (often not only individuals but also their families) and also those who have influence over the people and contribute towards keeping them united and making them feel the presence of the state: schoolteachers, nurses, village chiefs, catechists, leaders of the cooperatives, unionists, youths from the pacification teams, etc. I myself, walking about the villages in the morning, saw two examples of this: a catechist and, in another village, a twenty-year-old nurse, both killed during the night by the Viet Cong.[19]

I collected dozens of examples of evidence of this nocturnal terrorism from most creditable persons, since it was a question of daily experiences for those living in the country regions or on the plateaus. One missionary told me: "The expression we find in Sunday Lauds in the breviary—*gallo canente spes redit* (when the cock crows, hope returns)—perfectly describes the situation in our villages: at night, people sleep with one eye open, ready to take flight at the least sign of danger; the more influential people, who know they are in the Viet Cong's black book, never sleep two nights running in the same village."

Here are a few concrete facts, for which I would be able to give the date and the place where they happened, in order to give an immediate picture of the terrorism that is annihilating the people's spirit. One village chief, who had urged the population to vote in the elections of September 1967, was assassinated and his head fixed to a pike in the center of the village; the body of another assassination victim was divided into many pieces which were then scattered through the streets of the village for the dogs to eat (the most serious offense to the soul of the dead person); another was crucified at the door of his hut and tortured throughout the night before being killed (his screams awakened the population). In one large center, in one night, 18 people were assassinated, in another, 14. At times all the members of a family were killed, from the oldest to the unweaned, women included.[20]

One priest told me: "All of those who show some personality in the villages and stand out from the masses will sooner or later be eliminated if they are found to be at home at the right moment. There is no middle way for the most prominent people: either they are in good relations with the Viet Cong, or else they know what destiny awaits them.

We must point out, however, that the priests and the sisters are an exception to the rule and are generally respected (only those priests are eliminated who really cause trouble by taking an overt stand against communism, but these cases, after the first experiences, are now most rare). However, Catholic catechists, whose assassinations do not receive international coverage, are struck down indiscriminately. One bishop told me that in his diocese he no longer could find anyone who was willing to be a catechist in the villages, since this meant he had to expose himself as a leader of the community and therefore a target for the Viet Cong, who were most concerned with having the rural communities without leaders. And a well-informed priest of a diocese in central Vietnam told how in the last six or seven years almost all the most influential leaders of the Catholic laity were killed or gravely wounded in Viet Cong attacks:

I do not know how they got to know all of them so precisely, but we in the center of the diocese became aware, everything considered, that the most educated, most steadfast and most important Catholics of each village are no more. It is a continual, slow process which is not noticed in the individual village in its true scope, since at the most, on an average, there are five or six killings per village, spread out over several years. But when you put all the facts together, all the reports that come from the country areas, you get a frightening picture that shows the desire to exterminate not the little people but the leaders or those who show qualities to become such.[21]

The president of the Vietnamese Confederation of Labor, the Buddhist Tran Quoc Buu, whom we have already mentioned, told me literally: "The major problem for our trade union organization is this: our best people are killed or threatened with death by the Viet Cong, especially in the country areas, among the peasants, the fishermen, the rubber and coffee plantation workers."

Asked if these killings were ascribable to the eventual political propaganda of the trade unionists, Tran Quoc Buu answered:

We abstain from any political position: the trade unionists are killed like the government functionaries, the village chiefs, the doctors, the nurses, the teachers, and all who have influence over the population. For the Communists, the enemy no. 1 is neither the military, the Americans, nor the capitalists but those who live on the level of the people and have some public function or organizational ability. I maintain that our Confederation of Labor has paid up to now the highest price in these massacres by the Viet Cong; no week goes by without news of someone being killed. I know that my own life is threatened, but in the city it is easier to defend oneself and to change residence at night; in the country areas, however, one is completely defenseless.

The continuation of the war favors the Communists. The Viet Cong guerrilla war also has three aspects. For example, the collecting of taxes from the peasants, heavier taxes than the government succeeds in imposing; the Marxist indoctrination assemblies include all the adult inhabitants of a village (it even happens that priests and sisters have to take part in these night sessions). Propaganda has a most important part in the Viet Cong strategy, almost as much as terrorism, and in the villages already under their control, even more. For example, when a village is first approached by the Viet Cong, terrorism is the means most used to make the people understand who is in command and with whom they have to side if they do not want trouble, but afterwards, when the people are no longer in a mood to rebel, propaganda aims at winning over their assent, often with positive results. The propaganda themes used are in fact very simple and effective: anti-

Americanism (an incentive to nationalism), protest against the central government (and it is easy to get everyone to agree against a government that is unsuccessful in protecting its functionaries and its people), the struggle for social justice (against the local petty tyrants, etc.) and finally, the promise of a rosy future with the "building of socialism." The countryfolk, undefended and terrorized, end up by assenting, at least outwardly, to these themes. Certainly they would not want to live under a ruthless regime like that promised by the Viet Cong, but they are constrained, partially by force, partially by propaganda, to help the Viet Cong and to accept their extortions.

For example, boys of the ages of 12 and 13 are taken away and sent to training camps across the border in Laos, Cambodia, or in North Vietnam, where they remain for one or more years of indoctrination and military training. Several times, while visiting country or mountain villages, I heard the person accompanying me, who knew the people of the area well, say, "This woman has two sons with the Viet Cong, and that one only one . . ."

These are boys taken away at a very young age, and when they return to their region in Viet Cong formations, they become valuable assets for the Viet Cong themselves; they know the local language, the dialect, the customs, the paths through the forest, the people of the place, etc. Moreover, these youths return profoundly changed, partially because they have become fanaticized by what they have been newly taught, partially because they are terrorized by the threats made to them should they become traitors (their families would also pay), and partially because they have now become accustomed to seeing scenes of blood and violence. These boys, furthermore, now feel that they are "someone": they have arms in their hands, an idea for which to fight, they present themselves in their villages as "figures" far superior to the boys their own age who remained behind to do the farming. I heard precise accounts of young Christians, sons of good families and well educated in the mission schools, who came back with a real de-

moniacal hatred for religion after one or two years of indoctrination. Doubtless, these too are innocent victims of the war.

"I too have several of my Catholics in the Viet Cong formation,"
a Vietnamese priest told me, "boys taken years ago who now come
to find me and assure me that I have nothing to fear, but I found
them so changed in head and heart that I no longer recognized
them."

With similar people convinced of the cause for which they are
fighting and ready for everything, the Viet Cong successfully dominate the rural areas, leading a very effective underground fight,
even if it is not ostentatious, against any attempt by the government
to organize civilian life. They are in a position to impose their own
administration, their own justice, their own law, and gradually to
win the assent and the submission of the people. Here is what I
was told by a well-informed priest who lives north of Hué in a
zone almost completely occupied by the Viet Cong, when I asked
how did the Viet Cong become so all-powerful in the villages:

When a population is terrorized, a few violent and resolute types are
enough to dominate a whole region. If unexpectedly all the peasants of
this region decided to denounce the few Viet Cong that are in their
villages, I think that the guerrilla war would be over in a few days. But
here no one speaks, everyone thinks only of saving himself, because
everyone knows that whoever speaks or is seen with a soldier is finished. The Viet Cong could also leave a place, defeated for the moment,
but sooner or later they will be back. I know some people whose father
was killed, and although they knew very well who had done it, they
did not even dream of speaking. A Vietnamese proverb says: "For an
elephant who moves it is of no importance that he is so big," i.e., as
long as there is a way to keep alive, nothing else counts.

Why don't the South Vietnamese and American troops defend
the villages during the night? Such a question could be asked only
by someone who has not visited Vietnam, a country of forests and

rice fields, with few roads, now almost all blocked, with an area (very hospitable for the Viet Cong) more than 2,000 kilometers long and, finally, with very dispersed small villages of between twenty and thirty families each in which the majority of the population lives. To defend effectively all these little villages one would need an enormous military force, since an attack can be made by concentrating all the forces (100 or 200) on one village, and the defenders would be overwhelmed before others could come to their aid. The experiment of "fortified villages," at the time of Diem, with the people of a whole district brought together for the night in one fortified village, produced good results at the beginning but then became unbearable for the farmers and, furthermore, the Viet Cong could always infiltrate one of their own into the thousands of persons in a village; at night he could blow up the ammunition supplies or open some passageway to let the guerrillas in.

There still are villages that organize their own defenses, like a good part of the Montagnard villages on the plateaus: I have visited some of them myself, fortified with a double or triple fence of bamboo, with sharpened and poisoned sticks planted in the ground and in the grass. These are defenses that hold up well enough, but when the Viet Cong succeed in conquering one of these villages they make unheard of massacres, as in the case of Dak-Son in December 1967. Here, while I was still in Vietnam, they killed men, women and children without distinction, about 300 persons in all! After "demonstrative examples" of this kind, even the warlike Montagnards preferred to suffer the nocturnal visits of the Viet Cong and make the best of it rather than risk being exterminated en masse.

Even the cities are not safe from Viet Cong terrorism, which here reveals itself as really "scientific"; it strikes the victim without disturbing the rest of the population. This was true at least until last February, when the attack at the time of the Tet offensive even involved the city people. One ex-deputy who joined the opposition against the present government and who leads a semi-clandestine life in Saigon, since he is an important figure and therefore has many contacts with the political opposition forces, told me:

The more the war continues, the more the best people in Vietnam who tomorrow could control the country are either caught by Pro-American politics or else killed by the Viet Cong. In fact, the Viet Cong don't kill the generals who are waging the war but neutralists like me who in the future might be opponents of their designs. Their plan is well thought out: tomorrow, with the war over, in South Vietnam there will be only pro-American generals and politicians, i.e., people compromised by the present puppet government, and Communists; those known to be able men will all have been silently and gradually eliminated with a pistol shot at the back of their heads in Saigon itself. . . . The Communists know that sooner or later the war will have to end, that it can't last forever; and they know that the Americans, like the French, sooner or later will go away. Then it is clear that the fewer able persons that are still about, the sooner they will be able to put their plans into effect.

This politician told me that he often changed residence at night, not for fear of being arrested by the police but so as not to be caught off guard by the Viet Cong. Thus, many people come from the rural villages to sleep in the neighboring cities that are defended by the army and where it is easy to hide.

The Viet Cong seen close at hand. I apologize for the length of my treatment of this subject of the guerrilla methods. But for me, this was the real revelation of my trip to Vietnam, especially in the country areas, and the theme on which I collected the most eyewitness evidence. I think, therefore, that it is not possible to understand the present situation in Vietnam if one does not succeed in understanding this factor, which conditions all the other aspects of local life.

Again, I want to report, almost in its entirety, the interview I had with a French missionary who for about twenty years had lived in a large village in the Mekong delta in a zone almost completely controlled by the Viet Cong for several years. I was his guest, and I was able to converse at length with him, treating the subject of the guerrilla war exhaustively. I asked the priest how one could describe the mentality of the peasants toward the war and the warring sides:

The poor devil working in the fields wants only peace, and communism or anti-communism are of no importance to him. They are poorly educated people who have no political idea. Of course, they are terrorized by the Viet Cong and would not want to live in a regime dominated by them, but they also have had quite enough of the war that has lasted too long! The more the war goes on, the more opportunity the Viet Cong propaganda has to depict the Americans as foreign invaders and to promise peace and freedom if they themselves are the victors. The Americans have still not understood that this is a revolutionary war that is won more through propaganda on the level of the little people than by military action.

Can the Viet Cong's success with the country people be explained also by the social reforms they are bringing about in their areas or only by terrorism?

Terrorism does not explain everything. It does exist, but today, perhaps, it is no longer the chief means. But neither do the social reforms explain their success, since even if the Viet Cong have distributed some land, everybody knows that in North Vietnam and in China the Communists have taken back the land afterwards and given it to the control of the state: therefore, nobody is under any illusions. What is very effective, however, is the anti-American and antigovernment propaganda. In the beginning they did not believe it, but with the repetition of certain accusations and slogans they end up by feeling themselves psychologically on the side of the Viet Cong more than on that of the government, or at least they are disposed to collaborate more with the former than the latter, especially because the Viet Cong take inexorable revenge against any betrayal, while the government is unsuccessful in making its presence effectively felt. In the villages under my care, when the Viet Cong are in command there are always local people who commit themselves to being village chiefs, keeping order, collecting taxes for the Viet Cong; however, when the government troops arrive and are in command of the zone for some time, they never find anyone willing to take on any responsibility, and so they send functionaries from Saigon who are well paid but who remain there only by day and at night return to the cities or sleep in a military camp.

In the areas dominated by the Viet Cong, are they respectful of religion?

The Vietnamese people are profoundly religious, especially the country people. . . . The Viet Cong know this and always show deference to the priest and to religion. If you should walk there in black clothes, you could go into any Viet Cong area and no one would touch a hair on your head. But this is only the outward aspect, an accommodation: when they meet an aggressive priest who unmasks and condemns them, they also get rid of him. . . . But there is another side to the problem: where the Viet Cong establish themselves, they begin Marxist indoctrination which no one can escape; if they resist, they are eliminated, and then the people gradually end up by supporting the Viet Cong whether they want to or not. And once a person has pledged himself to the Viet Cong, he can never get away; even if the Viet Cong abandon the region, they leave behind a network of informers who control the people; whoever collaborates with the government, gives information, has a son in the army, has no way of escape, even over a period of years, unless he emigrates to other areas on the outskirts of the large cities where he can pass unobserved. For this reason there are very many emigrations to the city and displacements of populations from one part of the country to another.

Do the government forces use the same methods? Do they also take revenge on the relatives of the Viet Cong and on those who were forced to collaborate with the Viet Cong?

No. Absolutely not, because the government troops have to create confidence in the government, and in addition they do not have all the informers that the Viet Cong have. The Americans and the national soldiers do not use terror customarily: if somebody is suspected of being a Viet Cong, they are certainly not gentle with him and send him to the central police posts where he is interrogated and at times even tortured. . . . For this reason the government people are not feared by the population; from the point of view of their availability and collaboration, the populace is more on the side of the Viet Cong precisely because they fear them most.

But then, in such a situation, the people, basically, ought to be more against the Viet Cong than against the government?

In reality, yes. But the people have no possibility of expressing themselves freely. Not only this, but you must also realize that the Asians do not have the same reactions as do we Europeans. We, when faced with Nazi terror, rebelled because our moral sense of justice caused us to rebel. I was a chaplain with the maquis, the French patriots during the second world war, and I know that the French did not suffer Nazi terror passively. The Asian, however, is more inclined to admire violence than to rebel against it: the peasant sees that the Viet Cong are the most cunning, the most impartial, the most vengeful, the most informed; he understands that they can do him more harm if he is not on their side, and he ends up by standing with them. In Europe, people spontaneously go to the side that is most just, while in Asia, where there is no Christian spirit, people support the strongest and the most violent side.

But the Americans demonstrate that they are the strongest.

Yes, but their strength is silly and does not strike home. The Americans never kill a family in cold blood because it has a son with the Viet Cong, while the latter do away with everybody who opposes them in any way. There are incredible cases that happened in my own villages, which I know well. In one zone "liberated" by the Viet Cong, some landowners were killed "as an example." Then they brought together all the heads of the families and told them: "The owners of the rice fields who had more than what was necessary have been killed. Now the rice fields are yours." And they expound a plan for the distribution of the fields in which are also included the rice fields of the local church. One Catholic raises his voice and says: "The church's rice fields support our school and the medical dispensary, and can't be touched." The Viet Cong admit that they are useful to the people and don't touch them. But the day afterward the poor chap is found in the village square with his throat cut . . .

You can understand that after a similar happening no one will dare to utter one word of criticism. Something else: in one village—and I am always speaking of villages in my care which I therefore know well—the Viet Cong were holding a Marxist indoctrination session in which a girl who was a novice in some order of sisters and was home with her family on vacation had also to participate. The session is an invitation to hate, to get rid of traitors, etc. The girl, restrained in vain by her companions, raised her voice and confuted the speaker several times. She too was killed in the night, taken from her house and shot in the head with a pistol. In this village nobody will any longer do anything against the Viet Cong.

With us in Europe happenings of this kind would start a general uprising, or at least there would always be a courageous man disposed to risk his life to get to rid of the assassins. Here in Asia this kind of thing destroys a man and makes him passively accept the law of the strongest. Therefore, I say that the longer the war lasts the more the people will be submitted to the Viet Cong. Time is working for them.[22]

The Tet offensive in the cities. In the light of these facts, told by most trustworthy eyewitnesses, we can now better understand why the Viet Cong, although they represent only a minority of the population, are practically unbeatable.[23] We can also see why very few people in Vietnam are looking forward to their victory and their domination, although they foresee that it will be very difficult for the country to save itself from this experience.

The situation became still worse in the last months after the great offensive against the cities, which began in February 1968 and was still under way in the middle of that year. Up to January of that year the direct experience of the Viet Cong methods was almost exclusively confined to the country and plateau people. In the cities the situation was quite different. Here, Viet Cong terrorism was minimal and was aimed only at single individuals and not the whole city community, which actually lived in peace; for this reason the city populations swelled unbelievably. But now the escalation of the Viet Cong against the cities (which did not rouse the least protest in the West) involved millions of people in the hor-

rors of war, and since the Viet Cong could not hope to occupy the
cities permanently by driving out the national army, we think that
this was precisely their principal aim: to make the city people also
feel the weight of the war, and exasperate the weariness of Vietnamese public opinion which most counted (i.e., in the cities) in
order to spur them on to a "peace at any price."[24]

But if this were the political calculation behind the attack on the
cities, it seems that it proved to be completely mistaken. The city
elite, which had remained on the fringes of the war and who were
more inclined to see and criticize the faults of the government and
the Americans than those of the Viet Cong, now had their eyes
opened to the ruthlessness that had guided the Viet Cong's escalation in the cities: the bombardment of Saigon and the other cities
by shooting at random, day and night, at the citizenry, with the
sole aim of sowing terror; the unheard of massacres that characterized the attack on Hué and other cities in central Vietnam
particularly.

Stewart Harrison, the correspondent of the London *Times,* gave
a description of the common graves found at Hué and its environs,
filled with victims of the Viet Cong and the North Vietnamese,[25]
stating that, since he had always been against massive American
involvement in Vietnam, he did not want to believe the news from
an American source, and went personally to Hué and the surrounding area to see the graves of the victims (among the most terrifying
were those of Gia Hoi, each containing from three to seven
corpses). Harrison concludes that when one puts together the
obvious facts relative to the behavior of the Viet Cong and the
North Vietnamese army, one thing becomes abundantly clear and
ought to surprise no one. With their customary efficiency they put
into effect the traditional Communist policy of executing selected
leaders who were helping their enemies, the government of South
Vietnam and its American allies. Moreover, they also killed American civilian advisers, but this was merely to "encourage" the others.
In Hué, as in every place else, they did not succeed in capturing

and killing the most important functionaries, since the latter were careful to protect themselves by living in highly fortified places defended by soldiers and policemen. Thus, in Hué, as everywhere else, the victims were the defenseless "little people": village chiefs, teachers, policemen. But already many of these posts have been refilled, and it seems impossible to do justice to the courage of those who took the posts of the murdered.

At Hué, the price paid by the Catholics was especially high.

What was the Communists' attitude toward Catholics? [asks *L'Osservatore Romano*, March 14, 1968]. The facts speak well enough for themselves. At Hué they took possession of the minor seminary for the whole period that they remained and obliged the pupils to assist at daily evening courses on Marxism. From the quarter where the Catholics lived, hundreds of men and youths were deported and successively killed; the others suffered vexations and tortures; missionaries were subjected to lengthy interrogations, two priests were killed, two others wounded, five deported.

Recent news has confirmed the disaster of the Church at Hué in February 1968: 227 Catholics killed, 204 wounded and about 400 dispersed or deported by the North Vietnamese (without ever returning); among the dead were 4 priests, and another 3 among the dispersed; among the dead there were many members of the Legion of Mary, a particular target of the Communists.[26] Later there came the news of the death of 2 French Benedictines buried alive near their monastery of Thien An, near Hué.

Notes

1. In June 1968 the refugees of South Vietnam (i.e., apart from the million refugees that came from the North in 1954–1955 and who now had completely integrated into the life of the country) were calculated at two and a half to three million, i.e., one-fifth of the 16 million South Vietnamese. It is as if in Italy we had from 9 to 10 million people fleeing from one

region to another. North Vietnam has never published statistics on its refugees from the cities to the country areas following the American bombardment, but it is thought that they are from one to two million.

2. G. Girardi, "Intervista col vescovo di Dalat," *Le Missioni Cattoliche,* 1966, pp. 181–183.

3. We apologize for having at times to withhold the names of certain persons for reasons of prudence that are easily understood.

4. See the complete text in *Informations catholiques internationales,* February 1, 1966, p. 28.

5. *L'Italia,* Milan, May 16, 1968, p. 2.

6. Interview by J. P. Caudron, editor of *Informations catholiques internationales,* May 15, 1966, pp. 22–24.

7. Another very common error in the Italian press is that of idealizing the critical positions of the American Left on the war in Vietnam, insinuating that there are basic disagreements between these and the official position of the American government. Disagreements do exist, but certainly not of the kind one is tended easily to imagine. For example, in his speeches of November 1967 and February 1968, Robert Kennedy did not spare his severe criticism of the way the war was being conducted in Vietnam.

But the thrust of his message was this: a negotiated agreement (less than a victory for both sides) will bring to the discussion table at least one basic condition, one request which does not admit of discussion, one point on which no one is inclined to yield. And the preliminary condition for the United States is that they do not at any price abandon South Vietnam to the violent domination of a minority. . . . Today being today, they cannot withdraw. . . . Tens of thousands of Vietnamese have banked everything, their lives and their fortunes, on our presence and our protection: peasants in the villages, the keepers of the peace, the teachers and the doctors, people on the plateaus and the mountain tribes. There are many working for the good of their people, and although they do not support the Saigon government, they do not want to join up with the Viet Cong. And there are many who have already fled once from the dictatorship in the North. These people cannot, from one moment to another, be left at the mercy of the violent conquest of a minority. And again, Kennedy regrets the fact that some Americans romantically idealize the enemy to the point that kind "Uncle Ho" and the Vietnamese Communists are seen as a relatively harmless nationalist force. In terms of human values, only a dreadful lack of sensitivity to the cost can bring one to the point of holding that it is desirable for North Vietnamese nationalism to spread. The oppression of the North Vietnamese regime is much more severe and its government much more ruthlessly efficient than any South Vietnamese government. . . . Nothing of what the West calls freedom exists in North Vietnam today. In the South, the program of the Viet Cong was put forward through terrorism and the killing of women and children. . . . This is not a good reason to give it moral approval, and all the less is it an occasion to rejoice in the victories of the Viet Cong.

8. In Europe it is often written that the National Liberation Front is an organization representing many nationalistic political forces and not only the Communists. Doubtless, as we have already pointed out, the NLF orginated in 1960 in opposition to the Diem regime through the convergence of many political forces and representatives, but it is equally as certain that in South Vietnam today no one any longer believes that the NLF represents anything other than Communism. This is so true that after 1960 not one prominent political or religious figure sided with the NLF, although many were adversaries of Diem and of the military regimes that followed him and the Americans. This is an obvious indication that after its foundation the NLF assumed a clear Communist tone, even if in its leadership there continued to remain a few persons who in 1960 were not Communists. G. Chaffard, in an ample inquiry published in *L'Express,* May 2, 1965, pointed out that the posts of major responsibility in the NLF were entrusted to non-Communists but that the "numerical predominance of the Communists appears in all the intermediary groups where the proportion is about two out of three." And the "setting of the scene," already used by the Viet Minh in 1945 and the following years, which corresponds to a traditional Communist tactic, i.e., using local national forces for a revolutionary purpose and showing as composite a front as possible, although assured, underhandedly, of the reins of power. Chaffard points out further that everything in the NLF denotes the presence of Communism: the organized structures, the official vocabulary, the revolutionary teaching in the "liberated" areas, the methods of "liquidating" traitors, etc. Even F. Gigon, in his *Americani e Vietcong* (Milan: Mondadori, 1966), illustrates the identity between the NLF and Vietnamese Communism.

9. This position of Tri Quang is confirmed by other statements of his. Philippe Devillers wrote, *Le Monde diplomatique,* May, 1966, p. 6: "The position of Buddhism in regard to Communism is well-known and does not differ from that of the Vatican. But what Tri Quang reproaches certain "anti-Communists" for is that they are playing Communism's game. He states convincingly that by relying on "puppets," destroying Vietnamese sovereignty, getting deeply involved in the country's affairs, tolerating extortion, prostitution, the black market, etc., and having recourse to certain war

methods, the Americans are constantly bringing grist for the mill of Communist propaganda. In one word, what Tri Quang reproaches Washington and General Ky for is what the Vietnamese nationalists in 1948–1954 reproached Paris and Bao Dai for. What Tri Quang proposes is to lead the fight against Communism with more efficacious, adaptive and human means. In the same issue of *Le Monde diplomatique*, two disciples of Tri Quang, Huynh Cao Tri and Cao Huy Thuan (who was from Hué) wrote: "By tradition, the Cao-Dai and Hoa-Hao have no sympathy for Communism, and as for Buddhism, it leaders have more than once insisted upon the basic incompatibility existing between the methods of violence and the excesses of Communism and the doctrine of nonviolence and the 'just mean' of Buddhism." They report the opinion of Tri Quang, according to whom the Buddhist leaders are pledged to illustrate to their faithful "the peril" that would be present if the Communists took power or infiltrated into the national assembly.

10. Nhat Hanh, *op. cit.*, p. 87.

11. It may be pointed out that while in North Vietnam any opposition to the dominant regime has been totally eliminated, whether it was of a political, trade union or religious character, in South Vietnam, despite the dictatorships of Diem and Ky, the political, trade union and religious movements opposed to the government have been able to preserve a real vitality and activity in public control over the publication of newspapers and books, religious associations and centers, public opinion campaigns, etc. The difference between the two situations is remarkable, and it would be to go counter to historical truth to deny it.

12. Message reported in *World Buddhism*, Colombo, March, 1968, p. 202.

13. *La Luce*, the weekly of the Waldensian Church (Turin, May 3, 1968, p. 7). Similar evidence of a markedly anti-Communist tone can be found in these two books by English and American non-Roman Catholic clergymen: Gordon H. Smith, *Victory in Vietnam, Missions behind the Headlines* (Grand Rapids: Zondervan Publishing House, 1965); S. Harverson, *Doctor in Vietnam* (London: Lutterworth Press, 1968). On the Protestant missions in Vietnam, read E. Schloesing, "Missions protestantes en Indochine," *Le Monde non-chrétien*, Paris, 1955, pp. 245–272, 335–349; P. Medard "Catholiques et protestants au Vietnam," *Eglise vivante* Louvain, 1959, pp. 445–447.

14. For example, the *Kipa* agency of January 24, 1968, illustrated the "repression of the trade union activity in South Vietnam," reporting a communiqué of the International Conference of Christian Trade-Unions (CISC) of Brussels, which spoke of a "serious trade union situation" and of

"government repression," mentioning a police attack on the locals of the Vietnamese Confederation of Labor, and the "arrest of many union leaders, among whom was the secretary-general, Vo Van Tai," etc. The police had intervened to repress a strike of workers from the water and gas company and the Confederation of Labor had protested publicly, threatening a general strike throughout the country.

15. Interview published in *L'Italia*, Milan, January 18, 1968.

16. *Le Monde*, July 7–8, 1968, p. 2.

17. To the people of Vietnamese stock must be added the Montagnards, i.e., some two million tribal people of non-Vietnamese stock who occupy more than half the territory of South Vietnam, the plateaus covered with forests on the borders of Laos and Cambodia. These tribes are strongly anti-Communist and give a good contribution to the South Vietnamese army and the self-defense people's militia. Actually, it is in the Montagnard regions that one can visit the only villages that defend themselves at night against the Viet Cong. The anti-Communism of these warlike peoples, who live in a still very primitive state, comes from three factors: the Communists and the Viet Cong are Vietnamese and therefore for racial motives are hated by the mountain tribes (the South Vietnamese army rarely appears in the Montagnard regions, which are generally garrisoned by Americans or Koreans); the tribal races of North Vietnam were oppressed by the Communist regime, and there were refugees in the South who brought news of this oppression; finally, the Montagnards, whose religion is animistic (not Buddhist), are very much influenced by the Catholic and Protestant missionaries, the first people to show concern for them even in the past, defending them against the vexations of the Vietnamese. The Montagnards have their own political movement, the FULRO (United Front for the Liberation of Oppressed Races), which has sworn fidelity to the Saigon government, pledging itself to combat the guerrilla war. At the same time, and as a reward for their fidelity, the Montagnards sought greater autonomy from the Vietnamese government in Saigon (see P. O'Connor, "Montagnards back Saigon Regime," *Sunday Examiner*, November 18, 1966, p. 11).

18. After the attack on the cities, begun in February 1968, the situation has changed noticeably, as we shall soon see.

19. The American journalist Neil Sheehan gives a description of Viet Cong terrorism in the *New York Times*, February 27, 1966. He says that the Communist terrorism in Vietnam is not, as is commonly thought, the massacre of whole villages. Rather, it is a very selective and perhaps more effective terrorism precisely because of its selectivity, which spreads terror without alienating a great number of peasants through wholesale massacres.

Customarily the Communists kill a few well-known individuals in the villages: the village chief, a schoolmaster or a policeman. When the victim is killed, sometimes after a public trial before a so-called "people's court" for "crimes against the people," his death serves to terrorize many others, forcing them into silence or into cooperating with the guerrilla war. The Viet Cong cadres do not have to kill anyone else in the village, since the very fact that they can kill others at will is widely known and quite sufficient for their orders to be followed.

20. Someone may wonder why such facts are not known in the West or are known only summarily. I asked about this myself and have had various complementary responses. The Americans, I was told, do not know what is going on in the villages, and they therefore ignore generally this aspect of the guerrilla war. They are waging war on the grand style, and one death more or less in the villages is not something that impresses them (and this is the colossal mistake of the "American war," since the Viet Cong are aiming above all at the control of the population). The South Vietnamese government, which is aware of these facts, has no system of overseas propaganda, and anyway its voice is too suspect of partiality. (And finally, it does not give too much publicity to the Viet Cong terrorism so as not to confess its impotence and discourage the population even more). The foreign newspapermen are not in contact with the country people nor with the Vietnamese people in general, since they are covering the war from the press offices and by way of American airplanes (the only foreigners living with the people, the missionaries, take good care not to make public what they see for fear of reprisals. Whatever the missionaries told me was always preceded by the condition of never revealing a name nor reporting the place where I saw or heard something).

21. Nguyen Hong Giao, "The Church in Vietnam," The Tablet, London, September 11, 1965, p. 998, says that if it is also true that the Communist terrorism is directed against the Christians, it is understandable that the Christians had to suffer more, since the recruitment of fighters, the collection of taxes and the elimination of the faithful functionaries are not the unique objects of the rebels. An antireligious policy was begun in several regions under their control: propaganda, threats, false accusations against the leaders of the communities, priests or members of Catholic actions, notables, etc.

22. L'Italia, Milan, December 28, 1968.

23. For not a few Western commentators, this "unbeatability" of the Viet Cong would demonstrate that their revolt was heartily supported by the people, otherwise it could not last. Now, leaving aside the fact of the forced support of the people obtained through terrorism, we must report that in

countries with forests and without roads a guerrilla war can last for a long time even without any spontaneous support from the people. Cf. the case of 3,000 of Chiang Kai Shek's soldiers who, confined to Burma since 1948, waged a vast guerilla war there until 1965, when Chiang called them back to Formosa via Thailand. The people had great hatred for these Chinese invaders, the national army pursued them everywhere, but the guerrillas were practically invincible and they survived on terrorism, without any outside aid and without any friendly boundary to which they could repair in case of necessity. For the Viet Cong there are elements that are still more favorable: enormous aid from abroad both in means and in men, very long and friendly frontiers with Laos and Cambodia, guerrilla warriors familiar with the terrain which is their own country and, finally, the spontaneous aid of one part of the population that is certainly Communist.

24. *T.C.* June 20, 1968, p. 13. In regard to the Viet Cong operations against Saigon, C. Bourdet writes: "These operations seem to have a goal that is more political than military. . . . It is a question of bombarding the city with 122 mm. caliber rockets that are two meters long and cause terrible damage. It seems that the accuracy of these shots is bad, since the troops of the Front, dispersed on the outskirts, have no launching ramps but only makeshift set-ups from which they can fire only hastily and frenziedly and then immediately afterward change position in order to avoid being discovered. If we are to believe the Western correspondents, these bombs fell indiscriminately, causing civilian casualties, especially. Apparently the aim was to show that the Saigon government and the Americans were incapable of protecting the population and continually to develop the trend towards "peace at any price."

25. S. Harrison, "Mass Execution Policy Confirmed in Newly Discovered Hué Graves," the *Times*, London, March 27, 1968, p. 10.

26. P. O'Connor, "Agony of Hué Catholics," *Sunday Examiner,* Hong Kong, May 24, 1968, p. 2; *Fides,* April 17 and June 1, 1968.

X

The Vietnamese Church:
A "New Courage"
toward Peace

One fact that we don't think enough about in the West is this: that everything or almost everything that is written in books and magazines of some importance in the West on Vietnam is known in South Vietnam and discussed not only on an elite level but sometimes also among the students and the people. This is true— and I should say especially true—with the Christians who have a special interest here, since they feel themselves particularly bound by faith to the Christian West.

The Vietnamese Catholics feel themselves misunderstood and betrayed. In my contacts with Catholic circles in Vietnam and in my conversations with bishops, priests and educated laymen, I often heard questions of this type, with a very sorrowful tone: Why don't the Christians of Europe help us? Why do they misunderstand us and often attack us? Why do they take sides with the persecutors of the Church? . . . . From the other sister churches we have no moral help . . .

Material and financial assistance are not lacking, nor are missionaries, whether priests, sisters or laymen, but on the moral plane the Vietnamese Christians feel themselves misunderstood, betrayed —I do not like to write this word—*sold out* by their brothers in the faith. To some these words may seem too strong, but we must understand the state of mind of people who have been at war for twenty-seven years in order to comprehend the exasperation of their reactions to happenings which, undoubtedly, are much less serious.

It must be said that in Vietnam the French Catholic press is much read, for French is still the predominant foreign language and the links with the Church in France, which has been sending its missionaries here for many centuries, are still quite close.

When they read the French Catholic press (also the Italian and English presses, since, in addition to the bishops who know Italian well, some of the priests have studied at Rome), the Vietnamese Catholics are painfully struck by certain positions taken on the Vietnamese war which do not take any account of either the concrete realities of Vietnam nor the desire of the majority of the Vietnamese people, and particularly the Catholics, not to end up under a Communist dictatorship. A very highly thought of and prudent bishop told me:

I have read many appeals for peace in Vietnam published in the Western Catholic press and often signed by Catholic persons of note: they ask that the Americans stop the bombing of North Vietnam, they ask that the Americans leave Vietnam, they ask that the Vietnamese be "totally free from foreign interventions" to resolve their own problems among themselves. Rarely is there a mention of a peace that should be in justice and freedom, and still more rarely do they ask for international guarantees for this true peace. I have at times wondered whether the people making these appeals are in good or bad faith. I do not want to judge intentions, but how can people ignore to such an extent the danger of a Communist dictatorship which would be disastrous for our people and especially for us Catholics?

I heard similar statements repeated many times, often mentioning the situation in which Europe found itself during the Second World War, when American aid was indispensable to free our continent from Nazism. ("What if then the Americans had left the Europeans free to decide their own destiny and to resolve their own problems among themselves. . . ?" A bishop who was deploring some of the major French Catholic publications was asked why he had never written to specify the position of the Vietnamese Church. He answered with these words:

> I have written several times, sending letters and documentation, asking that they be published, but they were never satisfied with them: some answered that my letter was too long to be published, others told me that my experience was limited to only one region of Vietnam and therefore what I said was not, perhaps, valid for the whole country. . . . Then I stopped writing so as not to waste my time, but I wonder if this is honesty; I don't say Christian but merely human honesty . . .

Other bishops and priests confirmed to me that they had written to the major progressive French Catholic reviews, but their letters either were not published or else so cut as to render them of little or no significance. . . . On June 2, 1967—to take a concrete example from among so many that I could mention—the Paris daily *La Croix* published a "Letter to the ministers and priests of the U.S.A.," signed by 59 French priests, 8 professors of theology and 18 Protestant clergymen; the letter requested their American confreres to openly condemn the presence of the American troops in Vietnam and the war "which was crushing the revolt of a whole people against an unjust social order."

The Vietnamese Catholic lay committee, *Veritas*, sent a letter of particulars to *La Croix* which the Catholic newspaper did not publish (possibly because it really was too long and aggressive). In the letter they said that the French priests' appeal took literally the Communist version of the war in Vietnam, without any indication of a critical approach towards it, and completely ignored the fact that millions of Vietnamese were fighting against communism and another million had fled from the North to escape the Communist dictatorship. Here is the letter:

If you do not wish to believe us, ask any of our bishops. . . . The cause of the war is primarily the ambition of the Communist leaders of Hanoi, sustained by those of the Chinese. Since 1954, they have proposed to annex the whole of South Vietnam. . . . Our government, in accord with our people, requested the aid of the Americans, as your government and your people did in the two world wars. . . . They are to be censured who do not acknowledge that the Americans are here in Vietnam, as they were in France in 1917 and 1944, not as imperialists or colonialists but as defenders of a people in danger of being swallowed up! They are ready to leave Vietnam as soon as our security is assured; on this point a solemn pledge was made at an international conference, and you ought to know it . . .

We want peace, it is superfluous to say, with all our strength . . . but we reject the *sham peace* that serves to deceive the ingenuous. . . . The conditions for peace in Vietnam come down to one alone: make the Communist leaders abandon their plan to annex the South, and we shall immediately put down our arms. . . . With Paul VI we applaud the negotiations provided that they will restore peace to us without in any way endangering justice, freedom and human dignity. We do not want the humiliation of our adversary, but we also want our rights to be respected, and only our strict rights.

But if the Communists of the North continue to reject any peaceful means of ending the war and retain firmly their ambitious dream of occupying our territory in the South by force, put yourselves in our place and tell us what we can do! We are only imitating the example of courage, patriotism and love of freedom that you gave us with your heroic resistance to Nazi aggression, with the help of your allies at that time, who are also our allies today . . .

The *Veritas* document says again that the letter of the French clergymen, like several other documents of this kind, does not take into account the concrete realities of Vietnam and is nothing but an incitement to North Vietnam to continue in its intransigence. Another document of this kind—but we could mention dozens, almost all of which are unknown in the West, where they are ignored by this same Catholic press—is the "Open letter to the

American committee of clergy and laymen concerned about Vietnam," which the Catholic daily *Xay Dung* (Construction) had published in Saigon on January 25, 1967:

> We, too, are priests and laymen concerned about Vietnam. And we are Vietnamese. We live in the midst of the war in our own country. Our fathers, our mothers, our families live in Vietnam. . . . We have the right and the duty to speak out. You are foreigners with goodwill, certainly, but you live far away from the realities of Vietnam today. . . . It is you who worry us. Some of you have reached conclusions and made statements that are not in accord with the real situation in Vietnam today. The aggression is inspired, supported and directed by a Communist regime, that of North Vietnam, and we know this regime well. Those of us who thought we could work with this regime were deluded. The final objective of this aggression is certainly the imposition of the Communist regime in South Vietnam. . . . We beg you fervently to do nothing and to say nothing that could weaken Vietnam's resistance. Do not cooperate, especially in the name of religion, in imposing the Communist regime. None of you would want to live under a Communist regime. Why do you think that we should want to?

On the other hand, the West can harm the Vietnamese Catholics not only when it supports extreme "pacifist" positions but also when, on the opposite side, it makes warlike statements showing itself to have no confidence in negotiations but only hope in a military victory. The classic case is that of Cardinal Spellman, who at Christmas 1966, in his address to the American soldiers in Vietnam, had the unfortunate idea to make a statement to that effect. The gist of what he said was this: he felt that the war in Vietnam was a war for the defense of civilization; the Americans did not look for this war, it was imposed upon them and they did not wish to yield to tyranny. Their president and secretary of state had said that a war cannot be half-won. Therefore he prayed that the courage and commitment of the American soldiers would not be fruitless and that victory would soon come about, a victory that everyone in Vietnam and throughout the world would welcome.[2] "Any solution other than victory is inconceivable," the Cardinal concluded; "it is known that our leaders committed themselves to negotiating, but their offers were scornfully rejected . . ."

The statement was particularly serious in Vietnam, either because it was a very well-known Cardinal who made it, and in Vietnam itself, or because it came only two months after the peace mission of Mgr. Pignedoli, who had directed the Catholics to look favorably on the negotiations and to work for a peaceful solution of the war and who, furthermore, created in Vietnamese public opinion the clear impression that something was changing in the local Church. Cardinal Spellman's statement, reported in banner headlines in all the newspapers in South Vietnam, destroyed this image of the Church and drove Catholics back into their shell of fanatical anti-Communism. Despite all the later specifications made by the Cardinal which gave a better explanation of his remarks,[3] the initial impression predominated and caused considerable harm in the Vietnamese Church.[4] Cardinal Spellman was answered by the weekly *Song Dao*,[5] in addition, naturally, to many other reactions aroused throughout the world.

Unfortunately, Cardinal Spellman's case is not unique among the "Rightist" positions taken that harm the Church of Vietnam and Vietnam itself. Other publications and public figures support the continuation of the war to the point of victory over the "enemy" as the only solution to the Vietnamese problem. It is curious how, in the Catholic camp at least, positions are always so clearly divided into two: on one side "peace at any cost" and, on the other, "war until victory," while few people support the more upright and Christian solution of a "just peace in freedom" (that of Paul VI) which corresponds to the more profound aspirations of the Catholics and of the Vietnamese in general.[6]

The Church of the West and the drama of Vietnam. The erroneous positions taken in the Christian West among public figures, the press and movements of public opinion with regard to the war and the Vietnamese Church,[7] namely, in an extremist sense "Right" or "Left," are, we think, harmful in two senses: first of all because they weaken the Vietnamese Church by involving it in polemics, increasing the divisions within it, and by producing unacceptable solutions (continuation of the war or a Communist dictatorship). But the even graver harm is this: that the Christians of the West will end up by having no credability with their Vietnamese brothers and will no longer be able to supply them with that stimulus they so sorely need.

We repeat what we have already said: after twenty-seven years of war in Vietnam there is an enormous confusion of ideas, even among the Catholics who cling to the one sure thing, anticommunism, precisely in order to have a solid point of reference. Under the pressure of a thousand dangers and distresses, the Catholics (and often also the priests and bishops) no longer possess the tranquility and detachment that they so need in order to always choose the right path in the most intricate problems they must encounter.

In this difficult situation of the Vietnamese Church, the Christian West could play an important part by urging the bishops, priests and local lay Catholics toward peaceful solutions, in accordance with the spirit of the Council. But unfortunately the Western Catholic press is read almost exclusively, to say the worst about it since we are on the Vietnamese problem; it has assumed unjust and most partisan positions which are almost always biased to the harm of the Catholics and the anti-Communists generally and to the exclusive advantage of their political adversaries.[8]

Even Western bishops and Catholic movements find themselves at times taking these same positions, although with the best possible goodwill and right intentions, but without ever asking the opinion of the bishops of the Vietnamese Church, who are the chief people concerned by the problem.[9] The Archbishop of Saigon told me, "You are the first European Catholic journalist who in coming to Vietnam took the time to inform the bishops and then to ask their opinion on the problems of our country."

Many times in Vietnam I heard complaints about this lack of consideration shown by the West not only for the bishops but also for any representative of the Vietnamese Church; how could it happen that a Buddhist bonze—an undoubtedly most worthy person—could have been almost triumphantly greeted in Western Catholic circles, while no notice is given to the fact that a Catholic bishop may be in the area, nor is he invited to speak.[10]

It is easy to understand how all this is a source of grave moral suffering for a Church that feels its very existence threatened and sees itself misunderstood by its own brothers in the faith and even accused of mistakes for which it does not feel guilty. This is the worst trial possible.

It therefore seems more indispensable and urgent than ever that a fraternal dialogue be established between the Western churches and the Church of Vietnam. Dialogue means an exchange of experiences and ideas, it means giving and receiving. If the Vietnamese Church can give to the Christian West a magnificent example of faith and Christian practice, if it can make the West aware, through its painful experiences, of the concrete realities of the Vietnamese situation so as to make it avoid mistaken positions and judgments, undoubtedly the Western churches have much to give to the Vietnamese, and something essential for its renewal.

We have already said that the Vietnamese Church is still in great part unrenewed by the spirit and the decisions of the Council which should have made it examine itself and renew itself thoroughly. It is true, as I was told in Vietnam, that the Council grew to maturity in the West after many years of study and experience, and it therefore cannot be transported and imposed bodily on people who had not evolved their mentalities and structures gradually. But it is also true that time is going by very fast in Vietnam, and the Church cannot wait for the "long years" of maturation that were the case in the West.

For this sister Church the time of courage has come, a courage that is different from that to which it was accustomed by history. No longer fighting for the faith but making the faith an instrument of peace and service in Vietnam, it can no longer make crusades against the others but must initiate discussion with them and meet with them in a conciliar spirit, the spirit of the Gospel; it can no longer close into itself to defend its own traditions but must become open to dialogue with the others so as to build together a better Vietnam. It is along these new paths, the only ones that can lead to peace, that the churches of the West can help the Vietnamese Church to go by prayer, study, moral support, understanding and incentive. We must defend the freedom of the Vietnamese Catholics (of all the Vietnamese), but we must also show them in a brotherly fashion the blueprints for a post-conciliar renewal that cannot be delayed.

The courage to negotiate with the Communists. The first aspect of this "new courage" that is required of the Vietnamese Church is the rejection of negative, fanatical and blind anti-Communism, which, as the recent history of Vietnam shows abundantly, leads to the blind alley of a war to the finish. The Christians of Vietnam —like the great majority of South Vietnamese, for that matter— are dominated today by the fear of communism: an undoubtedly fully justified terror, but one that has no positive effect. Nothing is more disastrous, in politics especially, than to act under fear, and to consent to an evil—war above all—even though one knows it is an evil; one agrees to this out of fear of something worse, but the "worst" ends up by becoming inevitable in a more or less short space of time.

The courage of the Church is first of all in freeing itself of the fear of Communism. This is not easy for a bishop who hears day after day about the assassination of his Christians and his catechists; it is not easy for the Christian, or for the priest, who feel crushed by a force greater than their own. But it is the only way to bring about a positive solution both to the Vietnamese conflict and to the war. The continuation of the war to the bitter end is certainly not a positive solution but the most negative one possible, since, as everyone admits, the more the war continues in Vietnam the more the ultimate solution of a Communist dictatorship becomes inevitable. It is not a question, therefore, of merely postponing for as long as possible—with the war—the advent of a Communist dictatorship but of courageously setting out on a new path by putting an end to the war and accepting a compromise solution which would open up to Vietnam the hope of different solutions.[11] Let us repeat that we are well aware of how difficult it is to have a concrete idea of these different solutions, but people must also have confidence that just as war has its inevitable way of working things out (and we know in Vietnam this process leads to Communism), so peace, if it is built and not just experienced, can gradually open up new prospects that were not even thought of in the beginning.

It is necessary, then, that Christians become open to the idea of peace, and that they commit all their united and efficient forces to the task of peace and not war. But to do this people must not be motivated to act solely out of terror of communism, an attitude which simplistically divides men into two categories, Communists and anti-Communists, with the first to be fought and exterminated in order to save the second. This infantile way of looking at the reality of Communism is, in addition to being unjust, harmful to Vietnam itself. No one would dream of denying the danger of a Communist dictatorship—this whole book demonstrates that—but since the war cannot lead to a positive solution with a military victory of one side over the other, it is indispensable to come to an agreement, accept a compromise and be prepared to live with the local Communists in a position of collaboration and not of mutual extermination.

At the beginning of the Paris negotiations in May 1968, a Saigon newspaper wrote: "We are at the beginning of the end. It will no longer be possible to turn back and we must begin to be concerned about afterwards."

The war continues in Vietnam as before, perhaps more ruthless than before, but it is a war that is now meaningless—if it ever had any meaning! All it accomplishes today are more deaths and more destruction. There will no longer be any military victory, it will no longer be possible to turn back. And in order to be concerned about "afterwards," it is necessary to accept South Vietnamese Communism as a reality, certainly an unpleasant one, but it cannot be wiped away with a sponge. It is with this reality that Vietnam— and Catholics particularly—must be prepared to contend. So much will be gained by beginning immediately, as seems to be already indicated by the intentions of the new South Vietnamese prime minister, Tran Van Huong, who in June of 1968 called the Viet Cong "authentic patriots."[12]

Unfortunately, from the Catholic side, no similar attitude of relaxation of tension and a preparation for dialogue is yet noticeable. *La Croix's* correspondent in Saigon, Fr. Parrel, wrote recently:

Why do some people, among whom are certain Christians, stubbornly persist in not wanting to speak with the adversary, even if it is Communist? Because, in the last analysis, no one can dialogue by himself and every war must end with an encounter with the other side, even when dealing with Communists. Why refuse to speak with the NLF under the pretext that it is Communist? Certainly there are Communists in the Front and the Front is supported by the Communists from the North, but the Front is a reality and has its supporters—who are numerous—even among us. It is an undeniable fact. Therefore, why be obstinate, since it is impossible to wipe away something that exists?

Catholics and Buddhists united for peace. All observers agree in asserting that salvation for Vietnam can come only from a union of religious forces, the only ones that have any hold on the people not only in the cities but in the country areas as well, where 70 percent of the South Vietnamese live. No political party—with the exception of Communism, of course—has today, or can hope to have in the future, a strength and a hearing with the Vietnamese people comparable to that of the organized religions, especially Buddhism, Catholicism and the two sects Cao-Dai and Hoa-Hao (with small fringe-groups of Moslems, Protestants, Confucianists, Taoists). If the four most important religions were united in a close collaboration for peace and the building of peace, there is much hope that they would succeed in asserting themselves as the most important and widespread force and therefore give Vietnam the peace and security of a government based on the confidence of the people. But if these religious forces remain divided, as is the case up to this time, nothing and no one else will be able to be their substitute in the accomplishment of the task about which we have spoken.

The incomprehensible fact is this: that similar ideas are heard expressed by everyone in Vietnam, priests and bonzes, foreign observers and simple people, laymen and also government politicians. It is a common conviction that only the organized religions will be able to save Vietnam, but in practice the religions continue to ignore one another, polemicize, and at times even fight one another. It is true that progress along the way of understanding has been made (but almost exclusively at the top) among a few delegates of the various churches and religious organizations who have learned, after meeting every week, to get to know one another, to understand one another and to desire one another's good as well. For the rest, everything, or almost everything, is continuing as before. Even on the occasion of the great Viet Cong offensive against the cities (February 1968) a noticeable rapprochement between the religions was reported: charitable and religious services in common, communiqués in the press, meetings between prominent people, etc. It seemed almost that the imminent danger served to awaken people from a long sleep, but afterwards nothing concrete came of it all, no initiative with political consequences worthy of mention. On the occasion of the fifth anniversary of the coronation of Paul VI, the leaders of all the religions responded positively to the invitation of the apostolic delegate, Mgr. Palmas, to meet at the apostolic delegation's headquarters in warm and friendly conversation. In normal times, in a country at peace, this would be a good sign of religious "ecumenism." In Vietnam it is absolutely insufficient and has no other meaning than to publicize the photograph of the group of religious leaders in all the newspapers. This is not enough either to restore peace or to give the country a representative government.

The most profound division is that separating the "Neutralist" and pacifist current of Buddhism (that of Tri Quang) from the other religions, as we have already fully described in the preceding chapters. Tri Quang, even if he has lost much empathy among the Vietnamese elite from the summer of 1963 till today, is still the man who has succeeded in advancing the idea of peace and neutrality in Vietnam by clearly demonstrating his independence both in regard to Communism and to the government and the Americans. Catholics must ask themselves whether sincere collaboration with this man and his movement would not be the best contribution they have to bring to the future of the country and to the advent of peace. Some people have already moved in this direction. For example, the *Song Dao* group and Fr. Hoang Quynh, after a period of closedness and fanatical anti-Communism, has embarked upon, as we have seen, the most constructive road of understanding with the other religions without ever going back on his anti-Communism.[13] But the mass of Christians—and very often the priests and the bishops as well—still demonstrate that they are far from this "new courage."

One French student of Vietnam, M. Devillers, gives a good summation of the situation we are describing:

The religious forces are probably the only ones capable of obliging the Americans to change their methods and to respect the rights of Vietnam. Tri Quang, gifted with remarkable maneuverability, has understood

that the events could give Buddhism the opportunity to emerge as a
powerful, authentically national force capable of attracting the majority
of the people and thereby allowing it to combat Communism victori-
ously. . . . In order to begin this process, which through a civilian
government could restore sovereignty and national independence, the
Buddhists need the Catholics. . . . Apparently, the inspiration of the
Council has not yet reached Saigon, and the discordance between the
official position of the Vatican and that of the "Catholic forces" in Vietnam becomes more disturbing every week, to the point that many inhabitants of Saigon are asking themselves at times from whom do the
Vietnamese Catholics take their orders, from Rome or the American
embassy. *To speak of peace is no longer enough.* Today the concrete
problem is to know whether the Catholics will agree to work with the
Buddhists or not in restoring independence and facilitating peace.[14]

Although this was written in 1966, it is still fully up to date,
like this other statement prepared by a group of Vietnamese intellectuals in July 1965, in which we read that after the two realities
that alone count for something in Vietnam (the Communists and
the Americans), there is a third reality: the religions.

The nationalist political parties are reduced to "leadership groups" without followers, with each leader defining the party line in his own way
and according to his own interests. It is for this reason that in order to
give themselves a certain consistency, the successive governments have
relied on the religions. The religions are the third reality in Vietnam
since they have deep roots in the populace. Unfortunately it is not a
political reality since all religions proclaim their transcendent character
and detachment in regard to every regime and every political policy.
Moreover, it is a divided reality. . . . Two years ago, urged from every
side and confronted with the distressing problems of reality that put
their own existence in the balance, the religions were forced to assume
a political attitude that their members were trying more or less successfully to translate into political action. . . . Therefore, the religions can
be considered not as political forces but as spiritual forces able to influence with their weight the political line of a given historical mo-

ment. In this area experience has shown that the determining forces are the Buddhist and Catholic masses. United, they could constitute a formidable front; divided, they are barely capable of undermining a government. And only the Communists can gain by their divisions . . .

To make peace, two sides are needed. The two political reailties that count in South Vietnam are the United States and the NLF. At the peace table there will be the NLF. . . . But the other party cannot be the United States but rather a Vietnamese political force with a popular basis capable of being compared to that of the NLF. This force exists virtually in the masses of the religious membership. South Vietnam's concern and that of the non-Communists is that this become a reality: only then will the way to peace be opened. The key to the problem of peace, then, is to be found in the creation of a non-Communist movement that can negotiate on an equal footing with the NLF and that has enough strength to see that the conditions of the peace are respected in the future. The essential condition of peace can only be the establishment of a really democratic regime that is not subjected to any bloc and in which the essential freedoms will be respected, and where everyone, Communist or non-Communist, will be able to contribute towards the building of a society open to progress in accordance with the ideals of justice and freedom.

Utopia, people will say. How can anyone believe in the Communists' sincerity? In politics there is no question of sincerity but of a balance of forces. And in politics force comes from popular support.[15]

Nationalism and social justice. Terror of communism and the exclusive involvement in the anti-Communist struggle have made Catholics lose sight of other realities in Vietnam, even though they are most worthy of concern. Let us point out the two major ones: national independence and social justice which, being neglected by the non-Communist forces, have ended up by becoming the Communists' Trojan horse.

National independence is related, naturally, to the ever more massive American presence which is taking away all autonomy from the national government and supplies valid reasons for the Communists to proclaim themselves the only defenders of the country's freedom from any foreign invasion. For Catholics the problem is particularly grave, taking into account their history and the prejudice weighing against them as "agents of the foreigner," first with the French and now with the Americans. It is obviously not enough to forbid the priests to use the airplanes and the other means of communication of the Americans in order to demonstrate their independence; it is rather a question of having the courage not to be connected with the American war in defense of their own freedom and of being able to conceive the future of a neutral Vietnam free from any foreign presence.

Even here, we are perfectly aware of the difficulties of putting these general ideas into practice: when our existence is threatened, or when we see our own freedoms endangered, we attach ourselves spontaneously to the foreign ally who by his strength seems to be able to guarantee our rights. But this clearly shows a lack of confidence in the indigenous neutral and patriotic forces and a lack of that national dignity that in newly independent countries like Vietnam is strongly felt on all levels of the population.[16] Between the two extreme positions, of the Communists who want the immediate and unconditional withdrawal of the Americans and of those who have complete confidence in the American support, there is a middle way: that of justly appreciating the aid of the foreign ally against the attempt to deprive a people of their basic freedoms and, at the same time, looking upon this aid as temporary, without being bound to it hand and foot, and preparing a solution of replacement with national forces. A "middle way" which has still to be undertaken and pursued with courage.

The attitude of the South Vietnamese towards the Americans is most contradictory: everybody speaks ill of them but nobody wants them to leave. On the one side you have the exasperated nationalism of a people that have barely emerged from colonial domination and, on the other, the full realization that in the present state of affairs the American presence is indispensable for the safeguard of the South Vietnamese people's freedom to decide. The mistake is to bog down "at the present state of affairs" without taking any step forward to change a situation that cannot last forever. Often, even when speaking with highly placed and educated persons, I saw that they had no idea as to how to be able to prepare for the "post bellum" period, or how the country could live without the Americans there. In other words, what could be a temporary situation, an acceptable momentary aid, has become for many a permanent condition, and they cannot imagine a different future . . .

The second element neglected in the anti-Communist struggle is social justice, which is also a strong point of the Viet Cong propaganda. South Vietnam is certainly not a country of extreme misery, as are several in Asia and Africa; in fact, it can be said that within the disconsoling picture presented by the "third world" it is a rich country that does not suffer from hunger, due to its flourishing agriculture, and enjoys the advantage of only a small percentage of illiterates. Neither do we find in South Vietnamese society those frightful social injustices and class differences that are immediately evident in other parts of the "third world," nor are there large landed estates, as in Latin America (I am told that the tilled land—not the export plantations—is rather well distributed).

In normal times, therefore, South Vietnam would be a prosperous, orderly country without deep class conflicts. But, clearly, these are not normal times for Vietnam. The guerrilla war has caused destruction and misery, the Viet Cong propaganda has exaggerated social conflicts, the exceptional times through which the country is living have matured the consciences of the poor and have aroused in them a strong desire for greater social justice. But the governments which have succeeded one another in power in Saigon —as we have already said about the Diem government—were rarely concerned about making Vietnamese society more just: the war and the military needs prevailed over everything. It is easy to understand that in this way the Viet Cong have a free field to present themselves as champions of social justice, all the more so since where they have succeeded in establishing themselves they put into effect a certain distributive justice, in their own way, which in regard to the local landowners is also punitive. Certainly, for a tolerant and good-hearted people like the Vietnamese these summary and violent methods are not very pleasant, but in the face of government inefficiency the conviction is spreading that only the Communists are capable of working efficiently towards the establishment of justice.

The fault of the non-Communist nationalists—and particularly of the Catholics—is precisely their neglect of the theme of social justice, leaving it almost completely in the control of the adversaries. In the Church—as we have shown—there is much charity but little concern for justice; in the Christian masses an open awareness of social problems has not yet been formed.

If Vietnam wishes to survive as a free country, it has to be able to offer its people a social doctrine that is different from that of capitalism and naturally also from the Communist doctrine. Diem himself understood this need, and his "personalism" (which we explained in Chapter IV) was nothing else but the unsuccessful attempt to find an autonomous path between Communism and capitalism for the solution of the Vietnamese social problems. After him there was no longer any attempt to do anything, even though the Catholics had available to them examples of solutions that were in accord with the Christian spirit and which were put into effect in other countries, as well as pontifical and conciliar documents which were just waiting to be put into practice.[17]

The report of the Vietnamese intellectuals in 1965, quoted above, gives a good description of this situation:

The people of South Vietnam are not for the Communists . . . communism as a doctrine and as a regime goes against the national traditions and the immediate concerns of the population, composed by and large of deeply religious peasants eager for property. But anti-Communism would have taken hold on the population only if it was really accompanied by antifeudalism and anticolonialism, i.e., profound changes that would be aimed at substituting new social structures for the old and which would be capable of satisfying aspirations of justice and freedom. In this area, however, nothing has been done. Actually, South Vietnamese society has remained a feudal and colonial society after ten years of independence: the same mandarins continue to govern, the rich have become richer and the poor have still remained poor.

Certainly, the American aid has been generous and has prevented South Vietnam from falling into economic and financial chaos. But it has grave defects: it is conceived as a defense prop; it has created a class of middlemen in business who are greedy and parasitical and whose shameless ostentation is a permanent insult to the sentiment of justice; American economic aid keeps South Vietnam in a permanent state of dependence instead of helping it to really build a sound and vital economy.

These are the accusations that the South Vietnamese Catholics ought to have been able to make not only in words but also with their concrete commitment to greater social justice and the economic progress of the country, obtained also with American aid, but using this to make the national economy self-sufficient and not to create a new kind of neocolonial economic dependence.[18]

For a conciliar renewal of the Vietnamese Church. Finally, the last aspect of the "new courage" that our times require of the Vietnamese Church is that it take decisive steps along the paths indicated by Vatican Council II to all Christian peoples for their deep and evangelical *aggiornamento,* not only liturgical reform, however important it may be, but also all the others: the acknowledgment of past mistakes, a spirit of service to all men, the rejection of triumphalism, the caste spirit, clericalism, etc.

We shall not dwell on these themes since they have already been amply treated. We have pointed out that on account of its own historical vicissitudes, the Vietnamese Church is enclosed in its traditions and has not yet been renewed by the conciliar spirit. The Catholics present themselves as a unique bloc[19] separated in part from the rest of the country. In a country in rapid evolution like Vietnam, a Church of this kind is destined to be unable to survive in the long run, or at least no longer represents in the eyes of non-Christians the sign of the presence of Christ among men.

The tasks awaiting the Vietnamese Church are immense, and one trembles to think that it might fail either because of a lack of preparation and because of being too slow in bringing itself up-to-date in the historical moment in which it is living, or because out of blindness it did not perceive the "signs of the times" which require a Church that is humble, open, dedicated to the service of others, the bearer of peace and understanding, ready to be questioned and not closed up in its ivory tower with its defensive and conservative positions.

This is why the conciliar renewal of this Christian community is extremely important and cannot be put off. This renewal must not only involve Catholics together with all the other Vietnamese in the building of a free and peaceful Vietnam but also permit the Church to continue successfully its task of evangelization. If this does not happen, the Church will have lost in the Orient, perhaps definitively, another great historical opportunity, besides all those it lost in the past. I say in the Orient and not only in Vietnam because I am convinced that the future of Christianity in East and South-East Asia will in great part be won or lost in the rice fields and the forests of Vietnam, i.e., it depends upon the attitude of Vietnamese Catholics.

This should not seem to be a strange view. The Vietnam war has assumed an importance in Asian public opinion that is far greater than it has achieved in the West. And for the first time in the recent history of the Asian continent the Church finds itself having to assume the role of protagonist in the ups and downs of a country in Asia. This is tantamount to saying that if the local Christian community fails in its goal of contributing to peace in Vietnam, sad days will be in sight not only for the Vietnamese Church but for the Church in many other oriental countries.

The responsibility of world public opinion. The war in Vietnam is a problem that should be of concern to everyone, especially Christians. It is true that there are so many other wars, minor and major, in the world, but this one, involving the great powers, is the most dangerous and is also the most authentic test case in measuring man's desire for peace. The commitment of everyone to peace in Vietnam is therefore one of the essential conditions for the return of peace to this tormented country. Never before, in fact, has world public opinion so demonstrated its efficacy in promoting a peaceful solution to the conflict.

However, it must be a commitment to true peace for the welfare of the Vietnamese people and not in favor of one of the two sides in conflict. Hence, the firm conviction that there cannot be a military solution to the Vietnam war but only a political one must be spread and upheld; not a military victory of one side over the other but a political compromise.

Obviously, people go counter to this peaceful solution if they support a war and a one-sided victory to the bitter end, the American "hawks" on the one hand and the Communist "hawks" on the other, with all their supporters in the world—no small number on either side![20] We therefore condemn any escalation in the war, including the American bombings of the North and the escalation of the North Vietnamese and the Viet Cong in the South pointed at bringing the war into the cities, with tragic consequences for the civilian population. If we condemn the militarism of the generals, which constantly spurs the war on, we must also condemn all militarisms, and not only that of one side.

A compromise peace, without victors or conquered, essentially means two things: (1) that the NLF be recognized as one of the political forces present among the South Vietnamese, and that it therefore enjoy all those democratic rights that all political forces ought to enjoy in a country to which peace has been restored— with the agreement, however, that the NLF accept and respect the ways of democracy and that it not propose to set up its own dictatorship. (2) That the people of South Vietnam be guaranteed the ability freely to decide their own destiny in freedom, and that the peace, therefore, not be the equivalent of seeing a dictatorship impose itself, which the majority of the people do not want.

It is right, therefore, to recognize that the Communists represent a living and working force in South Vietnam. It is right that they too collaborate in the building of the country. It is right that they be admitted to the peace table and to the future civilian coalition government. But it is equally right that the peoples of South Vietnam have serious guarantees that the strongest, most organized and most violent do not impose themselves upon the majority with violent and oppressive methods, as North Vietnam has done.

The major obstacle to peace today comes precisely from this danger, clearly observed by the South Vietnamese: that peace, including the withdrawal of the American forces, may leave the road open for a Communist dictatorship, as happened in North Vietnam after 1954 and the departure of the French forces. It is necessary, then, that there be serious international guarantees that this will not happen. Without these guarantees it is vain to hope that the South Vietnamese will stop fighting and resisting a dictatorship imposed by force. Indeed, does peace exist in slavery?

In Europe it is sometimes said, even by Catholics sincerely desirous of peace, that between the two evils of a Communist regime and a war that endangers world peace it would be better to stop resisting communism and to allow a regime to be set up like the one in the North. Communism, it is said, would both establish social justice and make the Catholics' faith stronger and more mature.[21]

This is the proposal of the "at any cost" pacifists, which may have many merits but which has one very grave defect: it is proposed for others from whom they are tranquilly and safely at a distance of 15,000 kilometers! Everybody is capable of being a hero when others have to pay.

A Vietnamese bishop told me: "What the French Catholic progressives [and also the Italians, I might add] lack is the concrete experience of having lived for at least a year or two under a Communist regime here in Asia."

Our reasoning is based on an inculpable but abysmal ignorance of the facts and of Asian Communism. The South Vietnamese, who know it well, prefer war to a Communist peace. They will stop fighting once they have serious international guarantees that they will have peace in freedom and justice and not the peace of a dictatorship. Certainly they must prepare themselves for such a peace—as we have already pointed out—and not merely wait for it as a present from the outside. But this does not release us, who live outside Vietnam but who are deeply interested in the welfare of this people, from having to desire this peace and not another one, a peace in freedom and not under a dictatorship, in neutrality and not in any political bloc, and with serious international guarantees that all of this will be enabled to last and to be strengthened without being threatened by the stronger side, which is also more inclined to dictatorial methods.[22]

In Vietnam, I asked what judgment could be given of the demonstrations for "Peace in Vietnam" often organized in Europe by Catholics together with the Communists, and of clearly and exclusively anti-American demonstrations and writings. This was the response:

Such demonstrations, such books or articles, which put all the wrong on America and exalt the opposite side are not only false insofar as they do not take into account the historical reality and the will of the South Vietnamese, but they are also harmful insofar as on the one side they arouse a reaction with America and South Vietnam who see the basic reasons for their struggle misunderstood; and on the other, they spur on the opposite side with the favor of world public opinion to remain intransigent in their idea of total conquest.

What then? Are we to remain indifferent to the Vietnamese tragedy? Of course not. We can organize demonstrations and debates, write articles, demand peace through negotiations, but let us demand it of both contenders and not of only one. To cry out only against America as if it were the only one responsible for the Vietnamese war is false and a huge blunder.[23]

Let us demand peace as the pope has always done. He has always addressed himself with equal force to both sides in the conflict. In his Christmas radio message of December 23, 1966, Paul VI implored the belligerents to extend the Christmas truce: ". . . We ask this respectfully and warmly of both contending sides, that they both equally lend their support."

Notes

1. In April, 1967, 225 Vietnamese public figures, Catholics and non-Catholics, signed a motion of *Veritas* protesting against the request signed by 166 members of the Catholic University of Louvain for the immediate withdrawal of the American troops from Vietnam (among them were Canon Leclerq and Mgr. Houtart). The Vietnamese motion said: "Try to remember your state of mind during the Second World War with regard to the presence on your soil of the American and other allied troops. With what indignation would you not have denounced in 1917 and in 1941 all those who would have sought to keep the United States neutral! And so, just as you hoped for the intervention of the American army in 1941, we do the same today as non-Communist Vietnamese—i.e., the majority of the Vietnamese people—who fear the departure of the Americans as the result of partisan or ill-informed foreigners. The United States armed forces came here because they were called by our government and in accord with the ardent wishes of our people. To seek for them to leave would mean to change your devotion into irreparable cruelty. . . . Acknowledge our right to have our generous defenders. . . . May God will that you come to our defense by requesting the end of aggression or by asking for new help or, above all, by praying for peace, a peace that does not end up in Communist slavery" (see P. O'Connor, "Vietnamese reply to Louvain University's 'Motion' on War," *Sunday Examiner,* April 28, 1967, p. 2.

The rector of the University of Louvain, Mgr. Deschamps, in answering the Vietnamese motion of protest, said: "I am displeased in thinking that you have supposed that the signers of the motion represent a considerable part of the personnel of the university and that in some way the university has adopted this attitude. The academic and scientific personnel of our university includes some 2,000 persons [for 22,000 students]; this signifies that the 166 signatories of the motion only represent a small group . . ."

2. It must be added that from the Communist side there has never been talk of anything but final victory. See again the last message of Ho Chi Minh in July 1968, on the occasion of the anniversary of the Geneva accords, in which he speaks of "fighting still harder to bring back still greater victories," and of "fighting and conquering the cruelest enemy in the world." *Le Monde,* July 21–22, 1968, p. 1.

3. Upon his arrival in New York on January 7, 1967, Cardinal Spellman declared: "Our American soldiers, sailors and airmen, whom I met, ardently desire peace as much as anyone else in the world, but they are also resolved to fight until a peace based on justice is attained. . . . The victory they intend does not mean the complete destruction or crushing of the enemy. Nor does it mean the conquest of North Vietnam. It means rather to convince the adversary to come to the discussion table with the sincere disposition of finding a just and honorable solution." *L'Osservatore Romano,* January 15, 1967.

4. I was told in Vietnam that after Spellman's speech, which was styled by the most skillful in the Vietnamese press to mean more than what the poor Cardinal even meant to say, it became impossible for many months to reestablish friendly contacts with the neutralist currents of Buddhism, who had lost confidence in the Church's ability to change and were even disorientated by the fact that two public figures like Pignedoli and Spellman had come to Vietnam to make such contrary statements such a short distance apart. Even Tri Quang, in the long talk I had with him, asked me repeatedly for information about Spellman and Pignedoli and on the significance that would be given at Rome to their conflicting statements. It was enough for me to say that while the former came to Vietnam as the chief chaplain of the American armed forces, the second was the special envoy of the pope.

5. The open letter of the *Song Dao* was published in *Testimonianze,* January–February 1967, pp. 19–21.

6. The secretary general of the *Vietnamese Buddhist Associations Abroad,* Vo Van Ai, during a recent lecture tour in Europe, stated: "I look upon the spiritual forces, which I call a third force, as the only ones capable of producing a concrete solution. . . . This third force agrees to negotiate with the Communists but does not agree that they can run and lead the whole country of South Vietnam by themselves and denies their claim to do so. This force still less agrees with the suppression of the other anti-Communist forces that are not in agreement with the Hanoi regime . . . When I speak of a third force, I am not speaking only of a third force existing in South

THE CROSS AND THE BO-TREE

Vietnam, but I am also thinking of the third force existing in the rest of the world. Actually, as I said, Hanoi's politics is supported in the whole Communist bloc, and the politics of the present Saigon government is supported by America and the Western bloc, at least in part. The result is that press agencies and the radio always speak of these two contending forces, i.e., Communists or anti-Communists, who in reality are two minority forces with us. No press speaks of this powerful third force that gathers together the majority of the South Vietnamese people. In fact, this third force does not belong to either of the two blocs, and yet it is the one force that can know the Vietnamese problem. It has to be much talked about and made known everywhere: it is the force that must be supported. Even the demonstrations in the public square are always for one of the two contending forces and never for this third force which is the only one that can bring peace since it is a force that is directed towards giving peace to people's minds. . . . When people are engaged in these public demonstrations, they shout and fight to uphold their own ideology. . . . For example, the demonstration the other day in Rome: it cannot be denied that the participants and the organizers had goodwill and had also made great sacrifices, but think of those who saw it from the outside. They saw red banners, large portraits of Ho Chi Minh, cheers for red Vietnam, etc., which would make the onlooker think it was a demonstration in favor of a Communist Vietnam. In this demonstration there was not one cheer or one single expression in favor of the struggle being waged by the nonviolent in Vietnam, the Buddhists and the Catholics. Therefore, since it appeared to be a completely Communist demonstration, it will be thought in Washington that it is just one of the many Communist demonstrations and therefore in favor of America's enemies. Nor will American public opinion be shaken, while it would have been if they knew that the manifestation was in favor of the pacifist third force, that it was not directed against America, but that it was concerned with bringing peace to Vietnam and with the neutralization of South Vietnam. Therefore, there ought to have been demonstrations without one red banner or one cheer for red Vietnam, demonstrations where people speak only of the peaceful aspirations of all citizens of Vietnam," (*Gioventù*, Rome, March 1968, pp. 25–27).

7. One particularly irritating criticism of the Vietnamese Church, whether for Christians from there or for someone who has a minimum of good sense and Christian charity. In reading certain "histories" of the Church in Vietnam, often in very short articles, this idea essentially appears: the Church has always done the wrong thing and never did anything right or good; it did wrong with the Portuguese "patronage," then with French

colonialism, then in not supporting the guerrilla war against France (even when the Catholic patriots were being massacred by the Viet Minh!); then, naturally, the Catholics continued their mistake by fleeing en masse from North Vietnam, supporting the Diem regime and not dialoguing with the Buddhists, etc. In a word, even just criticisms are exaggerated in the extreme and especially presented without the counterweight of the positive aspect that the Church undoubtedly has in Vietnam, even in relation to the country itself. Articles or books of this type make the Vietnamese Catholics furious (and I mean, of course, priests and bishops as well), with the result that they lose all confidence in the Western Christian press.

8. Read, for example (only one of the very many examples that could be mentioned), the series of articles: L. Saurel, "Vietnam: Histoire d'un martyre," *T.C.,* from the July 1967 issue onwards. In Vietnam it was pointed out to me that the whole history of the country is interpreted according to the version given of it by the Communists, while the certain facts that go counter to this interpretation are minimized or just not mentioned. Examples of this kind abound in the French and Italian press.

9. To Cardinal Cardijn, following his participation in a demonstration for peace in Vietnam in which the withdrawal of the Americans was demanded, as we have already seen, the Bishop of Danang, Mgr. Pham Ngoc Chi, sent a telegram calling his choice "adventurous and harmful," all the more so because it was done "without consulting the Vietnamese episcopate and the apostolic delegate." There were visits of bishops that are remembered with gratitude in Vietnam. For example, in addition, naturally, to that of Mgr. Pignedoli, the visit of Mgr. Ancel, the apostolic administrator of the Diocese of Lyon, who in his statements has in fact always held a very balanced position in regard to Vietnam (see, for example, *La Documentation catholique,* coll. 1223–1226, 1967). Also the article of Mgr. Gouyon, president of the French section of *Pax Christi, op. cit.,* coll. 269–270, 1968. Which is also very balanced and aligned with the positions of the pope and the Vietnamese episcopate. Read also the statement of the American episcopate on the war in Vietnam (November 1966), which was fully acceptable to the Vietnamese.

10. In Italy, for example, no Vietnamese bishop has ever been invited to speak or be interviewed by radio or TV, and it should be remembered that the bishops of Vietnam speak Italian very well and were in Italy for many months during the Council, or came often to Rome for contacts with the Holy See.

11. The principle of condemning the war as a solution to the conflicts and of accepting a compromise solution has already been stated several times by

the Vietnamese bishops, but it is still not accepted by the Christian community in general.

12. *Le Monde,* June 25, 1968, p. 23.

13. In June 1968, Fr. Hoang Quynh launched an appeal for a cease-fire while strongly emphasizing that it ought not to be a question of peace at any cost, especially not for the benefit of the Communists (see the *Kipa* communiqué of July 8, 1968). On the relations between Fr Quynh and the religious leaders, especially with Tri Quang, we have already spoken. One more recent piece of news appeared in *Le Monde,* August 13, 1968, p. 2, reporting that the Catholic representatives led by Fr. Quynh and Buddhist representatives led by Tri Quang met to join forces in order to be "ready to fight the political battle that will be unleashed in Vietnam after the cease-fire." Fr. Quynh, considered as the leader of the Catholic moderates, endeavored to get the president of the Republic, Van Thieu, to free Tri Quang, whom the police had "taken under protection" in February 1968 during the days of the attack on Saigon by the Viet Cong.

14. *Le Monde diplomatique,* May 1966, p. 6.

15. *Mémorandum sur la guerre actuelle au Vietnam remis par un groupe d'intellectuels vietnamiens à la délégation universitaire américaine de passage à Saigon en juillet 1965, Kipa,* July 15, 1965; *France-Asie,* Paris, Spring, 1966, pp. 363–372.

16. Anti-Americanism, which is much more widespread that we may imagine, has many causes. The first is undoubtedly the intense Viet Cong propaganda and that of the North Vietnamese radio, which is almost completely devoted to the Americans (the government at Saigon is ignored); second, there is the humiliation of local nationalism (the American presence even in civilian jobs, etc.), the immorality of money and prostitution brought by the Americans, the damage done by the American bombings in the country areas and the cities, the bombing of North Vietnam, which is almost always condemned in the South, etc. To all of this there is added the idea that the Americans in Vietnam are fighting their own war against China and this was the reason why they eliminated Diem who, nationalist as he was, did not want to give a free hand to the American troops. The individual American soldier knew how to make himself likeable, often by helping the people. (A bishop told me: "In the last thirty years we have had many foreign armies in Vietnam: the Japanese, the French, the Chinese, the English, the American; none of them has behaved better than the Americans in regard to the civilian population.") But the American political policy is condemned, often categorically, even though in present circumstances the American military presence is held to be the lesser evil. Catholics are not

different from their other fellow countrymen in this anti-American sentiment.

17. One very interesting study on the social problems in Vietnam and on a middle solution between capitalism and Communism is that of Nguyen-Van-Can, *Viet-nam, prends garde de ne perdre corps et âme,* printed by the author, 17, rue de Javel, Paris-15e, 1967, p. 118. The author, a former diplomat and professor, advances precise proposals on the "post bellum" period, especially in regard to social organization and for the progress of the country, calling for a "communalist" solution which would take the good and leave out the bad of both capitalism and Communism.

18. The Vietnamese Confederation of Labor, founded and still today supported by Catholics, and by great masses of the South Vietnamese people is in a good position in regard to the struggle for greater social justice in the country, but it seems too bound up with the American presence in Vietnam. Even its chief leaders and cadres live in terror of Communism, and with good reason, we must add since, as we have already said, the trade unionists are among the most aimed-at victims of Viet Cong terrorism. The Catholics involved in the unions are, however, a minority in the Christian community: the rest seem to have failed to achieve an alert social awareness.

19. In these last pages of the conclusion of this book I am making some simplifications of things that are actually more nuanced. For example, I speak of Catholics as of a unique bloc. Although this was perhaps the situation of some years ago, it is certainly not the case today. The Christian community began to move, to assume different positions, and to feel itself free in its political and social involvement and not chain-bound by caste or religion. Especially among the youth one notices greater opening out to others, a new "conciliar" sensitivity that gives good hope for the future. According to an interesting inquiry on South Vietnamese Christianity, "Vietnams Katholiken in schwerer Entscheidung," *Herder Korrespondenz,* July 1968, pp. 315–317, these currents of renewal are constantly growing, and under the influence of the Archbishop of Saigon, Mgr. Binh, they have already overcome the influence of the more conservative currents. Even if we do not know anything of this, I point it out as a good omen.

20. *Pax Christi; Journal de la Paix,* Paris, April 1968, p. 3. Mgr. Paul Gouyon, Archbishop of Rennes and national president of *Pax Christi,* wrote: "One part of public opinion, after having demanded peace in Vietnam, seems today to have reversed positions and to side this time with the solution that was justly criticized when it was formulated by Cardinal Spellman: 'peace through victory.' Today, this part of public opinion no longer says 'peace in Vietnam' but 'war in Vietnam.'

Some people marvel that we do not commit ourselves to this path since, according to them, to do so is the only way to pronounce oneself in favor of the poor. Actually, we are not so sure. We believe that the poor want peace since they understand that they have nothing to gain from war. They want peace, at least a peace in conformity to that requested by Paul VI in the encyclical *Christi Matri,* a peace that assures respect of the rights of persons and of communities. With them, we also wish this."

Mgr. Gouyon's statement, like other positions taken by *Pax Christi,* was criticized by Fr. François Biot, O.P., in *T.C.,* March 28, 1968. In Fr. Biot's view, one cannot be neutral in the Vietnamese conflict, but in the struggle between the rich and the poor one had to choose the side of the poor, whom the author identifies with the Viet Cong and the North Vietnamese (actually, to assert a priori that the rich are wrong and the poor right is a rather curious way of performing justice: we may wonder, then, whether in the last world war the "rich" Americans, English, French, etc., were wrong and the "poor" Italians, Japanese and Germans (i.e., Fascism and Nazism) were right.

21. Fr. André Marillier M.E.P., who stayed for some years in North Vietnam after the advent of Communism, writes in *Parole et Mission,* no. 16, Paris, January 1962, pp. 59–61: ". . . Some conclude that Communism can play a providential role in the missionary world. Is it not, perhaps, for a Christianity too closed in on itself, entrapped in certain mental and social habits, a crucible out of which it will come rejuvenated and purified? Is not Communism preparing the way for the progress of Christianity by sweeping away the last vestiges of the pagan religions?

This outlook can produce serious illusions since it takes only one aspect of reality into account. All persecution brings spiritual combat and a high degree of tension, goals become clarified, and the essential frees itself from the accidental. Several parishes in North Vietnam experienced a kind of spiritual spring during the first years of the Communist regime. But Communism maintains its poison and its efficaciousness, and cannot be measured over the course of merely a few years. It puts its strength into the carefully worked out calendar of its programs and in the patience to allow situations to come to maturity. . . . If it does not convince the parents, it counts on winning over the children. . . . And the most courageous among the Christians who suffer under its yoke have no illusions as to its harmful power. Alongside the spiritual good that God helps them derive from their trial, they cannot forget the moral disasters that the Communist regime has already accumulated, nor lose its mortal risks from sight . . ."

Speaking of the "long range" in which Communism puts its goals into effect, Fr. Marillier adds: "Then, the admirable dedication and spiritual progress that Christianity was able to register in a transitory period of semi-freedom are radically compromised. The ecclesial body is paralyzed in its vital organs; the priesthood and the Christian family. . . , will gradually be disjointed and dismembered; the soul of the faithful is wounded by a propaganda that is so contrary to the maxims of the Gospel; the hatred of the enemies of the people becomes a civic duty, and the collective will for power is masked with the name of patriotism. . . . This soul becomes gradually anesthetized, deprived as it is of the sacred Word and of any interior quiet. Day after day, thanks and praise are noisily given to 'The Party, the President and the Government,' a human trinity dispensing one's daily bread and guaranteeing future well-being. The Party is infallible, the police omniscient, the government faithful to all its promises. Consequently, the state merits an unconditional faith, a blind trust, and a complete giving of self; the atheistic system will adopt the theological life of believers to its own profit. . . . At the same time, Communism perverts the pagan soul and thus compromises the possibilities of evangelization. Certainly, it causes the old cults which were an obstacle to Christianity to disappear, but it does so like the fireman who demolishes the house in order to put out the fire. Traditional religions do not prevent the people from preserving a basis of moral soundness from which Christianity can profit. . . . Marxist materialism inculcates in the new generations an obsession with production, the worship of technology . . . and the confused notion that these pagans might have had about their dignity as being spiritual beings is derided and oppressed every day by a state that decides for them what is true or false, just or unjust, and which reduces their existence and their destiny to that of a drone working in a collective beehive."

22. Many give Cambodia as an example of successful neutrality without any international guarantee. In newspaper articles Cambodia is often idealized as the country that has been able to maintain its freedom from Communist subversion thanks to its friendship with China and North Vietnam. This is a completely ideal way of looking at the Cambodian situation (we shall not speak of Laos, neutralized at Geneva in 1962 and now with two-thirds of its territory occupied by the internal Communist party helped by the North Vietnamese). In a letter to *Le Monde,* March 7, 1968, the political leader of Cambodia, Sihanouk, spoke about the regions bordering on Vietnam: "This province has been occupied for many years by the Viet Minh, which has indoctrinated certain elements . . . who oblige the population, under threat of death, to abandon their villages to go and live in the depth of the forests. . . . It is perfectly clear that Asian Communism does not permit us to remain neutral and outside the conflict between the Chinese-Vietnamese

and the Americans. Since it cannot make of us allies who would support them unconditionally, it is attempting to destroy our regime from within." If the Vietnamese war ends in the victory of the Communist side, what will become of Cambodia, Laos, Thailand and Burma?

23. Following the aggression of the five Warsaw pact countries against Czechoslovakia (August 1968), North Vietnam approved this military action, asserting on its radio that "the armed forces of the U.S.S.R. and its four allies have penetrated Czechoslovak territory . . . for the noble aim of defending the socialist regime against counterrevolutionary forces." It is true that North Vietnam has been somewhat constrained to take a position in favor of Soviet aggression, since it is dependent on Soviet military aid. But, as *Le Monde* wrote (August 23), if Hanoi could not condemn Moscow, we might rightfully expect it to have remained silent or at least give less warm and decided support. But the total approval is logical: Soviet intervention in Czechoslovakia is fully in line with the mentality and the actions of the North Vietnamese Communist leaders; the goal to be reached is uncontested and absolute domination by the Communist party, and to achieve this "noble aim" every means is good, even the armed oppression of a people, even the imposition of a regime that is not wanted. What we do not yet succeed in understanding is how, while the armed imposition of Communism is condemned by all when it happens in Czechoslovakia or Hungary, this same armed imposition of Communism is praised as a "people's" victory even by sincere democrats when it happens in Vietnam!